WOMEN AND GENDER IN ISLAM

Leila Ahmed

WOMEN AND GENDER IN ISLAM & Historical Roots of a Modern Debate

Yale University Press   New Haven & London

Published with assistance from the foundation established in memory
of Calvin Chapin of the Class of 1788, Yale College.

Designed by Jill Breitbarth.
Set in Sabon type by Brevis Press, Bethany, Connecticut.
Printed in the United States of America by BookCrafters, Inc.,
Chelsea, Michigan.

Library of Congress Cataloging-in-Publication Data
Ahmed, Leila.
   Women and gender in Islam : historical roots of a modern debate /
Leila Ahmed.
     p.   cm.
   Includes bibliographical references and index.
   ISBN 0-300-04942-0 (cloth)
         0-300-05583-8 (pbk.)
   1. Women—Arab countries—Social conditions.   2. Sexism—Arab
countries—History.   3. Women, Muslim—Attitudes.   4. Feminism—
Arab countries.   I. Title.
HQ1784.A67   1992
305.48'6971—dc20   91–26901
                                                            CIP

The paper in this book meets the guidelines for permanence and dura-
bility of the Committee on Production Guidelines for Book Longevity
of the Council on Library Resources.

10   9   8   7   6   5   4   3

CONTENTS

ACKNOWLEDGMENTS

I WORKED ON THIS BOOK FOR MANY YEARS, AND I AM indebted to numerous people and institutions. Colleagues and students at the University of Massachusetts at Amherst, especially in women's studies and Near Eastern studies, provided a challenging and supportive intellectual community and also generously allowed me the leaves that enabled me to carry the project forward. I am very grateful to the National Humanities Center, Research Triangle Park, North Carolina, and to the Bunting Institute, Radcliffe College, for fellowships that were critical to my being able to complete it. Colleagues in the Five College community and at numerous campuses where I have presented ideas in one way or another related to this book provided stimulating and provocative discussions that challenged and broadened my thinking. I particularly benefited from seminars at the Center for Contemporary Arab Studies at Georgetown University, the Pembroke Center at Brown University, the Center for Middle Eastern Studies at Harvard University, the Near Eastern Studies Program at Cornell University, and the Noun Symposium at Grinnell College.

My debt to the work of others, in Middle Eastern

studies and feminist studies, is immense, a debt my notes partially suggest. Here I can only acknowledge those who have contributed directly to my work. Several people read the manuscript and helped me improve it. I am especially grateful to Judith Tucker for the critical care with which she read the entire manuscript and for her many detailed and insightful suggestions; Nikki Keddie, who read most of the manuscript and whose comments helped me focus my ideas; and Elizabeth Fox-Genovese, who read several chapters and offered comments that stretched and enriched my thinking. I am fundamentally indebted, too, to conversations, arguments, and editorial suggestions from many friends and colleagues. I want to thank in particular Frédérique Apffel Marglin, Tosun Aricanli, Elizabeth Davis, Elizabeth Fernea, Peter Gran, Ahmad Al-Haidar, Giselle Hakki, Heba Handoussa, Mervat Hatem, Azizah Al-Hibri, Angela Ingram, Suad Joseph, Eileen Julien, Angelika Kratzer, Jane Lund, Afaf Mahfouz, Daphne Patai, Janice Raymond, Lisa Selkirk, Catharine Stimpson, Dorothy Thompson, and Sandra Zagarell.

I also owe much to Yale University Press: to the readers to whom the press sent my manuscript and whose comments, both critical and appreciative, helped clarify and sharpen my thinking; to Charles Grench, who took an interest in the book from early on and gave me encouragement and support through its various stages; and Mary Pasti, whose painstaking editing improved the manuscript in many ways and whose cheeriness and enthusiasm certainly made the labor of preparing the book for press far pleasanter than it might have been.

I am grateful, too, for the assistance of the staff at the libraries of the University of Massachusetts at Amherst; Amherst College; and Widener Library, Harvard University, particularly those working in the reference and interlibrary loan departments.

And I want finally to thank the University of Chicago Press for permission to reprint chapter 3, which appeared in an earlier version in *Signs: Journal of Women in Culture and Society* 11, no. 4.

A NOTE ON TRANSLITERATION
Wherever possible, I have used the familiar English forms of Arabic words and names; otherwise, I have used a simple system based on that of the *International Journal of Middle East Studies*. No diacritical marks are used. The letter *ayn* is indicated by ', and the *hamza* is indicated by '.

INTRODUCTION

I BEGAN THIS BOOK WITH THE INTENTION OF BRING-
ing together such information and insights as were currently available on the conditions and lives of women
in Middle Eastern Arab history. The only general accounts of women in Arab or Muslim history available
when I started to research this book (some ten years
ago) were such works as Wiebke Walther's *Woman in
Islam,* an attractively illustrated book, more anecdotal
than analytical, which took little if any notice of the
perspectives on women in history that contemporary
feminist research on Western women, and to some extent on Arab women, had begun to elaborate.[1]

I soon realized that my task would not after all be
as simple as I had first imagined and that a key focus
of the book must be the discourses on women and gender, rather than, more straightforwardly, the presentation of a synopsis of recent findings on the material
conditions of women in the different periods of Middle
Eastern Arab history. Throughout Islamic history the
constructs, institutions, and modes of thought devised
by early Muslim societies that form the core discourses
of Islam have played a central role in defining women's
place in Muslim societies. The growing strength of Is-

1

lamist movements today, which urge the reinstitution of the laws and practices set forth in the core Islamic discourses, made the investigation of that
heritage on women and gender seem particularly urgent and relevant.

Other factors contributed to my sense that a prime focus of this study
of Middle Eastern Arab women in history must be the discourses and the
changes in, and varieties of, the discourses on women. The debates going
on in the contemporary Arab world between Islamists and secularists—
between advocates of veiling and its opponents—and the ways in which
the issues of the veil and women as they figured in these debates were apparently encoded with political meanings and references that on the face
of it at least seemed to have little to do with women, again brought the
issue of discourse to the fore. Similarly, the way in which Arab women are
discussed in the West, whether in the popular media or the academy, and
the sense that such discussions often seem to be centrally even if implicitly
engaging other matters through the discussion of women—such as the merits or demerits of Islam or Arab culture—also highlighted the importance
of taking the discourses themselves as a focus of investigation.

Discourses shape and are shaped by specific moments in specific societies. The investigation of the discourses on women and gender in Islamic
Middle Eastern societies entails studying the societies in which they are
rooted, and in particular the way in which gender is articulated socially,
institutionally, and verbally in these societies. Some charting of the terrain
of women's history and the socioeconomic and historical conditions in
which the discourses are grounded was thus in any case a necessary first
step. This in itself was a considerable task. Knowledge about women's history and the articulation of gender in Muslim societies is still rudimentary,
although in the late 1980s there was a spurt of new research in that area.
Nonetheless, existing studies of periods before the nineteenth century deal
with random isolated issues or scattered groups and thus illuminate points
or moments but give no sense of the broad patterns or codes. A recent
authoritative tome on the history of the Islamic peoples by Ira Lapidus
makes no reference to women or the construction of gender prior to the
nineteenth century and devotes only a small number of pages to women
after 1800. This treatment exemplifies the status of research on women
and gender in Islam, reflecting the absence of work attempting to concep-
tualize women's history and issues of gender in any Islamic society before
the nineteenth century and also the progress that has been made in conceptualizing a framework of women's history with respect to more recent
times.[2]

Unearthing and piecing together the history of women and the articulation of gender in Muslim societies, areas of history largely invisible in Middle Eastern scholarship, thus was a primary and major part of this enterprise. Both historically and geographically the field to be covered was potentially vast, precluding any comprehensive account. The broad framework of this inquiry, with its principal objective of identifying and exploring the core Islamic discourses on women and gender and exploring the key premises of the modern discourses on women in the Middle East, served to set the geographic and historical limits.

Within the broad limits of the Arab Muslim Middle East it was in certain societies most particularly, and at certain moments in history, that the dominant, prescriptive terms of the core religious discourses were founded and institutionally and legally elaborated, so it is these societies and moments that must here be the focus of study. Crucial in this respect were Arabia at the time of the rise of Islam and Iraq in the immediately ensuing period.

Some examination of concepts of gender in the societies that preceded and adjoined the early Islamic societies was also necessary to understand the foundations and influences bearing on the core Islamic discourses. A review of these was additionally desirable because the contemporary Islamist argument, which maintains that the establishment of Islam improved the condition of women, refers comparatively to these earlier and neighboring societies.

The region comprises a kaleidoscopic wealth of the world's most ancient societies, but the organization of gender has been systematically analyzed in few of them. Those surveyed in the following pages—at times extremely briefly and only to point to salient features or note parallels with Islamic forms—include Mesopotamia, Greece, Egypt, and Iran. They were picked for a variety of reasons, among them their importance or influence in the region, their relevance to the Islamic system, and the availability of information.

In more modern periods, crucial moments in the rearticulation and further elaboration of issues of women and gender in Middle Eastern Muslim societies occurred under the impact of colonialism and in the sociopolitical turmoil that followed and, indeed, persists to our own day. Egypt in this instance was a prime crucible of the process of transformation and the struggles around the meanings of gender that have recurrently erupted in both Egypt and other Muslim Arab societies since the nineteenth century. In many ways developments in Egypt heralded and mirrored developments in the Arab world, and for the modern period this inquiry therefore focuses on Egypt. Which moments and societies in the course of Muslim history assumed a central or exemplary role in the development of the core or dominant discourses fundamentally determined which societies are focused on here.

The findings presented in the following pages are essentially provisional and preliminary and constitute in many ways a first attempt to gain a perspective on the discourses on women and gender at crucial, defining moments in Middle Eastern Muslim history. Part 1 outlines the practices and concepts relating to gender in some exemplary societies of the region antecedent to the rise of Islam. The continuities of Islamic civilization with past civilizations in the region are well recognized. Statements to that effect routinely figure in histories of Islam. Lapidus's *History of Islamic Societies* notes that the family and the family-based community were among the many institutions inherited and continued by Islam, others being "agricultural and urban societies, market economies, monotheistic religions."[3] The author might also have noted that the monotheistic religions inherited and reaffirmed by Islam enjoined the worship of a god referred to by a male pronoun, and endorsed the patriarchal family and female subordination as key components of their socioreligious vision. Judaism and Christianity, and Zoroastrianism, were the prevailing religions in the Byzantine and the Sasanian empires, which were the two major powers in the area at the time of the rise of Islam. In instituting a religion and a type of family conforming with those already established in such adjoining regions, Islam displaced in Arabia a polytheist religion with three paramount goddesses and a variety of marriage customs, including but not confined to those enshrined in the patriarchal family. That is to say, Islam effected a transformation that brought the Arabian socioreligious vision and organization of gender into line with the rest of the Middle East and Mediterranean regions.

Islam explicitly and discreetly affiliated itself with the traditions already in place in the region. According to Islam, Muhammad was a prophet in the Judeo-Christian tradition, and the Quran incorporated, in some form or other, many stories to be found in the Bible, those of the creation and fall among others. As a consequence, once Islam had conquered the adjacent territories, the assimilation of the scriptural and social traditions of their Christian and Jewish populations into the corpus of Islamic life and thought occurred easily and seamlessly. Converts brought traditions of thought and custom with them. For instance (to give just one example of how easily and invisibly scriptural assimilation could occur), in its account of the creation of humankind the Quran gives no indication of the order in which the first couple was created, nor does it say that Eve was created from Adam's rib. In Islamic traditionist literature, however, which was inscribed in the period following the Muslim conquests, Eve, sure enough, is referred to as created from a rib.[4] The adoption of the veil by Muslim women occurred by a similar process of seamless assimilation of the mores of the conquered peoples. The veil was apparently in use in Sasanian society, and segregation of the sexes and use of the veil were heavily in evidence in the Christian Middle East and Mediterranean regions at the time of the rise of Islam. During Muhammad's lifetime and only toward the end at that, his wives were the only Muslim women required to veil (see chap. 3). After his death and following the Muslim conquest of the adjoining territories, where upper-class women veiled, the veil became a commonplace item of clothing among Muslim upper-class women, by a process of assimilation that no one has yet ascertained in much detail.

What is or is not unique, specific, or intrinsic to Islam with respect to ideas about women and gender has already, then, become a complicated question. It is also clear that conceptions, assumptions, and social customs and institutions relating to women and to the social meaning of gender that derived from the traditions in place in the Middle East at the time of the Islamic conquests entered into and helped to shape the very foundations of Islamic concepts and social practice as they developed during the first centuries of Islam. All these facts emphasize the importance of considering Islamic formulations of gender in relation to the changing codes and practices in the broader Middle East. They suggest, too, that the contributions of the contemporary conquered societies to the formation of Islamic institutions and mores concerning women need to be taken into account, even with respect to mores that have come to be considered intrinsically Islamic.

For these reasons it was important to some extent to relate practices taking shape in early Islam to those of earlier and adjoining societies and thus to relate Islamic practices to the pattern of practices in the region. Moreover, to omit consideration of that larger pattern altogether would constitute a serious distortion of the evidence, for it would falsely isolate Islamic practices and by implication at least suggest that Islamic handling of these matters was special or even unique. (The variety and wealth of languages and cultures in the region and the consequent variety of disciplines, entailing specialist linguistic skills and other knowledges through which those cultures are explored, has perhaps contributed to the facility with which the Islamic and other societies of the region tend to be treated in scholarship as if they constituted separate, self-contained societies and histories.) Conceptually, therefore, it was important to outline practices in some earlier and contemporary cultures, even though in my discussion of non-Islamic or non-Arab cultures I would be compelled to rely entirely on secondary sources.

Part 2 deals with Arabia at the time of the rise of Islam, tracing changes that occurred when Islam was instituted and changes that accompanied its spread to the wider Middle East. It then explores the conceptual and social organizations pertaining to women and gender in Iraqi society in the Classical age—the region and period that witnessed the elaboration of the prescriptive core of Islamic discourses on women. The section concludes with an overview of salient features of the socioeconomic expression of the Classical Islamic system of gender and their consequences for the lives of women in some subsequent societies in premodern times. The societies examined are mainly those of Egypt and Turkey, primarily for the practical reason that some preliminary scholarship and data are available.

Part 3 takes as its starting point the turn of the nineteenth century and outlines the socioeconomic, political, and cultural changes that accompanied European encroachment on the Middle East. The focus here is almost entirely on Egypt. As numerous students of the modern Arab world have noted, there is compelling justification, culturally and intellectually, for regarding Egypt as mirror of the Arab world in the modern age, and this is certainly the case in analyzing the Arab world's dominant discourses on women.[5] Egypt was the first Middle Eastern Arab country to experience the consequences of European commercial expansion and to experiment socially, intellectually, politically, and culturally with the range of ideas that have tellingly marked or that have proved to be of enduring significance in the modern era, not only for Egypt but also for Arab societies as a whole.

The first region in the Arab world to experiment with social change for women, Egypt played and continues to play a central role in developing the key Arab discourses on women, while developments within Egypt with respect to women (as in other matters) continue to parallel, reflect, and sometimes anticipate developments in other Arab countries. Part 3 first describes the progress of social change for women over the course of the nineteenth century and traces the impact of those changes on women and on ideas about women. It next analyzes the eruption, in the late nineteenth or early twentieth century, of the first major debate on women and the veil in the Arab world and the emergence, in effect, of a new discourse on women—here called the discourse of the veil—in which issues of culture and class, and imperialism and nationalism, became vitally entangled with the issue of women. The political and discursive elements from which the new discourse was forged and the conflicts of class and culture with which it was inscribed are also analyzed.

The remaining chapters trace the impact on women of the socioeconomic changes that have occurred over the course of the twentieth century and then follow out the appearance and evolution of feminist discourses. Part 3 concludes with an account of the social background to the "return of the veil" and an analysis of the social and intellectual grounds informing the different perspectives on Islamism and Islamic dress, and an analysis, too, of the divisions between feminist women and women adopting Islamic dress.

It is unusual to refer to the Western world as the "Christian world" or the "world of Christendom" unless one intends to highlight its religious heritage, whereas with respect to the Islamic Middle East there is no equivalent nonethnic, nonreligious term in common English usage, and the terms *Islamic* and *Islam* (as in the "world of Islam") are those commonly used to refer to regions whose civilizational heritage is Islamic as well as, specifically, to the religion of Islam. My falling in with this usage is not intended to suggest that Middle Eastern "Islamic" civilization or peoples are more innately or unalterably religious than any other civilization or peoples.

The very structure of this work declares that ethnic and religious groups other than the Muslims belonged to and shaped the Middle East and its cultures as centrally as the Muslims did. The focus here on Islam and on Muslim communities connotes simply the intent to explore the dominant cultural tradition in the Middle East and is in no way intended to imply that the Middle East is or should be only Islamic. Although the issue of minorities is not specifically explored, the question of minorities has close notional ties to the question of women. In establishment Islamic thought, women, like minorities, are defined as different from and, in their legal rights, lesser than, Muslim men.[6] Unlike non-Muslim men, who might join the master-class by converting, women's differentness and inferiority within this system are immutable.

Of course, differences of class, ethnicity, and local culture critically qualify the experiences of women and give specificity to the particular ways in which they are affected by the broad discourses on gender within their societies.[7] Without in any way denying the fundamental role of such variables I should note here (in view of the lively current discussions and myriad interpretations of what "woman" is and who "women" are) that by definition, in that this is a study of the discourses on women in Muslim Arab societies and of the histories in which those discourses are rooted, "women" in this work are those whom the societies under review defined as women and to whom they applied legal and cultural rules on the basis of these definitions. They are those who—in Nancy Cott's useful retrieval of Mary Beard's phrase—"can't avoid being women, whatever they do."[8]

Part One

THE

PRE-ISLAMIC

MIDDLE EAST

Chapter 1 MESOPOTAMIA

THE SUBORDINATION OF WOMEN IN THE ANCIENT Middle East appears to have become institutionalized with the rise of urban societies and with the rise of the archaic state in particular. Contrary to androcentric theories proposing that the inferior social status of women is based on biology and "nature" and thus has existed as long as human beings have, archaeological evidence suggests that women were held in esteem prior to the rise of urban societies and suffered a decline in status with the emergence of urban centers and city-states. Archaeologists often cite Çatal Hüyük, a Neolithic settlement in Asia Minor dating from circa 6000 B.C.E., to substantiate women's elevated and (some have argued) dominant position. Within this settlement the larger of the burial platforms found in the houses contained women, and the paintings and decorations on the walls of the numerous shrines prominently featured female figures.[1] Çatal Hüyük, moreover, is not the only early culture of the area to provide evidence of women's having held a favorable and possibly even a privileged position. Archaeological findings indicate that cultures throughout the Middle East venerated the mother-goddess in the Neolithic pe-

11

riod, into the second millennium B.C.E. in some areas. Also, studies of the ancient cultures of the region show that supremacy of a goddess figure and elevated status for women were the rule rather than the exception—in Mesopotamia, Elam, Egypt, and Crete, for example, and among the Greeks, the Phoenicians, and others.[2]

Male dominance had already gained ground prior to the rise of urban societies, or so some scholars, including feminist theorists, have speculated. Theories as to why this occurred abound. Among the more compelling feminist theories is that put forward by Gerda Lerner, who suggests that the importance of increasing the population and providing labor power in early societies led to the theft of women, whose sexuality and reproductive capacity became the first "property" that tribes competed for. Warrior cultures favoring male dominance consequently emerged.[3]

The first urban centers of the Middle East arose in Mesopotamia—in the valleys of the Tigris and Euphrates rivers in the southern half of modern Iraq—between 3500 and 3000 B.C.E. The region, inhabited by Ubaidians who established the village settlements that developed into the urban centers of Sumer, was infiltrated by Semitic nomads from the Syrian and Arabian deserts, who were often politically dominant in the ensuing periods. The Sumerians arrived (probably from southwestern Asia) about 3500 B.C.E. and gained ascendance in the following period. Writing was invented, urban centers grew in complexity, and city-states arose. There was frequent warfare between the city-states, several of which in turn gained supremacy with the decline of Sumerian power (circa 2400 B.C.E.).

The growth of complex urban societies and the increasing importance of military competitiveness further entrenched male dominance and gave rise to a class-based society in which the military and temple elites made up the propertied classes. The patriarchal family, designed to guarantee the paternity of property-heirs and vesting in men the control of female sexuality, became institutionalized, codified, and upheld by the state. Women's sexuality was designated the property of men, first of the woman's father, then of her husband, and female sexual purity (virginity in particular) became negotiable, economically valuable property. This led (some have argued) to the emergence of prostitution and to the enforcement of a rigid demarcation between "respectable" women (wives), whose sexuality and reproductive capability belonged to one man, and women who were sexually available to any man. The increasing complexity and specialization of urban society and the growth of populations comprising artisans and merchants as well as agricultural laborers contributed to women's further subordination by facilitating their exclusion from most of the professional classes. This exclusion contributed to the further decline of their economic contributions and consequently of their status. The decline in women's status was followed eventually by the decline of goddesses and the rise to supremacy of gods.[4]

As different city-states successively dominated the Mesopotamian region, laws governing the patriarchal family changed, tending to become progressively harsher and more restrictive toward women. For example, the Code Hammurabi (circa 1752 B.C.E.) limited the time for which a man could pawn his wife or children to three years and expressly forbade beating or oppressing these debt-pawns. But later Assyrian law (circa 1200 B.C.E.) omitted these protective measures and explicitly permitted beating debt-pawns, piercing their ears, and pulling them by the hair.[5] Assyrian law also permitted a husband to "pull out (the hair of) his wife, mutilate (or) twist her ears, with no liability attaching to him," when punishing her ("Laws," 185). Again, in the Code Hammurabi men could easily divorce their wives, particularly if they had not borne children, but were liable to fines ("divorce money") and were required to return the dowry. The later Assyrian law codex apparently allowed the husband to decide whether the wife received anything following the divorce: "If a seignior wishes to divorce his wife, if it is his will, he may give her something; if it is not his will, he need not give her anything; she shall go out empty" (183).[6] According to the Code Hammurabi women could obtain a divorce only with great difficulty. "If a woman so hated her husband," the code states, "that she has declared, 'You may not have me,' her record shall be investigated at her city council, and if she was careful and was not at fault, even though her husband has been going out and disparaging her greatly, that woman, without incurring any blame at all, may take her dowry and go off to her father's house." Even asking for a divorce entailed risk, however. If on investigation the council found that "she was not careful, but was a gadabout, thus neglecting her house (and) humiliating her husband, they shall throw that woman into the water" ("Code," 172).

In any case, throughout the period of successive city-states, power and authority resided exclusively with the husband and father, to whom wife and children owed absolute obedience. A text from the middle of the third millennium B.C.E. said that a wife who contradicted her husband could have her teeth smashed with burnt bricks, and the Code Hammurabi decreed that a son should have his hand cut off for striking his father ("Code," 175).[7] The head of the family had the right to arrange marriages for his children and to dedicate his daughter to the gods, in which case she became a priestess and resided in the temple with other priestesses. He also had the right, mentioned above, to pawn or sell his wife and/or children to repay a debt; and if he then failed to pay the debt, they could be turned into debt-slaves. The concepts underlying many of the laws were evidently that the man's rights and power over wife, children, and slaves were absolute (though he could not kill them without good reason) and that he could substitute them for himself in case of indebtedness or punishment.[8] For example, if a creditor killed the pawned son of his debtor through ill-treatment, the creditor's punishment (in the Code Hammurabi) was to have his own son killed—that is, the son was expendable in payment for the father's crimes ("Code," 170). Similarly in the case of rape in Assyrian law, the penalty for a married rapist was to have his own wife "dishonored" and permanently taken away from him. Further, the rules of the Assyrian code indicate that conceptually, the rape of a virgin was viewed as a crime that above all economically damaged the victim's father: the penalty for an unmarried rapist was to pay the father the price of a virgin and to marry the woman he had raped ("Laws," 185).

Marriages were generally monogamous, except among royalty, though commoners might take second wives or concubines if the first wife was childless. In any case, men were permitted to have sexual intercourse with slaves and prostitutes. Adultery by the wife (and her partner), however, was punishable by death, although according to the Code Hammurabi, the husband could choose to let her live ("Code," 171). If the father recognized the children of a concubine as his, those offspring had the right to inherit equally with the children of the wife; if the father did not recognize them, they and their mother nevertheless gained their freedom when the father died (173). Royalty often maintained large harems consisting of both wives and concubines, though they were considerably smaller than harems under the Persian Sasanids, who ruled the region from 224 to 640 C.E., immediately prior to its conquest by the Muslims. The harem of an Assyrian king of the twelfth century B.C.E., for example, consisted of approximately forty women; that of a Sasanian king shortly before the Muslim conquest (Khusrau I, 531–79 C.E.) consisted of some twelve thousand women.[9]

The rules on veiling—specifying which women must veil and which could not—were carefully detailed in Assyrian law. Wives and daughters of "seigniors" had to veil; concubines accompanying their mistress had to veil; former "sacred prostitutes," now married, had to veil; but harlots and slaves were forbidden to veil. Those caught illegally veiling were liable to the penalties of flogging, having pitch poured over their heads, and having their ears cut off ("Laws," 183). The law on this matter is analyzed at some length by Gerda Lerner, and it is to her analysis that we owe the insight that the veil served not merely to mark the upper classes but, more fundamentally, to differentiate between "respectable" women and those who were publicly available. That is, use of the veil classified women according to their sexual activity and signaled to men which women were under male protection and which were fair game. Lerner's analysis makes clear, as she goes on to point out, first, that the division of women into "respectable" and "disreputable" was fundamental to the patriarchal system and, second, that women took their place in the class hierarchy on the basis of their relationship (or absence of such) to the men who protected them and on the basis of their sexual activity—and not, as with men, on the basis of their occupations and their relation to production.[10]

In spite of the unequivocal conceptual subordination of women codified in the laws governing the patriarchal family, upper-class women did enjoy high status and legal rights and privileges. Indeed, women of all classes within the legal systems just discussed often enjoyed such rights as owning and managing property in their own name, entering into contracts, and bearing witness.[11] As Lerner and others have argued, the high status and economic rights of kin and dependent women were not in conflict with the patriarchal system but rather served the interests of ruling patriarchs by establishing power through a "patrimonial bureaucracy." The security of their power, Lerner writes, "depended on their installing family members in important subordinate positions of power. Such family members were . . . quite often women—wives, concubines, or daughters. . . . Thus emerged the role of 'wife-as-deputy.'" Such women influenced events and had real power over men and women of lower ranks—and could indeed even emerge as rulers, as did Queen Semiramis of Babylon, wife of Shamshi Adad (824–810 B.C.E.), and Naqiʾa, wife of Sennacherib (704–681 B.C.E.). As Lerner stresses, however, their power derived entirely from the male on whom they depended or to whom they were related.[12]

In addition to marrying other members of the elite and wielding power and influence on public and economic life by virtue of natal or marital status, upper-class women could also play an important role in the economic and legal life of the society as priestesses (*naditum*), or servants of the gods. Women, mostly from the upper classes, became naditum by being dedicated to the gods in childhood by their fathers. They not only owned property but also had advantages over other women in that they could inherit property "like a son," their property returning to their patriarchal family on their death. They engaged in business, leased fields and houses, bought slaves, entered into contracts, gave loans, and so on. Naditum women lived together in conventlike institutions; marriage was rare but not forbidden.[13]

Besides playing an important part in the economic life of the community and ensuring that property remained within the patriarchal family, the institution of naditum clearly served the interests of the ruling class by cementing ties between the elite and the temple priesthood.

The laws giving women property rights and allowing them to enter contracts, bear witness, and engage in business benefited women of other classes as well. Women worked as potters, weavers, spinners, hairdressers, agricultural workers, bakers, singers, musicians, and brewers and occasionally even in occupations requiring lengthy training periods, such as that of a scribe. Documents attest to their buying, selling, and renting property and buying and selling slaves, including slaves who were used as prostitutes to provide an income for their mistresses. Contracts were sometimes used to modify the terms of marriage, as in the marriage of Amusakkal to a priest (circa 1737 B.C.E.), which gave her equal rights to and equal penalties for divorce. Contracts could also protect the wife from being liable to enslavement for her husband's debts, though this safeguard was presumably confined to classes that had the leverage to impose such terms.[14]

Many of the Mesopotamian laws were to have their parallels in Hebrew law (parallels that Lerner in particular has explored), as well as in Islamic law. Obvious similarities with Islamic law include giving the right to divorce almost exclusively to men, except when the contract stipulates otherwise (a contractual stipulation that Muslim women in some schools of law may also make); giving concubines who have borne children, and their children, rights to the father's property and to freedom; and giving women the right to testify (a right that was curtailed in the later Babylonian period).[15] Regarding the last-mentioned instance, Mesopotamian law, at least in its earlier form, was apparently more generous toward women than is Muslim law, or at least than Muslim law as traditionally interpreted, according to which the testimony of two women is equal to that of one man.

Mesopotamian civilization, it should be noted, spanned several millennia and included the rise and fall of a series of specific cultures and peoples— Sumerian, Akkadian, Babylonian, Assyrian—each of which successively dominated the region. Its mores and laws regarding women have yet to be comprehensively examined by a scholar of that civilization. To date, only Lerner has systematically reflected on the theoretical implications of the societal organization of gender. Further, it should be noted that even though many women, in particular slave and lower-class women, doubtless suffered unspeakable brutalities, as allowed by law, artifacts from the civilization nevertheless attest to the mutuality, love, and affection that existed between husbands and wives, fathers and daughters, and also attest that these were indeed qualities that the culture cherished and celebrated. Artists depicted loving couples "calmly standing side by side, hand in hand, or one arm around the other's shoulders." Letters that husbands and wives wrote to each other while separated are also extant, attesting to their devotion. Documents survive in which, for example, husbands make donations to wives for the stated reason that "she has cared for him and worked for him"; other documents safeguard the wife's livelihood in case of the husband's premature death or introduce clauses protecting her against the objections of relatives and children.[16]

In 539 B.C.E. the Achaemenid king Cyrus II conquered Babylon and much of Mesopotamia, Syria, and other regions of the Middle East. Between this date and the Muslim conquest in 640 C.E. the region was conquered by Alexander, then by the Parthians, and finally became part of the Iranian empire once again under the Sasanians, who reigned from 224 C.E. until the Muslim conquest. The cultural and social changes that followed these successive invasions were generally not abruptly imposed but occurred gradually as indigenous mores fused with those of the conquerors.

Although little is known about women during the period of these successive invasions, the exchange of mores following from them appears to have led to a decline in the status of women and to the broader dissemination of the more negative attitudes toward women. For instance, A. L. Oppenheim singles out a decline in the position of women as one of the few "key points" of change after the Iranian conquest of Mesopotamia; women could no longer serve as witnesses, and new restrictions were placed on their participation in the legal transactions of their husbands, among other things.[17] The lives of royalty also suggest the possibility that the series of conquests and ensuing cultural exchanges that occurred in the Middle Eastern and Mediterranean regions from about the middle of the first millennium B.C.E. to the Islamic conquests led to a decline in the status of women and the spread of practices implying their further devaluation. Alexander, for example, vastly increased the size of his harem after he defeated King Darius of Persia in 333 B.C.E. The harem he captured from Darius consisted of the king's mother and wife, each traveling in her own car and attended by her own troop of women on horseback; fifteen carriages carrying the king's children, their nurses, and a crowd of eunuchs; and more carriages carrying Darius's 365 concubines. (By this time the custom of secluding women was in place: the carriages carrying them were closed.) Thereafter, presumably in imitation of the ruler he had conquered, Alexander kept a harem of exactly the same number of concubines as Darius, in addition to a number of eunuchs accustomed to being "used like women." The size of royal harems was to grow so large that by Sasanian times, when concubines numbered in the thousands, a harem of 365 concubines would come to seem modest ("niggardly," as one scholar described it).[18] Similarly, following the Muslim conquests of regions in which large harems were the norm among royalty, the size of royal Muslim harems also vastly increased.

The exchange of mores was not confined to royalty and the elite, although only these classes had the means to keep large harems that were secluded and guarded by eunuchs. Veiling and the confinement of women spread throughout the region and became the ordinary social practices, as did the attitudes to women and to the human body (such as a sense of the shamefulness of the body and sexuality) that accompanied such practices. During the first Christian centuries the notion of women's seclusion—architecturally realized as a building or area for women in the residence, guarded by eunuchs—together with veiling and attitudes about the proper invisibility of women, became features of upper-class life in the Mediterranean Middle East, Iraq, and Persia. Indeed, such attitudes and practices were found as much on the northern shores of the Mediterranean—in Byzantine society, for example—as on the southern shores. Widespread by the early Christian era, they did not emanate (as is often suggested) solely from the Persian world but seem rather to represent a coalescence of similar attitudes and practices originating within the various patriarchal cultures of the region. Mesopotamian, Persian, Hellenic, Christian, and eventually Islamic cultures each contributed practices that both controlled and diminished women, and each also apparently borrowed the controlling and reductive practices of its neighbors. Cultural exchange seems to have led above all to the pooling and reinforcement of such ideas and to the triumphant endorsement throughout the region of a notion of woman in which her humanity was submerged and all but obliterated by a view of her as essentially and even exclusively biological—as quintessentially a sexual and reproductive being.

The spread of reductive and controlling practices and misogynist ideas at this time and in this region is striking. And it is also striking that attitudes that apparently recognized women's humanity as well as their biological capacity—attitudes that had also existed in this region (as will be discussed in chapter 2)—conversely did *not* spread and were *not* copied and exchanged from one culture to another. Indeed, even within each particular culture—Mesopotamian, Hellenic, Christian, and Islamic—it was the more humane ideas regarding women that apparently were consistently lost and those increasing male control and diminishing women that consistently gained ground. For both the West and the Middle East the societies of this period and this region and the ideas to which they gave rise have exercised and continue to exercise a controlling power over history.

Sasanian society, which prevailed in the Iraq-Iran region, is particularly important to the present work in that the Muslims conquered its people and directly inherited its culture and institutions. The mores of the incoming Arabs and the existing society fused after the conquest, and the new Muslim society that arose in Iraq played a key role in defining Muslim law and institutions, including many which are still in place today.

Customs of the Persian royalty at the time of the first Persian conquest of Mesopotamia continued to be practiced and became even more elaborate under the Sasanians. Harems grew vastly larger and were kept by the elite as well as by royalty, their size reflecting the owner's wealth and power.[19] The Achaemenid practice of sending women from the provinces to the king's harem on approval continued in Sasanian times. As an additional refinement, certain kings circulated their specifications of ideal beauty throughout their territories. Another carryover from Achaemenid times into at least early Sasanian times was the practice of incestuous marriage, in which a man was permitted to marry his sister, his daughter, or even his mother. These unions were "not merely tolerated, but indeed regarded as acts of piety and great merit, and even efficacious against the demonic forces."[20]

The paramount religion among the upper classes was Zoroastrianism, a monotheistic religion perhaps dating as far back as the first millennium B.C.E. During the Sasanian period Zoroastrianism grew in power and influence and eventually became the state religion, establishing the regulations that governed male-female relationships among the upper classes. The patriarchal family, as endorsed by this church (at least in this period of its history), demanded the wife's total obedience to her husband. She was required to declare, "I will never cease, all my life, to obey my husband," and was subject to divorce if she failed to do so. She was also required "every morning on rising" to "present herself before her husband and nine times make her obeisance . . . arms extended . . . in greeting to him, as men did praying to Ohrmazd."[21] Producing a male heir was religiously enjoined, and the various marriage arrangements that were possible reflected the priority placed on men's producing male heirs, if not directly, then through their daughters or other female kin. Thus the daughter of a man who had produced no male offspring had to be given in a form of marriage in which the offspring, and in particular the male offspring, belonged to her father, or to her patriarchal family if he was dead. In such a marriage a woman had fewer rights than in a *patakhashae* marriage, in which the children belonged to her husband. Similarly, widows of men who had produced no heirs (even women whose betrothed husband had died in childhood) entered into marriages in which the offspring belonged to the deceased husband's family and in which they did not have the rights of patakhashae wives, the only type of wives entitled to be treated as mistress of the house. A man could also loan his wife to another man without her consent, the terms of the loan being specified by contract. This practice was recommended in particular when a widower could not afford to marry yet required a woman to supply sexual services and to raise his children. Any offspring that might ensue belonged to the husband, according to the belief that a "woman is a field. . . . All which grows there belongs to its owner, even if he did not plant it."[22] Wife loaning was regarded by Sasanian jurists as a "fraternal" act, an act of "solidarity with a member of one's community which was sanctified as a religious duty."[23]

Husbands had rights to property acquired by the wife after the marriage unless a contract had specified otherwise. If she disobeyed him, she lost even these contractually specified rights. Her disobedience had to be proved in court; then the court issued a "certificate of disobedience." A woman inherited the share of her father's property that belonged to her, although the husband was the usufructuary; if she died childless, it reverted to her father's family. A *patixsayih* widow had the right to a share of her husband's estate equal to her sons. When widowed, she passed to the guardianship of an adult son or the nearest agnate of the deceased husband.[24]

Divorce generally required the agreement of both parties, unless the wife was guilty of a misdemeanor, in which case her consent was not necessary. Divorce became compulsory if the woman was needed to supply heirs for her father, brother, or other male relative, in which case she had to marry an agnate of that relative. (While scholars of the subject commonly state that women might thus be compelled into such marriages, to the point of having to divorce a current husband to fulfill this duty, they also make the apparently contradictory statement that women could not be given in marriage against their will.)[25] The strict class system of the Zoroastrians also played an important part in controlling marriage and women's status in marriage. Class distinctions were rigidly demarcated (even dictating who could and who could not wear silk), and women were required to marry within their social class.

Elements of these Zoroastrian regulations suggest that notionally women were somewhere between personhood and thingness—as evidenced by wives being legally loaned for sexual and other services. An account of the Mazdakian revolutionary movement that arose in Iran during the Sasanian era also suggests that women were regarded in some sense as things, as well as, perhaps, persons. Mazdakism was a religious movement that flourished in the late fifth and early sixth centuries C.E. It was populist and egalitarian, preaching the equitable distribution of wealth and the "breaking of barriers which made for the concentration of women and wealth in the hands of the privileged classes."[26] As the Arabic historiographer Tabari reports, followers of this movement declared that "God placed the means of subsistence . . . on earth so that people divide them among themselves equally, in a manner that no one of them could have more than his share," and therefore that "it was absolutely necessary that one take from the rich for giving to the poor, so that all become equal in wealth. Whoever possesses an excess of property, women or goods he has no more right to it than another." Because such accounts of Mazdakian beliefs are not their own, originating for the most part in sources hostile to them (their own accounts were destroyed in the course of their persecution), and because they have filtered down to us through yet another civilization, we cannot assume that the clear equation between women and things was indeed Mazdakian.[27]

The notion of women as things as well as persons nevertheless appears to inhere in the Zoroastrian laws just described that govern women, even without reference to Mazdakian thought. One student points out that slaves "belonged to the category of things" but that because of internal contradictions running through legal thought, they were also regarded as persons to some extent. He goes on to observe that even when the slave was considered not only as an "object of right" but also as a subject, his legal standing never exceeded "that of a subordinate person—a woman, a ward."[28] While the thingness versus the personhood of slaves has received scholarly attention, there is no comparable exploration of the ambiguities in the status of women. The same author confines his remarks on this matter to the observation that "in connection with the legal personality, it should be noted that the scope of a person's legal capacity and competence varied with sex and age: women and minors had a limited (passive) legal capacity."[29]

Zoroastrianism in Iraq (as distinct from Iran) was principally the religion of the Persians, who predominantly constituted the ruling, warrior, and priestly classes. The population as a whole was religiously diverse and included Gnostics, pagans, Manichaeans, Jews, and, in increasing numbers from the second century on, Christians. Both Jewish and Christian communities were self-governing under the Sasanians and were generally tolerated along with other non-Zoroastrian groups, although they also underwent periods of persecution. The fortune of Christians in particular, including the extent to which they were persecuted, tended to depend on the relation of the Sasanian empire with its arch rival, the Byzantine empire, which adopted Christianity as the state religion in 330 C.E. It also varied with the degree to which the Zoroastrian church felt threatened by Christianity at a given moment. Spreading first, perhaps chiefly, among the Aramaean and Arab populations of Syria and Iraq, Christianity was increasingly adopted by Iranians as well, including members of the highest-ranking elite. For example, King Khusrau II (591–628 C.E.) had two Christians among his wives.[30]

Women as well as men were among the early Iranian Christian martyrs. Although the Christian church endorsed male dominance, the narratives of the female martyrs suggest that it nevertheless introduced ideas which opened new avenues of self-affirmation and independence to women and validated ways to resist the belief that women were defined by their biology and existed essentially to serve the function of reproduction. Thus Christianity promulgated ideas that were fundamentally subversive of the Zoroastrian social order in two ways: it enabled women to claim spiritual and moral authority and affirm their own understanding of the moral order, in defiance of male priestly authority, and it undercut the notion on which Zoroastrian laws on women were grounded—that reproduction was their primary function.

With one exception, every case of Christian martyrdom collected by Sebastian Brock and Susan Harvey in *Holy Women of the Syrian Orient* features a woman who took a vow of chastity. The issues of chastity and of resistance to marriage were the central conflict in the battle of wills between the prosecuting Zoroastrian priests and each woman. To Martha, martyred in the fourth century, a Zoroastrian priest even declared that she might continue to be a Christian; all that he required was that she renounce her virginity—a condition "particularly abhorrent to Zoroastrian mores," observe Brock and Harvey.[31] The priest proclaimed:

> "Listen to me and don't be stubborn and obstinate, following your own perverted wishes in everything. Instead, seeing that you are set on not giving up your religion, act as you like, but do this one thing only, and you shall live and not die: you are a young girl, and a very pretty one—find a husband and get married, have sons and daughters, and don't hold on to the disgusting pretext of the 'covenant' [that is, the vow of chastity]."

The wise virgin Martha replied, "If a virgin is betrothed to a man, does the natural law order that someone else should come along, attack her fiancé and snatch away this girl who has already been betrothed? Or does it say that such a virgin should give herself up to marry a man who is not her fiancé?"

"No," answered the Mobed.

Briefly taken in and believing Martha to be betrothed to a man, the priest was momentarily sympathetic, until he realized that she was speaking of Christ, whereupon he exploded in rage, saying, "I will spatter you from head to toe with blood, and then your fiancé can come along and find you turned into dust and rubbish." Martha went to her death thanking Jesus for "preserving my virginity sealed up with the imprint of the seal-ring of our promise, and for preserving my faith in the glorious Trinity" (69–70, 71).

Tarbo, the exceedingly beautiful sister of the martyr Simeon (d. 341), bishop of Seleucia-Ktesiphon, had also taken a vow of chastity. She, her sister, who was married but lived in chastity, and her servant were accused of putting a spell on the queen, who had fallen ill. The priest who examined them sent Tarbo word that he would save them if she consented to be his wife. Tarbo replied:

"Shut your mouth, you wicked man and enemy of God; don't ever again utter anything so disgusting. . . . I am the betrothed of Christ. In his name I am preserving my virginity. . . . I entrust my life to him since he is able to deliver me from your impure hands and from your evil intentions concerning me. . . .

"Foul and perverted man, why do you crazily rave after something that is neither proper nor permissible? I shall die a heroic death, for thus shall I obtain true life; I will not live in an ignominious way and then eventually die." (74–75)

She and her companions were then subjected to gruesome deaths.

Other martyrs were similarly chaste or virgin women living together or, like Anahid, daughter of the Magian Adurhormizd, in a cell alone. (The one exception, Candida, the second-century martyr and emperor's wife, died as a result of harem machinations.) The prosecuting priests made marriage, rather than the verbal renunciation of faith, the condition of their release. Among the constant features of these narratives are the priests' explosive anger and the women's derisive challenges to priestly and male authority. For instance, one priest turned "green with anger and shame" when in reply to his question "What are you?" his victim (Martha) said, "I am a woman as you can see" (68); and Anahid's reply to the priest persecuting her begins, "You silly and senseless man" (93). In another narrative the woman's refusal to make herself sexually available and to be equated wholly with her sexual being figures in her torture and her response to it. At one point her breasts are severed. "Her two breasts were quickly cut through and hung each by a mere sinew. The holy woman stretched out her hands, grabbed her breasts, and placed them in front of the Magian, with the words, 'Seeing that you very much wanted them, O Magian, here they are, do with them whatever takes your fancy. If I have any other limbs you would like, give the order and I will cut them off and put them in front of you'" (95). The value placed on virginity in early Christianity by religious thinkers in particular was to a certain extent an expression of a rejection of physicality, of the body, and in particular of sexuality, and it was a rejection that comprehended an element of misogyny in that notionally women were seen as more implicated in physicality and the body than men—they were by cultural definition essentially sexual and biological beings. This misogynist element, moreover, was given clear expression in the writings of early Christian religious thinkers, as will be discussed in chapter 2. Nevertheless, the church's emphasis on the merit of transcending the body and its valuing virginity and sexual purity in women (as well as in men) at the same time radically struck at the roots of the definition of women—as essentially and exclusively biological beings—that prevailed in many of the cultures of the region in this period. Celibate, independent women—women who consulted only their own will and that of their God (whom they consulted directly)—constituted a challenge and a threat both to male authority and to the fundamental notions enshrined in the socioreligious order of the day.

THE

Chapter 2
℘

MEDITERRANEAN

MIDDLE EAST

BY THE FIFTH AND SIXTH CENTURIES C.E. SOCIETIES of the Mediterranean Middle East essentially comprised Christian and to some extent Jewish populations. Like the societies of the Mesopotamian region, the societies of the Mediterranean Middle East have a history long predating the rise of Christianity. Indeed, the Christian societies of this region were heir to such a diversity of cultures that it would be impossible to review them comprehensively here. In the following survey I will review salient features of the mores of only some cultures of the area: those of Byzantine society, as the dominant imperial power in the eastern Mediterranean, and those of Classical Greece and ancient Egypt, as two other major cultures of the region. My survey concludes with a review of the practices and ethos of early Christianity in the eastern Mediterranean in the period immediately preceding the Arab conquests.

As already suggested, ideas fundamental to Christianity—the intrinsic value of the individual, the equal spiritual worth of men and women, and slaves and masters, and the superiority of virginity even to wifely obedience—in some ways subverted ideas fundamental

25

to the reigning patriarchies of the age. Indeed, the mere notion that virginity was superior to reproductiveness undercut the idea that women's bodies and their reproductive capacity defined the limits of their duties and proper aspirations.

The subversiveness of these ideas, however, with respect to Christian as well as non-Christian formulations of male dominance was mainly discreet and implicit. A few women were able to invoke the Christian ideals of virginity and celibacy to gain control over their lives. Elaine Pagels and others have pointed out that celibacy, or "renouncing the world," offered women immediate rewards on earth, not just rewards in heaven. Women were able to use the ideals of celibacy and worldly renunciation, Pagels observes, to "retain control of their own wealth, travel freely throughout the world as 'holy pilgrims,' devote themselves to intellectual pursuits, and found institutions which they could personally direct."[1] For the majority of women, however, such paths were not available, and despite this potentially liberating element in Christian thought, the mores determining the lives of Byzantine and other women of the eastern Mediterranean in the early Christian era, at least on the level of the normative ideal, were thoroughly restrictive.

The study of Byzantine women is still a new and developing field. The account offered by Grosdidier de Matons, one of the few authors to attempt an overview, describes mores, life-styles, and attitudes toward women that are commonly associated with Muslim rather than Christian societies. Thus, as de Matons notes, citing Michael Psellos (an eleventh-century Byzantine author and political figure), the birth of a boy was greeted with cries of joy, but not that of a girl. Daughters (and even sons) could be betrothed in infancy, and girls generally married by the age of twelve or thirteen. Middle- and upper-class girls were taught to read, write, count, and sing, but their education was generally rudimentary compared to that of their brothers. Proper conduct for girls entailed that they be neither heard nor seen outside their home. Women were not supposed to be seen in public and were kept as "cloistered as prisoners," although women and young girls might be allowed to leave the house to attend marriages, births, or religious events or to go to the public baths. Barring some general disaster, women were always supposed to be veiled, the veil or its absence marking the distinction between the "honest" woman and the prostitute. To exemplify how rigidly Byzantine society viewed the veiling and seclusion of women, de Matons again cites Psellos, who, writing in praise of his mother, observed that she raised her veil in the presence of men for the first time in her life when, at her daughter's funeral, she was too distraught to care that she did so. Psellos also commended the Cesarissa Irene for so scrupulously observing the imperative of concealing the flesh that she covered even her hands (like some zealous Muslim women of today who have taken to wearing gloves).[2] Another Byzantine patrician, of the tenth century, defending his daughter's custom of going to the baths, explained that he made sure that she only went out "veiled and suitably chaperoned." The system of using eunuchs to enforce the separation of the sexes and to guard the enclosed world of women was fully in place. The only occupations regarded as proper for women were those that she might undertake in the home—spinning, weaving, and other activities involved in making cloth.[3]

Paradoxically, as one student of Byzantine society has remarked, the strict segregation that effectively kept women apart from men other than their immediate family also created openings for women. Every institution for women, such as the public bath, required female attendants, and the existence of women midwives and doctors further reflected the societal belief that it was improper for men to attend to feminine bodily matters.[4]

The preceding two paragraphs might without modification describe the normative ideals and the practices of the middle and upper classes of Muslim societies of the Middle East from about the eighth century to the eighteenth. A study of Byzantine women by Angeliki Laiou notes that the enormous emphasis on reproduction undoubtedly correlates in part with the high infant mortality rate; Laiou also argues that the view of Byzantine women as isolated and secluded has been overemphasized because of the weight given to the written accounts of such famous figures as Psellos. The "active economic role of women presupposes a general involvement in the society and a much greater interaction with men than scholars have believed," and thus the functional reality, Laiou argues, differed from the ideal.[5] Byzantine women, she points out, were active not only as bath attendants, midwives, and doctors but also as artisans and sellers of foodstuffs. Women also engaged in retail and long-distance trade and lent and invested money. Indeed, historians are noting the same kinds of facts with respect to women in Muslim societies and pointing out that the ideals of seclusion and invisibility were by no means fully realized as social reality. But ideals, even though undercut by economic and functional exigencies, are nevertheless an important and influential component of the system of meanings determining the psychosocial experience of being for both women and men. In addition to their impact on the real but often intangible domains of psychosocial experience, they constitute part of the conceptual ground upon which laws relating to marriage, divorce, property, and other matters are based; and indeed in matters of law as well as the social ideal, there are parallels between Byzantine and Islamic legal thought. (The Byz-

antine law limiting a woman's right to testify on matters relating directly
to women, such as childbirth, which women rather than men were likely
to witness, for example, has its parallel in Islamic law.)[6]

Not uncommonly, students of Byzantine society attribute the oppressive
customs toward women to "Oriental influences."[7] Indeed, the Greeks and
Byzantines did borrow some such customs from the Persians, for example,
Alexander's decision to keep a harem the same size as that of the Persian
king he had conquered. Still, Greek society, the most direct antecedent of
Byzantine society, also had a well-developed system of male dominance,
which was also oppressive toward women.

Pre-Christian Greek societies, and in particular Classical Greek societies, are among the few in this region in which women's lives have been
systematically studied. In outlining some salient features of Classical Greek
society, I have focused on customs regarding women that show continuity
with the Byzantine customs just described—which indeed were probably
in some degree common to the major urban centers of the eastern Mediterranean in the early Christian era, including those of Syria and Egypt.

Free women in Athens in the Classical period (500–323 B.C.E.), according to Sarah Pomeroy, "were usually secluded so that they could not be
seen by men who were not close relatives. An orator could maintain that
some women were even too modest to be seen by men who were relatives,
and for a strange man to intrude upon free women in the house of another
man was tantamount to a criminal act." Men and women led separate lives,
men spending most of their days in public areas, such as the marketplace
and the gymnasium, while "respectable" women stayed at home. Women
were expected to confine themselves to their quarters and to manage the
household, care for small children and servants, and supervise the weaving
and cooking.[8] Architecturally speaking, the sexes were segregated in separate quarters, with women inhabiting the rooms away from the street and
from the public area of the house. Their clothing concealed them from the
eyes of strange men: a shawl was worn that could be drawn over the head
as a hood. The qualities admired in girls were silence and submissiveness.
Orators praised women for their silence and invisibility and avoided men-
tioning the names of "respectable" women who were still alive. Infanticide,
particularly of females, was probably practiced on occasion.[9]

According to Aristotle, the purpose of marriage and the function of
women was to provide heirs. Under Athenian law a female "heir" was required to marry the next of kin on her father's side—even if she was already
married—to produce a male heir for her father's *oikos* (family, house).[10]
Athenian law regarded the wife as "a veritable child," having the legal sta-

tus of a minor relative to her husband. Males came of age at eighteen; females never did. They could not buy or sell land but could acquire property by gift or inheritance, even though such property was administered by male guardians. They did not even go to market for food because of the belief that "purchase or exchange was a financial transaction too complex for women" and because of the "wish to protect women from the eyes of strangers."[11]

Aristotle's theories conceptualized women not merely as subordinate by social necessity but also as innately and biologically inferior in both mental and physical capacities—and thus as intended for their subservient position by "nature." He likened the rule of men over women to the rule of the "soul over the body, and of the mind and the rational element over the passionate." The male, he said, "is by nature superior, and the female inferior; and the one rules and the other is ruled."[12] Man's nature "is the most rounded off and complete"; woman is more compassionate but also "more jealous, more querulous, more apt to scold and strike . . . more void of shame and self-respect, more false of speech, more deceptive."[13] These moral and mental differences were paralleled by biological ones. Thus Aristotle saw female bodies as defective, woman being "as it were an impotent male, for it is through a certain incapacity that the female is female." The female contribution to conception was inferior: the male contributed the soul and gave form to the secretion of the female, which merely provided the material mass.[14] Aristotle's influence was widespread and enduring. His theories in effect codified and systematized the social values and practices of that society. They were presented, however, as objective scientific observations and were received by both Arab and European civilizations (or by major figures within these civilizations) as the articulation of eternal philosophical and scientific verities.

During the subsequent Hellenistic empire, women's position in Hellenistic societies outside Athens improved. This improvement is thought to reflect not only Athenian interaction with other Greek societies that were less restrictive toward women but also the influence of other Mediterranean cultures on the Greek.[15] The best-documented and most-studied example of this improved status is that of Greek women in Egypt, which was a province of the Hellenistic empire at the time. Pomeroy, who devotes an entire work to their study, points to numerous ways in which these women were freer and treated more equally in law than women had been during any previous period in Greece.[16] Greek women were not secluded in Egypt, though Greek tradition "would discourage them from business contacts with strange men"; in contrast, the traditions affecting Egyptian women did not inhibit them from associating with men (154). Pointing out differences between Greek and Egyptian laws—for instance, Greek law required women to act through male guardians, and Egyptian law regarded women as capable of acting on their own behalf—Pomeroy notes that the status of Greek women slowly improved, either because Greek laws were altered along the lines of Egyptian ones or because Greek women chose to enter into contracts according to Egyptian law (119–20). Similar changes occurred in marriage contracts, making them far more favorable for women. For example, husbands were forbidden to be polygamous, were contractually bound not to entertain mistresses, concubines, or boy lovers, and were required to return dowries and pay fines for divorcing their wives without just cause. Women enjoyed the same rights to terminate marriages as did men (97, 94).

Broadly, Pomeroy finds that "there was less distinction between the genders in Ptolemaic Egypt than there was, for example, in Athens, or in Greek society in general of an earlier period. Parallels can be found scattered elsewhere, but no other Greek society of the Hellenistic period provides a comparable quantity and variety of documentation for women's increased participation in the economy and the improvement of their economic status" (173). Whereas Athenian democracy was based on the oikos, in which the female's role was the production of heirs, in Ptolemaic Egypt, according to Pomeroy, "there was no political concept of the *oikos*. A shared life, rather than reproduction, was the purpose of marriage" (xviii). In further contrast, she notes, there is little overt reference in Ptolemaic Egypt to the production of children as women's primary contribution to the domestic economy (72).

Unfortunately, Pomeroy compares Greek and Egyptian customs only in passing and never addresses the broad subject of the influence of the more egalitarian Egyptian laws and customs on Greek ones. Her resolute avoidance of a direct discussion of the subject is striking, given its centrality to her topic and findings. In another omission she deals only with the Greeks in Egypt, although the works of other scholars—such as Dorothy Thompson and Naphtali Lewis—show that it is quite possible to work solely through Greek-language sources and still take both the Egyptian and the Greek populations into account.[17] These omissions are particularly unfortunate in that they result in the invisibility of non-Europeans and in the glossing over of the more humane and egalitarian laws of the colonized non-Europeans as compared to those of their European overlords. Consequently, they also contribute to the endorsement of an Orientalist construct of the past and the origins, history, and nature of European civilization, especially in relation to African and "Oriental" civilizations.

As is clear even from Pomeroy's tangential references, Egyptian attitudes and laws regarding women at the time of the Greek conquest and for some time thereafter were remarkably liberal and egalitarian. As with ancient Greece, Egypt's is one of the few civilizations of the region that has been studied by a number of scholars with respect to women, though studies to date are generally descriptive rather than analytic. In a recent extended study of women in ancient Egypt, Jean Vercoutter unequivocally asserts, "It is beyond all doubt that the Egyptians never had any prejudice against the 'weak sex.'" Speaking specifically of the Middle Kingdom (2060–1785 B.C.E.), Vercoutter observes, "Man did not consider himself a priori as in essence superior. Consciousness of the equality of the sexes is profoundly anchored in Egyptian beliefs, and it was doubtless this which was to permit the progressive emancipation of women in the ensuing centuries [of the New Kingdom]."[18] Writing of a New Kingdom (1570–950 B.C.E.) document, he says: "In this text, the absolute equality before the law of the man and the woman appear clearly. Doubtless this equality is at the source of the general belief in the privileged position of the woman in Egypt, in comparison with the feminine condition in other civilisations of Antiquity, and this deserves to be examined more closely."[19]

The ancient Egyptian civilization endured for several millennia (from circa 3100 B.C.E. to the Greek conquest in 333 B.C.E.), and throughout the period the status of women naturally did not remain static. Although their position possibly declined during the Middle Kingdom and was at its best during the New Kingdom, the culture by and large accorded women high esteem and was remarkably nonmisogynist. By the time of the New Kingdom, the laws governing marriage and the rights to inherit, own, and manage property were pronouncedly egalitarian. All the evidence suggests, says Christiane Desroches Noblecourt, that juridically women were equal to men. For instance, women had the right to own, administer, and dispose of property, buy and sell, inherit and pass on property, testify in court, and act in all matters directly and without intermediary. Marriage was monogamous, except for the pharaoh's. It was a contract between the parties concerned and could therefore include conditions, such as the one included in an extant marriage contract between two workers dating from the New Kingdom, which stipulates that the husband would be liable to one hundred lashes and the loss of his property should he beat his wife. Both parties had the right to divorce, women being entitled to take their property with them in that event. Marriage and divorce alike were private agreements in which the state took no part, and no ceremonies were necessary, or even available, to sanction a marriage in religion or law.[20] The state appears to have regulated sexuality only to ensure public order, a point adduced by the Egyptologist C. J. Eyre on the basis of Ramses III's claim that "the woman of Egypt could go about wherever she wanted without being molested on the road." The state also interceded in the punishment of adultery, in the interest, Eyre argues, of "public order, and the restriction of vendetta," because the evidence suggests that an adulterer caught in the act might expect to be killed on the spot by the enraged husband.[21] Noblecourt and Vercoutter report that the penalty for adultery fell equally on both sexes, though they give examples of penalties affecting a man with whom a wife committed adultery, not penalties for a husband committing adultery. Eyre suggests that it can perhaps be presumed that "copulation with an unmarried and willing woman was of relatively neutral implication socially and legally." He also makes the remarkable statement that "actual evidence for prostitution in the New Kingdom is slight."[22] Women were neither veiled nor secluded, and they could socialize freely. Noblecourt and Vercoutter give numerous examples of women's autonomy, economic activity, and fair treatment in law and the enormously positive and even dominant role of female deities, in particular Hathor and Isis, and of priestesses, who commanded great respect and high salaries. Similarly, both authors, especially Noblecourt, give detailed accounts of the prestige of queens and even of the pharaoh's spouses and female relatives. As the example of the marriage contract suggests, worker-class women, as well as women of the more privileged propertied classes, benefited from the egalitarian spirit of the laws. Nevertheless, it should be noted that only women of the more privileged classes benefited from the property laws and that the society included slaves, a group that did not benefit from any of these laws.

The situation of women of the property-owning classes in Egypt thus appears to have been thoroughly anomalous in this region and time period. Evidently, Egypt was a male-dominated society, as the institution of kingship, the absence of women from administrative positions, and the domination of certain professions by men (women were rarely scribes) all make plain. Women, though equal in some areas, were also excluded from others. Still, male dominance was apparently not accompanied by misogyny or by laws systematically and comprehensively privileging men and oppressing women. That is, misogyny and the systematic oppression of women do not "naturally" result from male dominance once urban societies develop—although studies of the evolution and development of patriarchies and of patterns of male dominance, including Lerner's study, implicitly assume a necessary, perhaps even inevitable, relation between them. Pomeroy and Noblecourt both mention details that could be analytically telling—for example, that the Egyptian state took no direct part in marriage and divorce and did not regulate the family and that unlike the Greek conception, the purpose of marriage among Egyptians was apparently not the production of heirs for the patriarchal head of household but the shared life and the pleasures and comforts it had to offer. (This observation by Pomeroy is supported by an Egyptian adage quoted by Noblecourt, advising men not to divorce women because they have not conceived, a better solution being, the adage advises, to consider adoption.)[23] Why male dominance took such an apparently benign course in Egypt, compared to the course it took in Greece and Mesopotamia, and why it was the misogynist and oppressive models for treating women that eventually won over the entire region culturally and intellectually and not the more benevolent and egalitarian models are both questions deserving further attention.

The rights and egalitarian conditions enjoyed by Egyptian women shocked the conquering Greeks, says Vercoutter. He observes that as Greek and Roman mores and laws spread, Egyptian women lost most of their rights.[24] A number of points here are noteworthy. First, the decline of the position and rights of women in Egypt occurred under the influence of European dominance and laws. Second, this decline occurred long before Egypt was conquered by the Arabs and was apparently in place in the Christian era. Third, as we shall see, the laws that took shape under Islam in the centuries immediately after the Muslim conquest, far from bringing about an improvement for women as is commonly claimed, constituted rather a further, lamentable regression for Egyptian women and for the spirit of egalitarianism, humaneness, and justice. But it is also relevant to emphasize that although Islamic laws marked a distinct decline, a Greek, a Roman, and a Christian period had already brought about major losses in women's rights and status. In effect, Islam merely continued a restrictive trend already established by the successive conquerors of Egypt and the eastern Mediterranean. In inheriting the mores that by the time of the Arab conquest had become the mores of the dominant, Christian population, Islam accepted what was deeply consonant with its own patterns of male dominance. Islam, then, did not bring radical change but a continuity and accentuation of the life-styles already in place.

Evidence dating from the early Christian era, such as the representations of Syrian women in garments concealing them from head to foot and the wealth of misogynist Christian literature, points to the entrenchment of negative attitudes toward women in early Mediterranean Christianity. Christianity did carry the seed of a radical social and sexual egalitarianism, and its valuation of virginity allowed some women, as noted earlier, to defy the patriarchal authority of other religions, to claim an inner worth that transcended and even negated the primacy of their biological worth as reproducers, and to gain some autonomy in their lives. Still, it cannot be assumed that the spread of Christianity necessarily spelled a general improvement for women or that it necessarily brought about a more favorable order for women than would have pertained under other universalist religions popular at that time in the Mediterranean world. Two of the popular religions were based on the worship of the goddess Isis and, to a lesser extent, the goddess Ishtarte. Of Egyptian and Syrian origin respectively, they spread throughout the Mediterranean, including Greece and Rome, but were most deeply rooted in Egypt and the Middle East. Both goddesses were served by priestesses as well as priests. Some studies suggest that Middle Eastern Christianity had a more positive and liberal view of women and permitted them more active roles in the church than imperial Roman and Byzantine Christianity, possibly because of the rootedness of goddess worship and women's temple service. Early on, for example, Syrian and Egyptian Christianity emphasized the female aspect of the Godhead (God the Father and Mother) in ways that appeared heretical to the dominant imperial Christianity and were eventually outlawed by that church; similarly, the active role allowed women in the Eastern church was later curtailed.[25]

Politically dominant Christianity brought with it not only an implicit radical egalitarianism but also the patriarchal ideas of its originary Judaism, and with these the religious sanction of women's social subordination and the endorsement of their essential secondariness—through, for example, the biblical account of Eve's creation from Adam's rib. Jewish patriarchal ideas and regulations regarding women were related to ideas that developed in Mesopotamia, where the Hebrews probably originated. The cultural influence of Mesopotamia was also important in Palestine, where the Hebrews later settled. Judaism in the period preceding and around the time of the rise of Christianity permitted polygamy, concubinage, and unrestricted divorce for men and did not allow women to inherit or to play a role in religion, to mention only some salient features.[26] Some of these mores were accepted by Christianity; others—polygamy, for example— were not.

Jewish feminists have argued, perhaps with some justification, that Christians have tended to scapegoat Judaism as the source of Christian misogyny.[27] It would appear, for instance, that in terms of conceptualizing women's inferiority, the Greeks, as exemplified by Aristotle's reasoning in the fourth century B.C.E., had nothing to learn from the Hebrews. Thus, it is possible that the hellenization of the Mediterranean and the military, political, and cultural dominance of Greece and Rome were at least as important to the assimilation of misogyny and oppressive mores by Christianity as the Judaic heritage. After all, Christianity rejected other ideas fundamental to Judaism, so why not Jewish misogyny? To identify Judaism as the sole or even principal source of misogyny among Christians not only risks being simplistic and inaccurate but also evades the fundamental question of why such negative definitions of women found ready acceptance in this region at this time.

Whatever the cultural source or sources, a fierce misogyny was a distinct ingredient of Mediterranean and eventually Christian thought in the centuries immediately preceding the rise of Islam. One form it took in the pre-Christian era was female infanticide. The practice of infanticide, predominantly of girls, predated Christianity and was followed by the Greeks and the Romans. Greek and Roman authors reported it as a custom of their compatriots, but not of such aliens as the Egyptians and the Jews. (In the early Christian era it was also practiced in Arabia, where it was later banned under Islam). Among the Romans the discarding (through exposure) of female infants was even implicitly codified in the law: fathers were required to raise all their sons but only one daughter. Because infanticide was common among the Roman aristocracy, it was evidently not related to material need. Christianity was to view abortion, and even contraception, as sinful—in the sixth century the Justinian code of law defined abortion as homicide—developments that may have curbed infanticide.[28]

The church's attitude on abortion and contraception, however, formed part of a broader negative ethos concerning the body and sexuality—a sense of these as sinful and shameful and of sexuality as legitimate only for procreation.[29] The consequences for women were especially opprobrious, in that they were evidently perceived as innately more implicated in physicality and sexuality than men. The shamefulness of sex was focused most intensely on the shamefulness of the female body, which had to be totally concealed (the Syrian reliefs showing a woman so heavily swathed that no part of her, not even hands or face, is uncovered date from the early Christian era). Such ideas also meant that men had to avoid contact with women, even flee from them. Merely seeing a woman represented a danger— and therefore the veil, concealing clothing, and strict segregation became increasingly emphasized.[30] The fanatical repudiation of physicality and sex-

Christian leaders misogyny

uality, and of women as their quintessential representation, found expression in a patristic literature that developed to the full the misogynist possibilities of the Bible. The writings of such church fathers as Augustine, Origen, and Tertullian, for example, reflect the concept of the female as inferior, secondary, defined entirely by her biology, and useless to man— and, worse, as causing sexual temptation, corruption, and evil. Augustine, for instance, pondering the mystery of why God had created woman, considered that he had created her neither as man's companion, for another man would have filled this role better, nor as his helper, for again another man would have been more appropriate. He concluded, "I fail to see what use woman can be to man, . . . if one excludes the function of bearing children." He said women were also a source of sexual temptation.[31] More relentless in his misogyny, Tertullian wrote of woman: "*You* are the Devil's gateway. *You* are the unsealer of the forbidden tree. *You* are the first deserter of the divine Law. *You* are she who persuaded him whom the Devil was not valiant enough to attack. *You* destroyed so easily God's image, man. On account of *your* desert, that is death, even the Son of God had to die."[32]

Islam, arising in the seventh century C.E., explicitly identified itself as a monotheism in the tradition of Judaism and Christianity, indeed as a renewal of those faiths. Because at the time of the Muslim conquest the region was dominated by a Christian church that, to some extent, had legitimized and justified misogyny by reference to biblical stories, stories that Islam either openly or implicitly recognized as divinely revealed, the new religion could incorporate seamlessly an already-developed scriptural misogyny into the socioreligious universe it too would inscribe.

In the Introduction I noted that specialist disciplines and self-contained histories dealing with ancient civilizations, all within the Middle Eastern and Mediterranean region, had the effect of emphasizing their separateness and obscuring or erasing interconnections and continuities. Certain elements mentioned in the preceding pages, such as the tendency to attribute Byzantine seclusion to "Oriental influences" and to distance the oppression of women from European societies and represent it as originating among non-Europeans, suggest yet other barriers to understanding. In particular, they suggest that ideology and nationalism continue to play a role in the writing of history, and they indicate the need to develop an integrated approach, free of racial and nationalist bias, in the exploration of this crucial period in human history.[33]

Nor is it only the Western world that developed historical constructs to serve vested political and ideological interests. Islamic civilization developed a construct of history that labeled the pre-Islamic period the Age of Ignorance and projected Islam as the sole source of all that was civilized—and used that construct so effectively in its rewriting of history that the peoples of the Middle East lost all knowledge of the past civilizations of the region. Obviously, that construct was ideologically serviceable, successfully concealing, among other things, the fact that in some cultures of the Middle East women had been considerably better off before the rise of Islam than afterward.

Knowledge of the past was eventually recovered through the endeavors of Western scholars in search of the roots, ironically not of Islamic civilizations, but of Western civilization. The Western construct of Western civilization as the direct inheritor of the civilizations of the ancient Middle East—and the concomitant Western construct of Islamic civilization as disinherited from that past, or at least not its direct heir, a construct coinciding with the one that Islamic historiography created—still underlies many college courses and textbooks. Thus, brief accounts of ancient Middle Eastern civilizations frequently figure in Western courses and textbooks on the history of Western civilization—generally without acknowledgment that Islamic civilization has the same foundation—but they do not figure in courses and textbooks on the history of Islamic civilization. Feminist works may also replicate this perspective, as does, for example, Gerda Lerner's *Creation of Patriarchy*.[34]

Part &
Two

FOUNDING DISCOURSES

WOMEN

Chapter 3

AND THE

RISE OF ISLAM

IN THE SIXTH CENTURY C.E. ARABIA FORMED, AS IT were, an island in the Middle East, the last remaining region in which patrilineal, patriarchal marriage had not yet been instituted as the sole legitimate form of marriage; although even there it was probably becoming the dominant type of marriage, the evidence suggests that among the types of marriage practiced was matrilineal, uxorilocal marriage, found in Arabia, including Mecca, about the time of the birth of Muhammad (circa 570)—the woman remaining with her tribe, where the man could visit or reside with her, and the children belonging to the mother's tribe—as well as polyandrous and polygamous marriages.

Neither the diversity of marriage practices in pre-Islamic Arabia nor the presence of matrilineal customs, including the association of children with the mother's tribe, necessarily connotes women's having greater power in society or greater access to economic resources. Nor do these practices correlate with an absence of misogyny; indeed, there is clear evidence to the contrary. The practice of infanticide, apparently confined to girls, suggests a belief that females were flawed, expendable. The Quranic verses condemning infanticide

41

capture the shame and negativity that Jahilia Arabs associated with the sex. "When one of them is told of the birth of a female child, his face is overcast with gloom and he is deeply agitated. He seeks to hide himself from the people because of the ominous [bad] news he has had. Shall he preserve it despite the disgrace involved or bury it in the ground?" (Sura 16:58–61).[1] However, the argument made by some Islamists, that Islam's banning of infanticide established the fact that Islam improved the position of women in all respects, seems both inaccurate and simplistic. In the first place, the situation of women appears to have varied among the different communities of Arabia. Moreover, although Jahilia marriage practices do not necessarily indicate the greater power of women or the absence of misogyny, they do correlate with women's enjoying greater sexual autonomy than they were allowed under Islam. They also correlate with women's being active participants, even leaders, in a wide range of community activities, including warfare and religion. Their autonomy and participation were curtailed with the establishment of Islam, its institution of patrilineal, patriarchal marriage as solely legitimate, and the social transformation that ensued.

The lives and the marriages of two of Muhammad's wives, Khadija and 'Aisha, encapsulate the kinds of changes that would overtake women in Islamic Arabia. Khadija, Muhammad's first wife, was a wealthy widow who, before her marriage to Muhammad, employed him to oversee her caravan, which traded between Mecca and Syria. She proposed to and married him when she was forty and he twenty-five, and she remained his only wife until her death at about sixty-five. She occupies a place of importance in the story of Islam because of her importance to Muhammad: her wealth freed him from the need to earn a living and enabled him to lead the life of contemplation that was the prelude to his becoming a prophet, and her support and confidence were crucial to him in his venturing to preach Islam. She was already in her fifties, however, when Muhammad received his first revelation and began to preach, and thus it was Jahilia society and customs, rather than Islamic, that shaped her conduct and defined the possibilities of her life. Her economic independence; her marriage overture, apparently without a male guardian to act as intermediary; her marriage to a man many years younger than herself; and her monogamous marriage all reflect Jahilia rather than Islamic practice.

In contrast, autonomy and monogamy were conspicuously absent in the lives of the women Muhammad married after he became the established prophet and leader of Islam, and the control of women by male guardians and the male prerogative of polygyny were thereafter to become formal

features of Islamic marriage. It was ʿAisha's lot, rather, which would pre-
figure the limitations that would thenceforth hem in Muslim women's lives:
she was born to Muslim parents, married Muhammad when she was nine
or ten, and soon thereafter, along with her co-wives, began to observe the
new customs of veiling and seclusion. The difference between Khadija's
and ʿAisha's lives—especially with regard to autonomy—foreshadows the
changes that Islam would effect for Arabian women. ʿAisha, however, lived
at a moment of transition, and in some respects her life reflects Jahilia as
well as Islamic practice. Her brief assumption of political leadership after
Muhammad's death doubtless had its roots in the customs of her forebears,
as did the esteem and authority the community granted her. The acceptance of women as participants in and authorities on the central affairs of
the community steadily declined in the ensuing Islamic period.

The evidence regarding marriage practices in pre-Islamic Arabia is fairly
scant and its implications uncertain. Evidence of matriliny and of sexual
mores consonant with matriliny, including polyandry, is, however, distinct
enough for the nineteenth-century scholar Robertson Smith to have suggested that the society was matriarchal and that Islam therefore displaced
a matriarchal order with a patriarchal one. More recently, Montgomery
Watt has put forward a modified version of this theory. Gathering evidence
of the practices of uxorilocal marriage and polyandry in some parts of Arabia, he suggests not that pre-Islamic Arabia was matriarchal but that it was
predominantly matrilineal, a society in which paternity was of little or no
importance, and that the society was in the process of changing around the
time of Muhammad's birth into a patrilineal one—a change that Islam was
to consolidate. Watt speculates that the commercial growth of Mecca during the fifth and sixth centuries and the progressively sedentary ways of its
preeminent tribe, the Quraysh, led to the breakdown of tribal values, particularly the notion of communal property, which disappeared as individual traders accumulated wealth. Men now wished to pass on property to
their offspring, which gave new importance to paternity and led eventually
to the displacement of matriliny by patriliny.[2]

Smith's and Watt's theories aside, the evidence does at least unambiguously indicate that there was no single, fixed institution of marriage and
that a variety of marriage customs were practiced about the time of the rise
of Islam, customs suggesting that both matrilineal and patrilineal systems
were extant. Uxorilocal practices, for instance, can be found in Muhammad's background. His grandfather had been taken from his mother's clan
and appropriated by his father's only with difficulty. Muhammad's mother,
Amina, remained with her clan after her marriage to ʿAbdullah, who visited

her there, and after Muhammad's birth (ʿAbdullah died before his son was born). Muhammad passed to the care of his paternal kin only after her death.[3]

Other indications of a variety of types of union being practiced include al-Bukhari's account of ʿAisha's description of the types of pre-Islamic marriage. According to ʿAisha, there were four types of marriage in the Jahilia period: one was the "marriage of people as it is today," and two of the other types were polyandrous.[4] Instances of polyandrous marriages are known for both Mecca and Medina. Also, although there is evidence of polygyny before Islam, it is speculated, on the basis of lack of reference to the practice, that the virilocal polygyny that Muhammad practiced was rare and that, rather, polygyny in a matrilineal context probably entailed a husband's visiting his different wives where they resided with their tribes.[5] Similarly, some wives might have been visited by different husbands.

Divorce and remarriage appear to have been common for both men and women, either of whom could initiate the dissolution. *Kitab al-aghani* reports: "The women in the Jahilia, or some of them, divorced men, and their [manner of] divorce was that if they lived in a tent they turned it round, so that if the door had faced east it now faced west . . . and when the man saw this he knew that she had divorced him and did not go to her." Divorce was not generally followed by the *ʿidda,* or "waiting period" for women before remarriage—an observance Islam was to insist on—and although a wife used to go into retirement for a period following her husband's death, the custom, if such it was, seems to have been laxly observed.[6]

From early on, evidently, the institution of a type of marriage based on the recognition of paternity was part of the Islamic message. The pledge of allegiance to Islam, later formalized in the Quran (Sura 60:12, known as the Pledge of the Women; the men's pledge differed only in that it included the duty of defense), seems from the start to have included an undertaking to refrain from *zina,* a term usually translated as "adultery." What zina meant before the advent of Islam—in a society in which several types of union were legitimate—is not clear, nor, apparently, was it always clear to converts to Islam. After being conquered by Muhammad, the men of Taif complained in taking the oath that zina was necessary to them because they were merchants—in other words, they attached no stigma to the practice. One woman taking the oath said, "Does a free woman commit zina?"—a response construed to mean that she felt any union that a free woman entered into could not be termed zina.[7] When first used in Islam, therefore, the term may have referred to other types of marriage, including polyandrous ones, and to forms of "temporary" marriage also practiced in the Jahilia, which Islam would outlaw. ʿAisha, in her remarks about the different types of marriage in the Jahilia, concluded: "When Mohamad (God bless and preserve him) was sent with the Truth, he abolished all the types of marriage [nikah] of the pre-Islamic period . . . except the type of marriage which people recognise today."[8] If, in prohibiting zina, Islam was to some degree outlawing previously accepted practices, this perhaps would account in part for the otherwise surely extraordinary Quranic ruling (Sura 4:19) that four witnesses are required to convict anyone of zina. The ruling suggests both that those engaging in such sexual misconduct were doing so with some openness—the openness appropriate to relatively accepted rather than immoral or prohibited practices—and that Muhammad realized that such practices could not be instantly eradicated.

Islamic reforms apparently consolidated a trend toward patriliny in sixth-century Arabia, and particularly in Mecca, where, as a result of commercial expansion, the entire fabric of the old nomadic order was undergoing change. In addition to internal economic change, external influences no doubt played some part in transforming the culture. The infiltration of Iranian influences among the tribes of northern Arabia, along with Meccan trade linking Syria and the Byzantine empire to the north with Yemen and Ethiopia to the south, meant increasing contact with and exposure to the social organization of gender in these neighboring societies. A form of monotheism, characteristic of the predominant religions in these adjoining regions, as well as patrilineal marriage, in which men controlled women's sexuality, had also begun to gain ground in a hitherto polytheistic Arabia before Muhammad began to preach Islam. The mechanisms of control, seclusion, and exclusion of women from community affairs already elaborately developed in these societies must also have become familiar to Arabians, particularly traders.

The type of marriage that Islam legitimized was, like its monotheism, deeply consonant with the sociocultural systems already in place throughout the Middle East. Within Arabia patriarchal, patrilineal, polygynous marriage was by no means starkly innovative. Rather, Islam selectively sanctioned customs already found among some Arabian tribal societies while prohibiting others. Of central importance to the institution it established were the preeminence given to paternity and the vesting in the male of proprietary rights to female sexuality and its issue. Accordant customs, such as polygamy, were incorporated while discordant or opposing customs were prohibited. Through these changes Islam fundamentally reformulated the nexus of sexuality and power between men and women. The reconceptualization of marriage implied by the Islamic regulations might justly be regarded as critical to the changes in the position of women and to the crushing limitations imposed on them following the establishment of Islam.

The laws regulating marriage and women's conduct that were developed by later Islamic societies represent their interpretations of a series of Qur-anic verses revealed to Muhammad chiefly in the Medinian period and their decisions about the legal significance of Muhammad's own practices. The sources I draw on in exploring key moments in the development of marriage and in exploring those practices of Muhammad's in relation to women that were to prove decisive for Muslim women thereafter are largely the *hadith* and other early biographical literature on Muhammad and his Compan-ions. The hadith are short narratives about Muhammad and his Compan-ions and contemporaries collected into written form in the three or four centuries after Muhammad died. They are based (as the biographical lit-erature also is) on memorized accounts first related by Muhammad's contemporaries and transmitted by a carefully authenticated chain of in-dividuals of recognized probity. Although orthodox Islam has regarded certain collections as authentic accounts of acts or utterances of Muham-mad, Western and Western-trained scholars have revised their thinking on the matter; earlier this century most scholars regarded the material essen-tially as fabrications of a later age. More recently some Western-based scholars have come round to the view that some hadith probably did orig-inate in very early Muslim times—that is, in the period immediately after Muhammad's death, when many of his Companions were alive.[9] The nar-ratives cited below are drawn from texts generally considered among the most authentic, and the circumstances and behaviors described are typical of the life-styles portrayed in the hadith corpus.

In its account of pre-Islamic customs this early material has already been ideologically edited from an Islamic standpoint. All the material we have on the Jahilia dates from at least a century after Muhammad's death and thus was written down by Muslims. For example, when Ibn Saʿd asserts that none of Muhammad's foremothers through five hundred generations was a "fornicator" in the manner "of the Jahilia," he refers presumably to the forms of union, including polyandry, that were accepted practice (Ibn Saʿd, 1, pt. 1: 32). Practices endorsed by Islam, such as polygyny, are men-tioned without parallel censure. That is, the texts themselves discretely and continually reaffirmed the new Islamic practices and branded the old im-moral.

Furthermore, although these early reports were written down by men, a significant proportion of the accounts of Muhammad and his times—the literature revered as the authentic annals of early Islam and looked to for a model of Muslim conduct and as a source of Muslim law—were re-counted on the authority of women; that is, the accounts in question were traced back as having been first recounted by a woman of Muhammad's generation, a Companion, and often a wife or daughter, of Muhammad. Women therefore (and 'Aisha most particularly) were important contrib-utors to the verbal texts of Islam, the texts that, transcribed eventually into written form by men, became part of the official history of Islam and of the literature that established the normative practices of Islamic society. The very fact of women's contribution to this important literature indicates that at least the first generation of Muslims—the generation closest to Ja-hilia days and Jahilia attitudes toward women—and their immediate de-scendants had no difficulty in accepting women as authorities. It also means that the early literature incorporates at least some material expressing the views of women fairly directly, such as 'Aisha's indignant response to the notion that women might be religiously unclean. "You equate us [women] with dogs and donkeys!" she exclaims in one hadith. "The Prophet would pray while I lay before him on the bed [between him and the *qibla,* the direction of the Ka'aba in Mecca, which Muslims face when they pray]."[10] Obviously, this does not mean that opinions or actions unacceptable to the order represented by the men who transcribed women's words into written form were not suppressed and omitted.

In a cave in Hira, a hill near Mecca, to which he often retired for solitary contemplation, Muhammad, then forty years old, received his first reve-lation: a vision of the angel Gabriel, commanding him to read. Shivering from the experience, he hurried to Khadija, who comforted him physically and mentally, wrapping him in a blanket and assuring him that he was sane. Later she took Muhammad to her cousin Waraka (to whom she had been betrothed), a Christian versed in the Hebrew scriptures, who con-firmed what had evidently occurred to her: he said that Allah had also sent the angel Gabriel to Moses. Thereafter, the Judeo-Christian framework was to be that which Muhammad declared was the framework of his proph-ethood.[11]

Khadija became his first convert. The faith of this mature, wealthy woman of high standing in the community must have influenced others, particularly members of her own important clan, the Quraysh, to accept Islam (Ibn Sa'd, 8:9).[12] From the earliest years women were among the converts, including women whose clans were fiercely opposed to Muham-mad, such as Umm Habiba, daughter of Abu Sufyan, Muhammad's for-midable enemy. They were also among the Muslims who, under the

pressure of the growing Meccan opposition to and persecution of Muhammad and his followers, emigrated (circa 615) to Abyssinia. None of the
women, however, is mentioned as having emigrated independently of her
husband.[13]

It was during the period of persecution in Mecca that Muhammad spoke
verses sanctioning the worship, along with Allah, of the three Meccan goddesses, the "daughters of Allah," Allat, Manat, and al-ʿUzza, a development that briefly appeased the Meccans. The verses, however, were shortly
abrogated, having been "thrown" upon Muhammad's tongue by Satan,
according to tradition, at a time when Meccan persecution was growing
intense and the Meccans were offering Muhammad position and wealth to
cease reviling their goddesses. As they stand in the Quran, the verses in
their amended form (Sura 53:19–22) point out the absurdity of Allah's
having daughters when mortals could have (the preferred) sons—therefore
confirming what the practice of female infanticide indicated anyway, that
the existence of goddesses in the late Jahilia period did not mean a concomitant valuation of females above or equal to males.[14]

In 619 Khadija and Abu Talib, Muhammad's uncle and protector and
head of their clan, both died within days of each other. Muhammad himself
"went down into the pit" to place Khadija in her tomb in the Hujun, a hill
near Mecca that was the burial place of her people. Neither Muhammad
nor Khadija's daughters seem to have inherited anything from her, and it
is possible that she lost her wealth in the Meccan persecution.[15]

Abu Talib had not converted to Islam, but he nevertheless granted Muhammad the full protection of a clan member and thereby made it possible
for him to survive the Meccan persecution. His successor as head of the
clan was Abu Lahab, another uncle of Muhammad's, who was married to
Umm Jamil, sister of Abu Sufyan, Muhammad's enemy. Soon after Abu
Talib died, Abu Lahab sided with his wife's clan and refused to give Muhammad clan protection. When Abu Lahab and Umm Jamil were then
cursed in a Quranic revelation, the latter, carrying a stone pestle, went
searching for Muhammad and came to where he sat with his Companion
Abu Bakr, by the Kaʿaba. God made Muhammad invisible to her, so she
asked Abu Bakr where Muhammad was. "I have been told that he is sa-
tirising me, and by God, if I had found him I would have smashed his mouth
with this stone." She then declared herself a poet and recited:

> We reject the reprobate.
> His words we repudiate.
> His religion we loathe and hate.[16]

Bereft of the clan's protection, Muhammad began actively to seek converts and protectors beyond Mecca. He initiated a series of negotiations with people from Medina who, while on pilgrimage to Mecca in 620, had converted to Islam. The following year they returned with more converts, and in June 622 seventy-five Medinians, including two women and their husbands, came to a secret meeting with Muhammad at ʿAqaba, where they pledged to protect and obey him. Their allegiance meant he would be received in Medina not as the reviled leader of a sect seeking protection but as an honored prophet and designated arbiter of the internal tribal dissensions of Medina.[17]

Meanwhile, Muhammad had also set about his own remarriage—to Sawda and ʿAisha. The idea for the marriages reportedly came from Khawla, an aunt of Muhammad's who was a convert to Islam. After Khadija's death she "served" Muhammad, presumably seeing to the housework, along with his daughters. Muhammad had in the past intervened on her behalf, rebuking her husband for his celibacy and his consequent neglect of his duties toward his wife. When Khawla broached the idea of Muhammad's remarriage, he asked whom she would suggest. ʿAisha if he wanted a virgin, she said, and Sawda if a nonvirgin. "Go," he is said to have replied, "bespeak them both for me." Having two wives concurrently was not a new practice in that society, but it was new for Muhammad, leading some investigators to speculate that he may have had a marriage contract with Khadija specifying that during her lifetime she would be his only wife.[18]

Sawda, a Muslim widow and former emigrant to Abyssinia, described as "no longer young," sent back with Khawla the message "My affair is in your hands," indicating her consent (Ibn Saʿd, 8:36). This point confirms that as Khadija's case had suggested, widows in the Jahilia were apparently free to dispose of their persons in marriage without consulting any guardians (Ibn Saʿd, 8:36).[19] The marriage of Muhammad and Sawda probably took place shortly after Khadija's death.

ʿAisha's case was different. She was the six-year-old daughter of Muhammad's closest and most important supporter, Abu Bakr. Khawla took the proposal to Umm Rumman, ʿAisha's mother, who deferred the matter to her husband. He said that because ʿAisha was already betrothed, he would first have to release her from that commitment. There is no suggestion that anyone thought the marriage inappropriate because of the discrepancy in their ages, though ʿAisha's prior betrothal was evidently to a boy. Abu Bakr went to seek her release from the boy's parents and found the mother, who was not a Muslim, particularly anxious to release her son from that betrothal because she was afraid it might lead to his converting to Islam.

'Aisha later recalled that she had realized she was married (that is, that the marriage agreement had been concluded) when her mother called her in from her games with her friends and told her she must stay indoors; and so "it fell into my heart," she said, "that I was married." She did not, she recalled, ask to whom (Ibn Sa'd, 8:40). Muhammad thereafter continued his regular daily visits to Abu Bakr's house, but the marriage was not consummated until after the Muslims had migrated to Medina.

The Muslims migrated to Medina in small groups in the three months after the agreement with the Medinians at 'Aqaba had been concluded. Among the men, Muhammad and Abu Bakr left last, and secretly, to escape a Meccan plot to murder Muhammad, for the Meccans now feared that at Medina he would grow too strong for them. The two hid in the hills near Mecca, waiting for the search to be given up. Asma, 'Aisha's sister, took them provisions at night and helped load their camels when they were ready to depart. After they left, she returned home and found a group of hostile Meccans searching for the two men. When she denied knowledge of their whereabouts, she was slapped so hard, she related, that her earring flew off.[20]

Muhammad arrived in Medina with a large religious following and an important political standing. The year of the migration, or Hijra (Hegira), 622, is reckoned by Muslims as the first year of the Islamic era, and the migration did indeed inaugurate a new type of community, one that lived by the new values and the new laws of Islam—many of which were elaborated over the next few years.

Work was immediately begun on the building that was to be Muhammad's dwelling, the courtyard of which was to be both a mosque and the place where he would conduct community affairs. He meanwhile lodged on the ground floor of a two-room house belonging to the couple who lived nearest the construction. Some sense of the material privation of their lives and Muhammad's is suggested by the couple's response to breaking a jar of water: fearing it would leak through onto Muhammad and having no cloth to mop it up with, they used their own garments.[21]

Muhammad had Sawda and his daughters brought from Mecca. Like the dwellings built later for Muhammad's other wives, Sawda's was built along the eastern wall of the mosque and consisted of one room about twelve by fourteen feet, with possibly a verandalike enclosure giving onto the mosque courtyard; the courtyard had pillars of palm trunks and a roof of palm branches. Muhammad had no separate room, sharing in turn those of his wives.[22]

Abu Bakr also had his family fetched, and they joined him in a house in the suburb of Sunh. When 'Aisha was no more than nine or ten, Abu Bakr, anxious no doubt to create the further bond of kinship between Muhammad and himself, asked Muhammad why he was delaying consummation of the marriage. When Muhammad replied that he was as yet unable to provide the marriage portion, Abu Bakr forthwith provided it himself (Ibn Sa'd, 8:43). Thereafter, the marriage was consummated in 'Aisha's father's house in Sunh. As 'Aisha recalled the occasion:

> My mother came to me and I was swinging on a swing. . . . She brought me down from the swing, and I had some friends there and she sent them away, and she wiped my face with a little water, and led me till we stopped by the door, and I was breathless [from being on the swing] and we waited till I regained my breath. Then she took me in, and the Prophet was sitting on a bed in our house with men and women of the Ansar [Medinians] and she set me on his lap, and said, "These are your people. God bless you in them and they in you." And the men and women rose immediately and went out, And the Prophet consummated the marriage in our house.[23]

'Aisha became, and remained Muhammad's undisputed favorite, even when he had added beautiful, sought-after women to his harem. Her most recent scholarly biographer, Nabia Abbott, stresses Muhammad's tender care and patience with her; he joined even in her games with dolls. To modern sensibilities, however, such details, like 'Aisha's recollections of her marriage and its consummation, do not make the relationship more comprehensible. If anything, they underscore its pathos and tragedy. Nevertheless, Abbott is right to assume that the relevant matter is not the sensibilities of other ages but rather the accurate representation of the relationship. Consequently, other aspects, such as their apparent emotional equality and their mutual dependence, should also be noted. These are suggested by, for instance, Muhammad's sullen, wounded withdrawal following the famous necklace incident: 'Aisha was left behind at a campsite because she had wandered off looking for the beads of her necklace. Returning the following morning, her camel escorted by a young man, she was suspected by the community, and finally by Muhammad, of infidelity. Muhammad's distress over the matter became so intense that his revelations ceased for the duration of their estrangement; his first revelations at the end of that period were the verses declaring her innocence.[24] Complementarily, 'Aisha must have felt reasonably equal to and unawed by this prophet of God, for his announcement of a revelation permitting him to enter into marriages disallowed other men drew from her the retort, "It seems to me your Lord hastens to satisfy your desire!" (Ibn Sa'd, 8:112). In other words, in all its aspects their relationship was defined by the particular social context—not only in the sense of the mores of the society but also in the sense of the ways in which the mores of a society shape the inner psychic and emotional structures of its members.

The details of 'Aisha's betrothal and marriage indicate that parents before and around the time of the rise of Islam might arrange marriages between children, male or female, and their peers or elders. They indicate, too, that for girls betrothal entailed control and supervision of their sexuality, some form of seclusion ('Aisha understood she was married when told she had to stay indoors). A patriarchal notion of marriage and sexuality apparently, then, already pertained in 'Aisha's childhood environment. Similarly, the arrangements for Muhammad's simultaneous betrothal to two women were represented in the literature not as innovatory but, again, as ordinary. It is, however, possible that the reports, coming from the pens of Muslim authors, do not accurately reflect late Jahilia and early Islamic practices but rather conform to a later Islamic understanding of marriage.

'Aisha's removal to Muhammad's dwelling, where Sawda already lived and where they would soon be joined by more wives, introduced into Islam the type of polygyny—virilocal polygyny—that some investigators believe was Muhammad's innovation.

Three months after Muhammad's marriage to 'Aisha he married Hafsa, daughter of 'Umar ibn al-Khattab, who along with Abu Bakr was among Muhammad's closest supporters. Hafsa had lost her husband in the battle of Badr. The majority of Muhammad's wives thereafter were also widows of Muslims slain in support of Islam. Soon after this marriage, and after the battle of Uhud (625), which widowed many Muslim women, the Qur-anic verses encouraging polygyny—"Marry other women as may be agree-able to you, two or three or four" (Sura 4:3)—were revealed. Many of these widows were Meccan immigrants and so could not return to the support of their clans. The Muslim community consequently found itself with the responsibility of providing for them. Encouraging men to marry more wives both settled the matter of support for the widows and consolidated the young society in its new direction: it absorbed the women into the new type of family life and forestalled reversion to Jahilia marriage practices.

There was little intermarriage between Medinians and Meccans, perhaps chiefly because of their different attitudes toward marriage and especially toward polygyny. Medinian women apparently were noticeably more as-sertive than Meccan women. 'Umar ibn al-Khattab complained that before coming to Medina "we the people of Quraysh [Mecca] used to have the upper hand over our wives, but when we came among the Ansar [Helpers], we found that their women had the upper hand over their men, so our women also started learning the ways of the Ansari women."[25] One Medinian woman is said to have offered herself in marriage to Muhammad—who accepted—then to have withdrawn her offer when her family, who disapproved, pointed out that she could never put up with co-wives (Ibn Saʿd, 8:107–8).

Women's right to inherit property—generally speaking, a woman is entitled to about half a man's share—was another Islamic decree that Medinians found novel and apparently uncongenial. Medina's being an agricultural community presumably made the new inheritance law, involving the division of land, more complex in its consequences than for commercial Mecca, where property was in herds and material goods and where even before Islam it was apparently the custom for women to inherit.[26]

Accounts of the battle of Uhud portray women, including Muhammad's wives, actively and freely participating in the ostensibly male domain of warfare. One man described seeing ʿAisha and another wife of Muhammad's, their garments tucked up and their anklets showing, carrying water to men on the battlefield. Other women on the Muslim side are mentioned as caring for the injured and removing the dead and wounded from the field. On the opposing side Hind bint ʿUtbah, wife of the Meccan leader Abu Sufyan, led some fourteen or fifteen women of the Meccan aristocracy onto the battlefield, playing out women's traditional Jahilia role in war of singing war songs and playing tambourines.[27] The Meccans won, and Hind, who had lost a father and brothers to the Muslims in previous wars, cut out the liver of the man who had killed her father and cut off his nose and ears and those of other dead men on the field. Wearing necklaces and bracelets of the severed parts, she stood on a rock declaiming, in satirical verse, her triumphant revenge (Ibn Saʿd, 3:1, 5–6). The extreme ferocity attributed to her, reported in works compiled in the Abbasid age, perhaps owes its bloodiness to Abbasid hatred of the Umayyad dynasty, founded by Hind's son.

Such free participation in community affairs would soon be curtailed by the formal introduction of seclusion. The lives of Muhammad's wives were the first to be circumscribed, and during Muhammad's lifetime the verses enjoining seclusion applied to them alone. Early texts record the occasions on which the verses instituting veiling and seclusion for Muhammad's wives were revealed and offer vignettes of women's lives in the society Islam was displacing, as well as record the steps by which Islam closed women's arenas of action. These texts do not distinguish in their language between veiling and seclusion but use the term *hijab* interchangeably to mean "veil," as in *darabat al-hijab,* "she took the veil"—which in turn meant "she became a wife of Muhammad's," Muhammad's wives but not his concubines donning the veil—and to mean "curtain" (its literal meaning) in the sense of separation or partition. They also use the same term to refer generally to the seclusion or separation of Muhammad's wives and to the decrees relating to their veiling or covering themselves.[28]

The feast at Muhammad's wedding to Zeinab bint Jahsh, according to one account, was the occasion for the revelation of a number of these verses. Some of the wedding guests stayed on too long in Zeinab's room chatting, which annoyed Muhammad and thus occasioned the revelation of the verses instituting seclusion for his wives. At this or some other meal, according to another account, the hands of some of the men guests touched the hands of Muhammad's wives, and in particular ʿUmar's hand touched ʿAisha's (Ibn Saʿd, 8:126). The Quranic verses instituting seclusion read as if they followed such events: "O ye who believe, enter not the houses of the Prophet, unless you are invited to a meal, and then not in anticipation of its getting ready. But enter when you are called, and when you have eaten, disperse, linger not in eagerness for talk. This was a cause of embarrassment for the Prophet. . . . When you ask any of the wives of the Prophet for something, ask from behind a curtain. That is purer for your hearts and for their hearts" (Sura 33:54).

An account attributed to ʿAisha connects these and the further verses—which enjoined Muhammad's wives and Muslim women generally to draw their cloaks around them so that they could be recognized as believers and thus not be molested (Sura 33:60)—with another occasion. ʿUmar ibn al-Khattab, according to ʿAisha, had been urging Muhammad to seclude his wives, though unsuccessfully. One night she and Sawda went outside (there was no indoor sanitation), and Sawda, being tall, was recognized by ʿUmar from a distance. He called out to her, saying that he recognized her, and later again urged Muhammad to seclude his wives. According to one account, ʿUmar wanted Muhammad to seclude his wives to guard against the insults of the "hypocrites," a group of Medinians whose faith was lukewarm, who would abuse Muhammad's wives and then claim that they had taken them for slaves (Ibn Saʿd, 8:125–27).[29]

According to another account, ʿUmar urged Muhammad to seclude his wives because Muhammad's success was now bringing many visitors to the mosque.[30] (That several different occasions and reasons are given for those verses does not mean that they are all untrue but rather that they were part of the background to the new edicts and represented the kinds of situations that were becoming unacceptable to new Muslim eyes.) The mosque was the place where Muhammad conducted all religious and community affairs and the center of lively activity. Muhammad once received there the leaders of a tribe not yet converted to Islam; during the negotiations three tents were put up for them in the courtyard. Envoys from other tribes came there looking for Muhammad. Medinian chiefs spent the night there after a battle. One warrior brought the head of an enemy to the mosque. People without means slept in the arbor of the north wall. People also simply sat or lay about or put up tents. One woman, an emancipated slave, "put up a tent or hut in the mosque" and visited and talked with Muhammad's wives, according to ʿAisha. Many who came hoping for some favor from Muhammad approached one or another of his wives first to enlist their assistance.[31]

By instituting seclusion Muhammad was creating a distance between his wives and this thronging community on their doorstep—the distance appropriate for the wives of the now powerful leader of a new, unambiguously patriarchal society. He was, in effect, summarily creating in nonarchitectural terms the forms of segregation—the gynecum, the harem quarters—already firmly established in such neighboring patriarchal societies as Byzantium and Iran, and perhaps he was even borrowing from those architectural and social practices. As a successful leader, he presumably had the wealth to give his wives the servants necessary for their seclusion, releasing them from tasks that women of Muhammad's family and kin are described as doing: Asma, Abu Bakr's daughter, fetched water, carried garden produce, ground corn, and kneaded bread, and Fatima, Muhammad's daughter and ʿAli ibn Abi Talib's wife, also ground corn and fetched water (Ibn Saʿd, 8:182–83).[32]

Veiling was apparently not introduced into Arabia by Muhammad but already existed among some classes, particularly in the towns, though it was probably more prevalent in the countries that the Arabs had contact with, such as Syria and Palestine. In those areas, as in Arabia, it was connected with social status, as was its use among Greeks, Romans, Jews, and Assyrians, all of whom practiced veiling to some degree.[33] It is nowhere explicitly prescribed in the Quran; the only verses dealing with women's clothing, aside from those already quoted, instruct women to guard their private parts and throw a scarf over their bosoms (Sura 24:31–32).

Throughout Muhammad's lifetime veiling, like seclusion, was observed only by his wives. Moreover, that the phrase "[she] took the veil" is used in the hadith to mean that a woman became a wife of Muhammad's suggests that for some time after Muhammad's death, when the material incorporated into the hadith was circulated, veiling and seclusion were still considered peculiar to Muhammad's wives. It is not known how the customs spread to the rest of the community. The Muslim conquests of areas in which veiling was commonplace among the upper classes, the influx of wealth, the resultant raised status of Arabs, and Muhammad's wives being taken as models probably combined to bring about their general adoption.

There is no record of the reactions of Muhammad's wives to these institutions, a remarkable silence given their articulateness on various topics (particularly ʿAisha's, as the traditions well attest)—a silence that draws attention to the power of suppression that the chroniclers also had. One scholar has suggested that it was probably the wives' reaction to the imposition of seclusion that precipitated Muhammad's threat of mass divorce and the tense situation that culminated in the verses presenting Muhammad's wives with the choice of divorce.[34] Muhammad's wives were presented with the choice between divorce and continuing as his wives, which meant accepting the special conduct expected of them in this life and eventually receiving the special rewards awaiting them in heaven.

The threatened divorce was no mere domestic affair. During the month in which Muhammad remained withdrawn from his wives the community became gravely concerned over the potential consequences, because Muhammad's marriages cemented crucial ties with important members of the Muslim community in Medina and with tribal leaders outside Medina as well. The rumor of a possible divorce reportedly caused greater public concern than an anticipated Ghassanid invasion: Abu Bakr and ʿUmar, fathers of ʿAisha and Hafsa respectively (and the first and second caliphs after Muhammad's death), became so deeply perturbed that they reprimanded their daughters.

Given the seriousness of the situation, any of the purported causes of the breach were, as several scholars have noted, astonishingly trivial. The described activities and rivalries seem to have been part of ordinary life and therefore do not seem to be grounds enough for precipitating a serious political crisis. According to one account, Muhammad's wives were clamoring for more worldly goods than he had means to provide. Another account blames the bickering between ʿAisha and Zeinab over the equitable distribution of a slaughtered animal. Yet another claims that Hafsa had caught Muhammad with Miriam, his Egyptian concubine, in her own (Hafsa's) apartment, but on ʿAisha's day. In spite of promising Muhammad that she would not tell ʿAisha, Hafsa broke her vow. Soon after ʿAisha confronted him, the entire harem was up in arms over the matter (Ibn Saʿd, 8:131–39).[35]

The verses, which specifically enjoin and stress the importance of "obedience," indeed suggest that some kind of protest or disobedience had been under way among Muhammad's wives.

> Say, O Prophet, to thy wives: If you desire the life of this world and its adornment, come then, I shall make provision for you and send you away in a handsome manner. But if ye desire Allah and His Messenger and the Home of the Hereafter, then Allah has prepared for those of you who carry out their obligations fully a great reward. Wives of the Prophet, if any of you should act in a manner incompatible with the highest standards of piety, her punishment will be doubled. That is easy for Allah. But whoever of you is completely obedient to Allah and His Messenger, and acts righteously, We shall double her reward; and We have prepared an honorable provision for her. Wives of the Prophet, if you safeguard your dignity, you are not like any other women. So speak in a simple, straightforward manner, lest he whose mind is diseased should form an ill design; and always say the good word. Stay at home and do not show off in the manner of the women of the days of ignorance. (Sura 33:29–35)

Muhammad first put the choice to ʿAisha, advising her to consult her parents before making a decision. Replying that she had no need to consult her parents—"You know they would never advise me to leave you"—she chose to stay. The other wives followed suit. Verses conferring on Muhammad's wives the title and dignity of Mothers of the Believers—perhaps in compensation—and forbidding them to remarry after his death also probably belong to the same period as the verses that put to his wives the choice of divorce.[36]

In 630 the Muslims took Mecca with little bloodshed. Abu Sufyan, after surrendering at the Muslim encampment, returned to Mecca and called on his people to convert to Islam. His wife, Hind bint ʿUtbah, enraged by his surrender, denounced him publicly and then, realizing the cause was lost, shattered the statues of her gods. Some sources say that Hind was among the three or four women condemned to death and that she saved herself only by hastily converting to Islam, but this may be an anti-Umayyad embellishment of her story.[37] In any event she spiritedly led the Meccan women in taking the oath of allegiance to Islam. Muhammad led, and Hind responded.

"You shall have but one God."
"We grant you that."

"You shall not steal."

"Abu Sufyan is a stingy man, I only stole provisions from him."

"That is not theft. You will not commit adultery."

"Does a free woman commit adultery?"

"You will not kill your children [by infanticide]."

"Have you left us any children that you did not kill at the battle of Badr?" (Ibn Saʿd, 8:4)

With the conquest of Mecca the Muslims received the key of the Kaʿaba, which at the time was in the hands of Sulafa, a woman. According to Muslim sources, Sulafa's son had merely entrusted her with it for safekeeping, just as Hulail, the last priest-king of Mecca, had previously—also according to Muslim sources—entrusted his daughter Hubba with the key. Although no other women are mentioned as keepers of the key, Sulafa's and Hubba's minimal role in Islamic records probably reflects Muslim assumptions projected onto the earlier society. However, in a society such as that of the Jahilia, which had *kahinas* (female soothsayers) and priestesses, Hubba may well have been at least in some sense a successor to her father or a transmitter of his powers.[38]

Muhammad died two years after the conquest, following a brief illness. Lying sick in his wife Maimuna's room, where his other wives visited him, he began asking in whose room he was due to stay the next day and the next, in an attempt, they realized, to figure out when he was due at ʿAisha's. Finally, he asked to be allowed to retire there, and a few days later, on June 11, 632, he died. His unexpected death precipitated a crisis in the Muslim community. Abu Bakr was able to settle the question of where he should be buried by recalling that Muhammad had said that a prophet should be buried where he expires (Ibn Saʿd, 2, pt. 2: 71). Thus, Muhammad was buried in ʿAisha's room, which is now, after the Kaʿaba, the most sacred spot in Islam.[39] Abu Bakr and ʿUmar were also buried there, as they requested, although ʿAisha had hoped to keep the last space for herself. After ʿUmar's burial, she had a partition built between her section of the room and the tombs: she had felt at home, she said, sharing the room with her husband and father, but with ʿUmar there she felt in the presence of a stranger (Ibn Saʿd, 3, pt. 1: 245, 264).

Muhammad's death sparked off a series of rebellions in various parts of Arabia, most of which had converted to Islam by then. At least one armed rebellion was led by a woman, Salma bint Malik, and one of the "false prophets" who appeared as leaders of revolts against the Islamic state was a woman, too. Captured by the Muslims in a battle led by her mother in

628, Salma bint Malik was given to 'Aisha by Muhammad. She served 'Aisha for a time and later married a relative of Muhammad's. Upon Muhammad's death she withdrew and returned to her people, who were among those now rebelling against Islam. Her mother, when captured by the Muslims, had been executed by having each foot tied to a different beast, which then rent her in two. Salma, determined to avenge her or die, led her soldiers in person, riding on her mother's camel. She was finally killed, but not before "a hundred others" had fallen around her.[40]

The false prophet was Sajah bint 'Aws, of the Tamim, whose mother was of the Banu Taghlib, a largely Christianized tribe. The Tamim were divided between supporting and opposing Islam. Those wanting to throw it off supported Sajah. When her faction lost in a civil war and she was forced to leave Tamimi territory with her army, she headed for Yamama, the capital of another false prophet, Musailamah, and apparently made a treaty with him—but nothing is known of her after that. Her deity was referred to as Rabb al-sirab, "The Lord of the Clouds," but her teachings have not been preserved.[41]

Salma and Sajah were, it seems, a rebel and a prophet who happened to be women. But in Hadramaut women may have rebelled as women, rejoicing at Muhammad's death because of the limitations Islam had brought to them. "When the Prophet of God died," reads a third-century (Islamic) account of this rebellion, "the news of it was carried to Hadramaut."

> There were in Hadramaut six women of Kindah and Hadramaut, who were desirous for the death of the Prophet of God; they therefore (on hearing the news) dyed their hands with henna and played on the tambourine. To them came the harlots of Hadramaut and did likewise, so that some twenty-odd women joined the six. . . . [The text then lists the names of some women, including two it describes as grandmothers.] Oh horseman, if thou dost pass by, convey this message from me to Abu Bakr, the successor of Ahmad [Muhammad]: leave not in peace the harlots, black as chaff, who assert that Muhammad need not be mourned; satisfy that longing for them to be cut off, which burns in my breast like an unquenchable ember.[42]

Abu Bakr sent al-Muhagir with men and horses against the women, and although the men of Kindah and Hadramaut came to the women's defense, al-Muhagir cut off the women's hands. This account is intriguing, for why should the opposition of harlots have been threatening enough to Islam to merit sending a force against them? Three of the women listed were of the nobility, and four belonged to the royal clan of Kindah. Their status and the support of their men suggest that they were priestesses, not prostitutes, and that their singing and dancing were not personal rejoicing but traditional performances intended to incite their tribespeople to throw off the yoke of the new religion. They were evidently successful enough in gathering support to constitute a threat worthy of armed suppression.[43]

Furthermore, some Arabian women at the time of the institution of Islam, and not only priestesses, doubtless understood and disliked the new religion's restrictions on women and its curtailment of their independence. For them Muhammad's death would have been a matter for celebration and the demise of his religion a much desired eventuality. That some women felt Islam to be a somewhat depressing religion is suggested by a remark of Muhammad's great-granddaughter Sukaina, who, when asked why she was so merry and her sister Fatima so solemn, replied that it was because she had been named after her pre-Islamic great-grandmother, whereas her sister had been named after her Islamic grandmother.[44]

Muhammad's wives continued to live in their mosque apartments, revered by the community as the Mothers of the Believers. Financially they seemed to depend on private means, on their families, or on money they earned through their skills. Sawda, for instance, derived an income from her fine leatherwork. They apparently inherited nothing from Muhammad, Abu Bakr maintaining that Muhammad had wished his modest property to go to charity. In 641, as a result of the immense revenues brought by the Arab conquests 'Umar, the next caliph, initiated state pensions and placed the Mothers of the Believers at the head of the list, awarding them generous sums. This recognition further confirmed their already prominent status. 'Aisha, as Muhammad's favorite wife, received the state's highest pension. Acknowledged as having special knowledge of Muhammad's ways, sayings, and character, she was consulted on his *sunna*, or practice, and gave decisions on sacred laws and customs.[45] Other wives were also consulted and were cited as the sources of traditions, though none was as prominent and prolific as 'Aisha.

'Umar's reign (634–44) is regarded as the period in which many of the major institutions of Islam originated, for 'Umar promulgated a series of religious, civil, and penal ordinances, including stoning as punishment for adultery. He was harsh toward women in both private and public life: he was ill-tempered with his wives and physically assaulted them, and he sought to confine women to their homes and to prevent their attending prayers at the mosques. Unsuccessful in this last attempt, he instituted segregated prayers, appointing a separate imam for each sex. He chose a male imam for the women, another departure from precedent, for it is known

that Muhammad appointed a woman, Umm Waraka, to act as imam for
her entire household, which included, so far as can be ascertained, men as
well as women (Ibn Saʿd, 8:335).[46] Moreover, after Muhammad's death
ʾAisha and Umm Salama acted as imams for other women (Ibn Saʿd, 8:355–
56). Contrary to Muhammad's practice, ʿUmar also prohibited Muhammad's wives from going on pilgrimage (a restriction lifted in the last year
of his reign). This prohibition must have provoked the discontent of the
Mothers of the Believers, although "history" has not recorded any, just as
it has not recorded any opposition on the part of Muhammad's widows to
ʿUmar's attempt to prevent women from attending prayers at the mosques
(Ibn Saʿd, 8:150).[47] The consistent silence on such issues now speaks eloquently. Given the harsh suppression at Hadramaut, there can be little
doubt that the guardians of Islam erased female rebellion from the pages
of history as ruthlessly as they eradicated it from the world in which they
lived. They doubtless considered it their duty.

ʿUthman, the third caliph (644–56), allowed Muhammad's wives to go
on pilgrimage and revoked ʿUmar's arrangement for separate imams. Men
and women once again attended mosque together, although women now
gathered in a separate group and left after the men (Ibn Saʿd, 5:17). ʿUthman's restoration of some liberties to women, however, but briefly stayed
a tide that was moving inexorably in the reverse direction. ʾAisha still took
an active and eventually public role in politics, though acting out a part
that in reality belonged to a dying order. When ʿUthman was murdered,
she delivered, veiled, a public address at the mosque in Mecca, proclaiming
that his death would be avenged. She proceeded to gather around her one
of the two factions opposing the succession of ʾAli ibn Abi Talib; the controversy over his succession gave rise eventually to the split between Sunni
and Shiite Muslims. Factional opposition culminated in the Battle of the
Camel—named after the camel on which ʾAisha sat while exhorting the
soldiers to fight and directing the battle, like her Jahilia forebears. ʾAli, realizing her importance, had her camel cut down, causing her army to fall
into disarray. The victorious ʾAli (who became the fourth caliph, 656–61)
treated ʾAisha magnanimously. Nevertheless, the important role that she
had played in this controversial battle—the first in which Muslims shed
Muslim blood—earned her the reproach of many. Charges that the opposition had made from the start—that ʾAisha's going into battle violated
the seclusion imposed by Muhammad, who had ordered his wives to stay
at home, women's proper place in this new order—seemed more fully vin-
dicated by her defeat.[48]

We have surveyed key moments in the shaping of Islamic marriage, as well as in the elaboration of the mechanisms of control that the new relationship between the sexes necessitated, and we have seen the participation and independence of women in the society in which Islam arose and the diminution of their liberties as Islam became established. Jahilia women were priests, soothsayers, prophets, participants in warfare, and nurses on the battlefield. They were fearlessly outspoken, defiant critics of men; authors of satirical verse aimed at formidable male opponents; keepers, in some unclear capacity, of the keys of the holiest shrine in Mecca; rebels and leaders of rebellions that included men; and individuals who initiated and terminated marriages at will, protested the limits Islam imposed on that freedom, and mingled freely with the men of their society until Islam banned such interaction.

In transferring rights to women's sexuality and their offspring from the woman and her tribe to men and then basing the new definition of marriage on that proprietary male right, Islam placed relations between the sexes on a new footing. Implicit in this new order was the male right to control women and to interdict their interactions with other men. Thus the ground was prepared for the closures that would follow: women's exclusion from social activities in which they might have contact with men other than those with rights to their sexuality; their physical seclusion, soon to become the norm; and the institution of internal mechanisms of control, such as instilling the notion of submission as a woman's duty. The ground was thus prepared, in other words, for the passing of a society in which women were active participants in the affairs of their community and for women's place in Arabian society to become circumscribed in the way that it already was for their sisters in the rest of the Mediterranean Middle East.

Marriage as sanctioned or practiced by Muhammad included polygamy and the marriage of girls nine or ten years old. Quranic utterances sanctioned the rights of males to have sexual relations with slave women (women bought or captured in war) and to divorce at will. In its fundamentals, the concept of marriage that now took shape was similar to that of Judaic marriage and similar, too, in some respects to Zoroastrian marriage, practiced by the ruling Iranian elite in the regions bordering Arabia.[49] Not surprisingly, once the Islamic conquests brought about an intermingling of these socioreligious systems, Islam easily assimilated features of the others.

So far I have focused on the practices of the first community with respect to women and marriage, omitting from consideration the broad ethical field of meaning in which those practices were embedded—that is, the ethical teachings Islam was above all established to articulate. When those teachings are taken into account, the religion's understanding of women and gender emerges as far more ambiguous than this account might suggest. Islam's ethical vision, which is stubbornly egalitarian, including with respect to the sexes, is thus in tension with, and might even be said to subvert, the hierarchical structure of marriage pragmatically instituted in the first Islamic society.

The tensions between the pragmatic and ethical perspectives, both forming part of Islam, can be detected even in the Quran, and both perspectives have left their mark on some of the formal rulings on women and marriage made in the ensuing period. Thus some Quranic verses regarding marriage and women appear to qualify and undercut others that seemingly establish marriage as a hierarchical institution unequivocally privileging men. Among the former are the verses that read: "Wives have rights corresponding to those which husbands have, in equitable reciprocity" (Sura 2:229). Similarly, verses such as those that admonish men, if polygamous, to treat their wives equally and that go on to declare that husbands would not be able to do so—using a form of the Arabic negative connoting permanent impossibility—are open to being read to mean that men should not be polygamous. In the same way, verses sanctioning divorce go on to condemn it as "abhorrent to God." The affirmation of women's right to inherit and control property and income without reference to male guardians, in that it constitutes a recognition of women's right to economic independence (that most crucial of areas with respect to personal autonomy), also fundamentally qualifies the institution of male control as an all-encompassing system.

Thus, while there can be no doubt that in terms of its pragmatic rulings Islam instituted a hierarchical type of marriage that granted men control over women and rights to permissive sexuality, there can be no doubt, either, that Islamic views on women, as on all matters, are embedded in and framed by the new ethical and spiritual field of meaning that the religion had come into existence to articulate. I discuss the resultant ambiguities, and the different light cast on the issue of gender when the ethical meanings of the Quran are considered, in the next chapter.

Chapter 4
&

THE

TRANSITIONAL

AGE

THE EGALITARIAN CONCEPTION OF GENDER INHERING
in the ethical vision of Islam existed in tension with the
hierarchical relation between the sexes encoded into
the marriage structure instituted by Islam. This egalitarianism is a consistent element of the ethical utterances of the Quran. Among the remarkable features of
the Quran, particularly in comparison with the scriptural texts of other monotheistic traditions, is that
women are explicitly addressed; one passage in which
this occurs declares by the very structure of the utter-
ance, as well as in overt statement, the absolute moral
and spiritual equality of men and women.

> For Muslim men and women,—
> For believing men and women,
> For devout men and women,
> For true [truthful] men and women,
> For men and women who are
> Patient and constant, for men
> And women who humble themselves,
> For men and women who give
> In charity, for men and women
> Who fast (and deny themselves),

64

> For men and women who
> Guard their chastity, and
> For men and women who
> Engage much in God's praise,—
> For them has God prepared
> Forgiveness and a great reward. (Sura 33:35)[1]

Balancing virtues and ethical qualities, as well as concomitant rewards, in one sex with the precisely identical virtues and qualities in the other, the passage makes a clear statement about the absolute identity of the human moral condition and the common and identical spiritual and moral obligations placed on all individuals regardless of sex.

The implications are far-reaching. Ethical qualities, including those invoked here—charity, chastity, truthfulness, patience, piety—also have political and social dimensions. (The social and political dimensions of virtue were well recognized by Aristotle, for example, whose gender-based understanding of the nature of virtue might serve as a foil against which the Quran's ethical egalitarianism appears even more clearly.)[2] Other Quranic verses, such as the one declaring the identicalness of men and women and indicating the equal worth of their labor ("I suffer not the good deeds of any to go to waste, be he a man or a woman: The one of you is of the other"; Sura 3:195), are similar in their emphasis and thrust.

Additionally, as others have pointed out, both Quranic and hadith passages imply an egalitarian view of human biology, in terms of the male and female contributions to conception. Hadith passages, for example, indicate that women as well as men have "semen," or "fluid" (this was why, according to one hadith, "the son resembles his mother"). Other hadith indicate that male semen was not special (as it is in the Hebrew tradition, which forbids the "spilling" of male seed) or of superior importance to conception; in one, a soldier asks Muhammad whether it was permissible to practice withdrawal (a male contraceptive method) with female prisoners of war. Muhammad said it was, for if God wanted to create something, no one could avert it. This view of conception was important to the theological position on abortion (discussed below) and divided Muslim theologians and philosophers, the latter choosing to endorse the Aristotelian theory of conception, according to which the male secretion was superior to the female secretion and contributed the soul while the female secretion provided the matter.[3]

There appear, therefore, to be two distinct voices within Islam, and two competing understandings of gender, one expressed in the pragmatic regulations for society (discussed in the previous chapter), the other in the articulation of an ethical vision. Even as Islam instituted marriage as a sexual hierarchy in its ethical voice—a voice virtually unheard by rulers and lawmakers—it insistently stressed the importance of the spiritual and ethical dimensions of being and the equality of all individuals. While the first voice has been extensively elaborated into a body of political and legal thought, which constitutes the technical understanding of Islam, the second—the voice to which ordinary believing Muslims, who are essentially ignorant of the details of Islam's technical legacy, give their assent—has left little trace on the political and legal heritage of Islam. The unmistakable presence of an ethical egalitarianism explains why Muslim women frequently insist, often inexplicably to non-Muslims, that Islam is not sexist. They hear and read in its sacred text, justly and legitimately, a different message from that heard by the makers and enforcers of orthodox, androcentric Islam.

The debate as to which voice to hear and what kind of faith and what kind of society Muhammad meant to institute has gone on throughout history, beginning shortly after the death of Muhammad. It was intense from the start, through the age of the conquests to the end of the Abbasid era (750–1258) in particular. From the beginning there were those who emphasized the ethical and spiritual message as the fundamental message of Islam and argued that the regulations Muhammad put into effect, even his own practices, were merely the ephemeral aspects of the religion, relating only to that particular society at that historical moment. Thus, they were never intended to be normative or permanently binding for the Muslim community. Among the groups that to some degree or other took this position were the Sufis, the Kharijis, and the Qarmatians (Qaramita). As will be discussed below, their views on women and their rules and practices pertaining to them differed in important ways from those affirmed by the Islamic establishment; implicit to all of them was the idea that the laws applicable to the first Muslim society were not necessarily applicable to or binding upon later ones. The Kharijis and the Qarmatians, for instance, rejected concubinage and the marriage of nine-year-old girls (permitted by the orthodox), and the Qarmatians banned polygamy and the veil. Sufi ideas, moreover, implicitly challenged the way establishment Islam conceptualized gender, as is suggested by the fact that they permitted women to give a central place in their lives to their spiritual vocation, thus by implication affirming the paramountcy of the spiritual over the biological. In contrast, the legal and social vision of establishment Islam gave precedence to women's obligations to be wives and mothers.

Does Ethics worry power?

However, throughout history it has not been those who have emphasized the ethical and spiritual dimensions of the religion who have held power. The political, religious, and legal authorities in the Abbasid period in particular, whose interpretative and legal legacy has defined Islam ever since, heard only the androcentric voice of Islam, and they interpreted the religion as intending to institute androcentric laws and an androcentric vision in all Muslim societies throughout time.

In the following pages I contend, first, that the practices sanctioned by Muhammad within the first Muslim society were enunciated in the context of far more positive attitudes toward women than the later Abbasid society was to have, a context that consequently tempered the androcentric tendencies of Islamic practices; those tendencies were further tempered by the emphasis the religion placed on spiritual egalitarianism. Second, I argue that the decision to regard androcentric positions on marriage as intended to be binding for all time was itself an interpretive decision, reflecting the interests and perspective of those in power during the age that transposed and interpreted the Islamic message into the textual edifice of Islam. Finally, I argue that the social context in which this textual edifice was created was far more negative for women than that in Arabia, so the spiritually egalitarian voice of the religion would have been exceedingly difficult to hear. The practices and living arrangements of the dominant classes of the Abbasid era were such that at an implicit and often an explicit level, the words *woman,* and *slave,* and *object for sexual use* came close to being indistinguishably fused. Such practices, and the conceptions they gave rise to, informed the dominant ideology and affected how Islam was heard and interpreted in this period and how its ideas were rendered into law.

Within ten years of Muhammad's death Arab conquests had carried Islam to lands far beyond, and fundamentally different from, Arabia—to societies that were urban and that already had elaborate scriptural and legal traditions and established social mores. These societies were more restrictive toward women and more misogynist; at least their misogyny and their modes of controlling women by law and by custom were more fully articulated administratively and as inscribed code. The differences between the fundamental assumptions about women in Arabia at the time of the rise of Islam and elsewhere in the Middle East are suggested by the contrast between the Quranic verses *addressing* women and unambiguously declaring the spiritual equality of men and women and certain remarks of the supreme theologian of the Abbasid age, al-Ghazali (d. 1111). Al-Ghazali prefaces his account of eminent religious women with the following advice to readers, whom he presumes to be male: "Consider the women who have struggled in the path of God and say, 'O my soul, be not content to be less than a woman, for it is despicable for a man to be less than a woman in matters of religion or of this world.'"[4] That is, in the spiritual (as well as in the material) realm, the most ordinary of men should expect to surpass the most gifted and percipient of women. *That hurts to read*

Noticeably, al-Ghazali's sentiments about women were far closer to those of Tertullian or Augustine (see chap. 2) than to those that found expression in the Quran. Thus the attitudes to women expressed in the urban centers of the Mediterranean Middle East appear to have formed part of a cultural continuum extending over the territories that had formed part of the Byzantine and Sasanian empires. Through its conquests Islam was to inherit not only the Iraq-Iran region, which was to bring forth an al-Ghazali, but also the Mediterranean Middle East, which had nurtured such figures as Augustine and Origen. It was in these societies that major Muslim institutions and the edifices of Muslim law and scripture were to be given shape over the next centuries.

As we saw, Jahilia women participated actively in society, a habit that necessarily carried over into early Muslim society; after all, these were the people who, by conversion and by conquest, became the first Muslims. Until the latter years of Muhammad's ascendancy, and perhaps later for women other than his wives, women mingled freely with men; even in the last years of Muhammad's life they were not veiled, except for his own wives. Against the background of these mores, the pronouncements and broad recommendations of the Quran would be heard one way in Arabia and quite another way in the societies to which it was transposed. Arab mores themselves, moreover, changed as the Arabs adopted the ways of the conquered peoples and were assimilated into their new environments.

In the following pages I review the changes in mores as they affected women. I shall focus first on the transition of Islam to Iraq and on tracing the progression of changes in mores over the transitional period, then on the subsequent Iraqi Muslim society and in particular on the mores of its dominant classes. Following the establishment of the Abbasid dynasty in 750 and for approximately four centuries thereafter, Iraq was the seat of the major Sunni Muslim empire and had a central role in developing the thought and institutions that took shape at this crucially influential period in Muslim history. (Other regions, such as Egypt and Syria, also naturally made important contributions to the dominant understanding of the role of women, contributions that have yet to be studied.)

My object here is to identify the ideology of gender in that age and the

assumptions about women and the relations between the sexes silently informing the texts and interpretations of Islam articulated then. I therefore
focus in particular on the mores of the dominant classes of urban Abbasid
society, mores that were a key influence on the ideology of gender in the
age. It is this ideology, I want to emphasize, and the nature of the interactions between the sexes in the dominant Abbasid society in which it is
grounded, that is the subject of my investigation, rather than the exploration and reconstruction of the social realities of women's lives in Abbasid
society. Women's experiences and economic activities naturally differed
across classes and from urban to rural contexts. The task of unearthing
and piecing together that history is a different project from the present one,
and one that remains to be undertaken.

Neither identifying and reconstructing mores and attitudes toward
women, and shifts in these, nor unearthing and piecing together women's
social history are enterprises for which the traditional materials of history
readily offer evidence. The invisibility or the merely perfunctory presence
of women in mainstream academic histories of the Middle East attests to
this, as well as, to be sure, to the androcentrism of the historical tradition.
Women's invisibility, and the invisibility of the concept of gender as an
analytic category, has meant not only that the import to women of historical
change has remained unexplored but also that the extent and the specific
ways in which dominant cultures and societies have been shaped—in all
areas of thought and social organization—by the particular conceptions of
gender informing them have similarly remained unexplored.

To reconstruct changes in mores and attitudes, I have drawn primarily
on the hadith narratives, on such early religiobiographical compilations as
Ibn Sa'd's *Kitab al-tabaqat,* and on various later literary productions. In
addition, I have drawn on Nabia Abbott's detailed studies of the lives of
some—chiefly elite—women in the Abbasid period. The sources permit us
to trace the limitations gradually placed on Arab women's active participation in their society, the progressive curtailment of their rights, and the
simultaneous development of practices detrimental to women and attitudes
indicating a decline in their status. Among the specific areas for which
fairly direct evidence exists are warfare, religion, and marriage.

Warfare

War was one activity in which women of pre-Islamic and early
Islamic Arabia participated fully. They were present on the battlefield principally to tend the wounded and to encourage the men, often with song

and verse. A number of women became famous for their poems inciting warriors to fight fiercely, lamenting death or defeat, or celebrating victory. Some women also fought. In the Muslim battles of Muhammad's lifetime, women functioned in all three roles, on both sides—even Muhammad's wives (see chap. 3). The conduct of Hind bint ʿUtbah at the battle of Uhud incensed Muhammad's Companion ʿUmar ibn al-Khattab. He reportedly observed to a fellow Muslim: "I wish you had heard what Hind was saying and seen her insolence as she stood on a rock reciting rajaz-poetry against us." He recited part of what she had said and then satirized her.

> The vile woman was insolent, and she was habitually base,
>   since she combined insolence with disbelief.
> May God curse Hind, distinguished among Hinds, she with the
>   large clitoris,
> and may he curse her husband with her.[5]

Umm ʿUmara also fought in this battle, on the Muslim side along with her husband and sons. Her courage and her effectiveness with weapons led Muhammad to observe that she had acquitted herself better than many men. Umm ʿUmara continued to fight in Muslim battles during Muhammad's lifetime and afterward, until she lost her hand in the battle of ʿUqraba (634). She was far from unique. The histories of the Muslim battles after Muhammad's death name other prodigious women warriors, Umm Hakim for example, who single-handedly disposed of seven Byzantine soldiers at the battle of Marj al-Saffar, as well as groups, even battalions, of women participating in the fighting. One account of an Arab expedition against a Persian seaport relates that the women, led by Azdah bint al-Harith, "turned their veils into flags and, marching in martial array to the battle-field, were mistaken for fresh reinforcements, and contributed at a critical moment to victory." Another group of Muslim women reportedly fought vigorously in the battle of Yarmuk (637). Hind bint ʿUtbah, on the Meccan side at Uhud but now a Muslim herself and mother of the Muslim governor of Syria, was also active at Yarmuk, along with her daughter, Huwairah, who was wounded. Hind was prominent in the battle, goading the Muslims on with cries of "Strike the uncircumcised with your swords!" Another woman, the famed poet al-Khansaʾ, whose weapons were words, was also present at the battle of Qadissiyya (636).[6]

In the early days of Islam women's participation in battle was evidently normal enough for one Islamic sect, the Khariji, to formalize that role and institute jihad (waging war) as a religious duty, along with prayer, pilgrim-age, fasting, and almsgiving, for women as well as for men.[7] Like the Shiite movement, the Khariji movement had its rise (in 657) following the dispute over political leadership that erupted in the Muslim community soon after Muhammad's death.

As with Shiism and other opposition movements in early Islam, dissent over political leadership connoted dissent over the meaning and proper interpretation of Islam and over the kind of society Islam was intended to found. Although, as for other opposition groups, the differences between the Kharijis and the politically dominant "orthodox" Muslims were about religion and political leadership, religion was the political idiom of the day and the language in which issues of political power, social justice, and private morality were discussed. The divisions, therefore, between orthodoxy and the Khariji and other opposition movements were about the nature and proper organization of society comprehensively and not merely about what we today call religious issues. To give one instance of a "religious" divergence with clear social implications for women, the Kharijis rejected concubinage and the marriage of nine-year-old girls, even though Muhammad had owned a concubine and had married 'Aisha when she was about nine. They argued that God had allowed his prophet privileges not permitted to other men.[8] Orthodox Muslims, in contrast, accepted both concubinage and the marriage of girls who were about nine, arguing that Muhammad's practice established a precedent for all Muslim men. These examples of radically different readings of the import of Muhammad's actions and words, and of the Quran, by passionately committed Muslims illustrate how matters merely of emphasis and interpretation in relation to the same acts and texts are capable of yielding what are in effect, for women, fundamentally different Islams.

With respect to women warriors, the Kharijis argued that, in this case, the practice was legitimate and indeed a religious requirement for women, because women had accompanied Muhammad on his military expeditions and fought in his battles. In fact, a number of Khariji women won renown for their prowess in battle, among them Ghazala, who defeated al-Hajjaj in a duel. The orthodox, who opposed jihad for women, killed and exposed naked the women captured in their battles with the Kharijis—conduct suggesting an attitude toward women on the battlefield far different from that of the first Muslim community. The strategy was effective in leading Khariji women eventually to withdrawing from the theater of war. The early Kharijis were Arabs, as distinct from *mawlas* (converts from among the conquered peoples attached to Arab tribal leaders as "clients") or Arabs intermingled with mawlas; this perhaps was a reason that the Arab tradition of women in battle endured longer among them than among orthodox Muslims, who, following the conquests, more rapidly assimilated with non-Arabs.[9]

Religion

Broadly speaking, the evidence on women in early Muslim society suggests that they characteristically participated in and were expected to participate in the activities that preoccupied their community; those included religion as well as war. Women of the first Muslim community attended mosque, took part in religious services on feast days, and listened to Muhammad's discourses. Nor were they passive, docile followers but were active interlocutors in the domain of faith as they were in other matters. Thus the hadith narratives show women acting and speaking out of a sense that they were entitled to participate in the life of religious thought and practice, to comment forthrightly on any topic, even the Quran, and to do so in the expectation of having their views heard. The hadith show what is equally important: that Muhammad similarly assumed women's right to speak out and readily responded to their comments. For example, his female followers, who, like the male, learned the Quran, reportedly complained on one occasion that the men were outstripping them and requested that Muhammad set aside additional time to instruct them so they could catch up. This Muhammad did.[10] Presumably he had been instructing the men while the women were attending to household tasks, not just at the times of public prayer.

The most important question the women asked Muhammad about the Quran was why it addressed only men when women, too, accepted God and his prophet.[11] The question occasioned the revelation of the Quranic verses explicitly addressing women as well as men (Sura 33:35; see above)—a response that unequivocally shows Muhammad's (and God's) readiness to hear women. Thereafter the Quran explicitly addressed women a number of times.

The habit of listening and giving weight to women's expressed opinions and ideas evident in Muhammad's attitude was doubtless reflective of attitudes forming part of the society more broadly. That women's words had weight, even concerning matters of spiritual and social import, continued to be a feature of the Muslim community in the years immediately following Muhammad's death, as is clearly demonstrated by the acceptance of women's contributions to the hadith. From the start the preservation of these narratives was an exercise in the regulation of social conduct rather than merely an expression of the impulse to collect and preserve sacred memories. For a community newly bereft of their leader, the hadith represented a means of searching out what was and was not acceptable conduct in situations for which Muhammad had left no explicit rulings. To accept women's testimony on the words and deeds of the prophet was to accept their authority on matters intended to have a prescriptive, regulatory relation to mores and laws. Indeed, in ensuing Muslim societies the hadith had a central place, next to the Quran, as sources from which to derive the law.

The women who made the largest contribution to that corpus were Muhammad's widows, though others are also cited as sources. 'Aisha in particular, with Umm Salama and Zeinab as distant seconds, was an important traditionist; all conceded that she had been particularly close to Muhammad. Soon after Muhammad's death the community began to consult her on Muhammad's practice, and her accounts served to settle points of conduct and occasionally points of law. For example, when Safia, Muhammad's formerly Jewish widow, died around 670, having willed a third of her estate to her nephew, a dispute arose as to whether his being a Jew nullified the bequest. 'Aisha, upon being consulted, sent word that the will should be honored. Even more important, 'Aisha's testimonies on the way Muhammad prayed or the way he recited a Quranic verse settled points regarding prayer and the correct reading of that verse. An eminent traditionist herself, 'Aisha transmitted hadith to several of the foremost early Muslim traditionists. Some 2,210 hadith are attributed to her. Al-Bukhari and Muslim, known for the stringency of their standards in hadith collection, included between them some three hundred hadith attributed to 'Aisha.[12]

Even more important than the extensiveness of 'Aisha's and other women's contributions to the hadith is that they contributed at all—that Muhammad's contemporaries and their immediate descendants sought them out and incorporated their testimony alongside and on a par with men's. This fact is remarkable. After all, how many of the world's major living religions incorporate women's accounts into their central texts or allow a woman's testimony as to the correct reading of a single word of a sacred text to influence decisions? Nor should the significance of this fact be minimized on the grounds that the testimonies came chiefly from Muhammad's wives and were accepted only by virtue of their connection with him. At many periods in Muslim history, including the Abbasid period, women were so debased that even their kinship with a great man would not have rendered their words worthy of note. Had the testimonies of women not already been considered authoritative by a previous age, it is entirely conceivable, for example, that al-Ghazali and his brother theologians and legists would have set aside the testimony of women, however well grounded, as to the correct reading of a Quranic verse or on any other matter of import, in favor of the opinion of a male authority. Similarly, the regulations recently introduced in Pakistan, where the testimony of two women is adjudged equal to that of one man, would have made it impossible, had such laws existed in early Islam, to accept the recollections of Muhammad's female kin unless the word of one was backed by the word of another. Fortunately, the attitudes of men and women in the first Muslim society made women's contributions part of the received texts; consequently, even in the most misogynistic periods women have been able to participate to some degree in the world of thought and learning. Women traditionists, usually taught by their fathers, were found in Muslim societies in all ages, including the Abbasid.[13]

Many other details attest to the esteem in which the community held Muhammad's widows and to the weight they gave their opinions. Awarded the highest pensions in the state, the widows lived together in the mosque apartments they had shared with Muhammad, now one of the most sacred spots in Islam. Some of them commanded prestige and authority; all were independent women—specifically, women who were not living under the authority of any man—a condition that orthodox Islam was to require for women. Thus a community of independent, celibate women (Muhammad had decreed that no man should marry his widows) occupied a prominent place at the material and spiritual center of Islam at this moment of its consolidation and expansion. It is somewhat ironic that such a configuration should mark the early history of a religion that, in the orthodox view, frowns on celibacy and requires women always to live under the authority of men.

'Aisha and Hafsa, as daughters of the first two caliphs, Abu Bakr and 'Umar, enjoyed even further prestige and influence. Both Abu Bakr and 'Umar, just prior to their deaths, entrusted their daughters, rather than their sons, with important responsibilities. During his last illness Abu Bakr made 'Aisha responsible for disposing of certain public funds and properties and distributing his own property among his other grown sons and daughters. At 'Umar's death the first copy of the Quran, which had been in Abu Bakr's possession and then in 'Umar's, passed into Hafsa's keeping.[14]

Nor was it only male relatives who respected the widows' opinions; the community at large sought their views and support even in matters of politics, an arena in which Muslim women did not participate during Muhammad's lifetime. For example, when 'Umar's successor, the caliph 'Uthman, was criticized for his nepotistic appointments, he promised not to appoint any governor except "him on whom the wives of the Prophet and those of counsel among you have agreed." When his critics were not pacified, he appealed to ʿAisha and the rest of Muhammad's widows for assistance. In this case Safia in particular offered help.[15]

ʿAisha herself ventured into the political arena, delivering a speech in the mosque at Mecca and in other ways playing a prominent and perhaps central role in focusing the opposition to ʿAli's succession to the caliphate (see chap. 3). Her venture is itself a sign of the community's acceptance of women as capable of leadership and is important in that it even occurred. The debate that it fanned—whether ʿAisha was disobeying Muhammad's injunction that his wives' place was in the home or whether she was taking an appropriate step in venturing into the political arena—is important for the same reason. Many denounced her—many more perhaps than might have been the case had she been victorious—but others came to her defense. When Zaid ibn Suhan spoke outside the mosque, saying, "She was ordered to stay in her home and we were ordered to fight. . . . Now she commands us to do what she herself was ordered to do while she rides out to carry out the orders given us," Shabth ibn Ribʿi replied: "You stole and Allah cut off your hand. You disobey the Mother of the Believers and Allah will strike you dead. She has not commanded except that which Allah most high has commanded, namely the setting of things right among the people."[16] That men followed ʿAisha to battle and that some reasoned like ibn Ribʿi did, show the contrast between this society and Abbasid society, where a debate about women's participation, let alone actually permitting a woman to deliver a speech in a mosque or lead a war, was inconceivable.

Marriage

During the transition from the first Muslim community to Abbasid society attitudes toward women and marriage changed extensively concerning everything from the acceptability of marrying nonvirgins, such as widows and divorcées—hideous and shameful matches in Abbasid literature—to women's legitimate expectations in marriage. The trend, as with women's participation in war and religious matters, was toward closure and diminution.

Ample evidence attests that in the first Muslim society women frequently remarried after divorce or widowhood and did so without stigma. The lives of Umm Kulthum and ʿAtika bint Zaid are examples. Umm Kulthum converted to Islam while single and emigrated from Mecca to Medina to join the Muslims. Her brothers followed her there and demanded that Muhammad hand her over to them. After she pleaded with him to remain, Muhammad received a revelation decreeing it unlawful to return women to unbelievers. Umm Kulthum eventually married Muhammad's adopted son Zaid. When he died in battle in 629, she married another Muslim, Zubair ibn al-Aʿwwam. He treated her harshly, and although he refused to grant her a divorce, she was able to trick him into pronouncing the necessary words. When she gave birth to a child, Zubair complained to Muhammad that he had been tricked into divorce but to no avail. Umm Kulthum then married Abdel Rahman and, when he died (652), ʿAmr ibn al-ʿAs, conqueror of Egypt. Umm Kulthum, who bore children to her first three husbands, was in her forties or older at the time of her marriage to ʿAmr.[17]

ʿAtika bint Zaid (d. 672), a woman famous for her beauty, intelligence, and poetic ability, also married four men. Her first husband, son of Abu Bakr, died leaving a substantial inheritance on condition that she not remarry. After rejecting numerous suitors, she finally accepted ʿUmar ibn al-Khattab, who was murdered in 642. Then she married Zubair ibn al-Aʿwwam, on condition that he not beat her or prevent her from attending prayers at the mosque. He died in battle in 656, so she took her fourth husband, Husain, son of the caliph ʿAli. ʿAtika was probably about forty-five at the time.[18]

Besides illustrating that no stigma was attached to marrying nonvirgins, the information on these two women also indicates that neither age nor previous marriage barred women from making socially prestigious matches. Of Muhammad's wives, Khadija, it will be recalled, was fifteen years his senior, and only ʿAisha had not been married before.

Umm Kulthum's conversion to Islam and emigration to Mecca also confirm a point previously noted—that Arabian women exercised some independence of judgment and action. She was a single woman defecting to the enemy camp in the teeth of family opposition. ʿAtika's stipulating conditions for her marriage to Zubair and Umm Kulthum's tricking Zubair into a divorce—and Muhammad's not compelling her to return to him despite Zubair's complaint—suggest that the stricter codes for women notwithstanding, the Islamic type of marriage introduced by Muhammad retained a degree of flexibility; there was some room for women to negotiate marriage terms acceptable to them. Such flexibility presumably stemmed in part from still-strong pressure of the less restrictive Jahilia mores and the prebureaucratic nature of the first Muslim community, unfettered as yet by the elaborate legal and administrative systems that Islam acquired with its migration to the urban societies of the Middle East.

Jahilia habits and expectations survived for a brief while against the background of the social transformation that was occurring. Frequent re-marriage, for example, and the expectation, at least among elite women, that they could enter into marriage on their own terms continued during the transitional age. The lives of two aristocratic women, ʿAisha bint Talha (d. 728), the niece of Muhammad's wife of the same name, and Sukaina bint al-Husain (d. 735), Muhammad's great-granddaughter, are exemplary. Both were celebrated for their beauty, wit, and literary ability. ʿAisha was also renowned for her knowledge of history, genealogy, and astronomy, knowledge acquired, she said, from her famous aunt. ʿAisha married three times, Sukaina four to six times. References suggest, moreover, that with respect to one marriage, Sukaina initiated the divorce, and that with respect to another, she insisted on stiff—almost capricious—terms in her marriage contract. Reportedly, her husband agreed to take no other wife, never to prevent her from acting as she pleased, to let her reside near her friend Umm Manzur, and not to oppose her in any of her desires (2:901, 602–23).[19] Even if her particular terms were unusual, having a marriage contract spelling out terms was perhaps not itself unusual, at least among the elite.

The experiences of Umm Salama and Umm Musa some two or three decades later show that elite women continued to stipulate conditions—conditions granting some degree of autonomy to themselves and some degree of reciprocity within the marriage—but only in the face of fierce and growing opposition. Umm Salama, a woman of aristocratic Arab descent who had been twice married, one day noticed a good-looking young man named al-ʿAbbas, or so goes the story. Learning that he was of noble descent but impecunious, she sent a slave to him with her proposal of marriage and a sum of money for her dowry. Al-ʿAbbas accepted the proposal, swearing to her that he would never take a second wife or a concubine (2:632–36). Founder of the Abbasid dynasty, al-ʿAbbas became caliph (750–54) of the Muslim empire, based in Baghdad.

Already heir to the mores of the Arabs, al-ʿAbbas was heir, too, to those of the Persian elite, for several centuries now the upper class in this region. Most of the Persian upper class not killed in the wars of Arab conquest converted from Zoroastrianism to Islam, the new state religion; they and their descendants retained their upper-class status and became the bureaucrats of the new state. Surely it is the accents and assumptions of that heritage—in which kings traditionally had concubines by the thousands and proclaimed far and wide the specifications of the women to be sent to them—that are most evident in the advice a courtier now offered al-ʿAbbas. The courtier, Khalid ibn Safwan, declared that he could not understand why the caliph contented himself with one woman. He was depriving himself of much pleasure in not sampling the varieties available in his empire, "the tall and slender, the soft and white, the experienced and delicate, the slim and dark, and the full-buttocked maid of Barbary" (2:633). This string of adjectives—which describes women as if they were objects to be sampled, like pieces of fruit in a bowl, and certainly not like persons who might stipulate terms and expect some degree of reciprocity in their marriage—betokens the fundamental change in attitudes toward women that had gradually taken place. Al-ʿAbbas, I might add, did not succumb. Umm Salama, entering soon after Khalid's departure and noticing that her husband was perturbed, persuaded him to reveal the cause, then dispatched some powerful slaves to beat Khalid within an inch of his life.

Umm Musa, the wife of al-Mansur (754–75), al-ʿAbbas's successor as caliph, encountered more serious resistance. Also of aristocratic Arab descent, she had stipulated in her marriage contract, which was witnessed by a number of people, that he could not take another wife or a concubine. When al-Mansur became caliph, he requested judge after judge to declare the contract invalid, but Umm Musa always succeeded in learning which judge he was approaching and sent them large gifts to rule in her favor. When she died, the courtiers presented al-Mansur with a hundred virgins. Meanwhile, Umm Musa had left an endowment for concubines who had borne only girls (3:1510).[20] Evidently she understood that her battle to preserve the right to contract a monogamous marriage was part of a general and sharp deterioration in the status and rights of women.

ELABORATION

Chapter 5   OF THE FOUNDING
  ℘

DISCOURSES

IN ABBASID SOCIETY WOMEN WERE CONSPICUOUS FOR
their absence from all arenas of the community's central affairs. In the records relating to this period they
are not to be found, as they were in the previous era,
either on battlefield or in mosques, nor are they described as participants in or key contributors to the cultural life and productions of their society. Henceforth,
women of the elite and bourgeois classes would live out
their lives in seclusion, guarded by eunuchs if wealthy.
Indeed, so confined and reduced were their lives that
Nabia Abbott, the preeminent historian of elite women
in the Abbasid era, was led to remark, in words that
might seem almost Orientalist in their portrayal of
Arab mores at this moment, that "the social and moral
standards which came to prevail" must be understood
"in the light of certain institutions and the general
weakness of human nature which, with luxury and
ease, tends on the whole to degeneration." These institutions

were the trio polygamy, concubinage, and seclusion of women. The seclusion of the harem affected the freeborn Arab woman to a greater
extent than it did her captive or slave-born sister.

The choicest women, free or slave, were imprisoned behind heavy curtains and locked doors, the strings and keys of which were entrusted into the hands of that pitiable creature—the eunuch. As the size of the harem grew, men indulged to satiety. Satiety within the individual harem meant boredom for the one man and neglect for the many women. Under these conditions . . . satisfaction by perverse and unnatural means crept into society, particularly its upper classes.[1]

The steps by which things came to this pass were gradual. The enormous social changes that occurred following Islam's expansion beyond the borders of Arabia encompassed all aspects of life, including relationships between men and women.

The conquests had brought enormous wealth and slaves to the Muslim centers in Arabia. The majority of the slaves were women and children, many of whom had been dependents or members of the harem of the defeated Sasanian elites before their capture. A few statistics may suggest how dramatically the conquests changed Arab life-styles: ʿAisha was paid 200,000 dirhams for her room, in which Muhammad was buried, while retaining the use of it during her lifetime. Five camels were required to transport the money. ʿAisha had inherited nothing from Muhammad, what little property he had left having gone to charity. A man of modest means, he had been unable, for example, to afford a slave or servant to help his daughter Fatima with the housework, though she had complained bitterly of being overworked. The number of slaves people might own in the wake of the conquests were, like the sums of money they acquired, huge. After the conquests a member of the Muslim elite might own a thousand slaves; ordinary soldiers might have from one to ten people serving them. Al-Zubair, ʿAisha's brother-in-law, left one thousand slaves and one thousand concubines when he died in 656. (Muhammad had had one concubine.) The caliph ʿAli, who had been monogamous until his first wife, Muhammad's daughter Fatima, died, acquired nine wives and several concubines after the conquests. His son Hasan married and divorced one hundred women.[2]

A similar acquisition of vast wealth and slaves, including concubines, took place in Iraq, where the capital of the Sasanian empire had been located prior to the Arab conquest. The population of Iraq at the time of the conquest was ethnically diverse. Large-scale Persian immigration had begun with the rise of the Sasanian empire in the third century C.E., and the Persians now constituted the elite and a small segment of the peasantry, Persian agricultural workers having been imported, particularly into upper

Iraq. Aramaeans, who constituted the peasantry, were ethnically the most numerous, with Arabs, who had migrated to Iraq mostly in the Classical period and in Late antiquity (circa 500 B.C.), constituting another element. The state church and the religion of the elite was Zoroastrianism, whose regulations regarding marriage and women were discussed earlier. Besides Zoroastrians, the population included Christians, Jews, pagans, Gnostics, and Manichaeans. Religious identities did not necessarily correlate with ethnic identities. Aramaeans, for example, might be pagan, Jewish, Christian, or Manichaean; and Arabs and Persians, not just Aramaeans, were Christian. Christianity was perhaps the most prevalent faith.[3]

The Arab conquest set in motion a dual process: the broad arabization and Islamization of the population of Iraq and the simultaneous integration of the culture, customs, and institutions of this culturally and administratively complex region into the emergent Islamic civilization. Fusion and assimilation took place in a broad variety of ways, including in the lives of individuals, in administrative and bureaucratic practice, and in the literary, cultural, legal, and intellectual traditions.

The conquest brought, in the first place, enormous numbers of Arab soldiers to Iraq. The Muslim regular army, together with bedouin auxiliaries, totaled over thirty-five thousand men at the important battle of Qadissiyya (636), to give one estimate. Soldiers founded and settled in garrison towns, such as Kufa and Basra, or were assigned to administrative centers in Iraq. Although a few Arab contingents were accompanied by dependents, the majority were not, so they took wives and concubines from the local non-Muslim population. Initially some soldiers were unclear as to the propriety of taking non-Muslim wives; some divorced their non-Muslim wives when they obtained Muslim ones, but others did not (236–53). In any case, cohabitation—the blending of lives, practices, and attitudes—took place, and offspring arrived.

Given the large numbers of captured Persians, the major assimilation was between Persians and Arabs. The captives were chiefly the dependents of military and elite men, women, children, and male noncombatants. Peasants were usually left unharmed, provided they did not resist, and were allowed to continue to work, though subject now to the tax levied on non-Muslims. Many captives were at first sent back to Arabia, where they flooded the slave markets, but as settlement in Iraq proceeded, soldiers kept more and more of the captives, including former royalty and aristocrats, as wives and concubines. Freeborn Persian women thus became a significant element in the garrison towns, and their children grew up to be slaves and clients of the Muslims. Captives from Iran, swiftly conquered by the

Arabs as well, augmented the flow of Persian slaves. By 657, one garrison town, Kufa, already had eight thousand clients and slaves registered as part of the military contingent (196).

Other factors further contributed to assimilation between Persian and Arab. A sizable number of Persian soldiers defected to the Muslims, and a not inconsiderable number of the Persian elite also made terms with the conquerors and converted to Islam, the new religion of the ruling class. Others became prominent members of the Nestorian Christian church and similarly survived without loss of class status (202–3).

Persian ways were thus woven into the fabric of Arab life, particularly in Iraq but also, by way of the Persian captives, in Arabia and in particular in Mecca and Medina. Some aspects of the fusion are relatively easy to document. Michael Morony, who explores the transitions of this age in some detail, describes, for example, the new dishes and luxury foods that Arabs now became accustomed to, such as meat, rice, and sugar, and the different fabrics and new styles of dress (259). Human interactions in matters of gender are as concrete, routine, and intimate as cuisine or clothing, but their physical, psychological, and political aspects are for the most part expressed in texts only indirectly. Tellingly, and in a way that exemplifies the textual invisibility of this concrete yet also intangible dimension of social being, Morony remarks on such interactions merely that the Persian women and children "introduced Persian domestic organisation into the Muslim Arab households" (208–9).

Textually invisible in some ways, the politics of gender of an age are nonetheless inscribed in its textual productions in the form of an implicit and explicit ideology of gender. All writers are hostage (in Elizabeth Fox-Genovese's phrase) "to the society in which they live."[4] The men creating the texts of the Abbasid age of whatever sort, literary or legal, grew up experiencing and internalizing the society's assumptions about gender and about women and the structures of power governing the relations between the sexes, assumptions and structures that were encoded into and manifested in the ordinary daily transactions of life. Such assumptions and practices in turn became inscribed in the texts the men wrote, in the form of prescriptive utterances about the nature and meaning of gender, or silently informed their texts simply as assumptions about the significance of women and gender. (Women were not, in this age, creators of texts in the way that they were in the first Islamic age, when they were among the authors of verbal texts, later written down by men.) The practices and assumptions regarding women that informed the social and psychological reality of Abbasid writers—theologians, legists, philosophers—reappeared in their texts as the prisms through which they viewed and understood women and gender. The texts the men of this period created are regarded as the core prescriptive texts of Islam. The practices and assumptions of this society, and in particular those that became the norm at the highest and most ideologically influential level of society, and the ideology of gender informing these practices and mores therefore are briefly reviewed in the first part of the chapter. Thereafter I explore the ways in which these mores and ideology affected the interpretation of the Islamic message.

Elite Muslim men in the Abbasid era (and indeed already in the Umayyad period) were materially in a position to acquire as many concubines as they wished and in numbers unimaginable in the Muslim society of Muhammad's day. As it became the norm among the elites for men to own large harems of slave women, so the ground of intersexual relationships inevitably shifted. Elite women, by virtue of their aristocratic descent, were able for a while to negotiate the terms on which they married. But once the new order had settled in and the law and their expanded means allowed men to purchase in the market as many exquisite and exquisitely trained women as they fancied, why should they choose to enter into marriages in which terms were stipulated? As Nabia Abbott notes, "Acquiring a wife was a much more serious undertaking than stocking up on concubines who could be discarded, given away, or even killed without any questions raised. A wife had her legal rights to property settlement. She had 'family connections.' . . . These considerations were to lead, in the none too distant future as history goes, to fewer and fewer royal marriages. With few exceptions the royal concubine reigned almost supreme in the caliphal palace."[5]

The practices and attitudes of the Sasanian nobility were adopted by Abbasid nobles. Keeping enormous harems of wives and concubines guarded by eunuchs became the accepted practice. The caliph al-Mutawikkil (r. 847–61) had four thousand concubines, Harun al-Rashid (r. 786–809) hundreds.[6] Evidently, even the moderately wealthy routinely acquired concubines; one young man, on receiving his inheritance, went out to purchase "a house, furniture, concubines and other objects." An emphasis on virginity and disgust at the idea of remarriage for women—ideas paralleled in Zoroastrianism, which formally designated wives as belonging to their first husband and therefore permitted them to enter into second marriages only as inferior wives—also found expression in the literature of the day.[7]

For women, being part of a harem meant emotional and psychological insecurity; and unless they happened to be free, not slave, and independently wealthy, it meant material insecurity as well. Inevitably they must have expended much of their energy and resourcefulness in attempting to ensure their own and their children's security and a modicum of psychological and emotional comfort in situations that, even for the most socially and materially privileged among them, were always precarious and stressful. Whereas in the age of transition Umm Salama and Umm Musa could curtail their husbands' sexual interests by legal contract and direct intervention, Zubaida, royal-born wife of Harun al-Rashid, jealous of his attachment to a particular concubine, was advised to stop nagging—and felt the need to make up for her jealous lapse by presenting al-Rashid with ten concubines. Rivalry between wives and concubines meant that poison was "the active agent" in many stories of harem life. For a concubine desperately seeking to acquire the status of wife and thus make reasonably secure her own and her children's lives, "a lie or two, black or white, as the occasion may demand," was a necessary risk.[8] Gone, obviously, was the forthrightness that went with the different assumptions of earlier Arabian women. With the new ethos of the Abbasid world, women were reduced to resorting to manipulation, poison, and falsehood—the means of the powerless.

Although women had little power over their sexual, psychological, and emotional lives, some elite women did command fortunes and consequently did have power over the lives of some men and women. The system of segregation also created employment opportunities for some women—in the service of harem women. They could be hair combers, bakers, reciters of the Quran, washerwomen, midwives, washers of the dead, mourners at funerals, and female spies. Al-Ma'mun (813–33) reportedly employed seventeen hundred old women to infiltrate and report on his harem.[9]

But in terms of the perception and conceptualization of the meaning of "woman" and gender in the age, perhaps the most significant difference distinguishing Abbasid society from that of the first Islamic society in Arabia lay in the view that elite men had of women and the relationship in which they stood to them. For elite men, the vast majority of the women with whom they interacted, and in particular those with whom they entered into sexual relationships, were women whom they owned and related to as masters to slaves.

The marketing of people, and particularly women, as commodities and as objects for sexual use was an everyday reality in Abbasid society. Most female slaves were sold into domestic service. Traders, however, first sorted through their stock, picking out those with good looks or prized skills to train and groom for the concubine market; potential musical or vocal abilities were particularly valuable. Investments in training paid off. In spite of the abundant supply of slaves such items as "the polished black or white gem" fetched fabulous sums.[10]

Although it was primarily elite men and, to a lesser extent, men of the urban middle classes who had the resources to purchase slaves for personal use, the thriving slave trade involved a fair number of people—those who obtained, transported, trained, and marketed slaves and purchased them as investments for later resale. Everyone in the society, including those not directly connected with the trade, knew how ordinary it was to buy and sell women for men's sexual use. For them all, by virtue of the knowledge of the ordinariness of this transaction, and for elite men in particular because of the intimate and direct level on which they experienced that knowledge, one meaning of *woman* in a very concrete, practical sense was "slave, object purchasable for sexual use." For everyone, too, and for elite men in particular, the distinction between concubine, woman for sexual use, and object must inevitably have blurred.[11] The text that described how a young man went out to buy "concubines and other objects" confirms that the notions "woman" and "object" blurred into each other. How completely elite men might treat concubines as possessions indistinguishable, on a practical level, from other objects is suggested by the story of Prince ʿAdud al-Dawla. He became infatuated with a concubine and neglected affairs of state. Annoyed at this weakness in himself, he decided, as he might have done about a too distracting toy, to get rid of her—and so he had her drowned.[12] *Can't just send her away?*

Not surprisingly the literature of the elite men of this age vividly expresses the horror and dread with which they contemplated the possible fate of their daughters and women relatives. One wrote to another on the death of his young daughter that after all, this was the best of fates for a daughter: "We live in an age . . . when he who weds his daughter to the grave has found the best of bridegrooms."[13] The verses addressed to Hasan ibn al-Firat on the death of his daughter read:

> To Abu Hasan I offer condolences.
> At times of disaster and catastrophe
> God multiplies rewards for the patient.
> To be patient in misery
> Is equivalent to giving thanks for a gift.
> Among the blessings of God undoubtedly
> Is the preservation of sons
> And the death of daughters.

(handwritten margin note, top right: "& men could & love females --")

Yet another wrote that his dread of his daughter's fate should he prematurely die overwhelmed him with tears.[14] These are eloquent testimonies of the precariousness of the lives of even elite (let alone lower-class) women in this society and of the clear sense that their male relatives had of the possibilities of humiliation and degradation that hemmed in their lives and which they evidently felt themselves powerless to protect them from.

Altogether, the prevalence and ordinariness of the sale of women for sexual use must have eroded the humanity from the idea of woman for everyone in this society, at all class levels, women as well as men.[15] The mores of the elite and the realities of social life, and their implications for the very idea and definition of the concept "woman," could not have failed to inform the ideology of the day, thus determining how early Islamic texts were heard and interpreted and how their broad principles were rendered into law. That the interaction between the sexes in the dominant classes was predicated on and chiefly defined by the availability and easy acquisition of women as slaves and objects constitutes therefore the distinguishing feature of this society—the feature that rendered it profoundly and perhaps, at a fundamental level, immeasurably different from either the societies of early Islamic Arabia or those of the contemporary, predominantly Christian Middle East.

(handwritten margin note, left side: "all class levels")

Although this fusion, on an experiential level, between the notions "object," "slave," and "woman" contributed its own specific and unique blend of objectification and degradation to the idea of woman in the ethos of the day, other types and manifestations of misogyny also, of course, formed part of the other traditions of the Middle East (described in chapter 2) that Islam inherited and that eventually came to be woven together seamlessly and indistinguishably to form the heritage of Islamic civilization. After the conquests all Muslims who did not come from Arabia were converts from other religions, including in particular Christianity, Judaism, and Zoroastrianism. They naturally heard and understood Islam in terms of the assumptions they brought with them from those heritages.

By definition, contributions from other religious traditions brought in by converts and the descendants of converts were discrete in that they were either unconscious or traceless, by deliberate intention, to any tradition other than the Islamic. Similarities between prior customs and Islamic ones attest to the fact of Islam's having absorbed such traditions. The ascetic vigils and prayers of Rabiʿa al-ʿAdawiyya (d. 801), for example, point to those of Christian mystics in the Iraq region, where Rabiʿa lived.[16] Apparently even the times and rituals of Muslim prayer—not finalized until after the Muslim conquest—may incorporate features derived from Zoroastrian practice. Other kinds of facts—such as the fact that Hasan al-Basri (d. 728), the eminent early Muslim mystic, was the son of Persian Christian parents captured by the Muslims and the fact that Harun ibn Musa, a convert from Judaism, was the first to write down the variations in oral renderings of the Quran—are suggestive of the routes by which the heritages of other traditions entered Islamic civilization and point to the discrete contribution from converts and the descendants of converts to the ideas and practices to become part of Islam. Ideas and prejudices about women were among those now shared and exchanged, to wit, the Quranic text on the creation was glossed with the idea that Eve was created from Adam's rib. Pursuing the tradition of origin of this or that misogynist idea found in Islam would be a tedious and also a massive task.[17]

To the various prejudices against women and the mores degrading women that were part of one or other tradition indigenous to the area before Islam, Islamic institutions brought endorsement and license. In an urban Middle East with already well articulated misogynist attitudes and practices, by licensing polygamy, concubinage, and easy divorce for men, originally allowed under different circumstances in a different society, Islam lent itself to being interpreted as endorsing and giving religious sanction to a deeply negative and debased conception of women. As a result, a number of abusive uses of women became legally and religiously sanctioned Muslim practices in a way that they were not in Christianity, the other major religion of the day in the Middle East.

The weight Abbasid society gave to the androcentric teachings over the ethical teachings in Islam in matters concerning relations between the sexes was the outcome of collective interpretative acts reflecting the mores and attitudes of society. The fact that some people, such as the Kharijis, could "read" the same events or words as not intended to permit concubinage or marriage to nine-year-old girls while the orthodox understood them as intending to permit either, makes clear the crucial role of interpretation. Nonetheless, a misogynist reading was undeniably one reading to which Islam plausibly lent itself.

The ideology of gender of Abbasid society, expressed in the mores of the dominant elite and in the texts of the politically and religiously dominant, did not necessarily command everyone's consent. Some groups, such as the Khawarij, rejected elements of the dominant ideology and its political and social ethos.[18] The Sufis and the Qarmatians also dissented; they are discussed below.

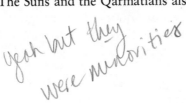

The Problem of Interpretation

Some dissenting sects understood Islam's ethical teachings to be the fundamentals of its message and regarded Muhammad's practices and the regulations he put into effect as relevant primarily to their immediate social context and thus as not necessarily binding (as orthodoxy considered them to be) on Muslim societies at all times in all places. Orthodox Islam, on the contrary, gave paramountcy, as it elaborated its understanding of Islam into laws, to the practices and regulations Islam had enunciated, paying little heed in elaborating laws regarding women to the religion's ethical teachings, particularly its emphasis on the spiritual equality of women and men and its injunctions to treat women fairly. As a result, the religion's emphasis on equality and the equal justice to which women were entitled has left little trace on the law as developed in the Abbasid age. And indeed in Abbasid society, whose mores were described in the preceding section, that ethical message would have been exceedingly difficult to heed. Had the ethical voice of Islam been heard, I here suggest, it would have significantly tempered the extreme androcentric bias of the law, and we might today have a far more humane and egalitarian law regarding women.

Quranic precepts consist mainly of broad, general propositions chiefly of an ethical nature, rather than specific legalistic formulations. As scholars have pointed out, the Quran raises many problems as a legislative document; it by no means provides a simple and straightforward code of law.[19] On the contrary, the specific content of the laws derivable from the Quran depends greatly on the interpretation that legists chose to bring to it and the elements of its complex utterances that they chose to give weight to. To illustrate the intrinsic complexity and ambiguity of the Quranic text and the crucial role played by interpretation, legal historians point to the Quranic references to polygamy. Polygamy, up to a maximum of four wives, is expressly permitted by the Quran, but at the same time, husbands are enjoined to treat co-wives equally and not to marry more than one wife if they fear they will be unable to so treat them. The legal base of marriage and of polygamy would be profoundly different according to whether the ethical injunction to treat wives impartially was judged to be a matter for legislation or one to be left purely to the individual man's conscience.[20]

Islamic law took shape over several centuries and by a variety of processes. Muhammad was the judge for his community and the interpreter of divine revelation. Upon his death the responsibility for interpreting Quranic precepts and translating interpretation into practical decisions devolved on the caliphs. The difficulties attendant upon interpreting and rendering ethical ideas into law were compounded by the Arabs' rapid acquisition of vast foreign territories. With the establishment of the capital of the Umayyad empire (661–750) in Damascus the Arab rulers adopted the administrative machinery of the Byzantine rulers they had succeeded, which facilitated the infiltration of foreign concepts into the still-developing and essentially rudimentary apparatus of Islamic law. Government-appointed judges, who, to begin with, combined the role of judge with that of administrator, tended to apply local laws (which varied throughout the territories) informed by the judge's own understanding of the Quran. Regional disparities soon arose. In Medina, for example, a woman could not contract a marriage on her own account but had to be given in marriage by a guardian, while in Kufa the law gave her the right to contract her own marriage. Differences of interpretation of Quranic injunctions also occurred. In one case the judge ruled that the Quranic injunction to "make a fair provision" for divorced wives should be interpreted as having a legalistic dimension and that therefore such a payment was obligatory. Another judge, hearing a similar case, ruled that the Quranic injunction was directed only at the husband's conscience and was not legally binding.[21]

During the Umayyad period local laws were modified and elaborated by Quranic rules and "overlaid by a corpus of administrative regulations and infiltrated by elements of foreign systems."[22] The growth of this legal and administrative corpus of rulings was haphazard; the materials and sources it drew on, heterogeneous; and the Quranic elements within it were largely submerged.

Scholars of religion voiced their views on the standards of conduct that expressed the Islamic ethic. They formed fraternities in the last decades of the Umayyad period, which were critical of the Umayyad legal establishment and which formed the early schools of law. Recognized and patronized by the new state when the anti-Umayyad Abbasids came to power in 750, they developed rapidly. With state sponsorship and the appointment of scholars to the judiciary and to posts as government advisers, the legal doctrines they propounded became the practice of the courts.[23]

A process of reviewing local practices piecemeal began in light of the principles the scholars believed to be enshrined in the Quran. Originating in the personal reasoning of individual scholars, a body of Islamic doctrine gradually formed and, as time passed, gained authority. The process of development and of the elaboration of legal doctrine and of juridical procedures continued into the ninth century. Some regional variation in the decisions of different regions continued to occur. For example, the Kufan school of law, formed in an environment influenced by the Sasanid sense of the importance of class, developed the doctrine that required a husband to be the social equal of his wife's family, a doctrine that formed no part of the law as it developed in Medina. By the tenth century the body of Sunni Muslim legal thought and practice achieved final formulation in four schools of law, representing to some extent the different regional origins of the schools and named after their major legal proponents—Hanafi, Shafi'i, Hanbali, and Maliki. The body of law and of legal thought embodied in the writings of those four schools was recognized as absolutely authoritative, in part by the application of a juridical principle that had gained general acceptance, *ijma'*, or consensus, according to which the unanimous agreement of qualified jurists on a given point had a binding and absolute authority. Once reached, such an agreement was deemed infallible. To contradict it became heresy; to repeal the consensus of a past age by a consensus of a later one, though theoretically possible, became, because of the authority vested in the existent body of law, highly unlikely. Further discussion was precluded not only on matters of consensus but also on matters on which the jurists had agreed to differ. Today the different regions of the Sunni Muslim Middle East follow, more or less exclusively, one or another of these four schools.[24]

In the early tenth century Muslim jurisprudence formally recognized the body of already formulated legal opinion as final. The duty of the jurist thenceforth was to imitate his predecessors, not to originate doctrine. In effect the law as it had evolved over the first Islamic centuries was consecrated as the complete and infallible expression of divine law. Even though, as the legal scholar Noel J. Coulson points out, "the great bulk of the law had originated in customary practice and in scholars' reasoning . . . and [the development] of classical theory . . . was the culmination of a process of growth extending over two centuries," traditional Islamic belief came to hold that the law as articulated in this literature was operative from the beginning. "The elaboration of the law," Coulson writes, "is seen by Islamic orthodoxy as a process of scholastic endeavour completely independent of historical or sociological influences."[25] The consequence, of course, is that the vision of society, the understanding of the nature of justice, and the view of the proper relationship that should pertain between men and women that were developed by the men of that age have been consecrated as representing the ultimate and infallible articulation of the Islamic notion of justice and have, ever since, been set in stone.

The claim is (as it must be if the body of legal thought as a whole is declared to represent the correct and infallible articulation in legal form of the ethical formulations of the Quran) that the different schools of law are essentially in agreement and that the variations that exist between them are only on matters of insignificant details. Some of these "insignificant" differences in interpretation, however, result in laws profoundly different in their consequences for women. For example, whereas all schools agree that marriage may be terminated unilaterally and extrajudicially by the male, Maliki law differs from the other three schools as to women's right to obtain judicial divorce. Maliki law allows a woman to petition not just on grounds of sexual impotence, as in Hanafi law, but also on grounds of desertion, failure to maintain her, cruelty, and her husband's being afflicted with a chronic or incurable disease detrimental to her. The differences for women obviously are fundamental. Similarly, Hanafi law differs radically from the other three in its view of marriage contracts and of a woman's right to stipulate terms such as that the husband may not take a second wife. The other three schools consider a man's right to unilateral divorce and his right to marry as many as four wives to be of the essence of marriage and therefore elements that may not be altered by the specific contractual agreements entered upon by husband and wife. The Hanafi school, however, considered that the Quranic utterances on polygamy, for instance, were permissive, not mandatory, and that it was therefore not contrary to the essence of marriage for a man to have only one wife; and it consequently saw the spouse's contractual agreement to this (or other matters) as valid and enforceable.[26]

Such differences make plain that the injunctions on marriage in the Quran are open to radically different interpretations even by individuals who share the assumptions, worldview, and perspective on the nature and meaning of gender typical of Muslim society in the Abbasid period. That groups of male jurists were able, in spite of the unquestioning androcentrism and misogyny of the age, to interpret the Quran as intending to enable women to bind men to monogamy, and to obtain divorce in a range of oppressive situations, is itself an important fact. It suggests that a reading by a less androcentric and less misogynist society, one that gave greater ear to the ethical voice of the Quran, could have resulted in—could someday result in—the elaboration of laws that dealt equitably with women. If, for example, the two dissenting doctrines just mentioned had been the view of the majority—and thus formed the basis of general legal practice in Islamic countries rather than that of a minority—they, particularly in combination, could have radically altered women's status in marriage.

Nor were those the only two points that the jurists interpreted to reflect the androcentric assumptions of their society while at the same time failing to give legal form to the ethical injunctions of the Quran. As two modern legal scholars remark:

A considerable step—a process of juristic development extending over more than two centuries—separates the Quran from the classical for-

it really seems out of the spirit of Islam was lost.

mulations of Islamic law . . . the modicum of Quranic rulings were naturally observed, but outside this the tendency was to interpret the Quranic provisions in the light of the prevailing standards. . . . In particular, the general ethical injunctions of the Quran were rarely transformed into legally enforceable rules, but were recognized as binding only on the individual conscience. Thus, for example, a husband was never required to show that he had any reasonable or proper motive before exercising his power to repudiate his wife. And while the Quran might insist upon impartial treatment of co-wives in polygamous unions, classical Islamic law did not elevate this requirement into any kind of legal restriction upon the husband's entrenched right to have four wives. The result was that the Quranic provisions concerning women's status and position in the family were dissipated and largely lost.[27]

Shoot

The rulings the jurists developed on women's rights in matters of sexuality (women were entitled to sexual satisfaction in marriage), contraception, and abortion, outlined by Basim Musallam in his important book *Sex and Society in Medieval Islam*, are interesting because in contrast to the laws regulating marriage, those governing contraception and abortion appear remarkably liberal in the measure of control they allow women in preventing and terminating pregnancy, and thus on the face of it, they might be construed as remarkably free of androcentric bias. In fact, although permitting women to exercise a measure of control in preventing and terminating pregnancy, when the broad legal environment of which they were a part is taken into account, these laws may also be seen as entirely in harmony with an androcentric perspective. The legal system that permitted polygamy and concubinage also stipulated, on the basis of clear Quranic rulings, that males were economically responsible for their offspring and that if a man's concubine bore him a child, the concubine could not thereafter be sold; she became legally free on the man's death, her child becoming the man's legal heir along with children born to his wives. Given this system, it was evidently economically to men's advantage that wives not bear many children and that concubines in particular not bear any children, for if they did, they ceased to be a profitable investment. And, in a system that permitted polygamy and unrestricted divorce and concubinage, a wife who did not give birth would present no hardship for the man, because he had the options of divorcing her, taking another wife without divorcing her, or taking a concubine.[28]

allowing contraception/abortion wasn't a women's freedom, oh so more like abortion to benefit men!

Interestingly, the law made sexual and other services a wifely duty but

★ very very strange

not necessarily the bearing of children, thus giving no special emphasis to women's generative capacity—in contradistinction to oral culture, past and contemporary, which stresses that capacity. Economically it was to women's advantage to reproduce: for slave women, bearing a child was almost a passport to freedom, and for wives, children bound up the husband's emotional and monetary resources and thus lessened his desire and ability to support other women. Arguably, then, oral culture expressed women's interests just as the law expressed men's.

Obviously an ideology such as that expressed in Islamic law emphasizing women's sexual function implies a conception of women that is no less biologically based than one that emphasizes their reproductive capacity. However, classical Islam's definition of wifely duties in terms of women's obligation to provide sex over and above their obligation to reproduce and mother is nevertheless noteworthy. *That is sad? I can't tell.*

The problem of interpretation and of the biases and assumptions that a particular age brought to its readings and renderings of a text is pertinent to all the central texts of Islam and not only to the texts of Islamic legal thought. With respect to the central texts at the core of the entire edifice of orthodox Islam, interpretation played a vital but more hidden role. Interpretation is of necessity part of every act of reading or inscribing a text. According to Islamic orthodoxy, the text of the Quran represents the exact words of the Quranic revelation as recited by Muhammad. Orthodoxy holds that the Quran was perfectly preserved in oral form from the beginning and that it was written down during Muhammad's lifetime or shortly thereafter, when it was collected and arranged for the first time by his Companions. The orthodox account of the process is that a complete written text was made after Muhammad's death, in the reign of the first caliph, Abu Bakr, and the authoritative version was established during the reign of the third caliph, ʿUthman. A dispute between Syrian and Iraqi troops as to the correct recitation of the Quran prompted the compilation of a single authorized version. ʿUthman obtained Hafsa's collection and commissioned four prominent Meccans to make a copy following the dialect of the Quraysh. Then he sent copies to the major centers and ordered other versions destroyed. This was complied with everywhere except in Kufa. The Kufans refused to destroy their version for a time, but eventually ʿUthman's became the canonical version and the final consonantal text. The final fully vocalized version was established in the tenth century.[29]

★ So the Quran did change?

Some Quranic scholars have speculated that the Quran may not be in the Quraysh dialect.[30] In addition, a number of other elements suggest that the process by which Muhammad's recitations were transformed from oral materials into written texts was not as seamless as orthodox accounts declare. For one thing, as these accounts themselves indicate, a number of different versions were evidently in circulation at the time of the compiling of the canonical version, including one sufficiently different for the Kufans to at first reject that canonical version. The physical transcription of a text in this place and period was also attended by difficulties, lending an element of uncertainty to readings. Not only were rough materials, such as animal shoulder blades, used to write down Quranic verses during Muhammad's lifetime but the Arabic letters used at this point were incomplete. The dots necessary to distinguish between the consonants were lacking, for example, so that in a group of consonants two or more readings were possible. Deciding which reading was the correct one on the basis of such notations and on the basis of oral memories, which orthodox belief also admits were divergent—a process not finalized according to orthodox account until at least fifteen years and many foreign conquests after Muhammad's death—was itself an act of interpretation. Similarly, deciding which vocalization and which meaning were to be the canonical ones with respect to a text in which only consonants were written was also an act of interpretation and could decisively affect meaning. As one important study of Muslim inheritance law has recently shown, in deciding between variant readings and finalizing one of two mutually exclusive readings as authoritative, the theologians and legists of the day were already choosing meanings from the perspective of their own environment, meanings perhaps profoundly different from those connoted by the same phrases in the early Muslim environment.[31]

The role of interpretation in the preservation and inscription of the Quran is, however, suppressed in orthodox doctrine, and the belief that the text is precisely as Muhammad recited it is itself a tenet of orthodox faith. Similarly, to question whether the body of consecrated Islamic law does in fact represent the only possible legal interpretation of the Islamic vision is surrounded with awesome interdictions. That its central texts do embody acts of interpretation is precisely what orthodoxy is most concerned to conceal and erase from the consciousness of Muslims. This is understandable, because the authority and power of orthodox religion, whose interests were closely bound up in the Abbasid period with those of the ruling elite, and the state, depended on its claiming a monopoly of truth and on its declaring its version of Islam to be absolute and all other interpretations heresies.

Various other interpretations of the Islamic vision from the start, however, developed and counterposed their reading of it to that of orthodoxy, even as orthodoxy gained control and denounced alternative visions as heretical. Among those that posed radically different interpretations were the Qarmatian and the Sufi movements, both of which drew many of their adherents from the underclass. The Qarmatian movement and some of the more radical varieties of the Sufi movement were persecuted as heretical until the former was entirely eradicated and the latter shorn of its more radical dimensions.

Movements of political and religious dissent often entailed different understandings of the social aspects of Islam, including matters directly affecting women, as was true of the early Khariji movement. Their divergence from the orthodox on a comprehensive range of matters, religious, political, and social, was rooted in a fundamentally different reading of Islam. Both the more radical forms of Sufism and the Qarmatian movement diverged in their interpretation of Islam from orthodoxy in particular in that they emphasized the ethical, spiritual, and social teachings of Islam as its essential message and viewed the practices of Muhammad and the regulations that he put into effect as ephemeral aspects of Islam relevant primarily to a particular society at a certain stage in its history. Again, therefore, the issue is difference of interpretation, not in the sense of different understandings of particular words or passages but in a more radical, pretextual or supratextual sense of how to "read" Muhammad's acts and words and how to construe their relation to history. Was the import of the Islamic moment a specific set of ordinances or that it initiated an impulse toward a juster and more charitable society?

The Sufi and Qarmatian movements are of specific interest in the present context because both broadly opposed the politics, religion, and culture of the dominant society, including, the evidence suggests, its view of women. Sufism was a movement in which pietism, asceticism, and mysticism were dominant elements. Possibly having its origins in the days of Muhammad, it gained ground and underwent important development in particular during the first three to four centuries of Islam, that is, over the same period that state-supported orthodox Islam developed. Sufi pietism had political dimensions, being a form of dissent and passive opposition both to the government and to established religion. Its oppositional relation to the society and ethos of the dominant is evident in the values it enunciated as fundamental to its vision. Asceticism, the renunciation of material goods and of money not earned by the labor of one's own hands and in excess of one's daily needs, and the emphasis on celibacy (though not an invariable requirement) precisely reverse the materialism, exploitation of the labor of others, and unbridled sexuality for men that were enshrined in the mores and way of life of elite society. Sufi emphasis on the inner and spiritual meaning of the Quran, and the underlying ethic and vision it affirmed, similarly countered the letter-bound approach of orthodoxy.

A number of elements in Sufism strongly suggest that the Sufi ethos countered that of the dominant society with respect also to their gender arrangements and their view of women. From early on, its proponents counted women among the important contributors to their tradition and among the elect spiritual leaders, honoring, for example, Rabiʿa al-ʿAdawiyya. Moreover, Sufi tales and legends incorporate elements that also suggest that they engaged with and rejected the values of the dominant society with regard to women.

The narratives about Rabiʿa al-ʿAdawiyya, for instance, exemplify distinctly countercultural elements with respect to ideas about gender. The notion underlying all male-female interaction in the dominant society—that biology and sexuality governed relations between the sexes—is, for example, clearly repudiated by one short Sufi narrative. In it the highly esteemed Sufi leader Hasan al-Basri declares, "I passed one whole night and day with Rabiʿa speaking of the Way and the Truth, and it never passed through my mind that I was a man nor did it occur to her that she was a woman, and at the end when I looked at her I saw myself as bankrupt [i.e. as spiritually worth nothing] and Rabiʿa as truly sincere [rich in spiritual virtue]."[32] Besides repudiating the notion of sexuality as governing male-female interactions, the tale also reverses the dominant society's valuation of male over female by representing not merely any man but one of the most revered male Sufi leaders describing himself as "bankrupt" compared with a woman of truly superior merits.

Many other short narratives depict Rabiʿa surpassing her male colleagues in intellectual forthrightness and percipience as well as in spiritual powers. One relates how Hasan al-Basri approached Rabiʿa, who was meditating with some companions on a bank. Throwing his carpet on the water, Hasan sat on it and called to Rabiʿa to come and converse with him. Understanding that he wanted to impress people with his spiritual powers, Rabiʿa threw her prayer carpet into the air and flew up to it; sitting there she said, "O Hasan, come up here where people will see us better." Hasan was silent, for it was beyond his power to fly. "O Hasan," Rabiʿa then said, "that which you did a fish can do . . . and that which I did a fly can do. The real work (for the saints of God) lies beyond both of these."[33]

Another tale tells how the Kaʿaba rose up and came forward to meet Rabiʿa when she was making her pilgrimage to Mecca. She commented,

"What have I to do with the house, it is the Lord of the house I need." Meanwhile an eminent fellow Sufi, Ibrahim ibn Adham, was taking many years over his pilgrimage to Mecca, piously stopping to perform ritual prayers many times along the way. Arriving in Mecca and seeing no Ka'aba, he thought his eyes were at fault until a voice informed him that the Ka'aba had gone forth to meet a woman. When Rabi'a and the Ka'aba arrived together, Rabi'a informed Ibrahim, who was consumed with jealousy that the Ka'aba had so honored her, that whereas he crossed the desert making ritual prayers, she came in inward prayer. The tale thus shows a woman not only surpassing a man but also gently undercutting the formalism and literalness of orthodox religion and the trappings of piety. Another remark attributed to Rabi'a, made about another Sufi, Sufyan al-Thawri, shows the same thing. "Sufyan would be a [good] man," she said, "if only he did not love the Traditions."[34]

Such narratives perhaps capture some qualities of the historical Rabi'a, but they are doubtless mainly legendary. It is highly unlikely, for instance, given their dates, that Hasan and Rabi'a ever met, let alone enjoyed the reported exchanges. The legendary nature of such stories, however, gives them greater rather than diminished weight as exemplars of Sufi thought, in that they are not records of mere happenings but full narrative structures deliberately devised to express thoughts. Among the thoughts distinctly expressed in the above narratives is that women may surpass even the ablest of men and may be men's teachers in the domain of the spiritual and that interactions between men and women on the intellectual and spiritual planes surpassed in importance their sexual interactions. This does not mean, of course, that all Sufi men were nonsexist or even that Sufi literature did not incorporate some of the misogynist elements present in its broad environment. The argument here is simply that it did include elements rejecting misogyny and transcending definitions of human beings on the basis of their biology.[35]

Other details in the legends about Rabi'a suggest reasons besides spiritual ones for women's being drawn to Sufism. For example, Rabi'a was, legend relates, either a slave or a servant of very poor origin, released by her master when he awoke one night to see the light of saintliness shining over her head and illuminating the entire house. She retired into the desert, then, reemerging, became a professional flute player. Thereafter, in the words of Margaret Smith, Rabi'a's twentieth-century biographer, the extant material "gives a clear idea of a woman renouncing this world and its attractions and giving up her life to the service of God."[36]

Smith focuses on Rabi'a's spiritual concerns, but Rabi'a's class background is worth noting, as is the fact that a female slave or servant was scarcely in a position to renounce worldly attractions. Sufism offered the chance of an independent and autonomous life otherwise certainly impossible for women, particularly women of low birth. Tales in which Rabiʿa rejects offers of marriage from numerous admiring Sufi companions similarly emphasize her autonomy and capacity to remain free of any male authority. Autonomy and a life free of male control—unattainable conditions for women in the dominant society—were thus available to them through Sufism. A spiritual vocation and celibacy (the latter the norm among Muslim women mystics), pursued no doubt for their own sake, functioned also as paths to autonomy and enabled women to resist the orthodox imperative to marry and live under male authority.[37] To remark such points in no way casts doubt on or belittles Rabiʿa's and other women's mysticism but only recognizes it as a complex and comprehensive response to their society and its mores.

As a mystic, Rabiʿa's major contribution was her emphasis on the centrality of the love of God to mystical experience.[38] She reputedly declared, for instance, that her love for God allowed no room for love even of his prophet. A famous tale relates how she carried a torch and a ewer through the streets of Basra intent, she explained, on setting fire to paradise and pouring water on the flames of hell, so that those two veils would drop away from the eyes of believers and they would love God for his beauty, not out of fear of hell or desire for paradise.[39]

Much less is known regarding Qarmatian views about women, but they, too, appear to have departed fundamentally from the prescriptions in orthodox Islamic society pertaining to the proper relations between men and women. Qarmatian writings have not survived, so one cannot base investigations of their beliefs or practices on their own accounts. The movement, which was rooted in the underclass, challenged the Abbasid regime militarily and for a time even succeeded in establishing an independent republic. It was eventually suppressed and its writings destroyed or lost. Nearly all the available information about Qarmatian activities and society comes from the pens of unsympathetic observers who supported the Abbasids.

Like other movements of dissent, the Qarmatian movement saw itself as representing the true realization of the Islamic message, as against the corruptions practiced by the dominant society. Qarmatian missionaries reportedly invited villagers to bring all they owned—"cattle, sheep, jewellery, provisions"—to a central place; after that, no one owned anything, and the goods were redistributed according to need. "Every man worked with diligence and emulation at his task in order to deserve high rank by the benefit he brought. The woman brought what she earned by weaving, the child brought his wages for scaring away birds."[40] In the republic they established, the communal property was administered by a central committee, which ensured that all had their needs for housing, clothing, and food taken care of.

Some writers asserted that the Qarmatians also practiced communism of women. Scholars today suggest, however, that such assertions represented misperceptions of the practices of Qarmatians—which were markedly different with respect to women from those of the writers' own society. The evidence adduced in support of their accusation was that Qarmatian women were not veiled, that both sexes practiced monogamy, and that women and men socialized together. These and similar practices apparently led the writers to assert that the Qarmatians were "debauched" and "obscene"; they themselves, of course, came from societies in which the "unobscene" norm among the elite was for men to keep, and relate sexually to, women by the dozen or so.[41] *hm . What a claim*

Thus Islam in this period was interpreted in ways, often representing the interests and vision of different classes, that implied profoundly different societies, including with regard to arrangements governing the relationship between the sexes. The dissent and "heresies" dividing the society were not so much about obscure theological points, as orthodox history generally suggests, as about the social order and the values inscribed in the dominant culture. The uniformity of interpretation and the generally minimal differences characterizing the versions of Islam that survived reflect not unanimity of understanding but rather the triumph of the religious and social vision of the Abbasid state at this formative moment in history.

One figure in particular deserves final mention, both because of his countercultural understanding of Islam with respect to women and because of his being probably unique among major Muslim scholars and philosophers in regarding women sympathetically. Ibn al-'Arabi (1165–1240), whose intellectual stature and range arguably surpass al-Ghazali's, was born in Murcia, Spain. He studied under Sufi masters in his native land in his youth, including two who were women: Shams, Mother of the Poor, and Nunah Fatima bint al-Muthanna. He said of Shams that "in her spiritual activities and communications she was among the greatest," and he described miracles performed by Nunah Fatima, with whom he studied when she was in her nineties. He helped build Nunah Fatima a hut of reeds.[42] Ibn al-'Arabi had a daughter whom he instructed in theology; she was apparently able to answer theological questions when scarcely one year old. He wrote movingly of her joy on seeing him after an absence. *Cute*

Ibn al-ʿArabi was persecuted as a heretic a number of times in his life. On at least one occasion the "heresy" that outraged the orthodox concerned his statements about women. His poem *Turjuman al-Ashwaq,* for example, is about a young woman he met in Mecca. He wrote that Nizam was "learned and pious, with an experience of spiritual and mystic life," and that but for "paltry souls . . . predisposed to malice, I should comment here on the beauty of her body as well as her soul." The memory of "the grace of her mind and the modesty of her bearing" and the "unwavering friendship" she offered him inspired his poem, the central metaphor of which (as in Dante's work two centuries later) is that the young woman is the earthly manifestation of Sophia, the divine wisdom that his soul craves.[43] The notion of divinity in the female face was profoundly offensive to the orthodox, and the antagonism that the poem earned Ibn al-ʿArabi led him later to write a commentary asserting that its meaning was entirely spiritual and allegorical. (The extent to which the different mores of Arab Spain shaped Ibn al-ʿArabi's different attitude to women—a question that naturally presents itself at this juncture—has yet to be explored.)

Ibn al-ʿArabi's emphasis on the feminine dimension of the divine and the complementarity of the sexes was a consistent element in his thought. He described Adam as the first female in that Eve was born from his side and gave an account of Mary as the second Adam in that she generated Jesus.[44] Using the Adam and Eve metaphor again, Ibn al-ʿArabi wrote of God drawing forth from Adam "a being in his own image, called woman, and because she appears to him in his own image, the man feels a deep longing for her, as something which yearns for itself." Ibn al-ʿArabi also construed the creative Breath of Mercy, a component of the Godhead itself, as feminine.[45] Although a controversial figure, one subjected to hostility during periods of his life, his intellectual power, as evidenced in a prodigious literature, has won him acknowledgment as a major Muslim thinker.

In sum, then, the moment in which Islamic law and scriptural interpretation were elaborated and cast into the forms considered authoritative to our own day was a singularly unpropitious one for women. The heritage of the Umayyad and in particular the Abbasid society played a significant part in determining the extent to which the elaboration of the law would be weighted against them. Even in this androcentric age, however, a reading of Islam that was fairer to women was possible, as the minority legal opinions indicated. The Sufi and the Qarmatian movements also show that there were ways of reading the Islamic moment and text that differed from those of the dominant culture and that such readings had important implications for the conceptualization of women and the social arrangements concerning gender.

These findings obviously have relevance to the issues being debated in *please!* Muslim societies today, especially given the trend toward interpreting Muslim Classical law yet more rigidly and toward endorsing, societally and governmentally, the orthodox Islamic discourse on gender and women. Now that women in unprecedented and ever-growing numbers are coming to form part of the intellectual community in Muslim countries—they are already reclaiming the right, not enjoyed for centuries, to attend mosque—perhaps those early struggles around the meaning of Islam will be explored in new ways and the process of the creation of Islamic law and the core discourse brought fully into question.

Chapter 6   MEDIEVAL ISLAM

MY AIM HERE IS TO DRAW TOGETHER THE AVAILABLE information on women's lives in the period subsequent to the establishment of Islam and to the consolidation of its founding institutions and the articulation of its dominant discourses. The focus here, geographically and with respect to the specific time-period, is largely determined by the availability of information. Thus the societies focused on are primarily those of Egypt, Turkey, and Syria and the sources and research drawn on relate chiefly to the fifteenth to the early nineteenth centuries (the Mamluk and Ottoman periods). The lives of women in these regions and periods appear to have been similar in their broad patterns and in particular with respect to the degree and nature of their involvement in the economy and with respect to the customs governing their lives, especially those relating to marriage. Research on Muslim women's history is, however, at a very preliminary stage: advances in the field may eventually enable us to discriminate between the lives of women in Turkey and Egypt and between those of Cairo in the fifteenth and eighteenth centuries.

The sources and scholarship I have drawn on consist chiefly of literary texts from the periods and societies under consideration, studies of documentary evidence, such as court records, from those societies, and accounts by European visitors. I have, in addition, drawn on S. D. Goitein's studies of the documentary collection of the Cairo Geniza records, which afford us, thanks to Goitein's prodigious labors, an unusually intimate glimpse of quotidian life in Cairo in the tenth to the thirteenth centuries. The Geniza documents, papers deposited in the Geniza by the Jewish community of Cairo, pertain to an earlier period than does much of the rest of the material drawn on here, and they give most information on the lives of the Jewish Cairene and Middle Eastern community. However, as Goitein notes, that community shared many of the practices, assumptions, and life-styles of the dominant Cairene and the broader Muslim society of the day; and in any case Goitein's findings on women are obviously relevant to the study of women in Muslim societies.[1] In incorporating material relating to that earlier age into this outline of the lives and activities of women of a somewhat later period, I again follow Goitein's example: Goitein liberally cites the nineteenth-century traveler Edward William Lane in confirmation or illustration of life-styles, practices, and customs of the Geniza people. Presently available information suggests that at least in their broad patterns and possibilities, the similarities of women's lives in this region did indeed extend from the tenth century to the early nineteenth century and the beginnings of Western economic encroachment and the ensuing erosion and eventual foundering of the social and institutional articulation of the dominant Muslim vision of gender.

Four factors, and the interplay between them, shaped the possibilities of women's lives in the Mediterranean Middle East in the period under consideration: (1) the customs and laws regulating marriage, in particular the laws permitting polygamy, concubinage, and unilateral divorce by the husband, (2) the social ideal of women's seclusion, (3) women's legal right to own property, and (4) women's position in the class system—this last determining how they were affected by the three preceding factors.

Because of the importance of class in framing and circumscribing the possibilities of women's lives, I shall describe how the mores and laws relating to marriage, the ideal of seclusion, and the laws regulating property affected women across classes, beginning with the upper classes. I shall follow my account of how these variables determined the *fundamentals* of women's personal and economic existence across the classes with an account of the tangible conditions of life: what their houses were like, how they were furnished, and how women dealt with matters of daily concern such as the purchase and preparation of food, and again I will discuss these within the framework of differences across classes. Then I will describe the mores with regard to socializing and entertainment, including such activities as shopping. In all these accounts, my concern is only with urban women, for almost all information at present available pertains only to them.

Most of the material I rely on here, whether documentary or literary, is remarkable in that it allows us to glimpse women only obliquely and only to guess at their subjectivity. All the Arabic source material I refer to was written by men, and none of it was written with the object of describing women or their lives; although such works as the biographical dictionary of the learned women of his age by the Cairene al-Sakhawi (1428–97) did aim at least to note their teachers and their scholarly achievements, as well as note such information as who they married. There are no works written by women from this period or these societies. The only accounts available to us describing how women were, what they said, and how they viewed their lives are the rare accounts by Europeans who visited them. Among the most detailed of these is that by Lady Mary Wortley Montagu. I conclude the chapter with some of her descriptions.

Some few practices in the matter of marriage appear to have been common to society as a whole and not to have varied by class. One of these was that marriage was the rule and celibacy extremely rare for either sex. Another was a marriage age for girls ranging between twelve and sixteen to seventeen at most; marriages at even younger ages were possible but were uncommon, insofar as we can tell from texts.[2] (As a rule, textual evidence relates chiefly to the upper and middle classes.) Beyond these two areas marriage customs were to an important extent class bound. Polygamy and concubinage occurred chiefly among the ruling classes; there they were the norm. Among the Mamluks, the rulers of Egypt from 1250 to 1517, keeping large harems of concubines and marrying the maximum number of wives probably expressed a man's class and power. (The Mamluks were military slaves who attained power and continued to replenish their number not only by intermarriage but also by buying and recruiting into their ranks slaves from their own Turkic region of origin.) Chroniclers of the day not infrequently mention that homosexuality was common among Mamluk men, yet this did not curtail the number of wives they had nor the size of their harems.[3]

For the wives of upper-class men the costs of polygamy and concubinage were generally emotional and psychological, rather than economic. The plight of the concubines of such men was, in addition, economically precarious, at least until they bore the master a child and thereby attained some security. A concubine's ethnic background could critically modify her lot. For instance, the Mamluks, who were an ethnic minority in Egypt, considered themselves superior to the natives, and married within their own caste and also took concubines from their Turkic region of origin; as members of an ethnic elite, such concubines were doubtless better treated.[4] Unsurprisingly, however, given the intrinsic rivalry of their situations— wives contending for position and status and concubines for security—the chroniclers tell tales of murders in the harem.

The biographies of two women suspected of being poisoned or bewitched into their sickness or death give a muted glimpse of the contention for status and power in the harem, where the rise of one favorite meant the displacement and fall of another, breeding resentment as surely as in the political arena. Julban, daughter of a Circassian woman, was bought by Sultan Barsbay; their son, Yousef, succeeded Barsbay to the sultanate. Barsbay married Julban after he married the chief princess, wife of his former master, Duqmaq; the chief princess was the mother of his other son, Nasir. After marrying the sultan, Julban became the new chief princess and received many further signs of his favor, including his having her family brought from Circassia and bestowing important positions on them. She died of poison, her murder doubtless following from her rise in the harem. She left a vast fortune (17).

The second woman, Shirin, was a Greek concubine who became the chief princess when her master became sultan and married her. As the new favorite, she took up residence in the Hall of Columns in the Citadel, replacing an earlier wife. Shirin had not been there long when she became ill and took to her bed. Some people were accused of having cast a spell over her; her son thought that some of the princesses, wives of his father, caused her illness out of envy and anger (69–70).

Divorce and remarriage were also common in this class and indeed in all classes. A table of the marriages of twenty-five Mamluk women shows that seven of them married four or more times and that not one married only once.[5]

Patterns of property endowments among Mamluk men suggest that the bonds of affection to daughters, sisters, and even wives were strong. It was fairly common for men to establish *waqf* endowments (endowments for the upkeep of charitable institutions that might also have relatives as beneficiaries) in favor of female relatives and for women to be named the administrators of such properties—which could be vast. Al-Masuna Tatarkhan was designated administrator by her father of an estate that included several hundred *fedans* of agricultural land, six townhouses, numerous shops, and other rental properties in Cairo.[6]

Women are named in nearly 30 percent of surviving waqf documents, either as donors of estates or, more commonly, as administrators. The naming of women as administrators was perhaps unusually high among Mamluks because of the peculiar terms of their relation to property. Mamluk men, who were slaves or of slave origin, were given land to which they enjoyed the usufruct and which reverted to the state upon their death. Because establishing waqf endowments forestalled the reversion of land to the state, they set up endowments for the upkeep of hospitals, schools, and other charitable institutions and endowments with relatives as beneficiaries. Furthermore, Mamluk men's mortality rate was high because their profession was soldiery. They were, in addition, vulnerable to political assassination, imprisonment, and confiscation of property.[7] Women were less vulnerable in these ways. Nevertheless, that women were named to receive and administer property indicates that men regarded them as capable of meeting the responsibility and that daughters were presumably raised to be competent managers.

Women of this class often commanded vast fortunes in their own right and must have sometimes administered their own estates.[8] In addition, Mamluk women ran their own households, which were huge establishments; one princess had seven hundred household staff. The staff of their households consisted entirely of women, including the treasurer (*khazindara*) and the general supervisor (*ra's nauba*). Like the men, the women in this class established endowments for schools, hospices, and mausoleums and also created endowments in favor of their female slaves.[9]

Among other classes as well, marriage at a young age and frequent divorce and remarriage were apparently commonplace. Furthermore, these patterns seemingly pertained in the different religious communities as well. Goitein reports a marriage age between twelve and seventeen for the Jewish community of Cairo and reports also that divorce was extremely common, more so than in any Jewish community in Europe or America until the latter half of the twentieth century. Both divorce and remarriage are reported for urban and rural Egypt for the fourteenth and nineteenth centuries.[10] Divorce nearly always occurred at the instigation of the husband. Occasionally references indicate that women in rare instances sought and obtained divorce, though generally at the price of relinquishing the right to see their children or after paying their husband a sum of money to divorce them or both; the arrangements usually entailed the help of the family—unless the woman was independently wealthy. One Meccan woman, presumably wealthy enough to take strong action, threw her husband out of the house and refused to take him back (64; see also 104, 62, 116). Whether women could obtain a divorce thus depended on their having the leverage of independent wealth or the support of their family. Similarly, only if they had money or family support might they be in a position to stipulate conditions in their marriage contract; if they could, they sometimes insisted that their husband agree in writing to take no second wife or any other bedfellow.[11]

Outside the ruling class polygamy and concubinage were relatively uncommon. Goitein speculates that among Muslims, as among Jews (whose laws, like those of Islam, permitted polygamy), monogamy was a characteristic of "the progressive middle class." European visitors to eighteenth-century Aleppo and nineteenth-century Cairo mention polygamy as rare, and one study of seventeenth-century Turkey found only twenty cases of polygamy in documents relating to two thousand estates.[12] Finances certainly curbed the practice among other than very wealthy men, for the law required that wives be treated equally; maintaining separate establishments for each wife, probably necessary for the sake of harmony, would be onerous, if not beyond most men's means. Even though accepted practice among the ruling class, the plight of women who shared their husband with other wives or concubines nonetheless appears to have been viewed as unhappy. When contemporary authors reported of a particular woman that she was in a monogamous marriage, they regularly went on to note how fortunate she was in this (68, 84–85, 44–45). Similarly, when families were in a position to stipulate monogamy for their daughters, they often did so. Both facts suggest that for members of this society polygamy was understood to be undesirable for women and that even though the law and elite social practice declared it permissible, it was nevertheless felt to be in some way a violation of what was due to women—at least when the women were one's own relatives. It is after all conceivable that some societies (societies in which, for instance, wives were more self-sufficient materially and in terms of food production) not only permitted polygamy but regarded the practice as a natural and happy one for all concerned. This distinctly does not appear to have been the case in the Muslim societies of the Mediterranean Middle East.

Polygamy figures only rarely in the lives of al-Sakhawi's subjects, and when it does, it generally precipitates drama or disaster. Habiba and Umm al-Husain, for example, found themselves in polygamous marriages. Habiba married her cousin, who secretly took another wife. When Habiba learned of this later marriage, her husband hastily divorced the second wife for fear of her anger (19). Umm al-Husain was a woman of scholarly attainments who reportedly lost her mind because her husband took another wife (140–41). Anger, secrecy, and madness—these bespeak a society that did not accommodate itself easily to polygamy. Even the language preserves a sense of the perception in that culture of the inherent unhappiness of the polygamous situation for women: the word for "co-wive," *darra*, is from the root "to harm."

Keeping concubines was obviously beyond the means of the worker class and was evidently uncommon in the middle class as well. Western travelers note its rarity, and contemporary Arabic sources scarcely mention it.[13]

For the most part, the extant records afford little information allowing a more intimate glimpse of the emotional and psychological costs of polygamy and concubinage. In one instance, however, nineteenth-century police records for Cairo yield details of a case that graphically illustrates the sexual vulnerability of slave women and the physical abuse to which they and their children were liable at the hands of other women as well as of men. (The case, it must be emphasized, figures in police records and thus represents criminal, not socially acceptable, practice.)

The slave dealer Deli Mehmet bought Semisgul in Istanbul. He took her to Egypt by sea and en route had sexual relations with her—his right because she was his property. In Egypt, Semisgul informed her master that she might be pregnant, and he, determined to sell her, illegal to do once she had borne him a child, gave her medicines to induce abortion—without success. He nevertheless sold her to the ruling house of Egypt. The women there noticed her condition and brought in a midwife to verify it; when she did, they returned her to the dealer.

Mehmet placed her next in the house of a fellow slave dealer, Mustapha. Mehmet's wife learned of the affair and went over to Mustapha's house. She reviled the girl, and though Mustapha's wife saved Semisgul from a beating on that occasion, the Mustaphas sent Semisgul to Mehmet's house a few days later. When a midwife refused to induce an abortion, saying the pregnancy was too advanced and when Mehmet refused to beat Semisgul until she miscarried, she undertook the business herself, beating Semisgul on her back and stomach with heavy objects (a clothespress and a mincing rod). A passing peasant woman heard Semisgul's screams and, after peering in, ran to a neighbor for help. The neighbor rushed over and took charge of Semisgul. Semisgul gave birth—to a boy, whom Mehmet's wife took away, indicating her intention to adopt him. He was dead within about a year. Mehmet meanwhile sold Semisgul again, this time to a fellow dealer—a sale that was illegal since she had borne him a child. The dealer who bought her, learning of the story, took her to the head of the slave dealers' guild, so that the matter might be investigated. The case was eventually referred to the Grand Mufti of Egypt: it is likely that Semisgul was granted manumission.[14]

For women of the middle and lower classes, uncushioned by personal wealth or wealthy families, polygamy could bring destitution, not just emotional and psychological stress, should a new wife gain enough ascendancy to bring about the divorce of the first wife. Even though middle- and lower-class women might own property independently of their husbands and families, the income was probably rarely substantial enough for economic self-sufficiency.

The plight of widows and divorcées and their children was perennially tragic. Those with grown sons were the luckiest. Al-Sakhawi mentions a number of women, whom he describes as the most fortunate of women, living with sons who treated them well: Khadija, widowed four times, lived with a devoted son, who "showed her a life of comforts beyond description," and Zeinab, now widowed, who had studied the Quran with her father and twice accompanied her husband on pilgrimage, lived with her son, "who treated her well and met all her needs" (25–26, 45). Widows and divorcées, in any case, had to live (like all women) under the guardianship of male relatives—if they had any. ʿAbida, divorced by two husbands, one of whom she had borne children to, lived under the guardianship of her maternal uncle, and al-Sakhawi's aunt Fatima, all of whose children had died, lived most of her life with her brother; she was skilled in embroidery and taught it to the neighborhood children (102, 72). Women without male relatives willing or able to take them in faced lives of mean poverty; that this was commonplace is suggested by the ubiquity with which it is mentioned in contemporary literature that such-and-such person was charitable to "the poor and the widows" or "the old and the widows."

Women in all ethnic groups faced a similar plight. Goitein writes of Jewish women: "The number of widowed, divorced, or deserted women who had lost their struggle for a decent livelihood, or who had never possessed one, was very considerable. They could not sit at home awaiting help. They had to 'uncover their faces,' as the phrase went, to show up in public, in order to secure their rights, or to obtain a minimum of sustenance." The synagogue made semiweekly distributions of bread and occasionally wheat, clothing, and even cash to registered persons. Among Muslims wealthy women sometimes established *ribats* (convents) for widowed or divorced women.[15]

The great historian and topographer of Cairo, al-Maqrizi (1364–1442), refers to some houses in the Karafa Kubra (grand cemetery), called ribats, he says, "in the manner of the houses of the wives of the Prophet." "Old women and widows and single women" lived in them. Al-Sakhawi also mentions ribats: a "fine" one in Harat Abdel Basit, constructed by Zeinab, wife of Sultan Ainal, for the benefit of widows, and another one, also "for widows," constructed by Khadija, daughter of Emir Haj al-Baysari, a woman who was good "to the poor and the aged" (44–45, 25–26).[16]

Religious communities, in the Christian sense of communities of celibate women or men, are not a feature of Islamic societies; nevertheless, convents that were in a sense religious communities and refuges for indigent women did exist. One such convent or ribat was mentioned by al-Maqrizi as a center of learning and religious knowledge. Al-Maqrizi defined *ribat* itself to mean a dwelling inhabited by those "in the way of God." It was founded by Princess Tadhkaray for Zeinab bint Abu'l-Barakat and "her women," Zeinab, known as al-Baghdadia, being a woman of distinguished scholarly and religious attainments. Dating from 1285, this convent was still active in al-Maqrizi's day, some 150 years later, though it had languished somewhat. The last woman to head it whose name he knew was Umm Zeinab Fatima bint al-ʿAbbas, who died in 1394. A woman of great learning, she influenced, inspired, and benefited many women in Cairo and Damascus. The women who lived in the ribat were, al-Maqrizi says, widows, divorcées, and women deserted by their husbands; they remained in the ribat until they remarried or returned to their husbands. The convent was strictly run and fell into decline only when "times became difficult" and when its proximity to a women's prison proved deleterious. Even in the author's day, when it was supervised by a Hanafi judge, it continued to be "of some good."[17]

Because Islamic law permits women to inherit and independently own property, women of the middle class often had property and engaged in various business activities, such as selling and buying real estate, renting out shops, and lending money at interest. A host of evidence attests to these activities. Studies of women in sixteenth- and seventeenth-century urban Turkey, eighteenth-century Aleppo, and nineteenth-century Cairo show that they inherited in practice, not merely in theory, and they were able and willing to go to court if they thought themselves unjustly excluded from inheriting estates.[18]

The pattern of women's involvement in property in all the regions studied shows their consistent involvement in real estate. In Aleppo and in Kayseri, Turkey, women were involved in 40 percent of all property transfers. They actively bought and sold commercial as well as residential property; they probably rented out shops (women shopkeepers were rare). In Aleppo a third of those dealing in commercial property were women and a third of these were buyers.[19] Evidence for Turkey and Syria shows women selling two to three times more often than they bought, a pattern that probably reflects their inheritance of shares in properties, which they then sold, and possibly reflects their chronic need for ready cash.[20]

Dealing in property did not entail large resources: people might own shares of houses as well as own them independently, and most people could afford to buy houses or shares of houses. Goitein reports that for medieval Cairo "even poor people possessed a house or part of one," and Abraham Marcus indicates the same for eighteenth-century Aleppo. Collectively women owned less real estate than men, though they apparently concentrated their assets in real estate, whereas men invested far more diversely. The disparity probably reflects the fact that although women inherited, they inherited a smaller portion of an inheritance than men did and that, frequent as property holding was among women, their holdings were generally modest.[21]

Whereas very wealthy women might invest in trade—the spice trade, for example, or the slave trade—or in commercial ventures as silent partners, middle-class women apparently invested largely in real estate. Other forms of investment included making loans at interest, often to family members, frequently to husbands, and sometimes to other women.[22] Such loans were secured in court, and if necessary, women went to court to reclaim them, whether from husbands or other family members or anyone else. Suers or the sued, women represented themselves in court and their statements had equal weight with men's.[23]

The scholarly establishment, especially in the West, has enthusiastically hailed the documentary evidence showing that women inherited and owned property and vigorously pursued their economic interests, even in court. The evidence attests that Muslim women were not, after all, the passive creatures, wholly without material resources or legal rights, that the Western world once imagined them to be. But women were active, let me emphasize, within the very limited parameters permitted by their society. For example, they were limited to acquiring property essentially through gift or inheritance. Areas of the economy in which wealth might be aggressively acquired were by and large closed to women—unless they had inherited the wealth to buy their way into those areas. Thus the evidence that women owned property and were economically active undermines the Western stereotype of Muslim women as passive and resourceless, but it also simultaneously confirms Muslim women's derivative and marginal relation to property. The number of women owning property substantial enough to render them financially independent of male relatives must always have been minute.

Women of all classes engaged in sewing, embroidery, and other forms of textile production. Embroidery, Goitein notes, was "the occupation most frequently referred to in connection with women" in the Geniza documents; and women (as well as men), he says, "were engaged everywhere in the unraveling and reeling as well as in the weaving and dying of silk."[24] In later periods it is clear that women could derive some income from textile work. Evidence for early nineteenth-century Cairo shows that women were economically involved to a significant degree in clothmaking, especially spinning and carding; this was in particular the case prior to the encroachment of European markets and the importation of European goods. The women purchased the raw cotton or linen, processed it in their own homes, and resold it, or they engaged in a "putting out" system, in which traders bought the cotton or linen, distributed it to the spinners and carders, then collected it from them for a piece rate for distribution to weaving workshops. Research on other urban regions of the eastern Mediterranean confirms the existence of similar patterns in earlier periods—in the seventeenth-century Turkish city of Bursa, for example, and in eighteenth-century Aleppo.[25]

The income derived from such labor was generally modest. Sewing and embroidery, as well as clothmaking, might also provide a modest income, though some women, at least on the evidence of early nineteenth-century Cairo, could make a good living embroidering women's jackets and other luxury items for the wealthy. An exceptionally successful woman might even employ young girls at low wages to serve as apprentices.[26]

Sewing and embroidery were widely taught. In the latter part of the nineteenth century girls were generally sent to sewing and embroidery schools to about the age of nine. Teaching those skills was one way to gain some income. Women, like al-Sakhawi's aunt, might also teach the neighborhood children informally. (Al-Sakhawi does not mention whether his aunt received any financial return.)

By the latter part of the period (the evidence relates specifically to the late eighteenth and nineteenth centuries), some girls were taught to read at such schools. If education was pursued after the age of nine, a female teacher was hired to come to the girl's home. Again, at least toward the end of the period, girls occasionally attended the *kuttab*, the school attached to the mosque and attended by boys, which taught reading and the recitation of the Quran.[27] A small minority of women advanced further in learning, and some became renowned scholars and even teachers of hadith and *tafsir* (interpretation). Women mentioned as having achieved advanced levels of education were mostly of the *ʿulama* class—the class of educated men which supplied the state with jurists, theologians, and administrators (at the upper end of the middle class, its members also occasionally intermarried with the ruling elite). Whether women of this class received an education or not apparently depended on whether a member of the family took the time to teach them. The family member most frequently mentioned in this connection is the father. Occasionally a grandfather or aunt instructed a female child, and sometimes even a husband instructed his wife.[28]

Women's initial education was obtained in the family, but at later stages they could have access to male scholars and teachers. Scholarship consisted in learning texts by rote—hadith, *fiqh* (juridical theology), and tafsir—and teachers awarded certificates attesting that the student had attained, and might teach, to a certain level. Umm Hani (d. 1466), who learned the Quran in childhood, received her first education from her grandfather; she later accompanied him to Mecca, and there, and again on their return to Cairo, she was "heard" in her recitations and "certified" by a number of male scholars. Al-Sakhawi reports that she knew hadith and fiqh and was one of the distinguished scholars of her day (156–57).

Another woman, Hajar (b. 1388), was educated by her father. She accompanied him when he visited scholars and engaged in discussions with them, and she too was heard by, and obtained certificates from, male scholars. Al-Sakhawi says she was among the foremost hadith scholars of her time, and students crowded to hear her. Because she did not wear the veil when she taught, a practice "common among many old women," of which he disapproved, al-Sakhawi did not study with her, although he did have some women teachers, as did his revered teacher and mentor, al-ʿAsqalani, and his contemporary al-Suyuti (131–32).[29]

Of another woman, Bayram, al-Sakhawi says that her father studied the Quran and mingled with the learned and that she grew up sharing in this, and that her studies included tracts by al-Nawawi and al-Ghazali. Her father also took her to Jerusalem; she "recited to the sheikhs there, and taught women of what she had studied." She married and then, al-Sakhawi cryptically concludes, "her life changed" (15).

Other learned women mentioned by al-Sakhawi include Khadija bint ʿAli (d. 1468) and Nashwan (d. 1468). Khadija, a scholar of the Quran and hadith and a calligrapher with whom the author studied, taught women as well as men (29). Nashwan had a number of friends among elite women on account of her erudition, which was such that her relative, Judge Kilani, who rose for no woman, rose for her when she entered his house. Nashwan enjoyed the friendship of Princess al-Bariziyya, whom she once accompanied on a pilgrimage. Nashwan's students praised her for her care and patience (129–30).

Other learned women acquired friends among the elite—Khadija bint Muhammad (d. 1389), for example, whose extensive scholarship included a knowledge of the hadith collections of al-Bukhari (31). One member of royalty, Princess Tadhkaray, as mentioned earlier, established a convent, in 1285, for the learned Zeinab bint Abu'l-Barakat and "her women." Elite women were sometimes distinguished scholars themselves: Bay Khatun (d. 1391), for example, who taught hadith in Syria and Egypt and whose teachers included distinguished male as well as female scholars (11–12).[30]

Evidently, then, scholarly interaction between men and women did take place, and women were taught by women and by men. But how and where is not clear. Apparently women attended men's lectures, and men studied with women, but histories of education in the Islamic world make no mention of women's attending any of the numerous *madrasas* (schools) or public institutions of learning.[31] A traveler in Cairo in the early nineteenth century wrote that women were to be seen at the renowned and ancient religious and educational institution of al-Azhar: "Contrary to the ideas commonly prevailing in Europe, a large portion of the votaries consisted of ladies, who were walking to and fro without the slightest restraints, conversing with each other, and mingling freely among the men." Could this freedom also have pertained in earlier periods? There is no suggestion, in any case, that women ever taught at such institutions, although they did obtain certificates, which, among men, was often a prerequisite to obtaining an entry-level position as an instructor. Such salaried positions were evidently not open to women.[32] And while women clearly had students, what remuneration they received, if any, is not indicated. Hajar, the eminent hadith scholar who had students crowding to hear her, was in such straits in her later years that she "did not hesitate to accept the wherewithal to live, and would even ask for more" (131). Women scholars possibly gave some sort of instruction for a stipend at the somewhat rare ribats for women and the even more rarely mentioned schools for orphans and widows, but the topic generally merits further investigation.

The pursuit of scholarship, whether for pleasure or remuneration, was evidently the prerogative of middle-class and elite women—even if in later life some of them fell on hard times. For lower-class women areas of remunerative employment included work as midwives, bakers, greengrocers, sellers of foodstuffs (cooked beans, flour, milk), *dallalas* (peddlers of clothes, embroidery, and jewelry to the harems), washers of the dead, mourners, and singers. They could work as bath attendants, as servants or orderlies in the *maristans* (hospitals for both male and female patients that employed orderlies of both sexes), and as prostitutes.[33] The prevalence of prostitutes in Egypt, Cairo in particular, is mentioned by many contemporary Arab authors, who note that prostitutes had to pay taxes in order to work. Alexander Russell, the English physician who practiced in Aleppo in the eighteenth century, mentions that the prostitutes in Aleppo were licensed by a state officer to whom they paid protection money, and he describes them as parading in the streets and on the outskirts of the town, "dressed in a flaunting manner, their veil flying loosely from the face, their cheeks painted, bunches of flowers stuck gaudily on the temples, and their bosom exposed; their gait is masculine, and full of affectation." Eighteenth-century and later sources mention guilds for prostitutes and for female singers and dancers, but the guilds were almost certainly little more than organizations whose function was to facilitate state control and taxation of those engaged in these professions. All these jobs were of a low to disreputable status.[34]

Women dwelling in ribats, and Sufi women in general, seem to have occupied a borderline status between the reputable and the disreputable. To some extent they, like their counterparts in the numerous ribats for men, were religious not merely in the general sense of observing the religious commands and leading a pious life but in the more specific sense of being members of a Sufi order. From the earliest times Sufism was the vehicle by which the mystical dimensions of Islam were expressed. By the thirteenth century bands of devotees lived together in convents and followed the "way" (*tariqa*) of a master revered in common; the heads of such bands or convents were known as sheikhs or sheikhas, depending on their sex. As their membership grew (as it did to the nineteenth century)—a membership drawn chiefly from among urban working people—Sufism took on many of the characteristics of a popular religion, including a reverence for saints and holy people and saints' tombs. Its characteristic qualities thus differed somewhat from those of both classical Sufism and the "rational" religion of the ʿulama class. Membership in the Sufi orders, however, was by no means confined to working people; in some, the members were mostly upper-class people or wealthy merchants. The elite, women as well as men, might be members; Shukrbay, wife of Sultan as-Zahir Khushqadam, for example, belonged to a Sufi order.[35] Mainly, however, the Sufism that now became widespread expressed working-class and lower-class cultural life. Many of its practices were disdained and denounced as "superstitious" by the ʿulama—the guardians of established religion. Among men, membership in a particular Sufi order had a pronounced connection with a particular line of work, but no such connection appears with respect to women.

Information about Sufi women in the premodern age is scant. One of the fullest accounts is by the jurist and scholar Ibn al-Hajj. In one passage he rails against sheikhas, their practices, and their followers—as indeed he railed throughout his work against any activity in which women were not silent, invisible, and subservient to men.

He denounces "those who are called sheikhas" for performing *dhikrs* (religious chants sometimes involving dance), which he views as illegitimate in that women's voices are *ʿawra* and should not be heard. (The word *ʿawra* is one of those words whose complicated layered meanings and range of possible referents are richly suggestive of the androcentrism of dominant Arabic culture and of the connections it made between women, sexuality, and shameful and defective things. Its meanings include blind in one eye; blemished, defective; the genital area; generally parts of the body that are shameful and must be concealed; women's bodies; women's voices; and women.) Ibn al-Hajj denounces the sheikhas for causing their women followers to adopt Sufi practices that were improper and were like those of Christian women in their convents, who did without husbands; that was against the law of the Prophet, who, according to Ibn al-Hajj, said, "Woman's strivings should be solely to the pleasing of her lord/husband."[36] In this period, then, as in others, the path of religion, celibacy, and sisterhood allowed some few women to escape male domination, at least in their personal lives; and it was evidently this fact—that even a few women lived outside the bounds of patriarchal rules—that most particularly provoked Ibn al-Hajj's diatribe.

The androcentrism of the culture and language, and the discourse broadly underlying the social organization, was directly manifested in the architecture of the upper class. The word *sakan*, or dwelling, from the root "quiet, tranquil," expresses the Islamic concept of a man's right to a haven of inviolable privacy, forbidden to and guarded from intrusion by other men. *Hareem,* from the word *haram,* "sacred, forbidden," refers to those apartments that were most particularly forbidden to other men—those in which his women resided.

Among the upper classes this ideal of a man's right to keep his women concealed—invisible to other men—was given architectural expression. The women's quarters were often designed to be the pleasantest part of the house, not just because the women spent most of their lives there but also because the master spent most of his time there when at home. Their rooms were distanced from the audience rooms and courtyards connecting with the outside world, and looked out onto interior gardens. The baths and kitchens were separate from but adjoining the harem. Sofas, cushions, and carpets constituted the main furnishings. In polygamous households, if wives did not have their separate palaces, they had their own self-contained apartments, and separate apartments housed the concubines.

Obviously, wealth was necessary for such constructions. Middle-class houses might or might not include a *haramiyya*—women's quarters. Some architectural remains from the tenth and eleventh centuries suggest that even fairly modest homes could have separate quarters for the women, but this arrangement appears to have been fairly rare in middle- and lower-class houses. The women's part of an average modest home was probably marked merely by a simple curtain over the doorway.[37]

Jews and Christians might occupy the same buildings as Muslims—there were no restrictions on who might live where—but they did not observe the seclusion of women in their domestic arrangements. In a Jewish home an unrelated man might come to the house and discuss matters with the woman of the house in the absence of the man. Such differences in custom occasionally caused friction. Geniza documents record that a Jewish family felt themselves inconvenienced when a Christian family they shared a house with converted to Islam and took to observing the seclusion for the women.[38]

As in upper-class homes, the chief furnishings in the middle-class home consisted of sofas, rugs, and cushions, with curtains sectioning off areas of the apartment, which might not have many rooms. The furnishings were brought by the bride to her new home; they and the bride's clothes were the chief items in her trousseau—all of which, in the Jewish community and no doubt among the Muslims as well, were carefully listed as the bride's property.[39]

Clothing, along with jewelry, often constituted the most expensive portion of the trousseau. Both men's and women's clothing could be gorgeous in color and texture. Outer garments, such as cloaks, could be worn interchangeably by either sex, though the authorities did not necessarily approve, condemning in particular a woman's adopting what was considered male attire. One edict issued in Cairo in 1263 forbade women to wear *ʿimamas* (male headgear) and other masculine clothing. But whatever their short-term effects, such edicts were apparently not effective in the longer term: Ibn al-Hajj, writing about a century later, criticizes his female contemporaries for wearing ʿimamas.[40]

The wealthy employed domestic slaves, most often female, to cook their food and clean their houses. People in the middle and lower classes who could not afford slaves probably purchased prepared food in the market most weekdays, given the expense of fuel and the enormous labor that cooking entailed. A large variety of prepared foods was available. As a rule it was probably a man of the family or a domestic slave that fetched the food from the market. Shopping, done among the upper classes entirely through merchants, who sent samples of their wares in to the harems, and through dallalas, the female peddlers, was also to some extent done through dallalas in the middle class. In Aleppo peddlers to harems were often Jewish or Christian women, but in Cairo, most were apparently Muslim women.[41] But middle-class and lower-class women evidently also did their own shopping, for clothing, textiles, and jewelry in particular, and often it was they (according to Ibn al-Hajj) who shopped for their men's clothing. On feast days they visited jewelry and other shops in such crowds that they outnumbered the men. Men consequently could only make their way through the souk with difficulty, and this appalled Ibn al-Hajj, who characteristically concludes that women ought therefore to be banned from visiting the markets; and indeed women were periodically forbidden to emerge into the streets at all. During such times the merchants, clothing and perfume merchants most of all, were reportedly in poor straits because of their inability to sell their merchandise.[42]

Women's social activities included visiting each other on formal occasions—weddings, births, funerals—and informally calling on each other and going to the public baths; public bathing, reported for all communities, was indulged in about once a week. Weddings and births involved elaborate festivities, perhaps with professional female singers and dancers performing within the harem (or whatever section of the house served to receive women) but placed to be also visible to the men or else performing in a court in the men's section that women might overlook from a balcony or window.[43] Funerals were also social occasions, and they could be substantial affairs, festive yet somber. Al-Sakhawi's biographical entries often conclude with the mention of the woman's funeral and a phrase such as "It was a lavish and solemn spectacle"; in one instance he even adds that there were "pleasant times and fine spectacles" and that poets delivered elegies (25–26). Professional female mourners might be hired to wail, beat their tambourines, and recite the fine qualities of the deceased. The proceedings would be inaugurated by the less dignified but equally ritualized abuse, even beating of the professional washer of the dead (a woman if the deceased was a woman); aware of what awaited her when she entered the house, she generally concealed herself, then she and the women engaged in a ritualized verbal exchange.[44]

Professional female mourners, prohibited by orthodox Islam, were periodically banned by the authorities, but without any prolonged success. On one occasion the ban was rescinded following the intervention of the *daminat al-maghani,* the female officer responsible for remitting to the government the taxes due from working women, such as singers, Sufi dhikr-chanters, mourners, and others.[45] The damina pointed out how much the treasury stood to lose in taxes if the government banned the hiring of mourners.

Women sometimes went further afield than each other's homes and the market, visiting cemeteries, attending the departure of the *mahmal* (the pilgrim caravan to Mecca), witnessing state spectacles, and going for outings along the river. All such excursions were periodically liable to banning or at least to stern and vehement censure from men of religion, like Ibn al-Hajj. Visits to cemeteries, especially to see famous tombs, were popular activities on feast days; going was not a mournful event but a chance to have fun and take the children out, and sometimes the women remained out overnight. Ibn al-Hajj says that women walked about at night visiting tombs in the company of men and "with empty spaces all about," even allowing their faces to be uncovered and talking and laughing with strange men. Gathering together among the tombs on moonlit nights, they set out lanterns and chairs and sat listening to storytellers—"all of which was forbidden for men and for women—and the visiting of tombs altogether is not for women."[46] When the censorious voices won out, as they periodically did, women were prohibited from visiting the cemeteries on feast days or from visiting them altogether.[47]

The annual departure of the mahmal also brought women out in large numbers. To assure themselves of a good view of the spectacle, including the rich caravans of elite women, those women not going along took up positions in well-situated shops a day before the departure and stayed there overnight, again mingling freely (too freely, in Ibn al-Hajj's opinion) with men.[48] Going to Mecca was a common ambition. Quite possibly, many of the lower-class women who came to watch the event would one day themselves make the pilgrimage, saving perhaps for a lifetime in order to do so. Al-Sakhawi's subjects, predominantly middle class, not uncommonly made the pilgrimage not once but several times.

Again, women were periodically prohibited from attending the departure of the mahmal. In certain times women were in fact forbidden even to leave their houses. In 1437, for example, the plague was raging, and the sultan, searching for ways to allay it, conferred in solemn assembly with the judges and jurists. He inquired of them what sin it was in the people that God punished with the plague. "Zina," they responded—adultery, sexual misconduct. Women these days were adorning themselves and freely going about the streets and souks night and day. They should be banned from going out, they said. Some debate ensued about whether the ban should apply to old women and to women who had no one to see to their affairs, but the sultan was inclined to apply the ban to all women, and this was done. "Women were forbidden on pain of death to leave their houses, . . . and women found [outdoors] were beaten."[49] How single women fared on this occasion is not reported, but accounts of other periods when women were ordered to stay at home say that some women starved to death.[50] Fortunately, extreme bans, though they were pronounced a number of times by one or other ruler over the centuries, were not very frequent and were not enforced for long periods of time. Such prohibitions—whether against women's wearing men's clothes or visiting cemeteries or appearing on the street—were evidently allowed to lapse, and women returned to former practices. Otherwise, complaints and bans would not have continued to be repeated.

Attending the baths appears not to have been prohibited, although some theologians frowned upon the practice for women and pronounced it un-Islamic.[51] Ibn al-Hajj censures the practice and instructs men not to let their women go to the baths. He argues that religious law required that women be covered from navel to knee when among other women but that women at the baths paid no attention to this and did not cover themselves at all. This indecency was compounded by the fact that Jewish and Christian women also attended the baths: Islam required that Muslim women's bodies not be seen by non-Muslims. All the women were there naked together, he complains. Among other objections, he mentions that women always put their best clothes on after bathing in order to show off to each other, then asked their husbands for better clothes. He concludes his criticisms with the remark that hammams led to numerous corruptions, including some he had not mentioned (and that were perhaps "unmentionable") that would be "clear to whomsoever reflects" on the matter.[52]

Women have left no written records, so we have no direct means of learning what it was like to live life thus. The most direct descriptions we have of women's lives and words come from the pens of European visitors. One in particular, Lady Mary Wortley Montagu, wife of the British ambassador to Turkey from 1717 to 1718, provides at least an impression of the lives of women in the period before the economic encroachment of the West and the changes that followed. Another British writer, Alexander Russell, also provides fairly detailed information on harem life. Russell, whom I have already referred to, was a physician and resident of Aleppo in the 1740s, and in his medical capacity he had access to harems normally denied to European men. The brief, intimate glimpses their works afford, however, relate essentially only to the upper classes, in the case of Montagu, and the upper and middle classes, in the case of Russell.

When Montagu visited upper-class harems, she was met by eunuchs who escorted her to the innermost rooms, where the woman of the household was generally seated with friends and relatives. The woman of the household would come forward to greet her. Dinner was served by female slaves, then other female slaves danced, accompanying themselves on instruments. The slaves, invariably beautiful, Montagu says, belonged to the women and were not accessible to their husbands. The quality of their performances reflected sometimes the wealth and sometimes the personality of the owner. One exceedingly rich woman in her fifties, whose performers put on a dull show, explained to Montagu, whom she received in the company of some five or six friends, that she no longer spent her money on superfluities, preferring instead to spend it on charity and to devote much of her time to prayer.[53]

The women that Montagu describes spent their time in the company of women friends and relatives and apparently formed close bonds with their female slaves, whom they acquired when the slaves were young and raised under their eye. In the home of the sultan's widow, Montagu observed ten child slaves, the eldest no more than seven and all beautifully dressed. They performed small tasks for the sultana—served her coffee, brought her water when she washed—and the sultana took great pleasure in them. Such slaves were well looked after; they were taught to embroider by the older slaves and were raised as carefully as daughters of the family. Because carefully raised slaves were very expensive, occasionally upper-class women bought girls as an investment, educated them, and sold them in their early teens

(1:384).[54] But it was apparently far commoner for upper-class women to raise them as their own personal slaves and to form close attachments to them. Montagu says that they never sold them (except "as a Punishment for some very great fault"); if they grew weary of them, they gave them to a friend or gave them their freedom. Russell says that they were sometimes married to a servant and, after being given their freedom, continued as adherents of the family, but the larger proportion of them remained single and "followed the fortunes of their mistress"; they were usually emancipated upon her death. In sixteenth-century Istanbul women made endowments for the benefit of their freed, generally female slaves more frequently even than for their own descendants, clearly indicating some attachment to and sense of obligation toward them (1:368).[55]

Other details in Montagu's descriptions show the easy, relaxed intimacies of women in the baths, where they were groomed by their slaves and conversed, drinking coffee and sherbet the while; she calls the bath "the women's coffee-house, where all the news of the town is told, scandal invented, etc." (1:314). Montagu also describes women of childbearing age as often preoccupied with the desire for children, resorting to love potions and magic to procure them.

Altogether the broad pattern of women's lives among the upper classes emerges as a series of stages. Early marriage, between the ages of twelve and sixteen, was followed by a preoccupation with childbearing and children. Then as the mother of grown sons and daughters, especially sons, a woman acquired security, status, authority, and respect within the family. In the last period of her life—which could constitute a good proportion of it, because marriage and childbearing occurred early—she quietly enjoyed the company of a few friends and occupied herself with acts of piety and charity. Making charitable endowments for the benefit of the poor, widows, or personal slaves, she thus arranged her soul and prepared for the hereafter and simultaneously earned the regard of her entourage and contemporaries as a person of piety and charity. (I am not here suggesting that their endowments were merely self-serving and did not express genuine feelings of piety and charity, but rather I am simply noting that such acts have multiple and complex meanings and motivations.)

Little other material is available from which one might surmise how the women of these societies felt about the world in which they were trapped. Two surviving descriptions, however, show them cogitating over the differences between their lives and those of women in other societies. In the first, an eighteenth-century account, we see them intensely curious about what it might be like to live in a different society. Alexander Russell, who attended women in the harem, describes how he would be persuaded "to protract his visit, and to gratify the curiosity of the ladies, who ask numberless questions concerning his country. They are particularly inquisitive about the Frank [European] women, their dress, employments, marriages, treatment of children, and amusements. . . . Their questions are generally pertinent, and the remarks they occasionally make on manners differing so widely from their own, are often sprightly, and judicious."[56]

The second description dates from the earlier part of the nineteenth century; it is from a work by Suzanne Voilquin, a French working-class woman, Saint Simonian, and ardent feminist, who served as principal (1834–36) of the women's college for doctors founded in Egypt in the 1830s. In her text, too, the women are intensely curious about European women, but their curiosity is now blatantly laced with envy and longing— feelings that Voilquin deliberately fans. During a two-year stay in Egypt, she attended a women's party. The household she was visiting was a Coptic one—there is no reason to think that the scene she describes would have differed much had it been instead in a Muslim or Jewish home.

> First we were presented with coffee [and] a nargheela (pipe) which were followed by sweetmeats and drinks. For the first few instants everyone was reserved: . . . but soon . . . they plied me with a thousand questions about the women of my country: I became an "agent provocateur" and set myself at criticising their thick and inconvenient veils, their seclusion, and then I tried to make them understand our polite and sociable customs. In France, I said . . . men constantly formed part of our gatherings, they accompanied us on our walks, everywhere we are placed first, faces uncovered and heads adorned with flowers! [Voilquin, as she later indicates, was not as innocent about the status of women in the West as she here pretends.] What sighs and exclamations escaped from their breasts listening to these tales of the West![57]

The women rounded out the evening with an entertainment: some of them dressed up as men and acted out roles that caused the company to laugh uproariously.

As Voilquin's presence in Egypt as principal of a women's medical school betokened, the world about which the women were curious was beginning to invade their own.

Part
&
Three

NEW DISCOURSES

SOCIAL AND

Chapter 7   INTELLECTUAL
ॐ

CHANGE

IN THE EARLY NINETEENTH CENTURY THE SOCIETIES
of the Middle East began to undergo a fundamental
social transformation. Economic encroachment by the
West and entrammelment in the global economy, the
emergence of "modern" states in the region, and the
domination, formal or informal, of much of the area
by European colonial powers in the late nineteenth and
early twentieth centuries formed the overarching economic and political parameters of the transformation.

As early as the first decades of the nineteenth century
some women, particularly rural workers and lower-
class women in countries, such as Egypt and Syria,
where European-made goods had made inroads, undoubtedly suffered as a consequence of the shifting
economic and political patterns. For women in general the effects of European political and cultural
encroachment were complicated and, in certain respects, decidedly negative. Nonetheless, in crucial ways
the outcome of the process of change the encroach-
ments set in motion was broadly positive, because the
social institutions and mechanisms for the control and
seclusion of women and for their exclusion from the
major domains of activity in their society were grad-

127

bad recipe

ually dismantled. The social system had combined the worst features of a Mediterranean and Middle Eastern misogyny with an Islam interpreted in the most negative way possible for women, and Middle Eastern women have no cause to regret its passing.

The changes ensuing from economic change and from state policies, whether promulgated by an indigenous or a colonial bureaucracy, and the cultural and ideological developments that followed, had an impact on the lives of both men and women. One development was of peculiar significance to women, however: the emergence of women themselves as a central subject for national debate. For the first time since the establishment of Islam, the treatment of women in Islamic custom and law—the license of polygamy, easy male access to divorce, and segregation—were openly discussed in Middle Eastern societies. The subject of women first surfaced as a topic of consequence in the writings of Muslim male intellectuals in Egypt and Turkey. From the start the treatment and status of women were intertwined with other issues that these intellectuals considered critically important to society, including nationalism and the need for national advancement and for political, social, and cultural reform. From the start the discussion of women and reform was embedded in considerations of the relative advancement of European societies and the need for Muslim societies to catch up. A new discourse on women emerged, overlaying rather than displacing the old classical and religious formulations on gender and often linking issues concerning women, nationalism and national advancement, and cultural change. In the new and, by the end of the century, dominant discourse on women these issues were inextricably connected.

There is no intrinsic or necessary connection between the issue of women and the issue of culture, as the history of Western feminism shows. The Western legacy of androcentrism and misogyny, though differing in its specificities, is nevertheless, generally speaking, no better than that of other cultures, including the Islamic. Indeed, in view of such occurrences as the extermination of thousands of women in the course of the European witch-hunts, Fatima Mernissi's formula describing how the Muslim order conceived of its enemies, "the infidel without and the woman within," seems at least as aptly to describe the European past.[1] Nevertheless, Western feminists do not therefore call for the abandonment of the entire Western heritage and the wholesale adoption of some other culture as the only recourse for Western women; rather, they engage critically and constructively with that heritage in its own terms. Adopting another culture as a general remedy for a heritage of misogyny within a particular culture is not only absurd, it is impossible. The complexity of enculturation and the depth of its encoding in the human psyche are such that even individuals deliberately fleeing to another culture, mentally or physically, carry forward and re-create in their lives a considerable part of their previous enculturation. In any case, how could the substitution of one culture for another be brought about for the peoples of an entire society or several societies?

Yet in the debate about women in the Islamic world, as in other parts of the non-Western world, those proposing an improvement in the status of women from early on couched their advocacy in terms of the need to abandon the (implicitly) "innately" and "irreparably" misogynist practices of the native culture in favor of the customs and beliefs of another culture—the European. (As I will discuss in the following chapter, it was no accident that the abandonment of native culture was posed as the solution for women's oppression only in colonized or dominated societies and not in Western ones.) This rhetoric became insistent and pronounced with colonial domination, and it was in this context that the links between the issue of women and the issues of nationalism and culture were permanently forged. They were fused initially in the context of Western economic and cultural encroachment and finally and most forcefully in the context of its political and discursive domination—a domination that was to precipitate new kinds of class and cultural conflict. The debate over women became a dominant mode through which these other profoundly divisive matters were contested. It was at this point that the veil emerged as a potent signifier, connoting not merely the social meaning of gender but also matters of far broader political and cultural import. It has ever since retained that cargo of signification. The fusion of the issue of women with issues of class, culture, and politics and the encoding of the issue of women and the veil with these further issues have been critical for women. Progress or regress in the position and rights of women has often directly depended on which side of the debates over nationalism and culture the men holding or gaining political power espoused. In this chapter I explore the developments that took place over the course of the nineteenth century and that set the stage for the emergence, in the late nineteenth century, of the discourse encoding gender with the conflicts of class and culture. The specific sources and evolution of that discourse form the subject of the next chapter.

Western economic encroachment and domination in the nineteenth century, the responses within Middle Eastern societies, and the economic and social changes that occurred were multileveled and intricate, as were the circumstances of the emergence and evolution of the debate on women. The direction of change was similar for the Middle East as a whole, though the pace of change differed from country to country. Egypt and Turkey and to a lesser extent Syria, where European products first entered the market, were in the vanguard, whereas the Arabian Peninsula was less directly affected until well into the twentieth century. Local factors accented developments differently as the various regions—with their various urban and rural, nomadic and tribal communities—were caught up in the global economy. Also shaping the specific social and political outcome in each country was the evolving political relation with European states—whether the Middle Eastern country remained independent or became submerged in colonialism or protocolonialism.

Rather than attempt to follow out developments in the region in all their local variations, a project hardly feasible except in the most superficial terms, I shall focus on their effects on women and on the new discourses on women in Egypt. Egypt was at the forefront of the changes overtaking the Arab world over the course of the nineteenth and twentieth centuries, and in many ways it was, and continues to be, a mirror of developments in the Middle East. The debate over the veil that erupted there at the turn of the nineteenth century, igniting a controversy within Egyptian society and touching off debate in other Muslim Middle Eastern capitals, marked the emergence of a new discourse. As formulated in Egypt at that time, when colonial ascendancy and class division were crucial issues, it proved to be a founding and paradigmatic discourse. Repeatedly throughout the twentieth century the issue of women and the veil, albeit occasionally in slightly different guise, has flared up in one or another Middle Eastern society—and indeed in Muslim societies further afield—and always the debate is charged with other issues—culture and nationalism, "Western" versus "indigenous" or "authentic" values—first drawn into the discourse on women at a past critical moment, a moment occurring in Egypt in the late nineteenth century. That is, it is a discourse on women and the veil in which another history is also inscribed, the history of colonial domination and the struggle against it and the class divisions around that struggle—a history affecting all Middle Eastern societies in one way or another and a discourse in which that history, those struggles, still live.

European economic encroachment was distinctly under way in Egypt by the late eighteenth century. By the 1770s local crafts, in particular textile production, were being adversely affected by imported European goods.[2] This trend steadily continued over the first decades of the nineteenth century, and by the 1840s a major shift was established, characterized by the import of finished goods and the export of raw materials and by an increase in trade with Western Europe at the expense of trade within the Ottoman empire. Egypt, which had traded chiefly with the Ottoman empire at the beginning of the nineteenth century, was trading predominantly with Europe by midcentury.

This imbalance was occurring for reasons external and internal to the Middle East. During the first half of the eighteenth century Europe underwent a technological revolution that culminated in the industrial revolution. Techniques improved, particularly in textile production, outstripping in efficiency and economy the techniques of the Middle East. At the same time, production in the Middle East was disrupted by a devastating series of plagues and by political unrest. In Egypt almost continuous warfare within the Mamluk ruling class, plus extortionist taxation, further contributed to a decline in production.[3]

Developments in Egypt played a key role in accelerating social change. Particularly important were the policies pursued by Muhammad ʿAli, who became ruler of Egypt, nominally under Turkish suzerainty, in 1805 and who stayed in power for forty-three years. Intent upon making Egypt independent, Muhammad ʿAli set about modernizing his army and increasing revenues. He introduced agricultural, administrative, and educational reforms and attempted to establish industries, his initiatives in these areas giving impetus to economic, intellectual, cultural, and educational developments important to women.

In their immediate impact, both Western economic advances and Muhammad ʿAli's policies adversely affected some women, particularly lower-class urban and rural women. In the first place European imports caused a decline in the local textile industry, competition from Western products putting pressure on those involved in textile work—one of the few areas of remunerative labor open to women.[4] This decline was exacerbated in the first decades of the nineteenth century by state trade agreements and later by state measures introduced to establish a state-run textile industry.[5] Bringing textile workers under state control and instituting state-run textile factories disrupted the local textile industry, previously dependent on autonomous workers. Even when most of the state-run factories had failed, by about midcentury, traditional textile crafts could not regain their former vitality, although some local production continued. The failure of the state venture into textile production accelerated the pace at which Egypt became essentially a supplier of raw materials—chiefly and increasingly cotton after 1840—and an importer of finished European goods.[6]

Some of the state factories had employed some women, in particular factories in provincial centers, such as the tarboosh factory at Fuwwa. There are no reliable figures on the number of women thus employed, but it is generally thought to be small. Women received about two-thirds of the wages received by men. Women, probably again only in small numbers, were also employed in other factories established by Muhammad ʿAli, sugar and tobacco factories, for example, and cotton-processing plants, some of which continued production into the twentieth century.[7]

Egypt's growing entrammelment in the global economy, however, initially decreased the opportunities for women to earn a livelihood or a supplemental income from textile production, whether by spinning, carding, or bleaching, as Judith Tucker has argued in her work on nineteenth-century Egyptian women. Tucker speculates, too, that the influx of European goods had a negative impact on other areas of local trade in ways that, again, harmed women and men. Thus she notes that while petty traders of foodstuffs, for instance, were probably unaffected, local merchants were pushed aside in favor of European companies and their agents. Consequently, women who invested in local trade would also have suffered.

The changes in land tenure laws that Muhammad ʿAli introduced in his pursuit of agricultural reform also adversely affected the peasantry, including women. The laws concentrated land in the hands of a few large landowners and led to peasant dispossession, which was exacerbated by other agricultural projects that Muhammad ʿAli vigorously pursued, such as digging and restoring dikes and canals. Although these measures significantly increased the area of cultivable land, they were carried out with forced male peasant labor, depriving the peasant household of essential agricultural labor and leading to further dispossession. Women and children, if they had no other means of support, sometimes worked alongside their men at the work sites. The pay was poor and often in arrears, and the conditions of work often appalling. Male peasants were also subject to forcible recruitment into the army, with once more the same consequences for their families; again, women and children with no other means of subsistence followed their men. They encamped in shantytowns and split the rations allotted to their men, and here, too, the conditions were often appalling.[8]

If not compelled by poverty to follow men fulfilling their corvée or military duties, women suffered in their men's absence, having to take on their agricultural tasks in addition to their own already onerous ones. Observers report seeing whole villages where cultivation was carried out by women.[9] Land left behind with no family to cultivate it might be taken over by someone else; at the very least the crop suffered.

Other measures, including state monopolies on agricultural produce, bore heavily on the peasantry, resulting in debt, loss of the right to work the land, or flight. All contributed to peasant dispossession and abandonment of the land, a trend that continued into this century. Peasant families fled to other villages or to the major towns, where they eked out a living as casual laborers and domestics—the outlawing of slavery in the later nineteenth century created a demand for domestics among the wealthier families.[10]

Broadly, then, according to Tucker, some of the changes ushered in by European imports and state reform measures worsened the lot of women, particularly women of the popular classes and rural women. However, other developments in the nineteenth century had enormous and more enduring consequences for women, in particular developments following from the state's aggressive pursuit of educational modernization and technological and social reform. Women were affected by such initiatives directly in the latter part of the century in that the state promulgated women's education and indirectly when men who were educated in the "modern" schools or who traveled to Europe to study called for reforms in the social arrangements regarding women. The questioning and rethinking of the role of women prepared the ground for the gradual expansion of educational opportunities for women and, eventually, professional opportunities as well. The initial beneficiaries of these intellectual and social changes were primarily upper- and middle-class women, but in the long term women of all classes had new opportunities.

Muhammad ʿAli's eagerness to acquire the technologies of Europe was an important catalyst. With the objective of strengthening and modernizing the country militarily and technologically and catching up with Europe, he sent student missions to Europe to learn military and engineering sciences and technologies such as shipbuilding and printing.[11] Schools and colleges for men were opened in Egypt, employing European teaching methods and presenting European subject matter, medical and military training in particular. Student missions were sent to Europe as early as 1809; a military school was established in 1816, and a medical school in 1827.

As part of the general enterprise of acquiring European knowledge, a school to train translators was established in Cairo in 1835. Its director, Rifaʿah Rafiʿ al-Tahtawi (1801–73), was a graduate of al-Azhar and a former member of an educational mission to Paris. In a descriptive work on French society, he recommended that girls be given the same education as boys, saying that this was the practice in the strongest nations, that is, in European ones. His was the first work to appear in Arabic associating reforms in social mores affecting women with the social and technological reforms for national renewal. Muhammad ʿAli much admired al-Tahtawi's book and recommended its general use with students. Shortly thereafter the state, at least rhetorically, adopted the view that educating women was desirable: in the late thirties the Educational Council of Egypt, of which al-Tahtawi was a member, issued a statement declaring itself "impressed by women's important contribution to the progress of civilisation in modern societies" and recommended public education for women.[12]

Aside from establishing a school to train women doctors in 1832, the state took no steps to institute education for girls until the 1870s. The impetus to found the School for Hakimas (women doctors) was a practical consideration: training medical practitioners who would have access to women. A shortage of labor power and the prevalence of epidemic and endemic diseases led Muhammad ʿAli to see the importance of organizing sanitary services and training doctors. The school was established under the directorship of Antoine Clot-Bey, a French physician; its first female principal was Susan Voilquin (see chap. 6).[13] Training at the school, generally called the Midwifery School because it emphasized obstetrics, took six years—the same length of time as the training at the School of Medicine, which was for men. At first the school had difficulty in recruiting students—it had places for sixty—but by 1846 it achieved enrollment to capacity and apparently maintained it at that level for the remainder of the century. Graduates, awarded a license to administer vaccinations, perform deliveries, and treat women and children free of charge, were appointed government employees with the rank of second lieutenant. The government also arranged marriages for the hakimas from among the graduates of the School of Medicine, for initially no marriage offers were forthcoming. One year, 1844, the director of the School of Medicine was ordered to submit the names of appropriate spouses among the medical officers for prospective graduates of the School for Hakimas. Once married, the couple were appointed to the same district and received a small house furnished at government expense.[14]

Hakimas treated indigent women at the Civil Hospital in Cairo, in an outpatient clinic as well as in the hospital, and they vaccinated children both at the hospital and in private homes, including those of the upper classes. About six hundred children were vaccinated at the Civil Hospital each month and over all about fifteen thousand per year. When the government established quarantine stations at ports in the 1830s and 1840s, the hakimas took over the physical examination of women; they also verified the cause of death, which was essential in planning preventive programs. The effectiveness of these women, even if the vaccination program they carried out is the sole measure of that effectiveness, was enormous. Furthermore, as Yacoub Artin, minister of public instruction in Egypt later in the century, noted, their active presence in society helped spread notions of the value of education for women and women's ability to be competent and earning professionals along with notions of basic hygiene. In addition to serving as medical practitioners, some of the women became instructors in the school from which they had graduated. One former student, Jalila Tamrahan (d. 1890), became the principal of the school and published a work on her experiences in obstetrics as a guide to students in 1871.[15]

Although the School for Hakimas remained the only state-sponsored venture in women's education until the 1870s, the openness toward women's studying European subjects was reflected in the practices of the upper classes. Muhammad 'Ali's daughters and their retinues received instruction from European tutors as well as the traditional instruction in Arabic and religion.[16] Upper-class families followed suit, though employing teachers for daughters was evidently a sporadic rather than a routine practice. 'Aisha Taymour (1840–1902), a distinguished poet and a member of the Turkish-Egyptian upper class, received an education, despite her mother's opposition, because of her own persistence and her father's support.[17] Nazli Fadl (d. early 1900s), eldest daughter of a prince, who hosted the first salon in Egypt frequented by leading intellectuals and members of the ruling class later in the century, was presumably tutored in childhood by European teachers as well as Egyptian or Arab instructors.

Among the middle and lower classes, a small percentage of girls continued to attend the kuttabs, or traditional schools, which taught reading and the recitation of the Quran. But European-type education began among these classes as well, initially by way of missionary schools, first established in the 1830s and 1840s. By 1875 an estimated 5,570 girls were attending missionary schools, among them 3,000 Egyptians; and by 1887 about 4,000 of 6,160 were Egyptian.[18] The majority of Egyptian girls attending missionary schools were Copts, but a small number of Muslims also attended, though most Muslim parents were reluctant to entrust their daughters to missionary schools, which were established for the purpose of winning pupils to Christianity. Occasionally when missionary-run schools set out to recruit from the poorest classes, among whom they felt able to resort to aggressive recruiting measures, Muslims could predominate. This was the case with Miss Whately's school. Mary Louisa Whately (daughter of the bishop of Dublin) recruited pupils by accosting poor people, parents and children, that she met in the street and persuading the children to attend. With the aid of Syrian Christian women teachers, she taught Christianity, Arabic reading, and needlework. The free instruction she offered in needlework earned her the animosity of Egyptian needlework teachers, who lost pupils to her; they came to the school to attempt to forcibly take them back.[19]

The zeal with which missionary schools pursued their proselytization, which they directed at local communities of Christians and Jews, as well as Muslims, spurred these communities to establish schools themselves. Two Coptic girls' schools opened in Cairo in the 1850s, constituting the first native European-style schools opened for Egyptian girls. Next came Jewish girls' schools, which opened in Alexandria and Cairo; and in the 1850s other communities, like the Greek, opened their own girls' schools in Cairo and Alexandria.[20]

Khedive Ismael (r. 1863–79), who declared schools to be the "base of every progress," instituted an Educational Committee soon after his accession. It recommended the establishment of schools throughout Egypt, including schools for girls, to be made available to all according to their means, and it proposed the modernization of kuttab schools and their incorporation into the state system. ʿAli Mubarak (1824–93), a member of this committee who had studied in France, was particularly supportive of women's education, stating that women had a right to pursue knowledge to its limits and a right to work, although their first task, he believed, was raising children and counseling spouses.[21]

The committee commissioned al-Tahtawi to write a textbook suitable for schoolchildren of both sexes. His *Al-murshid al-amin lil-banat waʾl-banin* (A guide for girls and boys), published in the 1870s, announced in its title that education was for both sexes. The text was a collection of pieces on a variety of subjects, including the education of women. Educating girls as well as boys, it stated, would make for harmonious marriages and would enable women, when necessary, "to take up occupations that men take up, to the limit of their strength and ability." Women and men differed only in those features of their bodies "pertaining to femininity and masculinity," women's intelligence being in no way limited to matters of the heart but on the contrary extending to the most abstract ideas. On the marital relationship al-Tahtawi wrote that spouses should endeavor to love each other completely: "Neither should raise their voice to the other, and each should give in to the other's will, men out of love, women out of obedience. . . . Neither should reproach the other with a past error. . . . Neither should part from the other even for a day without a parting word of love to be a reminder during the absence . . . and [a spouse should] never let the sun go down on anger."[22] It is worth noting here that al-Tahtawi, an elderly man by now, had contractually bound himself to live up to the ideal of reciprocity that his text preached: he had given his wife a document in which he undertook not to exercise his rights in law to take further wives or concubines or to divorce her as long as she remained with him "in affection and loyalty, looking after his children, servants and slaves."[23]

In 1873 the government established the first girls' school, a primary school, and in 1874 it established a secondary school. By 1875, out of 5,362 pupils attending government-run primary schools, some 890 were girls.[24] Ismael planned more girls' schools, but they did not materialize owing to the financial difficulties of the state and Ismael's subsequent abdication, in 1879.

With the British occupation, which began in 1882, the thrust toward educational expansion generally, including girls' education, slowed down. The finances of the country improved, and the British administration expended some of the increased revenue on irrigation and other projects, deliberately keeping down expenditure on education for both financial and political reasons, even though the demand for education was steadily intensifying. Nationalist intellectuals like Jamal al-Din al-Afghani (1839–97) and Muhammad ʿAbdu (1849?–1905) were urging the importance of education, and men of all sorts eagerly sought an education as a means of upward mobility and as a route to positions in government administration and teaching. The British did little to meet this growing demand; rather, they introduced measures to curb it. Immediately after occupying Egypt, they had continued the policy of the previous administration—providing education for both sexes at government expense—but as demand grew, they instituted tuition charges. In 1881, just before they took over, 70 percent of the students at government schools received government assistance for tuition, clothes, and books; by 1892, barely ten years later, 73 percent paid all their own expenses. Similarly, when it was pointed out to Evelyn Baring, British consul general (later Lord Cromer), in 1901 that many male primary-school graduates were unable to go on to secondary school and consequently could obtain employment in government service only with difficulty, he responded not by expanding the number of secondary schools but by raising the tuition fees at primary schools to cut enrollment.[25] The same policy was implemented at girls' schools. Increased demand led to even higher tuition fees. For men and women alike, education could lead to gainful employment, and public demand for more girls' as well as boys' schools had been voiced, but government-sponsored secondary-school education for girls was not expanded until the end of the century. When a teacher-training college for women finally opened at the turn of the century, there were 138 applicants for thirteen places.[26]

In response to the pressing demand for education and to the British curbs on attaining it, such figures as Muhammad ʿAbdu founded Muslim benevolent societies and private committees for the purpose of establishing schools. These institutions catered to more students of both sexes than did government schools, though the places available for males vastly outnumbered those for females. In 1897 government schools provided for 11,000 male students, and the benevolent societies for 181,000; government schools for 863 female students, and the societies for 1,164. The societies had established more schools for girls in provinces throughout the country by 1909, while the government opened its first primary school for girls in Alexandria in 1917. In 1914 the number of girls at state schools had actually dropped under the figure for the 1890s, to 786. Private schools and missionary schools were growing, however. In 1912 there were 5,517 girls attending American Mission schools alone. Also meeting the growing demand were the numerous foreign schools of all sorts that sprang up.[27]

State rhetoric and eventually state action in the matter of women's education paralleled the ideas being expressed in the discussions and writings of male intellectuals, such as those of al-Tahtawi and Mubarak. Similar ideas were being expressed elsewhere in the Middle East, notably in Turkey, which in matters of social and educational reform followed a course that closely paralleled Egypt's.[28] The intellectuals in the two societies shared and exchanged ideas. During the decades when al-Tahtawi, Mubarak, and Muhammad ʿAbdu were putting forward their ideas on women, education, and reform, in Turkey the writer Namik Kemal (1840–88) championed women's education, and the encyclopedist Semseddin Sami (1850–1904) published a book entitled *Kadlinar* (Women) in 1880 similarly emphasizing the importance of education for women and also advocating reform in the matter of polygamy, which, he argued, though permitted by the Quran, was not recommended, and he quoted verses to substantiate his view.[29]

Among the most influential thinkers on reforms with respect to women was the Egyptian Muhammad ʿAbdu, an intellectual of considerable stature and with an extensive following (not only in Egypt) who began to make his mark as an editor of a newspaper, *Al-wakaʾiʿ al-misriyya,* in the early 1880s. ʿAbdu was a student of al-Sayyid Jamal al-Din al-Afghani, a figure of enormous intellectual influence in both Egypt and Turkey, as well as in Iran and in other parts of the Islamic world. Al-Afghani was concerned in his teachings and writings to reform and revive Islam from the condition of "ignorance and helplessness" into which it had lapsed and which had resulted in Islamic lands becoming prey to Western aggression. Reform from within, the acquisition of modern sciences, adaptation to the demands of the modern world, and unity among Muslims were all essential, he thought, if Islamic countries were to beat off Western aggression and exploitation. Freed of the incubus of "foreign domination," they would "work out a new and glorious order of affairs without dependence on or imitation of European nations."[30]

Like his teacher, ʿAbdu was an ardent and committed religious thinker. He argued for the acquisition of "modern" sciences and for "modernisation," for the promotion of widespread education, for reforms in the intellectual and social fields, and for the elevation of women's status and changes in marriage practices, and he emphasized the importance of the need to throw off the ignorance and misinterpretations of Islam that had accrued over the centuries. ʿAbdu addressed the need for reforms with respect to women at various points in his life, principally in articles published in *Al-wakaʾiʿ al-misriyya* in the 1880s and in *Al-manar,* a weekly publication, in the 1890s and early 1900s. He was probably the first to make the argument, still made by Muslim feminists today, that it was Islam and not, as Europeans claimed, the West, that first recognized the full and equal humanity of women. ʿAbdu argued that the Quranic verse on the equal rewards of labor showed that "men and women are equal before God in the matter of reward, when they are equal in their works. . . . There is therefore no difference between them in regard to humanity, and no superiority of one over the other in works." Furthermore, he argued:

Anyone who knows how all nations before Islam gave preference to the man, and made the woman a mere chattel and plaything of the man, and how some religions give precedence to the man simply because he is a man and she a woman, and how some people consider the woman as incapable of religious responsibility and as possessing no immortal soul—any one who knows all this, can appreciate at its true value this Islamic reform in the belief of the nations and their treatment of woman. Moreover, it will be clear to him that the claim of Europeans to have been the first to honor woman and grant her equality, is false. For Islam was before them in this matter; and even yet their laws and religious traditions continue to place the man above the woman. . . . To be sure, the Muslims have been at fault in the education and training of women, and acquainting them with their

Islam's disconnect w/ practice

rights; and we acknowledge that we have failed to follow the guidance of our religion, so that we have become an argument against it.[31]

ʿAbdu argued that the regulations affecting women, such as those concerning polygamy and divorce, like other "backward" and "degraded" customs that had led the Islamic nations into a deplorable state of ignorance, had their source not in Islam but in the corruptions and misinterpretations that had beset Islam over the centuries. The regeneration of the Islamic nation as a whole lay in a return to the essentials of Islam. Such a return would make evident that "such matters as divorce, polygamy, and slavery do not belong to the essentials of Islam."[32] Polygamy, for example, was only permitted, ʿAbdu argued, because of the conditions of the day, although monogamy was clearly the Quranic ideal. The original intent of the Quran had been ignored, however, and it was necessary to pursue reforms, including legal reforms, to correct the harmful practices that had developed.

ʿAbdu, unlike most of the other mainly secular intellectuals and reformers of his age, had a thorough grounding in religious thought and could knowledgeably argue the case for reform and modernization in terms that represented such reform as in harmony rather than in conflict with a "true" Islam. His formulations therefore authoritatively articulated the case for Islam and modernization for other intellectuals. And indeed ʿAbdu associated with and was counted among the group of leading modernizing politicians and reformers, though he was perhaps more cautious and conservative than others. He advocated the discriminating acquisition of the knowledge, skills, and intellectual and other developments of the modern Western world in the cause of a national and Islamic renaissance. He deplored, however, the facile, unthinking imitation of Western ways—in dress, furniture, architecture, and the consumption of expensive luxuries—instead of the pursuit of a genuine transfer of knowledge and real social reform.[33]

By the 1890s the call for more education for women and for reforms affecting their status was clearly audible. Women began to present their own case in the newspapers and magazines for women that appeared in the 1890s—and indeed some appeals had appeared in print earlier in the century. The poet ʿAisha Taymour, for example, published a work, *Miʾrat al-taʾamul*, critical of upper-class men's conduct toward their wives, in 1874.

In 1892 the first magazine for women, edited by a woman, was published, and in 1898, a second, also edited by a woman, began publication.

The founder of the first, *Al-fatat* (The young woman) was Hind Nufal, a Syrian Christian woman from a family of journalists also working in Egypt. In its first editorial the journal declared its dedication to advancing the women of Egypt along the path that European women were taking, and it urged women to regard the journal as their defender, to write to it and not consider it shameful for women to be published. Journalism, the editorial declared, was a noble profession practiced by many distinguished European women. Invoking the names of Joan of Arc, Hypatia, and al-Khansa' (the Arab woman poet), it declared its concerns to be not politics and religion but whatever was of interest to women—science, literature, manners, morals, education, clothes, fashions, sewing, drawing, household management, and the raising of children. In its first year of publication the magazine printed an article titled "Knowledge Is Light" by the Lebanese Christian writer Zeinab Fawwaz in which the author stressed the importance of education for both men and women; an article by Labiba Habiqa, a medical practitioner at Kasr al-Aini Hospital, calling on women to look upon journalism and writing as a responsibility owed to their sisters; and a piece by Mohga Boulos of Tanta saying women had a right to be educated. Among the first articles in the second women's journal to begin publication, *Anis al-jalis*, was one, published in 1898, that cited statistics for literacy in Egypt—0.5 percent for women and 3.6 percent for men—and that urged the British administration to remedy this situation.[34]

By the 1890s women were also being published in magazines edited and published by men, and they were publishing their own works as well. Zeinab Fawwaz published articles on education in *Al-Nil* in 1892, in which she called on the British to give all Egyptians the opportunity to study, and to provide jobs for school graduates.[35] In 1888, Miriam Makarius, wife of the editor of *Al-lata'if*, published an article in her husband's journal on raising children in which she stressed the importance of educating women that they might acquire the skills and knowledge (hygiene, nutrition, and so forth) vital to this important task. Three years later Salma Qusatli, also of Syrian background, published an article in the same journal advocating women's education in more militant terms. She declared that women had been attending schools and were deciding to leave behind "their role of insignificance . . . and to give up the necessity of directing their thoughts and all their efforts to household tasks only." In 1891 the same journal reported the examination results at the American College for Girls in Cairo and the speeches made by the graduating schoolgirls. Adma Shuqra, graduating at the top of her class, gave a speech entitled "What Women of the East Have Gained in the Last Fifty Years," and Mariya Tuma, one entitled

"The Role of Women in Society." In 1896 another journal, *Al-muqtataf*, published an essay on women's rights by Princess Nazli Hanem.[36] Arab women's voices, even schoolgirls' voices, were raised with questions on redefining the role of women, the need for education for all, and a whole range of matters also preoccupying their male contemporaries; by the 1890s their opinions and ideas were part of the world of print and part of the fabric of intellectual life.

Not just talk about the need for change but actual change toward acceptance of Western styles and ways was in progress. As early as 1843, the British Orientalist Edward William Lane, resident in Cairo, noted to a friend that regarding furniture, architecture, manners, dress, "Cairo is rapidly becoming more and more unlike what it was." Only three years later he commented again on how the city was changing and how some viewed with alarm its increasing westernization and the adopting of Western fashions. "I told you of some instances of the 'march' of European innovation here," he wrote, "[and] the 'march' has now become a gallop. The officers of the Government . . . following the example of Constantinople, have begun to put themselves into the complete Frank dress; frock-coat, waistcoat, and trousers, the last as narrow as any of ours." The ʿulama were "very angry" at all this, "which they justly regard as indicating important changes."[37]

Egyptian contemporaries expressed anxiety over such visible changes in society. Like ʿAbdu, ʿAbdullah Nadim, another student of al-Afghani's, decried the facile imitation of Western ways everywhere in evidence in 1891. He noted in particular the consumption of alcoholic beverages, the adoption of European dress and foreign words, and the changes in women's manners and their greater freedom: women were increasingly to be seen on the streets "displaying their ornaments."[38] Qassim Amin, writing in the last years of the century, commented that "in recent years" men's domination of women had lightened with the advancement of their [men's] thought and that now one saw women going out to attend to their affairs and frequenting public gardens to enjoy the fresh air. Many women, he noted, now traveled abroad with their husbands.[39] Rashid Ridda, a disciple of Muhammad ʿAbdu's, also commented in the same year on changes that had taken place in women's lives. The imitation of European ways could be observed everywhere among the upper classes and "those that followed them from the people"; even the veil, he asserted, was being removed by degrees. This Europeanization had spread even to the houses of the sheikhs and the men of religion, where it appeared in the dress of their women. "Who knows," he concluded, "where it will lead?"[40]

References to changes in women's dress are plentiful for the first years of the new century, and some of these changes were evidently already in progress in the 1890s. Comments made early in the new century indicate that upper-class women traveling in Europe became accustomed to being unveiled, for they mostly veiled only when at home in Egypt. Among this class the veil became lighter and more transparent, apparently in imitation of the fashions of Istanbul.[41]

Other changes afoot for women would have been as obvious to contemporaries as changes in dress, though perhaps less easily pointed to or summed up as markers of change. Women, now more visible in public places, were not merely promenading to enjoy the fresh air but, as Amin observed, "going out to attend to their affairs." From the time the School for Hakimas opened in the 1830s, women had been medical practitioners and recipients of government salaries, treating women and children in homes and hospitals and quarantine stations. From the time missionary schools were founded in midcentury and increasingly over the last decades of the century as more schools of all sorts opened, women were active professionals—foreign teachers, governesses, and nuns at first, then Syrian Arab women, Coptic women, Jewish women, and eventually Muslim Egyptian women. By the end of the nineteenth century women in a variety of dress, veiled and unveiled, openly pursuing a range of professional activities, had begun to be features of this society. Schoolgirls were a feature of turn-of-the-century society, too. The number of literate women in Egypt in 1897 was estimated to be 31,200, including Europeans.[42] True, their number in proportion to the population of the country as a whole—an estimated ten million—was not large. But in the cities, and particularly in Cairo, they constituted elements in the society that most people, and certainly the male intellectuals of the era, could not have failed to notice.

THE

Chapter 8   DISCOURSE
𝔊

OF THE VEIL

QASSIM AMIN'S *TAHRIR AL-MAR'A* (THE LIBERATION OF
woman), published in 1899, during a time of visible
social change and lively intellectual ferment, caused intense and furious debate. Analyses of the debate and of
the barrage of opposition the book provoked have generally assumed that it was the radicalness of Amin's
proposals with respect to women that caused the fu-
rore. Yet the principal substantive recommendations
that Amin advocated for women—giving them a primary-school education and reforming the laws on polygamy and divorce—could scarcely be described as
innovatory. As we saw in the last chapter, Muslim intellectuals such as al-Tahtawi and 'Abdu had argued for
women's education and called for reforms in matters
of polygamy and divorce in the 1870s and 1880s and
even earlier without provoking violent controversy. Indeed, by the 1890s the issue of educating women not
only to the primary level but beyond was so uncon-
troversial that both state and Muslim benevolent societies had established girls' schools.

The anger and passion Amin's work provoked become intelligible only when one considers not the substantive reforms for women that he advocated but

144

rather, first, the symbolic reform—the abolition of the veil—that he passionately urged and, second, the reforms, indeed the fundamental changes
in culture and society, that he urged upon society as a whole and that he
contended it was essential for the Egyptian nation, and Muslim countries
generally, to make. The need for a general cultural and social transformation is the central thesis of the book, and it is within this thesis that the
arguments regarding women are embedded: changing customs regarding
women and changing their costume, abolishing the veil in particular, were
key, in the author's thesis, to bringing about the desired general social
transformation. Examining how Amin's recommendations regarding women
formed part of his general thesis and how and why he believed that unveiling was the key to social transformation is essential to unraveling the
significance of the debate that his book provoked.

Amin's work has traditionally been regarded as marking the beginning
of feminism in Arab culture. Its publication and the ensuing debate certainly constitute an important moment in the history of Arab women: the
first battle of the veil to agitate the Arab press. The battle inaugurated a
new discourse in which the veil came to comprehend significations far
broader than merely the position of women. Its connotations now encompassed issues of class and culture—the widening cultural gulf between the
different classes in society and the interconnected conflict between the culture of the colonizers and that of the colonized. It was in this discourse,
too, that the issues of women and culture first appeared as inextricably
fused in Arabic discourse. Both the key features of this new discourse, the
greatly expanded signification of the veil and the fusion of the issues of
women and culture, that made their formal entry into Arab discourse with
the publication of Amin's work had their provenance in the discourses of
European societies. In Egypt the British colonial presence and discursive
input constituted critical components in the situation that witnessed the
emergence of the new discourse of the veil.

The British occupation, which began in Egypt in 1882, did not bring
about any fundamental change in the economic direction in which Egypt
had already embarked—the production of raw material, chiefly cotton, to
be worked in European, mainly British, factories. British interests lay in
Egypt's continuing to serve as a supplier of raw materials for British factories; and the agricultural projects and administrative reforms pursued by
the British administration were those designed to make the country a more
efficient producer of raw materials. Such reforms and the country's progressively deeper implication in European capitalism brought increased

prosperity and benefits for some classes but worse conditions for others. The principal beneficiaries of the British reform measures and the increased involvement in European capitalism were the European residents of Egypt, the Egyptian upper classes, and the new middle class of rural notables and men educated in Western-type secular schools who became the civil servants and the new intellectual elite. Whether trained in the West or in the Western-type institutions established in Egypt, these new "modern" men with their new knowledges displaced the traditionally and religiously trained ʿulama as administrators and servants of the state, educators, and keepers of the valued knowledges of society. Traditional knowledge itself became devalued as antiquated, mired in the old "backward" ways. The ʿulama class was adversely affected by other developments as well: land-reform measures enacted in the nineteenth century led to a loss of revenue for the ʿulama, and legal and judicial reforms in the late nineteenth century took many matters out of the jurisdiction of the shariʿa courts, over which the ʿulama presided as legislators and judges, and transferred them to the civil courts, presided over by the "new men."

The law reforms, under way before the British occupation, did not affect the position of women. The primary object of the reforms had been to address the palpable injustice of the Capitulary system, whereby Europeans were under the jurisdiction of their consular powers and could not be tried in Egyptian courts. (The Capitulations were concessions gained by European powers, prior to colonialism, which regulated the activities of their merchants and which, with the growing influence of their consuls and ambassadors in the nineteenth century, were turned into a system by which European residents were virtually outside the law.) The reforms accordingly established Mixed Courts and promulgated civil and penal codes applicable to all communities. The new codes, which were largely based on French law, bypassed rather than reformed shariʿa law, although occasionally, concerning homicide, for instance, shariʿa law, too, was reformed by following an Islamic legal opinion other than the dominant opinion of the Hanafi school, the school followed in Egypt. This method of reforming the shariʿa, modifying it by reference to another Islamic legal opinion, was followed in Turkey and, later in the twentieth century, in Iraq, Syria, and Tunisia—but not Egypt—in order to introduce measures critically redefining and amending the law on polygamy and divorce in ways that fundamentally curtailed male license.[1]

Other groups besides the ʿulama were adversely affected by Western penetration and the local entrenchment of Western power. Artisans and small merchants were unable to compete with Western products or were displaced by the agents of Western interests. Others whose circumstances deteriorated or whose economic advancement was blocked by British administrative policies were rural workers who, as a result of peasant dispossession, flocked to the cities, where they swelled the ranks of urban casual laborers. A growing lower-middle class of men who had received a Western-type secular education up to primary level and who filled the lower ranks of the administration were unable to progress beyond these positions because educational facilities for further training were not available. The British administration not only failed to provide more advanced facilities but responded to the problem by increasing fees at primary level to cut enrollment. Measures such as these, which clearly discriminated in favor of the well-to-do and frustrated the hopes and ambitions of others, accentuated class divisions.[2]

The British administration pursued its educational policy in the teeth of both a popular demand for education for boys and for girls and the urgings of intellectuals of all political and ideological complexions that the administration give priority to providing more educational facilities because of the importance of education to national development. The British administration espoused its restrictive policy partly for political reasons. Cromer, the British consul general, believed that providing subsidized education was not the province of government, and he also believed that education could foster dangerous nationalist sentiments.[3]

Even this brief outline of the consequences of the increasing economic importance of the West and of British colonial domination suggests how issues of culture and attitudes toward Western ways were intertwined with issues of class and access to economic resources, position, and status. The lower-middle and lower classes, who were generally adversely affected by or experienced no benefits from the economic and political presence of the West had a different perspective on the colonizer's culture and ways than did the upper classes and the new middle-class intellectuals trained in Western ways, whose interests were advanced by affiliation with Western culture and who benefited economically from the British presence. Just as the latter group was disposed by economic interests as well as training to be receptive to Western culture, the less prosperous classes were disposed, also on economic grounds, to reject and feel hostile toward it. That attitude was exacerbated by the blatant unfairness of the economic and legal privileges enjoyed by the Europeans in Egypt. The Capitulations—referred to earlier—not only exempted Europeans from the jurisdiction of Egyptian law

but also virtually exempted them from paying taxes; Europeans consequently engaged in commerce on terms more favorable than those applied
to their native counterparts, and they became very prosperous.

Conflicting class and economic interests thus underlay the political and
ideological divisions that began ever more insistently to characterize the
intellectual and political scene—divisions between those eager to adopt European ways and institutions, seeing them as the means to personal and
national advancement, and those anxious to preserve the Islamic and national heritage against the onslaughts of the infidel West. This states somewhat simply the extremes of the two broad oppositional tendencies within
Egyptian political thought at this time. The spectrum of political views on
the highly fraught issues of colonialism, westernization, British policies,
and the political future of the country, views that found expression in the
extremely lively and diverse journalistic press, in fact encompassed a wide
range of analyses and perspectives.

Among the dominant political groups finding voice in the press at the
time Amin's work was published was a group that strongly supported the
British administration and advocated the adoption of a "European outlook." Prominent among its members were a number of Syrian Christians
who founded the pro-British daily *Al-muqattam*. At the other extreme was
a group whose views, articulated in the newspaper *Al-mu'ayyad*, published
by Sheikh 'Ali Yusuf, fiercely opposed Western encroachment in any form.
This group was also emphatic about the importance of preserving Islamic
tradition in all areas. The National party (Al-hizb al-watani), a group led
by Mustapha Kamil, was equally fierce in its opposition to the British and
to westernization, but it espoused a position of secular rather than Islamic
nationalism. This group, whose organ was the journal *Al-liwa,* held that
advancement for Egypt must begin with the expulsion of the British. Other
groups, including the Umma party (People's party), which was to emerge
as the politically dominant party in the first decades of the twentieth century, advocated moderation and an attitude of judicious discrimination in
identifying political and cultural goals. Muhammad 'Abdu, discussed in
chapter 7, was an important intellectual influence on the Umma party,
though its members were more secular minded; he had advocated the acquisition of Western technology and knowledge and, simultaneously, the
revivification and reform of the Islamic heritage, including reform in areas
affecting women. The Umma party advocated the adoption of the European
notion of the nation-state in place of religion as the basis of community.
Their goals were to adopt Western political institutions and, at the same
time, to gradually bring about Egypt's independence from the British.

Umma party members, unlike Mustapha Kamil's ultranationalists or the Islamic nationalists, consequently had an attitude, not of hostility to the British, but rather of measured collaboration. Among its prominent members were Ahmad Lutfi al-Sayyid and Saʿd Zaghloul.

The colonial presence and the colonizer's economic and political agenda, plus the role that cultural training and affiliation played in widening the gap between classes, provided ample ground for the emergence at this moment of the issue of culture as fraught and controversial. Why the contest over culture should center on women and the veil and why Amin fastened upon those issues as the key to cultural and social transformation only becomes intelligible, however, by reference to ideas imported into the local situation from the colonizing society. Those ideas were interjected into the native discourse as Muslim men exposed to European ideas began to reproduce and react to them and, subsequently and more pervasively and insistently, as Europeans—servants of empire and individuals resident in Egypt—introduced and actively disseminated them.

The peculiar practices of Islam with respect to women had always formed part of the Western narrative of the quintessential otherness and inferiority of Islam.[4] A detailed history of Western representations of women in Islam and of the sources of Western ideas on the subject has yet to be written, but broadly speaking it may be said that prior to the seventeenth century Western ideas about Islam derived from the tales of travelers and crusaders, augmented by the deductions of clerics from their readings of poorly understood Arabic texts. Gradually thereafter, through the seventeenth and eighteenth centuries, readings of Arabic texts became slightly less vague, and the travelers' interpretations of what they observed approximated more closely the meanings that the male members of the visited societies attached to the observed customs and phenomena. [Male travelers in Muslim societies had extremely limited access to women, and the explanations and interpretations they brought back, insofar as they represented a native perspective at all, essentially, therefore, gave the male point of view on whatever subject was discussed.]

By the eighteenth century the Western narrative of women in Islam, which was drawn from such sources, incorporated elements that certainly bore a resemblance to the bold external features of the Islamic patterns of male dominance, but at the same time it (1) often garbled and misconstrued the specific content and meaning of the customs described and (2) assumed and represented the Islam practiced in Muslim societies in the periods in which the Europeans encountered and then in some degree or other dominated those societies to be the only possible interpretation of the religion.

Previous chapters have already indicated the dissent within Islam as to the different interpretations to which it was susceptible. And some sense of the kinds of distortions and garbling to which Muslim beliefs were subject as a result of Western misapprehension is suggested by the ideas that a few more perceptive Western travelers felt themselves called upon to correct in their own accounts of Muslims. The eighteenth-century writer and traveler Lady Mary Wortley Montagu, for example, attacked the widespread belief among her English contemporaries that Muslims believed that women had no souls, an idea that she explained was untrue. (Montagu believed that many of the misapprehensions of her contemporaries about Islam arose from faulty translations of the Quran made by "Greek Priests, who would not fail to falsify it with the extremity of Malice.") She also said that having herself not only observed veiled women but also used the veil, she was able to assert that it was not the oppressive custom her compatriots believed it to be and in fact it gave women a kind of liberty, for it enabled them not to be recognized.[5] why shouldn't men use it too then?

But such rebuttals left little mark on the prevailing views of Islam in the West. However, even though Islam's peculiar practices with respect to women and its "oppression" of women formed some element of the European narrative of Islam from early on, the issue of women only emerged as the centerpiece of the Western narrative of Islam in the nineteenth century, and in particular the later nineteenth century, as Europeans established themselves as colonial powers in Muslim countries.[6]

The new prominence, indeed centrality, that the issue of women came to occupy in the Western and colonial narrative of Islam by the late nineteenth century appears to have been the result of a fusion between a number of strands of thought all developing within the Western world in the latter half of that century. Thus the reorganized narrative, with its new focus on women, appears to have been a compound created out of a coalescence between the old narrative of Islam just referred to (and which Edward Said's *Orientalism* details) and the broad, all-purpose narrative of colonial domination regarding the inferiority, in relation to the European culture, of all Other cultures and societies, a narrative that saw vigorous development over the course of the nineteenth century. And finally and somewhat ironically, combining with these to create the new centrality of the position of women in the colonial discourse of Islam was the language of feminism, which also developed with particular vigor during this period.[7]

In the colonial era the colonial powers, especially Britain (on which I will focus my discussion), developed their theories of races and cultures and of a social evolutionary sequence according to which middle-class Victorian

England, and its beliefs and practices, stood at the culminating point of the evolutionary process and represented the model of ultimate civilization. In this scheme Victorian womanhood and mores with respect to women, along with other aspects of society at the colonial center, were regarded as the ideal and measure of civilization. Such theories of the superiority of Europe, legitimizing its domination of other societies, were shortly corroborated by "evidence" gathered in those societies by missionaries and others, whose observations came to form the emergent study of anthropology. This same emergent anthropology—and other sciences of man—simultaneously served the dominant British colonial and androcentric order in another and internal project of domination. They provided evidence corroborating Victorian theories of the biological inferiority of women and the naturalness of the Victorian ideal of the female role of domesticity. Such theories were politically useful to the Victorian establishment as it confronted, internally, an increasingly vocal feminism.[8] *such. Bacdelagh already*

Even as the Victorian male establishment devised theories to contest the claims of feminism, and derided and rejected the ideas of feminism and the notion of men's oppressing women with respect to itself, it captured the language of feminism and redirected it, in the service of colonialism, toward Other men and the cultures of Other men. It was here and in the combining of the languages of colonialism and feminism that the fusion between the issues of women and culture was created. More exactly, what was created was the fusion between the issues of women, their oppression, and the cultures of Other men. The idea that Other men, men in colonized societies or societies beyond the borders of the civilized West, oppressed women was to be used, in the rhetoric of colonialism, to render morally justifiable its project of undermining or eradicating the cultures of colonized peoples.

Colonized societies, in the colonial thesis, were alike in that they were inferior but differed as to their specific inferiority. Colonial feminism, or feminism as used against other cultures in the service of colonialism, was shaped into a variety of similar constructs, each tailored to fit the particular culture that was the immediate target of domination—India, the Islamic world, sub-Saharan Africa. With respect to the Islamic world, regarded as an enemy (and indeed as *the* enemy) since the Crusades, colonialism—as I have already suggested—had a rich vein of bigotry and misinformation to draw on. *They didn't hear other's voices*

Broadly speaking, the thesis of the discourse on Islam blending a colonialism committed to male dominance with feminism—the thesis of the new colonial discourse of Islam centered on women—was that Islam was innately and immutably oppressive to women, that the veil and segregation epitomized that oppression, and that these customs were the fundamental reasons for the general and comprehensive backwardness of Islamic societies. Only if these practices "intrinsic" to Islam (and therefore Islam itself) were cast off could Muslim societies begin to move forward on the path of civilization. Veiling—to *Western* eyes, the most visible marker of the differentness and inferiority of Islamic societies—became the symbol now of both the oppression of women (or, in the language of the day, Islam's degradation of women) and the backwardness of Islam, and it became the open target of colonial attack and the spearhead of the assault on Muslim societies.

The thesis just outlined—that the Victorian colonial paternalistic establishment appropriated the language of feminism in the service of its assault on the religions and cultures of Other men, and in particular on Islam, in order to give an aura of moral justification to that assault at the very same time as it combated feminism within its own society—can easily be substantiated by reference to the conduct and rhetoric of the colonizers. The activities of Lord Cromer are particularly illuminating on the subject, perfectly exemplifying how, when it came to the cultures of other men, white supremacist views, androcentric and paternalistic convictions, and feminism came together in harmonious and actually entirely logical accord in the service of the imperial idea.

Cromer had quite decided views on Islam, women in Islam, and the veil. He believed quite simply that Islamic religion and society were inferior to the European ones and bred inferior men. The inferiority of the men was evident in numerous ways, which Cromer lists at length. For instance: "The European is a close reasoner; his statements of fact are devoid of ambiguity; he is a natural logician, albeit he may not have studied logic; he loves symmetry in all things . . . his trained intelligence works like a piece of mechanism. The mind of the Oriental on the other hand, like his picturesque streets, is eminently wanting in symmetry. His reasoning is of the most slipshod description."[9]

Cromer explains that the reasons "Islam as a social system has been a complete failure are manifold." However, "first and foremost," he asserts, was its treatment of women. In confirmation of this view he quotes the words of the preeminent British Orientalist of his day, Stanley Lane-Poole: "The degradation of women in the East is a canker that begins its destructive work early in childhood, and has eaten into the whole system of Islam" (2:134, 134n).

Whereas Christianity teaches respect for women, and European men

"elevated" women because of the teachings of their religion, Islam degraded them, Cromer wrote, and it was to this degradation, most evident
in the practices of veiling and segregation, that the inferiority of Muslim
men could be traced. Nor could it be doubted that the practices of veiling
and seclusion exercised "a baneful effect on Eastern society. The arguments
in the case are, indeed, so commonplace that it is unnecessary to dwell on
them" (2:155). It was essential that Egyptians "be persuaded or forced into
imbibing the true spirit of western civilisation" (2:538), Cromer stated,
and to achieve this, it was essential to change the position of women in
Islam, for it was Islam's degradation of women, expressed in the practices
of veiling and seclusion, that was "the fatal obstacle" to the Egyptian's
"attainment of that elevation of thought and character which should ac-
company the introduction of Western civilisation" (2:538–39); only by
abandoning those practices might they attain "the mental and moral development which he [Cromer] desired for them."[10]

Even as he delivered himself of such views, the policies Cromer pursued
were detrimental to Egyptian women. The restrictions he placed on government schools and his raising of school fees held back girls' education
as well as boys'. He also discouraged the training of women doctors. Under
the British, the School for Hakimas, which had given women as many years
of medical training as the men received in the School of Medicine, was
restricted to midwifery. On the local preference among women for being
treated by women Cromer said, "I am aware that in exceptional cases
women like to be attended by female doctors, but I conceive that throughout the civilised world, attendance by medical men is still the rule."[11]

However, it was in his activities in relation to women in his own country
that Cromer's paternalistic convictions and his belief in the proper subordination of women most clearly declared themselves. This champion of
the unveiling of Egyptian women was, in England, founding member and
sometime president of the Men's League for Opposing Women's Suffrage.[12]
Feminism on the home front and feminism directed against white men was
to be resisted and suppressed; but taken abroad and directed against the
cultures of colonized peoples, it could be promoted in ways that admirably
served and furthered the project of the dominance of the white man.

Others besides the official servants of empire promoted these kinds of
ideas: missionaries, for example. For them, too, the degradation of women
in Islam legitimized the attack on native culture. A speaker at a missionary
conference held in London in 1888 observed that Muhammad had been
exemplary as a young man but took many wives in later life and set out to
preach a religion whose object was "to extinguish women altogether"; and

he introduced the veil, which "has had the most terrible and injurious effect upon the mental, moral and spiritual history of all Mohammedan races." Missionary women delivered themselves of the same views. One wrote that Muslim women needed to be rescued by their Christian sisters from the "ignorance and degradation" in which they existed, and converted to Christianity. Their plight was a consequence of the nature of their religion, which gave license to "lewdness." Marriage in Islam was "not founded on love but on sensuality," and a Muslim wife, "buried alive behind the veil," was regarded as "prisoner and slave rather than . . . companion and help-meet." Missionary-school teachers actively attacked the custom of veiling by seeking to persuade girls to defy their families and not wear one. For the missionaries, as for Cromer, women were the key to converting backward Muslim societies into civilized Christian societies. One missionary openly advocated targeting women, because women molded children. Islam should be undermined subtly and indirectly among the young, and when children grew older, "the evils of Islam could be spelled out more directly." Thus a trail of "gunpowder" would be laid "into the heart of Islam."[13]

Others besides officials and missionaries similarly promoted these ideas, individuals resident in Egypt, for example. Well-meaning European feminists, such as Eugénie Le Brun (who took the young Huda Sha'rawi under her wing), earnestly inducted young Muslim women into the European understanding of the meaning of the veil and the need to cast it off as the essential first step in the struggle for female liberation.

Whether such proselytizers from the West were colonial patriarchs, then, or missionaries or feminists, all essentially insisted that Muslims had to give up their native religion, customs, and dress, or at least reform their religion and habits along the recommended lines, and for all of them the veil and customs regarding women were the prime matters requiring reform. And all assumed their right to denounce native ways, and in particular the veil, and to set about undermining the culture in the name of whatever cause they claimed to be serving—civilizing the society, or Christianizing it, or saving women from the odious culture and religion in which they had the misfortune to find themselves.

Whether in the hands of patriarchal men or feminists, the ideas of Western feminism essentially functioned to morally justify the attack on native societies and to support the notion of the comprehensive superiority of Europe. Evidently, then, whatever the disagreements of feminism with white male domination within Western societies, outside their borders feminism turned from being the critic of the system of white male dominance to being its docile servant. Anthropology, it has often been said, served as a handmaid to colonialism. Perhaps it must also be said that feminism, or the ideas of feminism, served as its other handmaid.

The ideas to which Cromer and the missionaries gave expression formed the basis of Amin's book. The rationale in which Amin, a French-educated upper-middle-class lawyer, grounded his call for changing the position of women and for abolishing the veil was essentially the same as theirs. Amin's text also assumed and declared the inherent superiority of Western civilization and the inherent backwardness of Muslim societies: he wrote that anyone familiar with "the East" had observed "the backwardness of Muslims in the East wherever they are." There were, to be sure, local differences: "The Turk, for example, is clean, honest, brave," whereas the Egyptian is "the opposite."[14] Egyptians were "lazy and always fleeing work," left their children "covered with dirt and roaming the alleys rolling in the dust like the children of animals," and were sunk in apathy, afflicted, as he put it, "with a paralysis of nerves so that we are unmoved by anything, however beautiful or terrible" (34). Nevertheless, over and above such differences between Muslim nationals, Amin asserted, the observer would find both Turks and Egyptians "equal in ignorance, laziness and backwardness" (72).

In the hierarchy of civilizations adopted by Amin, Muslim civilization is represented as semicivilized compared to that of the West.

European civilization advances with the speed of steam and electricity, and has even overspilled to every part of the globe so that there is not an inch that he [European man] has not trodden underfoot. Any place he goes he takes control of its resources . . . and turns them into profit . . . and if he does harm to the original inhabitants, it is only that he pursues happiness in this world and seeks it wherever he may find it. . . . For the most part he uses his intellect, but when circumstances require it, he deploys force. He does not seek glory from his possessions and colonies, for he has enough of this through his intellectual achievements and scientific inventions. What drives the Englishman to dwell in India and the French in Algeria . . . is profit and the desire to acquire resources in countries where the inhabitants do not know their value nor how to profit from them.

When they encounter savages they eliminate them or drive them from the land, as happened in America . . . and is happening now in Africa. . . . When they encounter a nation like ours, with a degree of

civilization, with a past, and a religion . . . and customs and . . . institutions . . . they deal with its inhabitants kindly. But they do soon
acquire its most valuable resources, because they have greater wealth
and intellect and knowledge and force. (69–70)

Amin said that to make Muslim society abandon its backward ways and
follow the Western path to success and civilization required changing the
women. "The grown man is none other than his mother shaped him in
childhood," and *"this is the essence of this book. . . . It is impossible to
breed successful men if they do not have mothers capable of raising them
to be successful.* This is the noble duty that advanced civilisation has given
to women in our age and which she fulfills in advanced societies" (78;
emphasis in original).

In the course of making his argument, Amin managed to express not just
a generalized contempt for Muslims but also contempt for specific groups,
often in lavishly abusive detail. Among the targets of his most dismissive
abuse were the rulers of Egypt prior to the British, whom he called corrupt
and unjust despots. Their descendants, who still constituted the nominal
rulers of the country, were championed by some nationalist anti-British
factions, including Mustapha Kamil's party, as the desirable alternative to
British rule. Amin's abuse thus angered nationalists opposed to the British
as well as the royal family. Not surprisingly, Khedive Abbas, compelled to
govern as the British wished him to, refused to receive Amin after the publication of his book. And Amin's eager praise of the British also inflamed
the anti-British factions: he represented British dominion in Egypt as bringing about an age of unprecedented justice and freedom, when "knowledge
spread, and national bonding appeared, and security and order prevailed
throughout the country, and the basis of advancement became available"
(69).

In Amin's work only the British administration and European civilization receive lavish praise. Among those singled out as targets of his abuse
were the ʿulama. Amin characterizes them as grossly ignorant, greedy, and
lazy. He details the bleakness of their intellectual horizons and their defi-
ciencies of character in unequivocal terms.

Our ʿulama today . . . takes no interest in . . . the intellectual sciences;
such things are of no concern to them. The object of their learning is
that they know how to parse the bismillah [the phrase "in the name
of God"] in no fewer than a thousand ways, and if you ask them how
the thing in their hands is made, or where the nation to which they
belong or a neighboring nation or the nation that occupied their coun-

try is located geographically and what its strengths and weaknesses are, or what the function of a bodily part is, they shrug their shoulders, contemptuous of the question; and if you talk with them about the organization of their government and its laws and economic and political condition, you will find they know nothing. Not only are they greedy . . . they always want to escape hard work, too. (74)

Those for whom Amin reserved his most virulent contempt—ironically, in a work ostensibly championing their cause—were Egyptian women. Amin describes the physical habits and moral qualities of Egyptian women in considerable detail. Indeed, given the segregation of society and what must have been his exceedingly limited access to women other than members of his immediate family and their retinue, and perhaps prostitutes, the degree of detail strongly suggests that Amin must have drawn on conceptions of the character and conduct of women based on his own and other European or Egyptian men's self-representations on the subject, rather than on any extensive observation of a broad-enough segment of female society to justify his tone of knowledgeable generalization.[15] Amin's generalizations about Egyptian women include the following.

Most Egyptian women are not in the habit of combing their hair everyday . . . nor do they bathe more than once a week. They do not know how to use a toothbrush and do not attend to what is attractive in clothing, though their attractiveness and cleanliness strongly influence men's inclinations. They do not know how to rouse desire in their husband, nor how to retain his desire or to increase it. . . . This is because the ignorant woman does not understand inner feelings and the promptings of attraction and aversion. . . . If she tries to rouse a man, she will usually have the opposite effect. (29)

Amin's text describes marriage among Muslims as based not on love but on ignorance and sensuality, as does the missionary discourse. In Amin's text, however, the blame has shifted from men to women. Women were the chief source of the "lewdness" and coarse sensuality and materialism characterizing Muslim marriages. Because only superior souls could experience true love, it was beyond the capacity of the Egyptian wife. She could know only whether her husband was "tall or short, white or black." His intellectual and moral qualities, his sensitive feelings, his knowledge, whatever other men might praise and respect him for, were beyond her grasp. Egyptian women "praise men that honorable men would not shake hands with, and hate others that we honor. This is because they judge according to their ignorant minds. The best man to her is he who plays with her all day and night . . . and who has money . . . and buys her clothes and nice things. And the worst of men is he who spends his time working in his office; whenever she sees him . . . reading . . . she . . . curses books and knowledge" (29–30).

One further passage about Egyptian women is worth citing for its surely unwarranted tone of authority. It is also interesting for the animus against women, perhaps even paranoia, that it betrays.

> Our women do nothing of housework, and work at no skill or art, and do not engage themselves in the pursuit of knowledge, and do not read and do not worship God, so what do they do? I will tell you, and you know as I do that what occupies the wife of the rich man and the poor, the learned and the ignorant, master and servant, is one thing . . . which takes many forms and that is her relationship with her husband. Sometimes she will imagine he hates her, and then that he loves her. At times she compares him with the husbands of her neighbors. . . . Sometimes she sets herself to finding a way to change his feelings toward his relatives. . . . Nor does she fail to supervise his conduct with the servant girls and observe how he looks when women visitors call . . . she will not tolerate any maid unless the maid is hideous. . . . You see her with neighbors and friends, . . . raising her voice and relating all that occurs between herself and her husband and her husband's relatives and friends, and her sorrows and joys, and all her secrets, baring what is in her heart till no secret remains—even matters of the bed. (40)

Of course, not many women would have had the wealth to be as free of housework as Amin suggests, and even wealthy women managed homes, oversaw the care of their children, and saw to their own business affairs, as I described in an earlier chapter, or took an active part in founding and running charities, as I will discuss in the following chapter. But what is striking about Amin's account (addressed to male readers) of how he imagined that women occupied themselves is that even as he describes them as obsessed with their husband and with studying, analyzing, and discussing his every mood and as preoccupied with wondering whether he hates them and whether he is eying the maid or the guest, Amin does not have the charity to note that indeed men had all the power and women had excellent reason to study and analyze a husband's every mood and whim. On a mood or a whim, or if a maid or a guest caught his fancy, they could find themselves, at any age, divorced, and possibly destitute. To the extent, then, that

Amin was right in his guess as to what women discussed when no men were present—and some women did endlessly talk about their husbands—perhaps those that did, did indeed need to be vigilant about their husbands' moods and conduct and to draw on their women friends for ideas.

On the specific measures for the "liberation" of woman that Amin called for, and even what he meant by liberation, the text is turgid and contradictory to a degree attributable variously to intellectual muddle on the part of the writer, to the intrinsic confusion and speciousness inherent in the Western narrative, which he adopted, and to the probability that the work was the fruit of discussions on the subject by several individuals, whose ideas Amin then threw together. Indeed, the contribution of other individuals to the work was apparently more than purely verbal: certain chapters, suggests Muhammad 'Amara, editor of Amin's and 'Abdu's works, were written by 'Abdu. One chapter that 'Amara argues was 'Abdu's is distinctly different in both tone and content and consequently will be discussed here separately. It may be noted in this context that one rumor in circulation when the book was published was that it had been written at Cromer's urgings. Given the book's wholehearted reproduction of views common in the writings of the colonizers, that idea was not perhaps altogether farfetched.[16]

Amin's specific recommendations regarding women, the broad rhetoric on the subject notwithstanding, are fairly limited. Among his focuses is women's education. He was "not among those who demand equality in education," he stated firmly, but a primary-school education was necessary for women (36). Women needed some education to enable them to fulfill their function and duty in life as wives. As Amin spelled it out: "It is the wife's duty to plan the household budget . . . to supervise the servants . . . to make her home attractive to her husband, so that he may find ease when he returns to it and so that he likes being there, and enjoys the food and drink and sleep and does not seek to flee from home to spend his time with neighbors or in public places, and it is her duty—and this is her first and most important duty—to raise the children, attending to them physically, mentally, and morally" (31).

Clearly there is nothing in this definition to which the most conservative of patriarchs could not readily assent. Amin's notion that women should receive a primary-school education similarly represented the conservative rather than the liberal point of view among intellectuals and bureaucrats of his day. After all, Amin's book was published in 1899, thirty years after a government commission had recommended providing government schools for both boys and girls and toward the end of a decade in which the demand for education at the primary and secondary level far exceeded capacity. In the 1890s girls, it will be recalled, were already attending schools—missionary schools and those made available by Muslim benevolent societies as well as government schools—and they flooded the teacher-training college with applications when it opened in 1900. In 1891 one journal had even published essays on the role of women by two women from the graduating class of the American College for Girls. Amin's call for a primary-school education for women was far from radical, then; no one speaking out in the debate sparked by his book contested this recommendation.

The demand that was most vehemently and widely denounced was his call for an end to segregation and veiling. Amin's arguments, like the discourse of the colonizers, are grounded in the presumption that veiling and seclusion were customs that, in Cromer's words, "exercised a baneful effect on Eastern society." The veil constituted, wrote Amin, "a huge barrier between woman and her elevation, and consequently a barrier between the nation and its advance" (54). Unfortunately, his assault on the veil represented not the result of reasoned reflection and analysis but rather the internalization and replication of the colonialist perception.

Pared of rhetoric, Amin's argument against seclusion and veiling was simply that girls would forget all they had learned if they were made to veil and observe seclusion after they were educated. The age at which girls were veiled and secluded, twelve to fourteen, was a crucial age for the development of talents and intellect, and veiling and seclusion frustrated that development; girls needed to mix freely with men, for learning came from such mixing (55–56). This position is clearly not compatible with his earlier statement that anything beyond a primary-school education was "unnecessary" for girls. If intellectual development and the acquisition of knowledge were indeed important goals for women, then the rational recommendation would be to pursue these goals directly with increased schooling, not indirectly by ending segregation and veiling so that women could associate with men.

Even more specious—as well as offensive to any who did not share Amin's uncritical and wholesale respect for European man and his presumption of the inferiority of native practices—was another argument he advanced for the abandonment of the veil. After asserting that veiling and seclusion were common to all societies in ancient times, he said: "Do Egyptians imagine that the men of Europe, who have attained such completeness of intellect and feeling that they were able to discover the force of steam and electricity . . . these souls that daily risk their lives in the pursuit of knowledge and honor above the pleasures of life, . . . these intellects and these souls that we so admire, could possibly fail to know the means of safeguarding woman and preserving her purity? Do they think that such a people would have abandoned veiling after it had been in use among them if they had seen any good in it?" (67).

In one section of the book, however, the argument against veiling is rationally made: the chapter which ʿAmara suggests was composed by ʿAbdu. ʿAbdu points out the real disadvantages to women of segregation and veiling. These customs compel them to conduct matters of law and business through an intermediary, placing poor women, who need to earn a living in trade or domestic service, in the false and impossible position of dealing with men in a society that officially bans such dealings (47–48).

The section as a whole is distinctly different in tone and ideas from the rest of the work, and not just in the humane rather than contemptuous prose in which it frames its references both to women and to the Islamic heritage. As a result, some of the views expressed there contradict or sit ill with those expressed elsewhere in the book. There is surely some discrepancy, for example, between Amin's view that women are "deficient in mind, strong in cunning" (39) and need no more than a primary-school education, on the one hand, and the sentiments as to the potential of both sexes that finds expression in the following passage, on the other: "Education is the means by which the individual may attain spiritual and material happiness. . . . Every person has the natural right to develop their talents to the limit.

"Religions address women as they do men. . . . Arts, skills, inventions, philosophy . . . all these draw women as they do men. . . . What difference is there between men and women in this desire, when we see children of both sexes equal in their curiosity about everything falling within their ken? Perhaps that desire is even more alive in girls than in boys" (22–23).

Passages suggestive of careful thought are the exception rather than the rule in this work, however.[17] More commonly the book presented strident criticism of Muslim, particularly Egyptian, culture and society. In calling for women's liberation the thoroughly patriarchal Amin was in fact calling for the transformation of Muslim society along the lines of the Western model and for the substitution of the garb of Islamic-style male dominance for that of Western-style male dominance. Under the guise of a plea for the "liberation" of woman, then, he conducted an attack that in its fundamentals reproduced the colonizer's attack on native culture and society. For Amin as for the colonizers, the veil and segregation symbolized the backwardness and inferiority of Islamic society; in his discourse as in theirs, therefore, the veil and segregation came in for the most direct attack. For Amin as for Cromer, women and their dress were important counters in the discourse concerning the relative merits of the societies and civilizations of men and their different styles of male domination; women themselves and their liberation were no more important to Amin than to Cromer.

Amin's book thus represents the rearticulation in native voice of the colonial thesis of the inferiority of the native and Muslim and the superiority of the European. Rearticulated in native upper-middle-class voice, the voice of a class economically allied with the colonizers and already adopting their life-styles, the colonialist thesis took on a classist dimension: it became in effect an attack (in addition to all the other broad and specific attacks) on the customs of the lower-middle and lower classes.

The book is reckoned to have triggered the first major controversy in the Arabic press: more than thirty books and articles appeared in response to its publication. The majority were critical, though the book did please some readers, notably members of the British administration and pro-British factions: the pro-British paper *Al-muqattam* hailed the book as the finest in years.[18] There were evidently many reasons for Muslims and Egyptians, for nationalists of all stripes, to dislike the work: Amin's adulation of the British and of European civilization, his contempt for natives and native ways, his insulting references to the reigning family and to specific groups and classes, such as the ʿulama (who were prominent among the critics of his book), and his implied and indeed explicit contempt for the customs of the lower classes. However, just as Amin had used the issue of women and the call for their unveiling to conduct his generalized assault on society, so too did the rebuttals of his work come in the form of an affirmation of the customs that he had attacked—veiling and segregation. In a way that was to become typical of the Arabic narrative of resistance, the opposition appropriated, in order to negate them, the terms set in the first place by the colonial discourse.

Analysts routinely treat the debate as one between "feminists," that is, Amin and his allies, and "antifeminists," that is, Amin's critics. They accept at face value the equation made by Amin and the originating Western narrative: that the veil signified oppression, therefore those who called for its abandonment were feminists and those opposing its abandonment were antifeminists.[19] As I have suggested, however, the fundamental and contentious premise of Amin's work was its endorsement of the Western view of Islamic civilization, peoples, and customs as inferior, whereas the author's position on women was profoundly patriarchal and even somewhat misogynist. The book merely called for the substitution of Islamic-style male dominance by Western-style male dominance. Far from being the father of Arab feminism, then, Amin might more aptly be described as the son of Cromer and colonialism.

Opponents with a nationalist perspective were therefore not necessarily any more antifeminist than Amin was feminist. Some who defended the national custom had views on women considerably more "feminist" than Amin's, but others who opposed unveiling, for nationalist and Islamist reasons, had views on women no less patriarchal than his. For example, the attacks on Amin's book published in *Al-liwa*, Mustapha Kamil's paper, declared that women had the same right to an education as men and that their education was as essential to the nation as men's—a position considerably more liberal and feminist than Amin's. The writers opposed unveiling not as antifeminists, it seems, but as cogent analysts of the current social situation. They did not argue that veiling was immutable Islamic custom, saying, on the contrary, that future generations might decree otherwise. They argued that veiling was the current practice and that Amin's call to unveil was merely part of the hasty and unconsidered rush to imitate the West in everything.[20] This perspective anticipates an incisive and genuinely feminist analysis of the issue of the veil and the accompanying debate offered a few years later by Malak Hifni Nassef, discussed in the next chapter.

Tal'at Harb's nationalist response to Amin, in contrast, defended and upheld Islamic practices, putting forward a view of the role and duties of women in society quite as patriarchal as Amin's; but where Amin wanted to adopt a Western-style male dominance, describing his recommendation as a call for women's liberation, Harb argued for an Islamic patriarchy, presenting his views quite simply as those of traditional, unadorned, God-ordained patriarchy. Harb invoked Christian and Muslim scriptures and Western and Muslim men of learning to affirm that the wife's duty was to attend to the physical, mental, and moral needs of her husband and children[21]—the same duty that Amin ascribed to her. Their prescriptions for women differed literally in the matter of garb: Harb's women must veil, and Amin's unveil. The argument between Harb and Amin centered not on feminism versus antifeminism but on Western versus indigenous ways. For neither side was male dominance ever in question.

Amin's book, then, marks the entry of the colonial narrative of women and Islam—in which the veil and the treatment of women epitomized Islamic inferiority—into mainstream Arabic discourse. And the opposition it generated similarly marks the emergence of an Arabic narrative developed in resistance to the colonial narrative. This narrative of resistance

So the West may have caused the veil to be solidified

veil resignified

appropriated, in order to negate them, the symbolic terms of the originating narrative. The veil came to symbolize in the resistance narrative, not the inferiority of the culture and the need to cast aside its customs in favor of those of the West, but, on the contrary, the dignity and validity of all native customs, and in particular those customs coming under fiercest colonial attack—the customs relating to women—and the need to tenaciously affirm them as a means of resistance to Western domination. As Frantz Fanon was to say of a later battle of the veil, between the French and the Algerians, the Algerians affirmed the veil because "tradition demanded the rigid separation of the sexes" and because *"the occupier was bent on unveiling Algeria"* (emphasis in original).[22] Standing in the relation of antithesis to thesis, the resistance narrative thus reversed—but thereby also accepted—the terms set in the first place by the colonizers. And therefore, ironically, it is Western discourse that in the first place determined the new meanings of the veil and gave rise to its emergence as a symbol of resistance.

Amin's book and the debate it generated, and the issues of class and culture with which the debate became inscribed, may be regarded as the precursor and prototype of the debate around the veil that has recurred in a variety of forms in a number of Muslim and Arab countries since. As for those who took up Amin's call for unveiling in Egypt (such as Huda Sha'rawi), an upper-class or upper-middle-class background, and to some degree or other a Western cultural affiliation, have been typical of those who became advocates of unveiling. In Turkey, for example, Ataturk, who introduced westernizing reforms, including laws affecting women, repeatedly denounced the veil in terms that, like Amin's, reproduced the Western narrative and show that his concern was with how the custom reflected on Turkish men, allowing them to appear "uncivilized" and objects of "ridicule." In one speech Ataturk declared: "In some places I have seen women who put a piece of cloth or a towel or something like that over their heads to hide their faces, and who turn their backs or huddle themselves on the ground when a man passes by. What are the meaning and sense of this behaviour? Gentlemen, can the mothers and daughters of a civilised nation adopt this strange manner, this barbarous posture? It is a spectacle that makes the nation an object of ridicule. It must be remedied at once."[23]

Similarly, in the 1920s the Iranian ruler Reza Shah, also an active reformer and westernizer, went so far as to issue a proclamation banning the veil, a move which had the support of some upper-class women as well as upper-class men. The ban, which symbolized the Westerly direction in which the ruling class intended to lead the society and signaled the eagerness of the upper classes to show themselves to be "civilized," was quite

differently received by the popular classes. Even rumors of the move provoked unrest; demonstrations broke out but were ruthlessly crushed. For
most Iranians, women as well as men, the veil was not, as a historian of
Iranian women has observed, a "symbol of backwardness," which members of the upper classes maintained it was, but "a sign of propriety and
a means of protection against the menacing eyes of male strangers." The
police had instructions to deal harshly with any woman wearing anything
other than a European-style hat or no headgear at all, and many women
chose to stay at home rather than venture outdoors and risk having their
veils pulled off by the police.[24] *That's rude*

Veil as protection

In their stinging contempt for the veil and the savagery with which they
attack it, these two members of the ruling class, like Amin, reveal their true
motivation: they are men of the classes assimilating to European ways and
smarting under the humiliation of being described as uncivilized because
"their" women are veiled, and they are determined to eradicate the practice. That is to say, theirs are the words and acts of men exposed to the
Western discourse who have accepted its representation of their culture,
the inferiority of its practices, and the meaning of the veil. Why Muslim
men should be making such statements and enacting such bans is only intelligible against the background of the global dominance of the Western
world and the authority of its discourses, and also against the background
of the ambiguous position of men and women of the upper classes, members of Muslim societies whose economic interests and cultural aspirations
bound them to the colonizing West and who saw their own society partly
through Western eyes.

   The origins and history, just described, of the idea of the veil as it informs
Western colonial discourse *and* twentieth-century Arabic debate have a
number of implications. First, it is evident that the connection between the
issues of culture and women, and more precisely between the cultures of
Other men and the oppression of women, was created by Western discourse. The idea (which still often informs discussions about women in
Arab and Muslim cultures and other non-Western world cultures) that improving the status of women entails abandoning native customs was the
product of a particular historical moment and was constructed by an androcentric colonial establishment committed to male dominance in the service of particular political ends. Its absurdity and essential falseness become
particularly apparent (at least from a feminist point of view) when one
bears in mind that those who first advocated it believed that Victorian

mores and dress, and Victorian Christianity, represented the ideal to which Muslim women should aspire.

Second, these historical origins explain another and, on the face of it, somewhat surprising phenomenon: namely, the peculiar resemblance to be found between the colonial and still-commonplace Western view that an innate connection exists between the issues of culture and women in Muslim societies and the similar presumption underlying the Islamist resistance position, that such a fundamental connection does indeed exist. The resemblance between the two positions is not coincidental: they are mirror images of each other. The resistance narrative contested the colonial thesis by inverting it—thereby also, ironically, grounding itself in the premises of the colonial thesis.

The preceding account of the development of a colonial narrative of women in Islam has other implications as well, including that the colonial account of Islamic oppression of women was based on misperceptions and political manipulations and was incorrect. My argument here is not that Islamic societies did not oppress women. They did and do; that is not in dispute. Rather, I am here pointing to the political uses of the idea that Islam oppressed women and noting that what patriarchal colonialists identified as the sources and main forms of women's oppression in Islamic societies was based on a vague and inaccurate understanding of Muslim societies. This means, too, that the feminist agenda for Muslim women as set by Europeans—and first devised by the likes of Cromer—was incorrect and irrelevant. It was incorrect in its broad assumptions that Muslim women needed to abandon native ways and adopt those of the West to improve their status; obviously, Arab and Muslim women need to reject (just as Western women have been trying to do) the androcentrism and misogyny of whatever culture and tradition they find themselves in, but that is not at all the same as saying they have to adopt Western culture or reject Arab culture and Islam comprehensively. The feminist agenda as defined by Europeans was also incorrect in its particularities, including its focus on the veil. Because of this history of struggle around it, the veil is now pregnant with meanings. As item of clothing, however, the veil itself and whether it is worn are about as relevant to substantive matters of women's rights as the social prescription of one or another item of clothing is to Western women's struggles over substantive issues. When items of clothing—be it bloomers or bras—have briefly figured as focuses of contention and symbols of feminist struggle in Western societies, it was at least Western feminist women who were responsible for identifying the item in question as significant and defining it as a site of struggle and not, as has sadly been the case with respect to the veil for Muslim women, colonial and patriarchal men, like Cromer and Amin, who declared it important to feminist struggle.

That so much energy has been expended by Muslim men and then Muslim women to remove the veil and by others to affirm or restore it is frustrating and ludicrous. But even worse is the legacy of meanings and struggles over issues of culture and class with which not only the veil but also the struggle for women's rights as a whole has become inscribed as a result of this history and as a result of the cooptation by colonialism of the issue of women and the language of feminism in its attempt to undermine other cultures.

This history, and the struggles over culture and between classes, continues to live even today in the debates on the veil and on women. To a considerable extent, overtly or covertly, inadvertently or otherwise, discussions of women in Islam in academies and outside them, and in Muslim countries and outside them, continue either to reinscribe the Western narrative of Islam as oppressor and the West as liberator and native classist versions of that narrative or, conversely, to reinscribe the contentions of the Arabic narrative of resistance as to the essentialness of preserving Muslim customs, particularly with regard to women, as a sign of resistance to imperialism, whether colonial or postcolonial.[25]

Further, colonialism's use of feminism to promote the culture of the colonizers and undermine native culture has ever since imparted to feminism in non-Western societies the taint of having served as an instrument of colonial domination, rendering it suspect in Arab eyes and vulnerable to the charge of being an ally of colonial interests. That taint has undoubtedly hindered the feminist struggle within Muslim societies.

In addition, the assumption that the issues of culture and women are connected—which informed and to an extent continues to inform Western discussions of women in Islam and which, entering Arabic discourse from colonialist sources, has become ensconced there—has trapped the struggle for women's rights with struggles over culture. It has meant that an argument for women's rights is often perceived and represented by the opposing side as an argument about the innate merits of Islam and Arab culture comprehensively. And of course it is neither Islam nor Arab culture comprehensively that is the target of criticism or the objects of advocated reform but those laws and customs to be found in Muslim Arab societies that express androcentric interests, indifference to women, or misogyny.

The issue is simply the humane and just treatment of women, nothing less, and nothing more—not the intrinsic merits of Islam, Arab culture, or the West.

I suggested in an earlier chapter that Western economic penetration of the Middle East and the exposure of Middle Eastern societies to Western political thought and ideas, though undoubtedly having some negative consequences for women, nonetheless did lead to the dismantling of constrictive social institutions and the opening up of new opportunities for women. In the light of the evidence reviewed in the present chapter it appears that a distinction has to be made between, on the one hand, the consequences for women following from the opening of Muslim societies to the West and the social changes and the expansion of intellectual horizons that occurred as a result of the interest within Arab societies in emulating Western technological and political accomplishments and, on the other hand, the quite different and apparently essentially negative consequences following from the construction and dissemination of a Western patriarchal discourse targeting the issue of women and coopting the language of feminism in the service of its strategies of domination.

True, reforms introduced by upper- and middle-class political leaders who had accepted and internalized the Western discourse led in some countries, and specifically Turkey, to legal reforms benefiting women. Ataturk's programs included the replacement of the shari'a family code with a code inspired by the Swiss family code, which at once outlawed polygamy, gave women equal rights to divorce, and granted child-custody rights to both parents. These reforms benefited primarily women of the urban bourgeoisie and had little impact beyond this class. Moreover, and more importantly, whether they will prove enduring remains to be seen, for even in Turkey, Islam and the veil are resurgent: militant Turkish women have staged sit-ins and hunger strikes to demand the right to veil.[26] Reforms in laws governing marriage and divorce that were introduced in Iran in the 1960s and 1970s, though not as far-reaching as Turkish reforms, have already been reversed. Possibly, reforms pursued in a native idiom and not in terms of the appropriation of the ways of other cultures would have been more intelligible and persuasive to all classes and not merely to the upper and middle classes, and possibly, therefore, they would have proved more durable.

THE

Chapter 9
✷

FIRST

FEMINISTS

CHANGE OCCURRED RAPIDLY IN THE FIRST YEARS OF
the twentieth century, change that was readily apparent
to the eye: women's and men's apparel changed, and
women were more commonly seen in the streets. A
transportation network was laid, linking the major cities and eventually the smaller agricultural centers. The
districts of cities were now linked by tramways and
paved roads, and sewer piping was installed. City populations expanded at a rate of 20 percent between
1907 and 1917—slightly higher than the population
growth rate for the countryside. The telephone was
brought to Egypt in 1884, and the first cinema opened
in 1906. These and similar imports must have lent European civilization a dazzling seductiveness, enhanced
by the exhilarating sense of progress these novelties
must have seemed to betoken. As Salama Musa, a distinguished journalist of the period, noted: "The town
of Cairo was in those years alive with encouraging por-
tents of the era. We saw an automobile for the first
time. . . ."[1]

Some classes of Egyptian society benefited by certain
policies of the British administration. Irrigation projects extended the amount of cultivable land, helping

landlords and peasants—as well as the colonialists and the manufacturers of Europe. At the same time, however, British colonial attitudes and discriminatory practices grew more marked and further fueled anti-British feelings. Even though Egypt had more material prosperity, the British held exclusive political control: British officials held all the key administrative positions and filled the top ranks of the civil service. However skilled an Egyptian, there were barriers beyond which he could not advance. The cleavage between the British and the Egyptians grew more severe over time. In schools, for example, British and Egyptian staff had separate common rooms, and it was "not done" for the British to mix with Egyptians.[2]

Resentment intensified against control by a foreign power contemptuous of Egyptians. Exacerbating that resentment was the uneven economic development: prosperity occurred essentially in those areas where it was beneficial to Britain and to foreign investors—agriculture, security—whereas local industries that might compete with European ones were stifled. Egyptians increasingly demanded a greater share in government and political control, and by the early 1900s there was pressure for an end to alien domination, a pressure fed in part by the spread of education that came in the wake of greater prosperity—by 1917 33 percent of the male population in major cities was literate.[3] Three political parties were formed in 1906–7, all planning, in different ways, to bring about an Egypt independent of British control. Both the National party, founded by Mustapha Kamil, and the Constitutional Reform party, founded by ʿAli Yusuf, were fiercely anti-British. The third party, the Umma party, the party of the secularist intellectuals, advocated gradual national reform and cooperation with the British toward that end and toward eventual political independence.

A number of events occurred that crystallized public resentment of the British. One, the Dinshawai incident, which whipped up intense nationalist ardor, will sufficiently convey a sense of the iron-fisted British rule and the tensions created. In June 1906 a contingent of the British army was marching through lower Egypt to Alexandria. While bivouacked near Tanta, some soldiers went off to shoot pigeons near the village of Dinshawai. The sport, popular among the British, was resented by the Egyptian peasants, who regarded pigeons as their own domesticated animals. Shortly after the soldiers began shooting, there was an altercation with the villagers, in the midst of which one soldier's gun went off accidentally, he claimed, wounding a peasant woman. The peasants turned on the soldiers, beating them with sticks after the soldiers allowed themselves to be disarmed. The soldiers believed that the village head, when notified, as required, that they intended to shoot, had passed the information on to the villagers and thus that the interference with their shooting expedition had been planned. One soldier managed to break away and run for help, but overcome by heat and the effects of a head wound, he collapsed and died.

When the news reached Cromer, the British consul general, and before he knew the details, he invoked a special military tribunal to try the case. The tribunal had been established in 1895 to try serious assaults against the occupying army because of the increasing number of such offenses. It was composed of British and Egyptian judicial officials, appointed by the British. The court met in late June 1906 and tried fifty-two men from the village. Thirty-one were found not guilty and released; the remainder were found to have shared varying degrees of responsibility. Because the court found their actions premeditated, it dealt harshly with them. Four were condemned to death by hanging, two to penal servitude for life, and the remainder to imprisonment for a varying number of years and to fifty lashes. The hangings and floggings were carried out just outside of Dinshawai, in front of the villagers.[4]

The barbarity of the sentence shocked Egyptians and caused even supporters of the British occupation, like Qassim Amin, to falter. Amin wrote, "Everyone I met had a broken heart and a lump in his throat. . . . Sadness was on every face. . . . The spirit of the hanged men seemed to hover over every place in the city."[5] Salama Musa wrote that the event stirred up a general nationalist feeling, as if Egyptians "were waking up from their sleep" (32).

According to Musa, people discussed only one other subject as much as nationalism and the British occupation: "Qassim Amin's movement for the liberation of women" (29). Although Musa says that he does not much care for the movement, elsewhere in his recollections he observes that there were "a few rays of light" in the years 1907 to 1912, and among these he lists two events he considered landmarks in women's progress: "we witnessed Miss Nabawiyya Musa's success as the first young woman who obtained her secondary-school certificate, though Dunlop had placed many obstacles in her way" (27, 50). Douglas Dunlop, British adviser to the Ministry of Education, had refused to admit her to the examination because she was a woman.[6] Nabawiyya Musa stood her ground, however, and in 1908 she took the examination and passed. The incident caused a stir and was reported in the papers.

The second "ray" Musa reported was that "for the first time, Egypt saw a woman contributing to newspapers" (49–50). This was Malak Hifni Nassef, who published her articles in *Al-jarida*, the newspaper of the liberal secularist Umma party, under the pseudonym Bahithat al-Badiyya (Seeker in the desert). Nassef was not the first woman to write for a newspaper; women, as we saw above, had been writing for and editing journals since the 1890s, and these activities intensified in the early 1900s, when women's journals multiplied. Nassef was perhaps the first woman to contribute articles regularly to the mainstream press.

As individual women and their ideas and achievements were becoming part of the educated person's consciousness, other changes affecting women were also afoot, both obvious and subtle ones. Styles of dress, particularly variations in the veil, from thick to flimsily light, were the most obvious. By 1910 or so unveiling was distinctly on the increase in Egypt, so that visitors from other Arab countries were struck by the prevalence of the phenomenon.[7] The women in Musa's Coptic family unveiled around 1907, and some other sources suggest that Muslim women also began to unveil around then (13). Also, schoolgirls and schools for girls were strikingly in evidence. An American visitor to Cairo in 1913 noted that it was impossible not to be "amazed" at the number of schools of all kinds, French, English, and Italian, that had been established for girls.[8]

In fact women's literary, intellectual, and social life began a period of enormous vitality, during which varieties of feminist activism emerged. Women wrote in the numerous women's journals published then, such as *Anis al-jalis* (1898–1908), *Fatat al-sharq* (1906–39), *Al-jins al-latif* (1908–24), *Al-ʿafaf* (1910–22), and *Fatat al-Nil* (1913–15), as well as, in some cases, in the mainstream press. They founded organizations for the intellectual improvement of women, the Society for the Advancement of Woman, established in 1908, being among the earliest; it took a conservative Islamic line.[9] Another, the Intellectual Association of Egyptian Women, founded in 1914, included among its founders Huda Shaʿrawi, the preeminent feminist leader of the 1920s and 1930s, and Mai Ziyada, a feminist intellectual and writer. Others followed: the Society of the Renaissance of the Egyptian Woman, the Society of Mothers of the Future (established in 1921), the Society of the New Woman (established in 1919). A lecture series for women, held at the Egyptian University on Fridays (when no male students or faculty were present), was inaugurated in 1908 by Huda Shaʿrawi with the assistance of other upper-class women. Shaʿrawi initiated the series in response to a question from Marguerite Clement, who was visiting Egypt under the sponsorship of the Carnegie Endowment, about the availability of lectures for women. Shaʿrawi invited Clement, the first speaker in the series, to compare the "lives of oriental and Western women and talk about social practices such as veiling." Egyptian women, including Nassef, as well as other European women, were later invited to speak.[10]

In the first decades of the twentieth century women also established dispensaries, nursery schools, and charitable associations for women, often also serving boys and men. Among the organizations that upper-class women instituted and ran were some that played a critical role in the medical services of the nation. The Mubarat Muhammad 'Ali, for example, launched by two princesses in 1908, provided clinics, hospitals, and dispensaries. Run by a group of rural and urban upper-class women from different religious backgrounds, who financed their activities with bazaars, fetes, sweepstakes, and donations from the members and their friends, this organization, which began with a small clinic, continued to thrive and by 1961 had created twelve hospitals in Egypt, in which one-quarter of the beds were free of charge, and eighteen dispensaries and clinics, where patients were treated and supplied with medication free or for a nominal sum. Over a period of twenty-one years the Mubarat institutions treated over thirteen million patients. In 1964 its hospitals were nationalized.[11]

Women became visible politically as the collaborators of prominent male politicians, members of women's political organizations paralleling and actively supporting men's parties, and participants in political riots and demonstrations. The 1910s, and indeed subsequent decades, were years of political unrest and agitation against the British, agitation in which both upper-class women and women of the popular classes took part. At the end of the First World War, when the British deported Sa'd Zaghloul, leader of the major political party in Egypt, along with two other prominent party members, the country erupted in riots, strikes, and acts of violence against the British, with women at all class levels openly participating. Peasant women appeared as active as the men, tearing up railway lines, destroying telegraph lines, and pillaging and burning throughout the countryside. Even schoolgirls demonstrated and sent telegrams of protest to the prime minister—and were reportedly more violent than the boys, some of the English women teachers apparently being subjected to "an extremely unpleasant time" by their mutinous pupils. Women were shot and killed along with the men when British soldiers opened fire to control the rebellion at Kafr el Shawm in Embaba and in the Fayyum on March 15, 1919, and more were killed in the provinces and in Cairo during the following weeks.[12]

Safia Zaghloul, wife of the exiled leader, addressed the crowds who had flocked to their home on the evening of the day of her husband's arrest.[13]

On March 15, wives and relatives of both the exiled leaders and members of the Wafd, the name by which Zaghloul's political party was thenceforth called, met at the home of Huda Shaʿrawi, whose husband, ʿAli Shaʿrawi, was among the founding members of the Wafd, to decide on a course of action. Notifying as many women as they could, they marched in protest the following day; some 350 women, from Alexandria, Fayyum, and elsewhere, were in the procession.[14] This emergence of a group of "invisible" upper-class women added a new, visually and politically arresting element to the situation. A correspondent for the London *Times* described the women as "descend[ing] in large bodies into the streets, those of the more respectable classes still veiled and shrouded in their loose black cloaks, whilst the courtesans from the lowest quarters of the city, who had also caught the contagion, disported themselves unveiled and arrayed in less discreet garments."[15]

Later in the same year when the Milner Commission, appointed to investigate the disturbances, arrived in Egypt, protests once more erupted, and again women participated. The *Times* correspondent wrote that one of the women's "favourite devices" was to take possession of tramway cars and drive through the city, "yelling 'Down with Milner!'" and waving paper flags.[16] Upper-class women marched through the streets and presented resolutions to the British authorities. When a women's branch of the Wafd political party was formed in 1919, the Wafdist Women's Central Committee elected Huda Shaʿrawi president.

Over the first three decades of the century feminism became visible intellectually, then organizationally and politically. The founding feminist discourses emerged in those decades, as did the articulation of the first complex and incisive feminist analysis, primarily and most eloquently in the work of Malak Hifni Nassef. Critical tensions also emerged within feminist discourse; of the two divergent strains of feminism, one became the dominant voice of feminism in Egypt and in the Arab Middle East for most of the century, and the second remained an alternative, marginal voice until the last decades of the century, generally not even recognized as a voice of feminism. The dominant voice of feminism, which affiliated itself, albeit generally discreetly, with the westernizing, secularizing tendencies of society, predominantly the tendencies of the upper, upper-middle, and middle-middle classes, promoted a feminism that assumed the desirability of progress toward Western-type societies. The alternative voice, wary of and eventually even opposed to Western ways, searched a way to articulate female subjectivity and affirmation within a native, vernacular, Islamic discourse—typically in terms of a general social, cultural, and religious renovation. The renovation was understood to be regenerative for the entire society, not just for women, hence the rights of women were not the sole nor even any longer the primary object of reform, but one among several. These divergent voices, incipient in the early 1900s, were perhaps best articulated by Sha'rawi and Nassef respectively. Nassef's premature death and the organizational and political success of Huda Sha'rawi and her Egyptian Feminist Union were perhaps both important factors in the emergence of the westernizing voice of feminism as the prevailing, uncontested voice of feminism in the Arab context in those early years.

For the entire twentieth century, massive quantities of material are available—published and unpublished documents and texts, oral histories, and so forth. Only when some substantial research has been done will it be possible to write an account of the discourses on women within Egyptian and other Arab societies that does even partial justice to its rich polyvocal diversity and complexity, and only then will it be possible to assess accurately the impact of the economic, social, and political developments on different classes of women and, from that, the nature of the forces shaping the societies in which those discourses are anchored. Here I merely note some main trends and identify issues worthy of further exploration.

As in the chapters analyzing the broad sweep of social change and the evolution of the discourse on women in the nineteenth century, the focus here is again on Egypt, justifiably considered the mirror or precursor of developments in the Middle East in this period. Still, each country is unique, its particular composition shaping and informing specific local developments. Among the features differentiating developments in Egypt from those in other Arab countries in the Middle East in the twentieth century, perhaps two should be remarked on. Even though in intellectual and social terms Egypt continued to play a pioneering role in women's issues, the struggle to institute legal reforms in the area of family law, and in particular to restrict polygamy and male access to divorce, met with virtually no success. In contrast, other Arab countries, notably Tunisia, Syria, and Iraq, did introduce measures to render polygamy and unilateral divorce more difficult; of the Arab countries Tunisia alone prohibited polygamy altogether. The closest Egypt came to instituting reforms in these matters was in 1927, when the cabinet approved draft legislation (based in the main on the views of Muhammad 'Abdu) to restrict polygamy and the male right to divorce. King Fuad refused in the end to endorse it.[17] The second important area of difference between Egypt and other Arab countries is with respect to culturally but not religiously sanctioned practices, in particular clitoridectomy. By and large this custom, practiced by some classes in Egypt, appears to be geographically confined, among Arab countries, to Egypt, the Sudan, and some parts of Arabia. It is not an Islamic custom, and in Egypt, for instance, is as common among Christians as among Muslims.

The organizational and political success of the feminist movement led by Huda Sha'rawi and the members of the Egyptian Feminist Union (EFU) helped bring about some significant gains for women. Sha'rawi (1879–1947) founded the EFU on March 16, 1923, prompted, according to one account, by the unwillingness of the Wafd to grant women suffrage. The Wafd had won Egypt's "independence" from the British in 1923, though the British retained the right of absolute control in certain matters, including national defense and the protection of foreign interests. The Constitution, proclaimed in April 1923, restricted suffrage to males, and Sha'rawi reportedly founded the EFU with the object of fighting for women's suffrage.

At any rate, whether the founding of the EFU was prompted by Wafd footdragging or, as another account suggests, by an invitation to Egyptian women to attend the forthcoming International Women's Alliance in Rome, a delegation from the EFU—consisting of Sha'rawi, her friend and protégée Saiza Nabarawi, and Nabawiyya Musa, the woman who fought for her right to sit for the Secondary School Examination—did attend the Rome conference in May 1923. It was upon their return from this trip that Sha'rawi and Nabarawi removed their veils, presumably in a symbolic act of emancipation, as they stepped off the train in Cairo. For Sha'rawi the gesture perhaps fulfilled a childhood aspiration. A member of the upper classes, she had been guided in her thought and in her French readings by her friend and mentor, a Frenchwoman, Eugénie Le Brun, from an extremely young age. Le Brun was married to Rushdi Pasha, an Egyptian. She had conveyed to Sha'rawi the common European belief that "the veil stood in the way of their [Egyptian women's] advancement," evidently inspiring in her a determination to one day cast off the habit.[18]

The EFU drafted a constitution and elected a board of directors and an executive committee to pursue its aims: to raise Egyptian women's "intellectual and moral" level and enable them to attain political, social, and legal equality. Specific goals were obtaining access to education at all levels for women, reforming marriage laws, in particular laws relating to polygamy and divorce, and setting a minimum marriage age of sixteen for girls. The job of financing the EFU initially and for some time to come fell largely to Sha'rawi, who enjoyed a large personal fortune. The membership of the union rose to about 250 by the late 1920s.[19] In 1923, in response to a petition from the EFU, the Parliament passed a law setting the minimum marriage age for girls at sixteen and for boys at eighteen. Thereafter, however, no progress was made toward modifying the marriage laws.

Important advances for women were made in the area of education, however. In 1923 the Egyptian Constitution declared education a priority. In 1925 the government decreed primary education compulsory for both boys and girls (though it did not have the resources to implement this decree, some significant progress in the matter was made, and the principle was thenceforth never to be retreated from). The government also opened a secondary school for girls. In the late 1920s women were admitted into the university for the first time; Huda Sha'rawi and the EFU had pressed for their admittance, and it occurred quietly and undramatically under the rectorship of Lutfi al-Sayyid—friend to Mai Ziyada and editor of *Al-jarida* when that journal published Nassef's work. When the first batch of women students graduated from the government secondary school, al-Sayyid arranged for their admittance to Fuad University (later to be called Cairo University).[20] In 1933 the first women university graduates from the Egyptian university took their degrees. They were not the first women university graduates in the country, for women had already graduated from universities in England and the United States.[21]

The EFU itself sent young women to Europe on scholarships beginning in the 1920s. It ran a primary school for girls, for which students paid no or minimal fees, and a program of aid for widows, which provided them with temporary monthly assistance, paid their children's way to school, and obtained medical treatment for them. It also ran a vocational-training workshop for economically deprived girls, teaching them sewing and rug weaving, and a dispensary for women and children. By 1928 the dispensary had treated about nineteen thousand cases with visceral diseases, eye diseases, and the diseases of women and pregnant mothers. These programs were run at the expense of Sha'rawi and other members of the organization and with the aid of volunteers.

Connections with Western feminists had always been Sha'rawi's forte, and from its founding the EFU regularly sent delegates to international women's meetings. The organizational habits and skills thus acquired were used later in the promotion of Arab feminism. In the 1930s, as the troubles in Palestine intensified, Sha'rawi issued an invitation to Arab women to an "Eastern" feminist conference to address and defend the Palestinian cause. The conference was convened in Cairo on October 15, 1938, and was attended by delegates from seven Arab countries. They issued firm resolutions in support of the Palestinians and, on a practical level, organized fund-raisers for the Palestinians. In 1944, at a second Arab women's conference, an Arab Feminist Union was founded, and Sha'rawi was elected its president. Upon her death in 1947, Ibtihaj Qaddus of Lebanon succeeded her as president.[22]

Sha'rawi's feminism, then, was politically nationalistic; it opposed British domination in the sense that the liberal intellectuals of her class and the upper-middle classes opposed it, rather than opposing the British and everything Western with the extremity expressed by other groups and parties that had a base among the popular classes. Broadly, this meant supporting gradual reform toward total political emancipation from British control and toward the adoption of Western political institutions and a secularist understanding of the state. Culturally and in her feminism, as is suggested by the fact that she construed the act of unveiling to be an important and significant act—although by the time she unveiled, the custom was apparently rapidly vanishing among women of her class—and by her close connections with Western women and Western feminism, her perspective was informed by a Western affiliation and a westernizing outlook and apparently by a valorization of Western ways as more advanced and more "civilized" than native ways.

This inclination is confirmed by details revealed in her autobiography. In contrast to Nassef, who wrote eloquently in Arabic, Sha'rawi's command of the Arabic language did not permit her to write her own memoirs: she dictated them to her secretary. She was in a sense, then, an exile, an outsider, within the universe of Arabic. Sha'rawi's valorization of the European—perhaps over the native—is suggested by the fact that in her public presentation of herself it is the influence of the West that she chose to bring into the foreground as critical at a formative period in her life. She presents her reading of French books (probably novels) and her friendships with French or French-educated young women as sources of intellectual nurturance at an important time—when she extricated herself from a marriage into which she had been forced, and devoted herself to music, books, and friends and to "creating" herself. Similarly, she is careful to acknowledge her debt to Eugénie Le Brun's discussion of the veil and the position of women as having guided her ideas. Even though it is those sources of strength and resolution that she explicitly acknowledges, it is also clear from her account that arguably her most daring and authoritative act—the act of leaving a marriage in defiance of husband and family—occurred when she was thirteen and when her exposure to Western ideas had been minimal. Evidently, therefore, there were sources within her background prior to her exposure to Western ideas that endowed her with a sense of her right to autonomy and her right to follow her own sense of what was morally correct in defiance of elders. That it is the influence of Western thought that Sha'rawi chose to emphasize is, then, revealing not only of the actual circumstances of her life but also of the value of being influenced by the West in her own eyes and in the eyes of the readers she had in mind— presumably members of her own class and of the upper-middle class, for whom to assimilate to a certain degree to Western ways also represented assimilating to more "civilized" ways. I am not here suggesting that her reading of French novels and her friendships with French or French-educated young women did not influence her life, nor that Le Brun's ideas were not important in shaping its course, but rather that the sources of Sha'rawi's feminism and her personality and motivations are doubtless much more complex and nuanced, and more imponderable, than Sha'rawi, in her public presentation of herself (and perhaps also in her own internal organization of self) chose to formally acknowledge. And I am suggesting that her organizing her past to show a turning toward things Western perhaps indicates a psychological inclination to admire the European more than the native and points to an area of complexity and ambiguity that requires investigation.

From Qassim Amin onward, the internalization of colonialism and of notions of the innate superiority of the European over the native—the colonization of consciousness, in short—could complicate feminism. For some feminists, such as, arguably, Doria Shafik, the ambiguity and destructive self-dividedness that internalized colonialism apparently gave rise to could be psychologically crippling. Other feminists, most notably Zeinab al-Ghazali, who at first looked to Sha'rawi for feminist leadership, reacted against the implicit valorization of the Western over the Arabic in Sha'rawi's feminism and turned away from it, seeking to forge a feminist path—or a path of female subjectivity and affirmation—within the terms of the indigenous culture.

Where Sha'rawi espoused a Westward-looking feminism, already in the 1900s and 1910s, Malak Hifni Nassef was articulating the basis of a feminism that did not automatically affiliate itself with westernization. Nassef was opposed to unveiling, and her views in this matter suggest the differences between her perspective on feminism and culture and Sha'rawi's, as well as give some sense of the incisiveness of Nassef's thought and the precision of her understanding of the new varieties of male domination being enacted in and through the contemporary male discourse of the veil.

Nassef (1886–1918) took up the subject of the veil within a decade or so of the publication of Amin's book, prompted by a series of articles by Abdel Hamid Hamdy, who, like Amin, advocated unveiling. After thanking the author for his concern for women, Nassef explained that she felt bound to comment, for the subject continued to provoke such a "battle of the pens." She was opposed to unveiling, though not for the usual conservative reasons: she neither believed that religion dictated anything specific on the matter to women nor that women who veiled were more modest than women who did not, for true modesty was not determined by the presence or absence of a veil. Men based their views on the veil on their "research and speculation" (literally, "imaginings"), but she based hers on "observation and experience and [accounts of] the experiences of a variety of women." In the first place, she points out, women were accustomed to veiling and should not be abruptly ordered to unveil. Moreover, she asks, "How can you men of letters . . . command us to unveil when any of us is subjected to foul language if she walks in the street, this one throwing adulterous glances at her and that one bespattering her with his despicableness so that the sweat of shame pours from her brow." Given "a collection of men such as we have at present, whose abuse and shamelessness a woman should not be exposed to, and a collection of women such as we have at present, whose understanding is that of babes, for women to unveil and mix with men would be an innovation that would lead to evil." [23]

Nassef goes on to observe that perhaps in response to the advocacy of Hamdy and others, some women were already venturing into the streets in European dress, congratulating themselves on being modern. For the most part, however, those who unveiled were upper-class women preoccupied with fashion; they were not motivated by a desire for liberty or persuaded that the veil hampered them in the pursuit of knowledge—indeed if those were their reasons "then it would be a duty to grant them their demand without reserve." As it was, Egyptian women were too "ignorant" and the men of such "corruptness" that unveiling and the mixing of the sexes was for the present a bad idea (1:26).

Although adopting Western ideas was neither good nor bad in itself, indiscriminate adoption of Western ways without reference to their suitability in a particular environment was unwise. What was essential, therefore, was not for intellectuals to debate the veil but for "you [men] to give women a true education and raise them soundly and rectify how people are raised and improve your moral character, so that the nation as a whole is well-educated and well-mannered. Then leave it to her to choose that which is most advantageous to her and to the nation" (1:25–28).

Nassef's words are carefully weighed, and the points she makes are not random or casual but part of a taut argument. She shows herself to be aware of the misogyny in contemporary male texts and the politics of male dominance being reenacted through the debate over the veil, and she exposes and rejects male arrogance in dictating what women ought to do and brings a critical and discriminating eye to the issue of adopting Western customs. Strikingly unlike Amin's text, in which it was the ignorant, base, and idle character of women that held Egyptian men back, Nassef's text presents men as corrupt and degenerate, as the ones who bespatter women with their despicableness. Women's ignorance is innocent, an ignorance of babes. It is men's moral character that stands in need of improvement. Not dictating to women about whether they should veil but enabling them to obtain an education and allowing them to decide for themselves was the course she commended to men.

Nassef's views on the veil and her critique of male writers on the subject, condensed in her article, are elaborated in an open letter to the young feminist Mai Ziyada. Ziyada, who initiated their correspondence, which was published over several issues of *Al-jarida,* had invited Nassef to advise young women on how to improve their lot. Nassef responded, saying that all at present "call for the advancement of woman and for the need to prepare her to be a good wife and mother," but each (that is, each man) has his own view on how this should be done. Some have decided that "all backwardness and ignorance has its source in the veil and that hence it is essential that Egyptian women unveil immediately—forgetting the wisdom of proceeding with due deliberation when wishing to move from a dark and familiar state to an as-yet-unknown state that looks astonishingly, dazzlingly attractive and brilliant" (2:8). Another group, Nassef said, was convinced that the veil was essential and that education would corrupt women. "Which path should we take, which group follow? The majority of us women continue to be oppressed by the injustice of man, who in his despotism commands and forbids us so that now we can have no opinion even about ourselves. . . . If he orders us to veil, we veil, and if he now demands that we unveil, we unveil, and if he wishes us to be educated, we are educated. Is he well intentioned in all he asks of us and on our behalf, or does he wish us ill? There is no doubt that he has erred grievously against us . . . in decreeing our rights in the past and no doubt that he errs grievously . . . in decreeing our rights now" (2:8). We cannot assume, she continued, that all men who write about women are wise reformers. Their words must be carefully scrutinized, and we must be wary of man "being as despotic about liberating us as he has been about our enslavement. We are weary of his despotism" (2:8–9).

The feminist subjects that Nassef gave priority to were education—she was a graduate of the Sannia Teacher Training College and worked as a teacher prior to her marriage—and educational reform and reform in the marriage laws and the conjugal relationship. In particular she denounced the evils of polygamy and men's unrestricted license to divorce their wives, early marriage for girls, and marriages with too great a disparity in age between the spouses. She wrote against these practices in language fraught with a sense of the terrible human cost these customs entailed for children as well as for women. On polygamy, for example—her article on the subject is subtitled "Or Co-wives"—Nassef writes:

> It [co-wife] is a terrible word—my pen almost halts in writing it—women's mortal enemy. . . . How many hearts has it broken, how many minds has it confused and homes destroyed, how much evil brought and how many innocents sacrificed and prisoners taken for whom it was the origin of personal calamity? . . . [It is] a terrible word, laden with savagery and selfishness. . . . Bear in mind that as you amuse yourself with your new bride you cause another's despair to flow in tears . . . and children whom you taught to sorrow, weep for her tears. . . . You hear the drums and pipes [at a wedding], and they hear only the beat of misery.

Women she has talked to have said "they would rather see their husband borne away on a bier than see him married to a second wife," and she details the miseries that the husband's selfishness brings to wives and children (1:41).

Nassef knew about polygamy all too intimately. After her graduation at the age of twenty-one, her father, who had encouraged her in her studies, accepted on her behalf an apparently suitable proposal of marriage from 'Abdel Sattar al-Basil Pasha, a prominent leader of Arab stock. Nassef's father was an intellectual and man of letters, a friend of Muhammad 'Abdu's and one of the founders of the Umma party—in whose organ, Al-jarida, Nassef's work first appeared. Only after she married and accompanied her husband to his residence in Fayyum did she learn that he already had a wife. She found the situation agonizing but revealed her pain to no one, not even her family, to whom she was close and of whom she was most protective: as the eldest child in a home where the mother was an invalid,

Nassef had taken on the responsibilities of running the household and mothering her siblings. She kept her marital unhappiness from her parents because she did not want to cause them distress and from others because she feared her "failure" in marriage would be pointed to as an example of the consequences of educating women and thus used to women's detriment.

When her articles inspired Mai Ziyada to write an open letter of impassioned admiration, Nassef replied that her writing arose out of pain, not a personal pain—she had never lost anyone nor had she any personal reason for sorrow, she declared—but a moral pain. Her heart was "cracked" at the corruption of society; she felt compassion for all who suffered and had sworn "to help Egyptian women, a vow that it is important to me to fulfill, even though its execution is arduous and the difficulties surrounding it are such that despair almost blocks my path" (2:7). In Ziyada's reply, in a literary conceit she wished Nassef more such moral pain, for that pain had ignited "a sacred fire," "a fire that raised the spirit on flaming wings to the sky of meanings" (2:10). Nassef responded: "How, Mai, can you wish me moral pain? Physical pain is lighter, more bearable. . . . I have known both. . . . You say because it is 'a sacred fire.' Yes, it has given me a measure of sacredness greater than is right for such as I and made the distance between me and this far-from-sacred world too great" (2:17).

Pain figures in the lives of the women who throughout this century have devoted themselves to the cause of women and who have played a significant part in defining the territory and articulating the discourses of female subjectivity—Nassef, Mai Ziyada, Huda Sha'rawi, Doria Shafik, Nawal El-Saadawi, Alifa Rifaat. All suffered directly from the system in place, whose destructiveness to women and, as Nassef pointed out, to children was explicitly set at naught, regarded as immaterial, when measured against the pleasures of men. Characteristically their writings and social activities, the charitable institutions they founded and to which they dedicated their energies, bear the mark of an impassioned desire to resist injustice, right wrongs, survive and assist others to survive, and serve others whom that system had crushed or destroyed. In comparison, the male-engendered debate about women, with its fixation on the veil, often seems preoccupied with abstractions and essentially oblivious of the appalling human cost to women and children and consequently to men exacted by the system of male dominance enshrined in the laws and institutions of Arab societies.

Nassef lectured and wrote prolifically. Her writings reveal a vision both lucid and penetrating and entitle her to be regarded as the major intellectual of the feminist movement of the first decades of the century. Her tragic death at the age of thirty-two, of Spanish flu, was a serious loss to the

struggle for women's rights and indeed to Arabic letters generally. Her contemporaries recognized her gifts: her funeral was attended by front-rank
feminists, government leaders, including the minister of education, and men
of the conservative ʿulama class, who delivered orations in her praise.[24] In
1924, on the seventh anniversary of her death, there was another gathering
to commemorate her, presided over by Huda Shaʿrawi, now the foremost
feminist. Elegies were read and speeches delivered by, among others, Nabawiyya Musa, Mai Ziyada, and the poet Khalil Mutran.[25]

In addition to lecturing and writing, Nassef was active in the political
field and in founding and running charitable societies. In 1911, when the
first Egyptian congress met to deliberate and issue recommendations on
the needs of the country, Nassef, noting that the points presented for the
congress to consider addressed every issue of importance except women's
issues, hastily drew up a list, which she presented to the congress. It included the demand that all fields of higher education be opened to women
and that space be made available in mosques for women to attend public
prayer. Among the institutes she founded were a women's association, intended to bring women together and disseminate information; an emergency dispensary and nursing service modeled on the Red Cross, for
emergency relief; and a nursing school for women, which she established
in her own home and at her own expense.[26]

Shaʿrawi and Nassef both advocated that society enable women to pursue
education to the limit of their abilities, and both pushed for fundamental
reforms in the laws governing marriage. Indeed, there appear to be no substantive differences between their goals. Nassef was no less committed to
fundamentally altering the position and rights of women in society, even
though she was cautious toward the West, comfortable within and well
rooted in the universe of Arabic language and Arabic culture, and disposed
to seek reforms in terms internal to the indigenous culture. A member of
the upper-middle class, Nassef was raised firmly within the native culture—perhaps unusually among the upper and middle classes—whereas
Shaʿrawi was raised to be bicultural, with French culture, at least from her
teens forward, receiving more emphasis and valorization than the Arabic.

Given the nature of the material available or becoming available, the detailed investigation of precisely these kinds of issues will soon be possible—
the constitution of identity and the sense of self, and the psychological and
personal dimensions of political views and affiliations, among others. The
records are quite different from those available for preceding generations
in that many women were now literate and able to record their thoughts
and experiences and in that new literary conventions, diary keeping and

autobiography, permitted and encouraged the recording of personal facts and opinions.

Consequently, we can anticipate exploring such questions as the nature of the relationships that existed between women, and the connections between feminists, and, generally, the meaning of friendship in the Egyptian and Arab cultural context and the ways in which the personal intertwined with the political in women's lives. It is to these early decades of the twentieth century that one may perhaps look for the first textual records of female friendships, and literary friendships, and female networks of support, and patterns of feminist mentorship. Links of friendship or mentorship, for example, not only bound Huda Sha'rawi, Nabawiyya Musa, and Mai Ziyada with each other and with Nassef but also linked some of these women to women of the succeeding generation who were to play an important role in developing further the discourses of feminism and female subjectivity. The intergenerational link might be a mentor relationship, such as that between Nassef and Ziyada, or a relationship of mutual support, such as that between Sha'rawi and Nassef. Sha'rawi in particular was mentor to a number of women, notably Amina al-Sa'id, later a distinguished journalist and writer and a dedicated feminist, and Doria Shafik, a journalist, activist, writer, and feminist intellectual. Sha'rawi was also a mentor, or rebelled-against mentor, to Zeinab al-Ghazali, founder of the Islamic Women's Association.

Further questions to explore concern the meaning of marriage and the affective weight carried by the marital relationship in the balance of extended familial relationships and relationships beyond the family and the meaning of family as a source of support and emotional satisfaction, validations of self, and even perhaps relationships of intimacy and passion. On the basis of her own testimony, we know that for at least one of the women mentioned above, Huda Sha'rawi, her relationship with her brother was the most intense and important in her life; and oral information from women of her society suggests that a strong emotional bond between sister and brother was fairly common.[27] Other areas worthy of investigation include issues of sexuality and the ways in which sexual and erotic experience, heterosexual and homosexual, shaped consciousness, and even more fundamentally the meaning of sexuality and whether the spectrum of emotional, erotic, and sexual experience within Egyptian and Arab society might be adequately or accurately captured by such modern Western terms as *heterosexual, homosexual,* or *lesbian.* The presumption that these terms are applicable to experiences regardless of the sociocultural framework shaping them and its specific structuring of the affective and psychic universe of its subjects, and that the range of experiences they connote is identical in all societies, is large indeed.

The subject of affectional, erotic, and sexual love between women has scarcely yet been touched. Warda al-Yaziji (1849–1924), a member of the well-known literary Christian Lebanese family who had migrated to Egypt and the subject of a biography by Ziyada, wrote love poems addressed to a grammatically feminine lover. Critics, assuming this to be a literary device, have judged her pronouncedly erotic poems therefore to be unconvincing because "unrealistic."[28] Using the feminine was perhaps a literary device, but perhaps it also corresponded to an experiential reality. The only explicit references to sexual relationships between women occur with respect to members of the highest level of the upper class. Jemileh Hanem, an aunt of Abbas II, khedive of Egypt, is described as an "outrageous Sapphist," whose involvements with "her ladies," including a particular Armenian, were matched by her husband's passion for his groom.[29]

Sexual excesses of all sorts are attributed to members of the ruling family, women as well as men. Khedive Ismael's (r. 1872–79) mother was rumored to have "a sharp eye for a good-looking young man." As she drove through Cairo, "she often noticed someone to whom she was attracted. Her Eunuchs were then promptly despatched with an appropriate message. Queer and disturbing rumours began to circulate about strange disappearances."[30] To give an example involving another kind of excess, Nazli, daughter of Muhammad ʿAli, was said to be so jealous over her husband that when he remarked on the long, wavy hair of one of her female slaves, she had him served the following evening with a covered dish on which lay her head.[31] Stories of this sort are even more common about the male members of the family. Such accounts, by definition about the use of power and the breaking of boundaries, cannot be used as the basis for speculation about the broader society, however.

Some few details of these women's psychological and affective lives are known. For example, Shaʿrawi, who was from an immensely wealthy upper-class family, felt rejected as a child because she was a girl, a rejection that bred feelings of exclusion, of being outcast from the human world, and led her to seek refuge from it in the world of animals and nature. She was compelled, at the age of twelve or so, to marry her guardian, a man in his forties, and her life on her wedding morning appeared to her devastated, desolate. And after she succeeded in bringing about a separation between herself and her husband, friendships, with European women in particular, played a vital part in her regaining a sense of herself and a sense of wholeness as she strove, as she put it, to "create" herself.[32] Such facts are known, but not their psychological significance.

Similarly, we know the bare fact that Mai Ziyada (1886–1941), who was a young girl when her Christian Arab family migrated to Egypt from Nazareth, never married. Remaining single was rare for men as well as for women. Ziyada, writer, intellectual, and feminist, was a prominent figure in the Egyptian intellectual world. She hosted a weekly salon, which she held from about 1912 on and which attracted many distinguished intellectuals, politicians, and men of letters from the Arab world (and indeed from the Western world: Henry James, for one, visited Ziyada). Salama Musa, an Egyptian intellectual and a friend of Ziyada's, implicitly attributes Ziyada's never having married to her not having received any offers because of the salon she hosted. "Our Libanese friends, modernised though they may be, had for that matter not yet ceased to be orientals. They could not put up with the idea of having a wife who received her guests in a literary *salon* where in discussion and social intercourse prevailed the freedom of the European tradition" (158). Still, at least two eminent men were reputedly in love with her.

The deprivations and penalties that society visited upon intellectual and feminist women are also still to be explored. As education became available to women, penalties probably became increasingly part of their experience. Their situation might well have fostered feelings of psychological alienation and isolation and of exclusion, even internal exile, for breaking the bounds of feminine conduct—being a writer or an intellectual—and for advocating feminism, thereby placing themselves explicitly, by advocating feminism, in opposition to the dominant Arab androcentric culture. Mai Ziyada voiced that feeling: "Despite my immense love for the country of my birth, I feel like a displaced person, a refugee with no homeland."[33] (The statement is not without ambiguity, though. Ziyada was born in Palestine and schooled in Palestine and Lebanon, and she moved to Cairo with her family when she was eighteen, where she remained for most of the rest of her life.) Interestingly, Virginia Woolf reflected along parallel lines, saying that while England was the country of Englishmen, Englishwomen had no country.[34]

Mai Ziyada, again like Woolf and like a remarkable number of intellectual women of the Anglo-American world, died "insane." A pacifist, she became convinced that she was being watched by agents with a murderous intent, a belief that arose after a visit to fascist Italy in 1934, when she was told, after she made a critical remark while waiting for an audience with the pope, that she was not welcome in Italy and that Il Duce was having her watched. In 1936, haunted by this fear and by depression, she attempted suicide. She refused to see anyone while in the hospital "because everyone who visits me talks to me as if he believes I am insane." Gradually she became distrustful of everyone, of her servants, whom she discharged, and of her friends. She died in 1941; her body was discovered in her lonely flat three days after her death.[35] Doria Shafik also underwent several mental breakdowns and, like Woolf and Ziyada, killed herself, in 1976. It would not be surprising if more such tragedies are unearthed.

Mental breakdown and suicide naturally have many causes. Among them doubtless are the punishing social and psychological effects visited by society on women who—breaking the bounds of femininity—become writers and thinkers and take their stand against the reigning dogmas of the culture, including a male dominance that trails in its wake emotional, psychological, and material brutality to women and children as religiously sanctioned law and accepted social practice and demands that such abuses be covered up in the name of loyalty to the culture.

Chapter 10   DIVERGENT VOICES

ALTHOUGH THE CONSTITUTION OF 1923 DECLARED education a priority and the government made primary education compulsory for both boys and girls shortly thereafter, the government did not in fact have the resources to make education generally available. The existing buildings and teachers were stretched to the utmost, however, and education expanded rapidly over the following decades. Urban areas fared better than rural ones, for they had more teachers and facilities and both could be used in double shifts—at inadequate pay, women teachers complained.[1]

By 1930 the number of girls attending school, 218,165, or 24 percent of the total school population, was much higher than in 1913, when the number was 31,000, or 10 percent of the school population, and the figures continued to rise thereafter. The increase in the numbers of women attending university rose at a "phenomenal" rate, an American contemporary observed, after the first five women matriculated in 1929. By 1937 there were 1,979 women holding university degrees; by 1947 there were 4,000 women; and by 1960 there were 24,800, secondary-school and university education having become free in the 1950s.[2]

In spite of increased enrollments the illiteracy figures continued to be high. In 1937 it was estimated that 74 percent of the male and 91 percent of the female population were illiterate; the rate improved slightly by 1947 to 67 percent for males and 87 percent for females. Educational expansion could not keep pace with the growth of the population, which had been rising steadily since the late nineteenth century, mainly because of improved health facilities and higher survival rates for infants and mothers. The population, over nine million in 1897, was over fifteen million in 1937.[3]

The number of graduates nevertheless outstripped the number of available jobs, and unemployment among educated males became a palpable problem. By 1937 an estimated eleven thousand secondary-school and university graduates were unemployed. Graduating women seeking to enter employment already confronted prejudice because of their sex, and the shortage of jobs exacerbated the situation. The subject of women taking jobs away from men was heatedly discussed in an exchange in the press (in which Nabawiyya Musa took part) as early as 1929.[4]

Women graduates who wanted a job also encountered resistance from their families. Even though progressive middle- and upper-class families (the background of an overwhelming proportion of women proceeding to university) were in favor of educating their daughters, the notion of their going out into the world to work was quite another matter: only poor women worked for a living, and it was improper for the well-to-do to work. Still, many women overcame family as well as societal resistance by arguing, as did Soheir al-Qalamawi, that they wished to work not because they wanted the money but because they wanted to work.[5] Beginning in the early 1930s, when the first women graduated from Fuad University, they began to enter the professions—including law, journalism, medicine, and university teaching. A striking number of those pioneers went on to become leaders in their fields and became household names: al-Qalamawi, writer and academic; Amina al-Saʿid, journalist and author, Bint al-Shati, the pen name of ʿAisha Abdel Rahman, writer and popular historian, to name but a few.

However, given high unemployment and low wages among lower civil servants, clerical workers, and industry employees, it was probably women secondary-school graduates seeking these jobs, rather than women university graduates seeking entry into the professions, who faced the greater difficulties. World War II helped break down the barriers. The presence of the Allied armies created employment; they employed two hundred thousand Egyptians, including eighty thousand male clerks and over four thousand women. The presence of foreign working women and the visible and vital volunteer work being done by Egyptian upper- and middle-class women in the medical and social services, in war relief, and in disaster relief, coping with the cholera and malaria epidemics that struck Egypt in the 1940s, helped make work socially acceptable.[6]

Women also worked in the cigarette, textile, and pharmaceutical industries that developed in the 1920s and 1930s. Industries remained small, employing, by 1947, about one million men, women making up about 3 percent of the work force. Most women workers were in agriculture; their next-largest category of employment was service, including domestic service.[7]

The period was one of mounting social unrest, generated by a large body of educated intellectuals with frustrated expectations to whom the system offered no hope of advancement, population pressure, and the escalating rural migration to urban areas, partly in response to the development of industries. From 1917 to 1937 the population of Cairo increased by 66 percent, rising from 791,000 to 1,312,000, and that of Alexandria by 55 percent, from 445,000 to 686,000. Egypt, by now thoroughly integrated into the world economy and dependent on exporting its agricultural products, was affected by the Great Depression of 1929 and underwent the same economic fluctuations as other national economies. The decline in agricultural exports helped stimulate the development of local industries, as did a growing sense among the elite that industrialization was essential for modernization and progress. Local capital began to be invested in industry, and the government, under pressure from nationalist leaders, negotiated a tariff reform that provided some protection for infant industries. Industrial growth itself, by drawing in workers, encouraging migration, and fostering uprootedness, also contributed to the unrest. Urban migration accelerated even faster as a result of the war and the presence of Allied armies. The population of the cities increased from 2,249,000 in 1937 to 3,416,000 in 1947. Causing even more political unrest was the army of unemployed—250,000 strong—created by the ending of the war and the withdrawal of the Allied armies.[8]

On the political level these decades were characterized by the decreasing effectiveness of the party in power, the Wafd; it lost control over events and steadily lost its appeal to the masses. There was a concomitant rise of popular nationalist groups with strong anti-British and anti-Western tendencies, which eventually came to challenge the established groups, including the Wafd. From its election in 1923 on, the Wafd was involved in a continual battle for power with the king, Fuad I. Representing itself as the champion of the Constitution, parliamentary government, and civil liberties against a monarch who wished to usurp popular power, the Wafd was able at first to mobilize mass sympathy. By 1935 the Wafd was riven by internal divisions, which led to the formation of splinter parties. Its negotiation of the Anglo-Egyptian treaty upon its return to power in 1936, a treaty that made provision for the continued posting of British troops in the Suez Canal zone, further alienated the most vehemently anti-British and nationalist elements and lost the party its monopoly of the leadership of the nationalist cause.

Meanwhile, other political groups sprang up, including a small Communist party. Two in particular gained in power and importance, the Young Egypt and the Muslim Brethren. Young Egypt, founded in 1933, was a fascist group, which preached the glory of the Egyptian past and an imperialist Egyptian future. It emphasized the importance of religion and morality and of imbuing youth with a martial spirit. Like the fascist European movements, it also gave importance to women as the mothers of heroes, stressing therefore the importance of educating women that they might rise to this glorious task.[9] It developed a paramilitary youth organization, the Green Shirts, and was vehemently anti-British and anti-Western.

Of far greater moment and future influence, however, were the Muslim Brethren (Al-ikhwan al-muslimun). Like Young Egypt, the Muslim Brethren, started by Hasan al-Banna (1906–49) in 1928, were fiercely anti-British and anti-Western. Al-Banna—whose father, an imam and a teacher in a mosque, had studied at al-Azhar in the days of Muhammad ʿAbdu, whom he had much admired—founded the society shortly after he was posted, upon graduating, to teach in Ismailia, a town on the Suez Canal. He had already helped establish the Young Men's Muslim Association in Cairo. Al-Banna was appalled to see the contrast between the luxurious villas of the foreigners and the "miserable" homes of the Egyptians; even street signs were in "the language of economic domination."[10] The first members of his new organization were six men who worked on the British camp; they expressed themselves "weary of this life of humiliation and restriction. . . . We see that the Arabs and the Muslims have no status . . . and no dignity. . . . They are not more than mere hirelings belonging to foreigners" (8).

The organization grew rapidly, with al-Banna establishing himself as the Supreme Guide, who would lead people back to a purified Islam, which would inform every aspect of personal and national life, and free the nation from Western domination. The Brethren were opposed to the government and to political parties, which they saw as importations of Western ideologies and as tools of British domination. The parties were monopolized by the upper classes, who were participants in and beneficiaries of foreign economic domination. Anger at Western domination and determination to attain independence from it were central to the movement.

The views of the Brethren clearly stemmed from the ideas of al-Afghani and 'Abdu. Like those nationalists of the previous century, the Brethren preached the defense of the faith through moral purification and internal reform, as well as through resistance to and rejection of external encroachment; indeed, internal reform and rearmament were necessary to the successful rejection of external, Western encroachment. Education was consequently an important part of their program, as it had been for 'Abdu, and they were active in establishing schools. But they were far more fiercely anti-Western than 'Abdu was, and far more rigid in their adherence to the legalistic tradition of Islam; even within Islamic positions they were intolerant of intellectual diversity.

Through the 1940s bitterness over the Palestinian issue spurred anti-Western feeling and enhanced the appeal of societies like the Brethren and Young Egypt, the pan-Islamic, fervently pro-Palestinian stand of the Brethren further helping it to gain adherents. For the Brethren, the developing situation in Palestine represented a Western imperialist and Zionist crusade against Arab and Islamic peoples, one the West had never ceased to wage; they confirmed their view by quoting what General Allenby said when he entered Jerusalem during World War I: "Only now have the Crusades come to an end" (230).

The membership of the society has been variously estimated; the society claimed a membership of two million at its peak in 1949, while its opponents set the figure at about two hundred thousand.[11] The size of the membership cannot be accurately known, for membership was often secret. Whatever their number, by the early 1940s the society constituted a force to be reckoned with. Through the 1940s its paramilitary organization increasingly resorted to tactics of violence against the authorities. The urban lower-middle and working classes and the rural working class were impressed by the activism of the Brethren in establishing schools and setting up mosques and cottage industries, among other projects, while the dispossessed found hope in its promise to end foreign exploitation and inaugurate a prosperous future in a just society. Its organization and the bonding between Brethren created a comforting sense of connectedness and community in a time of change.[12] Although its mass following was largely lower class, its leaders were for the most part members of the emergent urban middle classes, for whom foreign economic control and the internal allies of the West—the ruling classes and the Western resident minorities—represented limits to their personal advancement.

The message of the society was enormously attractive to men, but it was not similarly attractive to women. Although women were drawn into its activities as wives or relatives of Brethren, the active membership of the branch organization, the Society of Muslim Sisters, was small—about five thousand at its peak in 1948–49—notwithstanding al-Banna's early emphasis on the important role of women in the Islamic reformation and his attempt to promote membership among women by establishing an Institute for Mothers in 1933. Recruitment among male students was high, but this was distinctly not the case with women, the number of adherents among university women remaining "negligible." The Brethren were aware that "the Islamic feminist movement" had not succeeded in attracting "the educated type," who saw the movement as a "return to the harim," rather than, as the Brethren represented it, the path to "true female emancipation" (175).

Women who joined the branch organization, Muslim Sisters (Al-akhawat al-muslimat), wore a head covering, but the position on women taken by the Muslim Brethren in fact bore traces of 'Abdu's modernism. On polygamy, for example, they took a position close to 'Abdu's, arguing that to treat all wives precisely equally, as the Quran stipulated, was exceedingly difficult, hence the problems that polygamy engendered led to violations of other directives in the Quran associating marriage with love, kindness, and mercy. Similarly they held that divorce was, as a hadith declared, "the most hateful to God of the lawful things"; people abused the practice because they had fallen away from true Islam. The answer was not "to abolish what is permitted" but to return to the fundamentals of Islam (258–59).

The Muslim Brethren rejected Western women as a model for Muslim women, setting forth a critique that Muslims still make today. It maintained that the West used women and female sexuality to increase profits; advertisements with a beautiful secretary, model, or saleswoman exploited women in the service of capitalism (257). Even if Western women were not to be emulated, their educational attainments were. The Brethren stressed that education was as essential to women as to men, chiefly that they might fulfill their roles as wives and mothers, though this need not be their sole objective. The society took the view that Islam forbade women no subject of study: a woman might be "a merchant, a doctor or a lawyer" or anything else that brought licit gain, as long as she was rigorously decorous in behavior and dress. Though permitted, a profession, or even an education, was not necessarily the most desirable goal for a woman, whose real job was the home and family. Hasan Ismail Hudaybi, who succeeded al-Banna as leader of the Brethren, summed up their position on women:

> The woman's natural place is in the home, but if she finds that after doing her duty in the home she has time, she can use part of it in the service of society, on condition that this is done within the legal limits which preserve her dignity and morality. I remember I left my daughters freedom to choose the kind of education which fitted them. The elder entered the faculty of medicine, is now a doctor and practices professionally. The second is a graduate of the faculty of science and is now a teacher in the faculty. Both are married and I hope that they have found harmony between their homes and jobs. (258)

Hudaybi, who was of working-class background, became a lawyer and a judge before becoming the leader of the society. He was thus typical of the emergent middle-class leadership that ran the society, just as his views on the subject of women were typical of theirs. Evidently, fervent religious or religiopolitical commitment did not entail a negative attitude toward women's employment, let alone toward their education, nor apparently did the threat of women's displacing men in the work force shape fundamental attitudes on the subject. Rather, the virtues of gainful employment and a second income, of further consolidating middle-class status, seem to have been the main determinants.

Developments among political women, feminist and nonfeminist, paralleled and meshed with the broad sweep of national political developments. Women participated formally and informally in a wide range of political activities during these middle decades—as radical conservatives espousing Islam as both a nationalist and a feminist cause, as nationalists pursuing women's rights and nationalist issues, and as left-wing intellectuals and communists. A variety of approaches to the issue of women's rights also emerged, including the position among Islamist activists that feminism was only relevant to Western women and that the pursuit of female affirmation for Muslim women should come in other terms. So far, however, the activities and perspectives of these women are mostly unchronicled. The work of interviewing people, combing newspapers and magazines, and searching for unpublished materials to reconstruct these activities has only just begun.

Brief published excerpts from research currently in progress offer tantalizing glimpses of the extraordinary vitality of the period. Interviews with left-wing women whose activism took shape in the 1940s, for example, suggest the intellectual and political adventurousness of university women, their passion and idealism, and their practical, physical involvement in the sociopolitical life of the age. Inji Efflatoun (1924–87), later a distinguished artist, political activist, eloquent feminist, was the delegate of the League of Women Students and Graduates of Egypt, the communist women's organization, to the World Congress of Women held in Paris in 1945. She vividly conveys her exhilaration:

> I was chosen to lead the Egyptian delegation. I was very excited; I saw many brave and famous women. The Soviet delegation, I remember, came in their military uniforms with their medals shining; they had just come from the war. All of what we saw left a great impression. I made a very powerful speech in which I linked the oppression of women in Egypt to the British occupation and imperialism. I not only denounced the British, but the King and the politicians as well. It was a very political speech in which I called for national liberation and the liberation of women. My ideas were applauded.[13]

Latifa al-Zayat, later a distinguished novelist, was a student activist at Fuad University. According to a British Embassy report, communism was "spreading fast" at the university, and "female students in the Faculty of Arts were particularly inclined towards communism."[14] Known for her dynamism and eloquence, al-Zayat addressed audiences with men, not just women, in them. She ran for and was elected to office in the student communist organization, only to be harassed for her activities by "Muslim fundamentalists." They accused all communists of immorality and specifically "tried to defame my reputation—they called me a prostitute and other such things." Although she went home and wept, she steeled herself with the thought that her work was "public work" in which she must persist. Soraya Adham, another communist active in the 1940s, was searched and later arrested and imprisoned for ten months for her political activities.[15]

Two women who focused their energies on women's issues emerged as compelling figures in these middle decades in quite different ways: Zeinab al-Ghazali campaigned for women and the nation in Islamist terms, and Doria Shafik campaigned for women's rights and human rights in the language of secularism and democracy. The divergence in their perspectives repeats the divergence incipient in feminism at the turn of the century and articulates a persistent and ever-widening bifurcation within Egyptian and Arab "feminist" discourse—feminist in that it affirms women and women's subjectivity. A variety of social forces and personal circumstances always play a part in shaping particular paths taken. The following brief review of the politics and lives of these two women therefore constitutes merely a preliminary exploration of the factors shaping the differences between them and is perhaps suggestive also of the differences underlying the two primary and contrasting channels through which women have affirmed themselves and their subjectivity in the twentieth century in the Egyptian, and Arab, context. As this century draws to its close, the idiom developed by al-Ghazali, the Islamist founder of the Muslim Women's Association, is unexpectedly proving to have the greater resonance for those now shaping mainstream Egyptian culture, and the feminism of Doria Shafik, like that of Sha'rawi, Amina al-Sa'id, and others, secularist and westernizing, the indisputably dominant voice of Arab feminism for most of this century, appears to be now becoming the marginal, alternative voice.

Al-Ghazali (b. 1918) started her political life working for Huda Sha'rawi and what al-Ghazali (in an interview given in 1981) termed her "women's movement, which calls for the liberation of women."[16] She quickly found herself in disagreement with its aims and resigned to found, at the age of eighteen, her own organization, the Muslim Women's Association. The association helped women study Islam and carried out welfare activities, maintaining an orphanage, assisting poor families, and helping unemployed men and women to find useful employment. Within six months of its founding, Hasan al-Banna tried to persuade al-Ghazali to incorporate the association into his Muslim Brethren movement. He met with her after she delivered a lecture at the Brethren headquarters and exerted considerable pressure on her to make this move. In recounting how she and the association members refused, although they offered full cooperation in every other way, al-Ghazali refers to al-Banna's persistence in the matter and to his "anger" at their refusal.[17] By the time she wrote of these events in *Ayam min hayati* (Days of my life), the Muslim Brethren had been subjected to intense persecution, al-Banna had been murdered (in 1949), and she herself had been imprisoned and tortured for six years (1965–72) at the hands of the Nasser regime for her support of the Brethren cause.

Even after making an oath of allegiance to al-Banna when his brotherhood was undergoing its trials, al-Ghazali, and her association, remained independent. When the government ordered the Muslim Women's Association to dissolve in the late 1940s, in conjunction with its measures against the Brethren, al-Ghazali contested the order in court and won. By this time she was a figure to be reckoned with. She acted as an intermediary between al-Banna and her friend Mustapha al-Nahhas, leader of the Wafd, and through the 1950s and early 1960s she consulted with the senior leaders in the society, joining with them in devising its future program. The Muslim Women's Association continued to function until her imprisonment in 1965, when it was dissolved. It appears not to have been reconstituted, though al-Ghazali continues to lecture and work for the Islamic cause.

As al-Ghazali recalled it to her interviewer forty-five years later, she broke away from Sha'rawi's association to found her own because she believed Sha'rawi's approach to be a "mistake." She thought it was "a grave error to speak of the liberation of women" in an Islamic society. She believed that Islam provided women with "everything—freedom, economic rights, political rights, social rights, public and private rights," though these rights were unfortunately not manifest in Islamic societies. The goal of the association was "to acquaint the Muslim woman with her religion so she would be convinced by means of study that the women's liberation movement is a deviant innovation that occurred because of the backwardness of Muslims. . . . We consider Muslims to be backward; they must remove this backwardness from their shoulders and rise up as their religion commands" (235).

Besides helping women study Islam and carrying out benevolent activities, the association also took a political stand: "Egypt must be ruled by the Koran, not positivistic constitutions." The way to bring about a society in which women had freedom and human rights was also the way to revive the Islamic nation, which "possesses one third of the world" and which geographically speaking is "richer than the rest of the world": "Why are we backward? Because we are not following our religion, we are not living in accordance with our constitution and laws. If we return to our Koran and to the Sunna of our Prophet, we will live Islam in reality, and we will control the whole world" (235–36).

Al-Ghazali did not spell out how these comprehensive rights would be restored to women or whether a new Islamic law would be drafted to ensure them—for surely they are not provided for in shari'a law as commonly applied. There is, moreover, an implicit or potential contradiction between her declaration on the provision of these rights and other statements she has made on the role of women in Islamic societies. Her definition of their role essentially coincides with that expressed by the reformist wing of Brethren thought: although a woman's primary role is in the family, she is also entitled to a professional life and to full participation in political life. Al-Ghazali said:

Women [are] . . . a fundamental part of the Islamic call. . . . They are the ones who build the kind of men that we need to fill the ranks of the Islamic call. So women must be well educated, cultured, knowing of the precepts of the Koran and Sunna, informed about world politics, why we are backward, why we don't have technology. The Muslim woman must study all these things, and then raise her son in the conviction that he must possess the scientific tools of the age, and at the same time he must understand Islam, politics, geography, and current events. He must rebuild the Islamic nation. We Muslims only carry arms in order to spread peace. We want to purify the world of unbelief, atheism, oppression, and persecution. . . . Islam does not forbid women to actively participate in public life. It does not prevent her from working, entering into politics, and expressing her opinion, or from being anything, as long as that does not interfere with her first duty as a mother, the one who first trains her children in the Islamic call. So her first, holy, and most important mission is to be a mother and wife. She cannot ignore this priority. If she then finds she has free time, she may participate in public activities. Islam does not forbid her. (236–37)

What is unclear here is who is to see to it that women fulfill their first, holy, and most important mission. There is at least a potential contradiction between this view and her statements to the effect that Islam provides women with freedom and comprehensive rights. Al-Ghazali does not indicate whether she envisages that women themselves will have the autonomy and authority to decide whether or not they intend to fulfill their "first, holy, and most important mission" or whether she accepts the common notion of male-defined Islam that men are in authority over women and have the right of decision in such matters. Given the high regard in which she is held by the Brethren and by many eminent patriarchal leaders of the Arab world, including Prince ʿAbdullah Feisal of Saudi Arabia, who visited her in Egypt, it is doubtful that she challenges the idea of male authority and control. These statements, with their grand and idealistic vagueness, imply contradictory perspectives, and nowhere is that contradiction addressed.

The contradiction in al-Ghazali's position on women is not confined to words. Al-Ghazali's own life seems, on the one hand, to flagrantly undercut her statements on the role of women in Islamic society and, on the other hand, to demonstrate that all rights are available to the woman who knows her Islam even within the area legally of greatest peril for women, the laws governing marriage. Thus al-Ghazali entered into two marriages, she informed her interviewer, on terms that she set and that gave her control over the continuance of the marriage. She divorced her first husband because her marriage "took up all my time and kept me from my mission" (as Islamic activist, not as wife and mother) and because her husband "did not agree with my work." She had stipulated before marrying him that her mission came first and that they would separate if there was any major disagreement between them. Besides illustrating that al-Ghazali is correct in that women do have the right (in some schools of Muslim law) to stipulate conditions that are legally binding in their marriage contracts, these remarks about her marriage also indicate that apparently it is permissible for women, or, in any case, it was for her, to place their work before their obligations to raise a family and to devote themselves to their husband. The terms of her second marriage were similar to those of her first; indeed, her second husband not only agreed in writing that he would not come between her and her mission but also, in a complete reversal of conventional roles, agreed too that "he would help me and be my assistant" (237).

Al-Ghazali's autobiographical account spells out no less unambiguously than her statements to her interviewer how her calling took precedence over marriage. She writes that she made clear to her husband that

> if your personal or economic interests should conflict with my Islamic work and I find that my married life has become an obstacle to my fulfilling my mission and the establishment of an Islamic state, we would part. . . .
>
> I had decided to cancel the matter of marriage from my life, in order to devote myself completely to the mission. . . . I do not have the right to ask you today to join me in this effort, but it is my right to stipulate that you do not prevent me from continuing in my struggle in the path of God . . . the struggle to which [I] have devoted [myself] from the age of eighteen.[18]

Apparently al-Ghazali was raised with the expectation that she would be an Islamic leader. Her father in particular nurtured this ambition in her. A graduate of al-Azhar, he was a large-scale cotton merchant, who devoted his time, outside the cotton season, to touring the country and preaching in mosques on Fridays. He schooled her in the Islamic cultural heritage and told her that with God's help she would be a leader—not in the style of Huda Sha'rawi, she reports him saying, but in the tradition of the women leaders of Muhammad's time.

Al-Ghazali's account of herself shows her collaborating more and more closely with the leaders of the Brethren, Abdel Fattah Ismael, Hudaybi, and Sayyed Qutb. She met frequently with Ismael to study how "to restore this nation to its glory and its creed." She describes how they decided to promote their cause with pamphlets, study groups, and lectures for thirteen years ("the duration of the call in Mecca"), and then, after these years of "Islamic education for young men and old, and for women and girls," they would conduct a survey. If they found that "the harvest" of those believing in Islam as both "religion and state" was 75 percent, then they would call for the establishment of an Islamic state. If the harvest was less, they would renew their teaching for another thirteen years. It was unimportant if generations came and went; what was important was to continue working to the last and to pass on the banner of Islam to the next generation.[19]

As the testament of a religious revolutionary, al-Ghazali's account is striking in a number of ways. First, it is remarkable that a spiritual commitment to Islam seems to be absent. Islam figures as a path to empowerment, to glory, to a properly regulated society—but not as a spiritual path. Similarly, the qualities of a reflective consciousness, of an acuity of moral perception, which might be expected in someone with a religious mission, again seem to be absent. In justice to her, she does write of "good nights and unforgettable days, holy moments with God." These words occur in the context of group readings, when people met together to read verses of the Quran and review their meanings and implications. Those were days, al-Ghazali writes, "which were sweet and good, a blessing from God surrounding us as we studied and studied, educating ourselves and preparing men and youth . . . for the cause."[20] But again the cause and the exhilaration of working together in a common cause seem to be what the words are celebrating.

Al-Ghazali's account is striking in the second place for the openness with which it links the need to restore Islam with the need to restore a nation suffering from the humiliations of imperialism and for the openness with which it preaches that Islam is the path to power and glory. The call to Islam is not made to call souls to God or proclaim a fundamental truth but to restore to power and give "control [of] the whole world" to the nation of Islam.

Finally, her account is remarkable for the apparent naïveté and bland innocence with which she announces an agenda of intolerance, exemplified in her statement "We Muslims only carry arms in order to spread peace. We want to purify the world of unbelief, atheism, oppression, and persecution" (236). Surely even Muslims, let alone people of other faiths or none, have reason to fear such a statement, for perhaps their Islam will not precisely fit the desired mold. Al-Ghazali seems either unaware or unconcerned that some of the worst brutalities in history have been committed in the name of purifying society.

Al-Ghazali's contemporary Doria Shafik (1914–76) was in many ways her exact opposite. Where al-Ghazali's home environment nurtured in her a powerful sense of the rich resources, the repleteness, of the Islamic heritage, Shafik's underscored the superiority of the West and, at least by implication, the inferiority of the native. Shafik attended a kindergarten run by Italian nuns and at the age of eight was sent away from home to live with her grandmother in Tanta, so that she could attend the French mission school there—which her mother had attended—rather than the local Arabic school. Shafik's mother's family was, according to the daughter, "an old upper-bourgeois Egyptian family which had lost most of its fortune"; her father, of "a less well-known family," was a government employee.[21] On graduating, with brilliant distinction, Shafik was set on attending the Sorbonne, though by this time—1930—women had just begun attending the university in Egypt. Her father, who could not afford to send her, encouraged her to pursue her idea of presenting her case to Sha'rawi. Sha'rawi responded with an invitation to meet and informed her that she would arrange a scholarship for her.

Shafik's account of the interview reveals how her desire was focused not merely on continuing her education but on studying abroad—in the West— and it reveals how her adulation of the West was charged with an emotional intensity. Sha'rawi welcomed her with "such charm and simplicity" that Shafik, who had lost her mother when she was eleven, at once felt in her "a warmth that resembled that of a mother . . . a mother who would take my hand and guide me towards my future." Her account of the scene continues: "She saw how moved I was and did everything to make me feel at ease. . . . 'I am happy to see you are so smart,' she said; 'I am pleased that a girl of your standard will represent Egypt abroad.' 'Then you think my departure is possible?' I asked. 'Why not? Tomorrow someone will speak about you to the Minister of Education.' She saw so much emotion and gratitude on my face that she asked me: 'Why this ardent desire to study abroad?' . . . I was near to tears. She noticed it and without waiting for the answer, quickly changed the subject" (18).

Shafik did go abroad for her studies and returned with a doctorate from the Sorbonne in 1940. She taught briefly at the Alexandria College for Girls and at the Sannia School, then was a French-language inspector for the

Ministry of Education, after which she left this job for journalism. She founded three women's magazines, including one with Dr. Ibrahim ʿAbdu, the feminist journal *Bint al-Nil* (Daughter of the Nile), which appeared continuously from 1945 to 1957, when it was closed down by Nasser, who also placed Shafik under house arrest. The editorials that Shafik wrote were, to begin with, hesitant in their demands for equality for women; she was aware that such demands might endanger women's right to male economic support and that addressing them would entail finally resolving the question of who was responsible for the home (20–21). By 1948, however, her resolve was firm, and she founded the Bint al-Nil Union with the object of obtaining "full political rights for women" (22). She immediately affiliated the new organization with the International Council of Women, under the name the National Council for Egyptian Women, and was thereupon elected to the executive committee of the parent group. Because there were numerous women's organizations in Egypt by this point, others resented and contested Shafik's thrusting herself and her organization forward as representing all women's organizations, and the issue was publicly aired in the press of the day (30).

The Bint al-Nil Union took its first militant action in 1951, when Shafik led a thousand women in a demonstration at the Egyptian parliament, disrupting its session for three hours. They only dispersed when the presidents of both chambers promised to support their feminist demands. The action provoked outrage among the Islamic conservatives. The head of the Union of Muslim Associations in Egypt (which included the Muslim Brethren) sent a cable of protest to the king, demanding that he abolish women's organizations that called for participation in politics, that he force women to return to their homes, and that he enforce the use of the veil (23).

Shafik's union even had its own paramilitary unit of two hundred women who had received military training. In 1952, in the series of strikes and demonstrations that began on January 16, when students and others made clear their opposition to the government, to the king, and to the British, the paramilitary unit also joined in the action, surrounding Barclay's Bank and preventing employees and others from entering. Not long before, Shafik had heard a lecture on women in India emphasizing that women's liberation accompanied and followed from their struggle for national liberation, and thought the gesture against British domination would generate popular support. The British responded to the general disturbances, which included students' openly displaying arms and using them against the police, by deciding to occupy Cairo. When the British ordered the police to surrender their weapons, they refused, so the British destroyed the police compound and decimated its Egyptian defenders—over fifty police were killed and many more wounded. The next day, January 26, the mobs burned Cairo.

The government introduced martial law and scrambled to regain control. The king appointed al-Nahhas military governor-general of the country, then abruptly dismissed him. Another strong man of politics, ʿAli Maher, formed an independence government, which resigned on March 1. Parliament was dissolved and elections postponed indefinitely. It is in the context of this general instability that a military coup, on July 23, 1952, terminated the monarchy, exiled King Farouk, and brought Nasser to power.

The Free Officers, who had carried out the revolution, did not have a clear ideological or political agenda upon taking power but developed it as they consolidated their control. Their first declared objective was the expulsion of the British, and they immediately began negotiations for the evacuation of the canal zone. Domestically, the direction of their policy was suggested by the introduction, in 1952, of the agrarian reform laws limiting individual ownership of land to two hundred fedans. To eliminate possible opposition from the Brethren and the Wafd, all political parties were dissolved and banned in 1953. The monarchy was abolished, and Egypt was declared a republic. In 1954 an agreement was signed with Britain arranging British withdrawal from the Suez Canal but allowing Britain to use it as a base in case of war. In October, when Nasser was making a speech about the agreement, a Muslim Brother attempted to assassinate him—the Muslim Brethren had criticized him continually. The leaders were arrested, six were executed, and thousands were thrown into prison. In 1956 a new Constitution was promulgated; it replaced the parliamentary system with a presidential republican system. It defined Egypt as a democratic republic and—a novel elément—as an Arab state forming an integral part of the Arab nation and committed to socialist economic and social policies.[22] In 1956, too, in response to the abrupt withdrawal of a British and American loan for financing the High Dam project, Nasser nationalized the Suez Canal. The response to this was the Tripartite Aggression: the British, French, and Israeli invasion of Egypt. An international outcry—including a U.S. denunciation of the action, in terms suggesting that the Western powers were acting in a colonialist fashion, and a Russian threat to use force—ended the aggression. For the Arab world, and the larger third world, Nasser emerged from these events as a symbol of the struggle against Western domination.

Shafik continued her campaign for women's political rights during these events. In March 1954 a constitutional assembly was formed to adopt or reject a proposed new constitution, an assembly that included no women. Shafik felt that excluding them threatened them: "Lacking women, the Assembly might adopt a constitution in which women's rights were not guaranteed. . . . I decided to play the last card. I decided to go on a hunger strike to death for 'women's full political rights'" (25). She proceeded with her hunger strike, taking care to ensure that it would receive wide attention. She sent cables to the major leaders in Egypt and to Egyptian and foreign press agencies, stating that her objective was full political rights for women and declaring, "I protest against the formation of a Constitutional Assembly without women's representation. I will never agree to be ruled by a constitution in the preparation of which I had no say." She was joined in her strike by fourteen other women in Cairo and by members of the Bint al-Nil Union in Alexandria. The governor of Cairo was dispatched to inform her that the new Egyptian constitution would guarantee full political rights for women. Shafik asked him to put this in writing. He replied, "But Madame Shafik, I cannot ask the government to put this in writing. It is impossible." She then asked him to put in writing what he had been sent to announce. The governor agreed, and the strike ended. Shafik was gratified by this outcome and by the comment her action had drawn in the international press. She wrote the following month in *Bint al-Nil* that the press perceived the action "with what it implied of meanings greater and more profound even than the rights of women . . . the strength of the democratic trend and the rooting of a new popular consciousness in Egypt . . . the consciousness that could tolerate no longer to be patient about rule with no parliament, no constitution, no freedom" (26).

The 1956 Constitution granted women the vote, yet it limited the right to vote to women who asked for it, a condition that was not applied to men. Shafik filed a legal protest, declaring that the Bint al-Nil Union refused to accept a "fragment" of political rights. In 1957 she made a further, dramatic protest. She announced to President Nasser and the Egyptian and foreign press that she was going on a hunger strike to the death to protest "against the infringement of my human freedom on two fronts—the external and the internal: (1) the Israeli occupation of Egyptian land [Israel took its time about withdrawing from the Sinai after the Tripartite Aggression] and (2) the onset of dictatorship that is leading Egypt into bankruptcy and chaos," and to carry out her threat, she went to the Indian Embassy. This was Shafik's last public stand. Her associates at Bint al-Nil forced her to resign and, along with all other women's associations in Egypt, publicly denounced her as a traitor. Nasser placed her under house arrest and closed down the Bint al-Nil Union and journal (27). Shafik continued to write but underwent several mental breakdowns, which culminated in her suicide in 1976.

Shafik's gestures seem overdramatic and disproportionate, and her arrogant and contemptuous attitude toward Nasser is astonishing in its miscalculation and misreading of the political realities of her society. Nasser, abhorred in the West and especially in Britain, where he was regarded as an upstart dictator, was a national hero at home, and in protesting his dictatorship, Shafik was playing to the wrong—Western—gallery. In Egypt, where he was a hero, it was political suicide not to at least pay lip service to that dogma. Many of Shafik's political gestures, and the last most particularly, seemed to have been conceived and enacted with a Western audience in mind. Her immediate denunciation by her associates reflects the repressive atmosphere created by the regime, her associates presumably deeming it necessary for their own political survival to instantly denounce her as a traitor. Yet perhaps there was more at stake than immediate political survival, for denouncing her was in effect to collaborate with the regime in silencing radical criticism. Whether Shafik's gestures and criticisms were politically astute or not, they drew attention to genuine transgressions on the part of a regime growing more brutally repressive toward its critics every day; the society would doubtless have been healthier and state abuses perhaps somewhat curbed had there been many more Doria Shafiks.

Shafik and al-Ghazali are contrasting figures in some obvious ways. Al-Ghazali was tenaciously committed to indigenous culture and to pursuing feminism—or, at any rate, female subjectivity—in indigenous terms, and Shafik consistently exemplified, in her pursuit of education and Western-style feminist goals and in her public actions, a sense of the superiority of the West. The two appear also to have had contrastingly constituted personalities, in ways perhaps not unrelated to the different attitudes toward indigenous culture that imbued their childhood. Whereas al-Ghazali's life bespeaks a powerful self-confidence, an ability to rise to each new situation and negotiate it with astuteness to further her purpose, to always function with assurance, surviving imprisonment and torture and emerging the more determined, Shafik's life in almost every sense exemplifies the opposite. Shafik's postures vacillated between arrogance and timidity. In spite of her undeniable brilliance, she was singularly inept at accurately gauging the political and social realities of her world and seems often to have been at odds with that world. In the end she apparently underwent personal disintegration when faced with the tribulations that the Nasser regime inflicted on her. Shafik was, to be sure, an inwardly reflective individual, an intellectual, and a writer, with several books of poetry and prose (published in France) to her credit. The differences between the two women pointed to here are noted, not to diminish the fragile, reflective, and anguished consciousness in favor of the self-assured and determined, but rather to perhaps represent contrasting models of the possible psychological consequences of colonization and the ways in which these intertwined with and affected the feminist vision that a woman embraced and articulated. Al-Ghazali's conviction of the superiority of her culture, a conviction vigorously nurtured in childhood, is replicated psychologically as an unshakable sense of her own worth and a firm inner solidity—and a determination to find feminism within Islam. It stands in contradistinction to the adulation of the West and the disparagement of the native, implied or explicit, that formed Shafik's background and informed her childhood and was perhaps replicated psychologically as an internalized self-hatred and self-rejection (of the native in herself) and as a divided, disintegrative sense of self, with the inevitable agonies that must follow from a consciousness divided against itself.

It should not be concluded, however, that biculturalism in a colonized subject necessarily entails the internalization of a sense of the superiority of the colonizer's culture or that it necessarily results in an unstable, divided sense of self. Nor should it be concluded that the combination of feminism with biculturalism entails the internalization of a sense of colonial superiority or results in a precarious sense of self. Neither appears to have formed elements in Inji Efflatoun's life: she was bicultural, and she, too, was subjected to hardships by the regime—in her case, for her communist activities. She continued to paint during her imprisonment (1959–63), taking her fellow prisoners for her subject and creating a powerful record of women in prison.

THE

Chapter 11   STRUGGLE
ℒ

FOR THE FUTURE

IN THE SECOND HALF OF THE TWENTIETH CENTURY
the roles of Egyptian women underwent massive expansion and transformation. Women entered all arenas
of white-collar and professional work, including aeronautics, engineering, big business, and politics—even
becoming members of parliament. The only positions
they have not occupied are judge and head of state. The
nature and variety of their participation in the economy, in political life, and in the visible, dominant culture are now enormously complex. That participation,
plus their numbers in the work force and the economic
necessity that most middle-class families find their income to be, along with the man's, complicates, alters,
and informs the discourse on women. The complexity
arising from the changed social reality within the borders of the country is augmented by further dimensions
of complexity arising from realities beyond the national borders—for example, Egypt's relationship to
the West and the increased importance of regional and
transregional forces. All of these affect the local situation in a variety of ways. The wealth of the oil states
since the 1960s, for instance, has meant job opportunities for women as well as men, and perhaps it has

208

also meant the greater influence of Islam as a social idiom, another matter with an important impact on women. Similarly, the Iranian revolution and the spread of Islam as a political idiom in the Middle East and further afield, as in Pakistan, has potential implications for the situation in Egypt (and, indeed, in other Arab and Muslim countries). All these elements play a part in shaping today's discourses, in the Arab world generally and in Egypt. Only a full-length study focusing exclusively on these decades could adequately represent the complexity of the current reality and its discourses. Here I explore some major trends.

The 1952 revolution in Egypt inaugurated a new age for women by virtue of both its commitment to social egalitarianism and its proclaimed position on women. The first portent of the new socially egalitarian direction the government would take came with the Land Reform Law, issued in September 1952, limiting land ownership to two hundred fedans per person. The chief object of the law was to break the power of the landowners, two thousand of whom had owned 20 percent of the agricultural land before the revolution; at the same time, the further stipulations of the law that the surplus land was to be distributed among landless and small peasants also announced the intention of the government to pursue a policy of egalitarianism. After 1956, when the government had consolidated itself, it embraced "Arab Socialism" and embarked on a series of measures indicating its commitment to social and economic egalitarianism and to economic reform under state control, such as nationalization of foreign business interests and all big businesses in the industrial sector of the economy, rent control, minimum wage laws, and the introduction of social services. These measures eventually altered the class structure in Egypt in fundamental ways, in effect dissipating the old elite and drawing a new and broader segment of the population into the middle classes.

This transformation was as important for women as it was for men. The state proclaimed itself committed to opening the doors of opportunity to all its citizens, actively defined to include women. The National Charter, drafted and approved by the National Congress in 1962 (a charter reorganizing the political and constitutional life of the country), proclaimed that women and men should be considered equal working partners. The goals of socialism and social freedom could not be realized except "through an equal opportunity for every citizen to obtain a fair share of the national wealth"; and all citizens had the right and the obligation to work, women as well as men. "Woman must be regarded as equal to man and must, therefore, shed the remaining shackles that impede her free movement, so that she might take a constructive and profound part in the shaping of life."[1] Already, in 1956, the state had granted women the vote and the right to run for political office. By 1957 two women had been elected to the national assembly, and by 1962 a woman, Dr. Hikmat Abu Zaid, had been appointed minister of social affairs by Nasser.

Educational policy and the government's forcefully egalitarian actions in that arena were undoubtedly of enormous importance in bringing about change and expansion in women's roles. The first steps were a governmental decree in 1952 making primary education free and compulsory for all between the ages of six and twelve and the policy of coeducation at the primary level, which was thenceforth followed.[2] In the following years education was declared free at all levels, including the university level. Entry into coeducational departments at the universities was competitive, based on grades and regardless of sex. The state provided financial assistance to those in need, as well as to outstanding students in recognition of their excellence. It also virtually guaranteed employment to university graduates, adding a further incentive to the pursuit of a degree.

Additional incentives were scarcely needed. The demand for education for both girls and boys, women and men, particularly in urban areas, was immense. The supply could not meet the demand. Facilities and teachers served more than one daily shift, and the student-teacher ratio was stretched to the utmost.[3] As a result, whereas in 1952 only 45 percent of primary-school-age children attended school, by 1960 the figure had risen to 65 percent, and by 1967, to 80 percent. Thereafter, enrollment for both sexes dropped slightly, probably reflecting the congestion in the educational system and the increase of state spending on arms after the 1967 defeat by Israel. Female enrollment continued to rise faster than male enrollment, however, and the gap between the two rates gradually decreased, stabilizing by the 1970s at all levels to about two males to one female.[4]

The most dramatic increase in women's participation in education occurred in higher education—at universities and other institutes of higher education. Women's enrollment rose rapidly and at a much faster pace than men's. The ratio of males to females, which had stood at 13.2 to 1 in 1953–54, was 1.8 to 1 in 1976. In 1953–54 there were 6,121 women attending universities and institutes of higher education, and by 1962 this figure had risen to 19,762. By 1980 some 154,000 women held university degrees, and women degree-holders constituted a quarter of the university graduates in the nation.[5]

Women's access to education resulted in a radical change in the number of employed women and their pattern of employment. Women had formed 4 percent of the wage labor force in 1962, and the majority of those

618,000 women had been illiterate rural workers engaged in agricultural work. By 1982 over 15 percent of Egyptian women, or one million people, were in formal employment outside the home, with the majority concentrated in urban areas. The entry of educated women into the labor force accounts almost entirely for the increase.[6] The greatest proportion of them were found in professional, technical, and scientific fields, women holding 26 percent of such employment in the country. Teaching and health-related work were the foremost growth occupations, and clerical work and the civil service also significantly expanded as fields of employment for women. But women penetrate virtually all professions, notably aeronautics, engineering, politics, agriculture, medicine, law, journalism, film, business, radio, and television (radio and television being the ones in which women have achieved notable prominence).

In spite of these distinctly positive developments, Egypt's economic and population problems meant that the state fell far short of its objective of eliminating illiteracy. To begin with, some segments of the population were better served by the system than others. Urban areas, for instance, tended to be better provided with educational facilities than rural areas. Moreover, the educational system continued in some degree to perpetuate class bias by favoring the better-off as against the poorest classes, both urban and rural, for families at the lower economic level were often unable to provide children with books and clothes long past the age of six, and they even needed the child's financial contribution to help support the family. Nor were the benefits of the kind that primary education offered in terms of the labor the child was expected to perform, such as helping with agricultural work, entirely obvious.[7]

In this situation girls, for whom the benefits of education were even less obvious than for boys, tended to be held back from school at a higher rate than boys, particularly in rural areas. Literacy figures since the 1950s show improvement but also indicate the size of the illiteracy problem with which Egypt has to contend, and reveal the gap between female and male literacy rates. Overall, the illiteracy rate for the population dropped from about 70 percent to 56 percent between 1960 and 1976, male illiteracy dropping from 56 percent to 43 percent and female illiteracy from 84 percent to 71 percent.[8]

One important factor modifying the fight against illiteracy has been the rate of population growth: as educational programs expanded, so too did the population, rising from twenty-six million to thirty-eight million between 1960 and 1976. Passing the forty million mark in the early 1980s, it is growing at a rate of about 2.3 percent per year, nearly one million additional people annually.[9] The expansion of educational facilities has not kept pace.

Not until after the revolution did the state begin to take steps to control population growth by promoting birth control, opening the first family planning clinics in 1955. The government championed family planning through the 1960s, until the 1967 war, after which increased spending on arms led to the curtailment of funding in this area, as in others. Although in the early 1970s a government adviser declared that the threat from population growth was as great as the threat from Egypt's Zionist enemies,[10] and Sadat declared his support for family planning, it was not until late in the decade that funding for the programs again became available and a network of 3,675 clinics was established nationwide. Although the coverage is far from complete, it is considerably more extensive than in most developing countries. Nonetheless, birth control methods are still not widely adopted, estimates suggesting that no more than 5 percent to 8 percent of couples use them.[11] The reasons for this have never been adequately studied. The service may be inadequate: perhaps the clinics are not disseminating information widely or efficiently enough, for example, and perhaps they do not have the support of an adequate publicity campaign. It is possible that many believe (wrongly) that birth control is contrary to Islamic precepts.

Then, too, couples may not wish to limit fertility. The fairly high infant mortality rate (119 deaths per 1,000 births in 1967 and probably a higher rate in the countryside) and the wish to ensure that there will be surviving children are among many reasons to have large families. Children offer security against disability or old age, and the additional labor they provide can be significant, particularly in rural areas. Given the current legal situation, which allows men easy divorce, women may see additional children as psychologically likely to bind the man and to make divorce financially onerous, for a father is required to support his children. Studies on Egypt and elsewhere distinctly suggest a strong link between literacy and limited fertility, those on Egypt showing a correlation between more extensive use of contraceptives and smaller families among educated, urban couples.[12] But as population growth outstrips the rate of increase in literacy, the solution seems to lie in vastly increased expenditures on both educational and birth control programs, a solution that, given Egypt's somewhat bleak economic situation, seems at present scarcely feasible.

Thus an illiteracy rate that remains high because the education campaign cannot keep up with population growth coexists with the expansion of education and opportunities for a significant segment of the population, a segment large enough for real social and cultural change for both women and men to be effected. It has been estimated that increasing and equalizing educational opportunities, enlarging the pool of the literate and allowing new groups to send their children to school, thus enabling them to enter professional and white-collar occupations, markedly transformed the Egyptian class structure. In the first two decades after the revolution, it has been suggested, Egyptian society witnessed a social fluidity and upward mobility unequaled in any other period in this century.[13]

Higher educational attainment, upward social mobility among both men and women, and women's increasing presence in the urban work force have intersected with another concurrent demographic change: migration. Like many developing countries, Egypt has experienced substantial migration from rural to urban areas in the last decades, due, among other reasons, to population growth and overcrowding in rural areas, where there is little room for expansion in agricultural employment, and to education and the raised expectations it creates, for the kinds of employment and amenities considered suitable are not available in rural areas. Between 1960 and 1976 the population of Egypt doubled, while that of its urban centers—chiefly Cairo, Alexandria, Port Said, and Suez—tripled. Cairo in particular, the capital and the largest city in the Middle East, grew rapidly, nearly doubling its population between 1960 and 1976 (from 4.8 million to 8.0 million). In addition to laborers in search of work, and their families, sizable numbers of students also arrived (200,000 in 1975, for instance), often accompanied by family members and job seekers.[14] The population density of Cairo is now greater than New York's, although Cairo is not a city of high-rise buildings—a fact that may suggest something of its teeming over-crowdedness. Although this enormous swelling in the city's population is due in part to natural increase, the influx from rural areas is clearly sub-stantial. Some Cairenes naturally regard these developments with appre-hension. Not only are the physical facilities of the city strained, but also, Cairenes lament, this flood of migrants, to whom they critically refer as "rural hoards," are arriving at such a rate that instead of the city urban-izing the migrant peasantry the latter is ruralizing the city, overwhelming the mores of the city with those of village life.[15]

Together these trends in education, the broadening base of literacy, and upward social mobility meant that a significantly broadened segment of the population was increasingly politicized.[16] They meant, too, that this broad-ened segment of the population, drawn from rural as well as urban back-grounds and constituting the emergent middle classes, helped shape mainstream culture and its discourses on all the levels at which they manifest themselves, in literature, politics, and thought and in the language of custom and dress. Not only were mainstream culture and its discourses now being articulated from a broader social base but they were for the first time in many centuries also being shaped by significant numbers of women.[17] Television, film, and literature, as well as styles of dress, reflected the altered demography of cultural production and of the production of mainstream discourses.

With respect to women and the issue of women the cultural productions and discourses from the 1950s to the 1980s appear to fall into two distinct phases. The first phase was marked by a lively feminism, finding expression in organizational activities and in literary forms that showed a critical consciousness of the politics of male domination in psychological and other realms not previously explored. Whereas the first feminists of the century had addressed themselves primarily to contesting and attempting to reform the overt, formally sanctioned injustices to women enshrined in the law and in accepted social practices, by the 1960s and 1970s, in addition to continuing the battle to institute reform in the Personal Status Laws (the laws governing marriage), women now began to make visible the covert, unofficial aggressions and manipulations, both psychological and physical, to which they were subject and to address themselves to and organize around taboo issues, such as contraception and clitoridectomy.[18] Research currently under way indicates that in terms of formal and informal organizational activities as well as in literary terms, the 1950s, 1960s, and 1970s were an era of dynamic feminism.[19]

In literature the generation of women who came of age in the 1950s and 1960s produced a number of feminist writers, most from the urban middle classes, who addressed themselves to articulating the psychological manipulations of middle-class life, as well as to attacking the casual destruction of women permitted by the culture. Among the many writers who could be included in this group, two stand out as masters of the precise revelation of the discrete and destructive androcentric practices of the middle classes: Alifa Rifaat and Andrée Chedid. Rifaat's stories are ironic, cool, and merciless, dissecting with annihilating precision the culturally sanctioned destructive egotism of the Egyptian male. Chedid, with an equally seeing eye and more open mourning, chronicles the exploitation and abuse of women. The first writer, it may be noted, is of Muslim background and writes in Arabic, the other of Christian background and writes in French—but insofar as culturally sanctioned practices go, there is little difference in the abuse of women each presents as regarded as permissible by the community depicted, Muslim or Christian.

Besides addressing situations involving psychological aggression against women, Chedid also concerns herself with issues of child marriage and that grand, culturally sanctioned savagery, the murder of women for "honor." In her novel *From Sleep Unbound (Le Sommeil délivré)*, for example, a novel about a teenage girl married against her will to a middle-aged man, the story of the murdered Sayeda, though only briefly mentioned, occupies a central place in literary and psychological terms. Sayeda, a widow, is seen one evening by a palm grove, talking to a man, which casts shame on her. "The father and brother lost their heads. They killed her."[20]

In exposing hidden physical abuses, whether culturally sanctioned and openly performed, like the practice of clitoridectomy, or culturally invisible, furtively committed, and denied abuses, such as the sexual abuse of children, no writer has played a more important and eloquent role than Nawal El-Saadawi—nor has any feminist been more outspoken and done more to challenge the misogynist and androcentric practices of the culture. In more recent novels El-Saadawi has also dealt with such issues as prostitution and illegitimacy, as well as the psychological abuse of women.

Even this naming of the unnamed and invisible inhumanities toward women exposes no more than a fraction of the pervasive cruelties to which they may be subjected. Countless semisanctioned practices and unsanctioned but routine practices—many still unnoticed and unrecorded—are visited on women. Brief items such as the findings of a 1946 report on women workers at the Mahalla al-kubra spinning and weaving factory, which notes that 90 percent of the women there suffered from tuberculosis, hint at the textually invisible and largely unchronicled deprivations and inhumanities to which girls and women are subject.[21] Of course, not only women suffer from tuberculosis, malnutrition, and ill-treatment. The problems of poverty and human rights are generalized, affecting boys and men as well as girls and women in much of the Middle East. But among the economically deprived, females are routinely more deprived and more abused than males. Attitudes that permit the ill-treatment and unjust treatment of women in the law courts permit, in a continuum, their casual and systemic deprivation and ill-treatment in other ways and in informal domains.

It must be noted, however, that the existence of numerous and invisible practices destructive of women within Egyptian society does not mean that the generality of Egyptian or Muslim or Arab men can be assumed to be more brutal to women or more misogynist than Western men are. To read Nawal El-Saadawi's *Hidden Face of Eve* with its graphic exposures of the appalling abuses of women and girls that she encountered as a medical doctor, including cases of incest, and to conclude therefrom that it represents the lot of the generality of Egyptian women, which must consequently indeed be terrible, would be about as valid a reaction as if someone from an Arab culture reading works on rape or incest in the United States or books in one way or another focused on exposing extremes of misogynist conduct there concluded that the books described the common lot of American women, who were consequently deeply to be pitied.

Writers of the generation here discussed, then, took feminist discourse forward and into explorations and exposés of the sexual politics of domination and the victimization of women in the informal and personal realms of life. This overt concern with feminism seems distinctly absent among women of the succeeding generation, women coming of age in the 1970s and 1980s. It is among women of this succeeding generation—women of the second phase—that the use of the veil is most prevalent.

Over the middle decades of the century the veil, whether a covering for face or head, virtually disappeared from the Egyptian urban scene—though not from small towns and rural areas, where wearing a veil as a headdress continued to be the norm. Already abandoned before the Nasser era by the upper and middle classes of Cairo and other cities, it became rare to see the veil in urban areas after the revolution and its espousal of women's place as citizen and worker, except in popular quarters, and even there it was growing uncommon.

Investigators commonly fix on 1967, the year that Egypt was defeated by Israel, as the moment after which Islamism began to take hold. People seeking to make sense of the defeat, which had come as a shock, came up with a variety of explanations—that the military had grown elitist, corrupt, and bureaucratic, for example, or that Egypt was underdeveloped technologically. Investigators claim that one reason in particular found a general resonance: God had abandoned Egypt and allowed it to be defeated because the Egyptians had abandoned God. A vision of the Virgin Mary appeared, perhaps manifesting this mood of religiosity, in a small church in a suburb of Cairo marking the site of the holy family's resting place in their flight to Egypt. Hundreds of thousands of Egyptians, Christian and Muslim alike, flocked to see the vision, which continued to appear for several months. The Coptic clergy declared that the vision meant Mary was saying, "I know, Egyptians, you are very sad because you can no longer visit Jerusalem, and that is why I come to you instead."[22]

Another consequence of the defeat was the people's loss of faith in Nasser and in his entire secularist ideology and his "socialist" program, which were now judged to have been failures. The defeat came at a difficult moment for the government. For a variety of reasons the economy was in difficulties. The expense of the Yemeni War (1962–67) and the waste, mismanagement, and corruption that plagued some of the schemes at home, plus the long-term nature of some of the projects, which needed more time to give returns, all contributed to Egypt's finding itself in economic straits by 1964–65. The defeat of 1967 meant not only the burden of coping with the refugees from towns in the canal zone—about half a million of them—the expense of rebuilding the region, and the doubling of the military budget for arms replacement but also the weakening of the Nasser government: having lost the confidence of the people, it was no longer in a position to impose unpopular and austere economic measures. Those last years of the Nasser government consequently marked a turning point in Egyptian internal economic policies. The government began to make concessions to the affluent and powerful classes and to retreat from its socialist policies—a retreat that became flagrantly obvious after Nasser's death in 1969 and through the 1970s under Sadat.

Islamist groups grew stronger and more widespread in the 1970s and have continued to gain ground since, as has their visible emblem, Islamic dress, for both men and women—though the dress is more obvious and perhaps more widespread among women. A variety of factors have contributed to the spread of these groups and the new type of Islamic outlook. Sadat, who was under attack from Nasserists and leftists as the government retreated from socialist commitments, actively encouraged the Muslim Brethren (perhaps urged to do so by Saudi Arabia) so that it might serve as a base of opposition to his opponents. He permitted the Brethren to resume their activities, which Nasser had banned, and their publications soon reached a wide audience and helped disseminate the religious idiom as the idiom of political discourse. Furthermore, as their publications turned to criticizing not only Nasserism and communism but also Sadat's policies, particularly after the treaty with Israel, their religious idiom also became the language of political dissent and discontent. With other discourses of opposition silenced—leftist publications had been banned—the Islamic idiom became the only available vehicle of dissent. Once allowed to gain popularity and legitimacy, the Islamist position was difficult to limit: Sadat could take action against leftists and Nasserists, but once the Islamists had gained ground, he could not afford to lay himself open to the charge of being anti-Islamic. Sadat himself began to use the idiom of religion to gain support and legitimacy, declaring himself committed to a state based on the twin pillars of Iman (faith) and ʿIlm (science).[23]

In addition, external political interests doubtless played a direct part in fostering Islam as the medium of political discourse and as the language of social being. It was rumored, for instance, that Saudi Arabia and Libya used their oil wealth in Egypt and in other parts of the Middle East to boost the membership of Islamic groups as well as to promote the adoption of Islamic dress. Men and women said they were offered sums of money to affiliate with Islamic groups or to persuade others to do so. Some women related that they had been offered a small sum for every woman they persuaded to wear a veil, and rumors circulated of men who threatened to divorce their wives if they did not adopt Islamic dress.[24]

Conditions meanwhile were such as to breed discontent. The government had embarked on the Infitah, or open-door, policy and had promulgated a series of new laws, including ones that offered concessionary terms to foreign investors, the object of which was ostensibly to encourage foreign investments, both Western and Arab, and to promote growth. In practice, the concessions led to foreign investments lucrative only to foreigners and to a few Egyptian middlemen, in nonproductive areas like tourism, banking, and fast foods—Kentucky Fried Chicken and Wimpy's, for example—and to the flooding of the country with luxury and consumer goods to the detriment of the local textile, clothing, and tobacco industries. Some Egyptians made huge fortunes, particularly individuals connected with the government and in a position to maneuver matters to their and their foreign partners' advantage. Abuses and corruption, and ostentatious consumerism among some, were rife. A few major scandals exposing such deals rocked the country. In one of them an archaeologist, Dr. Nʿimat Fuad, a woman, emerged as the national hero who single-handedly publicized and succeeded eventually in bringing about the cancellation of one such scheme. The deal, worth hundreds of millions of dollars, involved a foreign property-development company and a newly formed Egyptian tourist company that acquired land near the pyramids at concessionary rates to develop a giant tourist complex along the lines of Disneyland. But for Fuad, this archaeologically rich area would have been destroyed, and a Disneyland-type development would have permanently loomed at the side of the Sphinx and the pyramids.[25]

A sense that corruption and moral breakdown were rife and were associated with foreigners, Arab and Western, began to be common among some Egyptians. This laxity was felt to be affecting personal as well as business mores. An unfamiliar and culturally offensive mixing of the sexes—drinking, dating, sex—were seen as in vogue. Rumor even suggested that in the pervasive materialist atmosphere respectable women were augmenting their income by selling sexual favors to wealthy Arabs.[26]

Besides retreating from a commitment to the lower half of society and to the democratization of opportunity, the government, in adopting the open-door policy, also veered away from the Soviet Union in favor of alignment with the West and conservative Arab oil-states and accommodation with Israel. The scandals involving corrupt Egyptian middlemen implicated Arab oil wealth as often as other foreign interests. Arabs were given rights to acquire property, and tourism from Arab oil-states increased, and with it more conspicuous consumerism.

The relaxation of restrictions, including restrictions on emigration, benefited some Egyptians of the professional classes, who left Egypt for the Arab oil-states, generally for a limited period of years. By 1980 an estimated one and a half million Egyptians worked abroad in the Arab world. Perhaps as many as a third of these were women, mostly professionals (teachers, nurses) but also domestics and nannies.[27] The government encouraged this migration in the belief that it would ease unemployment and earn Egypt much-needed hard currency. It did achieve the latter—remittances from Egyptian workers abroad soon became Egypt's major source of hard currency—but it did not reduce unemployment, bringing about rather a brain drain, for the most skilled and employable left, not the unemployed. (The repercussions of this brain drain, particularly its impact on education, have yet to be gauged.)[28] Returning workers, whose salaries vastly exceeded earnings for the same work at home, joined the ranks of conspicuous consumers, acquiring televisions, refrigerators, and washing machines. The markets of Cairo and Port Said filled with dazzling consumer items far beyond the reach of the majority of Egyptians.

While the open-door policy brought sudden wealth for a few, along with the spectacle of blatant corruption and avid consumerism, most Egyptians experienced its negative effects, exacerbated by the state's retreat from internal development and the public sector. These were high inflation; serious shortages, particularly in housing; low wages; reduced employment prospects; and poor working conditions. Matriculations at the university continued at the previous high rate and even increased—whereas the public sector, the chief source of employment, was cut back. The results were delays in employment, poor salaries and working conditions, and, for the educated, the increasing likelihood of unemployment. Sadat's promise of an "era of prosperity" and his assertion that every Egyptian would have a villa and a car was an extravagant and wildly unrealistic fantasy. Exemplifying the trend were the food riots when bread subsidies were cut in 1977: Sadat characterized the riots as "an uprising of thieves" and as a communist conspiracy, but the editor of the influential paper *Al-ahram,* which had previously supported the open-door policy, began to write critical editorials. The open-door policy had been such a success, the editor noted sarcastically, that plenty of German, Dutch, and Danish beer and foreign cigarettes were available and that an abundance of Kentucky Fried Chicken and other foreign fast-food chains were rapidly changing the eating habits of ordinary Egyptians, giving them a taste for hamburger instead of *ful* (beans). In other editorials he commented on the flaunting of waste and wealth in the midst of suffering.[29]

Veiling first made its appearance among university students in major urban centers, such as Cairo, Alexandria, and Assiut, and it is among these students and young professionals of both sexes that formal or informal affiliation with the Islamist trend, indicated outwardly by veiling among women, became most prevalent. Although the term *veiling* is commonly used in English to refer to the new "Islamic" dress—and in Arabic the women are referred to as *mutahajibat,* "veiled ones"—the clothing that women wear often in fact does not include a veil in the sense of a face covering, but rather includes a variety of styles of headgear and a variety of coverings for the face, which mask it to a greater or lesser degree—if worn at all. The garments, of whatever style, are intended to conform to the Islamic requirement that dress be modest, that is, not sexually enticing; the mandate applies to both men and women. It is generally taken to mean robes or loose-fitting, long-sleeved, ankle-length garments that do not reveal the contours of the body. Both men and women conforming to this code have developed styles of dress that are essentially quite new, neither the traditional dress of Egypt nor the dress of any other part of the Arab world, or the West, though they often combine features of all three. Although called Islamic dress (*al-ziyy al-islami*), the term means that they fulfill the Islamic requirement of modesty, not that they derived, as a style of clothing, from an Islamic society of the past.

Accordingly, men complying with the requirement of modesty may wear Arabian-style robes (rather than Egyptian robes), sandals, and sometimes a long scarf on the head, or they may wear baggy trousers and loose shirts.[30] Women wear robes in a variety of styles, all of which resemble Western styles more than they do traditional peasant dress, except that the skirts are ankle length and the sleeves long. With the robes they wear an assortment of headgear, ranging from scarves, hats, and bonnets to what might be described as wimples and fabric balaclavas; and some of them, depending on how they personally interpret the requirement for modesty, wear face veils, which again come in a variety of styles and degrees of thickness and length. Finally, some also wear gloves. The use of this last item is somewhat bizarre, for there were no gloves in Arabia in Muhammad's day, when the requirements for modesty of dress were set, but perhaps their wearers interpret the Islamic requirement as intending women to appropriate the latest inventions of modernity in the service of modesty.

The streets of Cairo consequently present a somewhat motley appearance. Many styles of female Islamic attire are seen there, that is, in addition to the Western-style clothing that some still wear—Western styles for women were always to some extent and are nowadays in particular interpreted conservatively in the sense of avoiding the display of bare flesh. One observer described the scene: "One is struck by the number of women wearing costumes rather similar to those of Catholic nuns before Vatican II, although their flowing dresses, coifs and long wimples are usually in light rather than dark colors. Occasionally the old-fashioned yashmak, or face veil, is also seen, though this is rarer. Other women wear pantsuits, often with long jackets and a wimple, or at least a large kerchief on their heads, leaving only the face and hands uncovered."[31] That al-ziyy al-islami does not resemble traditional dress, even though traditional dress fulfills all the requirements of Islamic modesty, is perhaps as significant a fact about it as any other. In modern times traditional dress has come to be confined to the lower classes and the peasantry; traditional dress therefore identifies the wearer as from these classes, whereas al-ziyy al-islami, which might be seen as a democratic dress, erases class origins.

Studies indicate that youth and a high educational achievement characterize adherents of the new Islamist trend. For men, who have been more fully studied and about whom we have more information, the age at which they joined an Islamic group was typically between seventeen and twenty-six, whereas university women in Islamic dress were generally in their late teens to early twenties, rarely older.[32] Women and men alike had generally attended or were attending university, often in the fields—medicine, engineering, military sciences, pharmaceutics—that require the highest grades to get into, though some are graduates of secondary or technical schools.

Two further factors emerge as crucial variables among the young people affiliated, formally or informally, with the contemporary Islamic movement: they are for the most part members of the new middle classes and, more typically, of the lower middle class and often have a rural background or come from families that have recently migrated to urban centers. (Class in these studies was determined by a combination of indicators, including the parents' level of education and type of employment.)

A study conducted among veiled and unveiled women at Cairo University, based on responses from about two hundred women from each group, clearly shows a direct correlation between veiling and a lower level of education in both parents, to the point that the educational level of the parents was a strong predictor of whether the daughter would be veiled. Thus a considerably larger proportion of fathers of veiled women had not progressed beyond basic literacy, or at best intermediate education, compared to the fathers of unveiled women, who more commonly were graduates of a secondary school or university. Similarly, a significantly larger proportion of the mothers of veiled women had had minimal schooling or were illiterate compared to the mothers of unveiled women (67 percent as against 47 percent). Importantly, the majority of veiled students (77 percent) came from families in which other women were veiled, and for a large proportion (82 percent) this included the mother.[33] That is to say, for the majority adoption of al-ziyy al-islami entailed not innovation and conformity to new, socially accepted codes of dress but, on the contrary, adoption of a "modern" version of the conventions of dress they and their families were accustomed to.

These findings regarding class and educational background also hold good for men affiliating with Islamic groups. As for the veiled university students, the men had typically attained or were in process of attaining a higher educational level than their father, and the mother was likely to be either illiterate or to have had minimal schooling. Mothers of men and women alike were important sources of "traditional" and "Islamic" values. The "typical" male member of an Islamic group, for example, had parents who were born in rural villages and who had retained, "particularly the mother, village manners and values" and had acquired from the mother "a strong dose of religion and tradition."[34]

Taken together, these studies suggest a number of commonalities in the psychosocial composition of people affiliating with the Islamic trend, in the problems confronting them, and in the strategies to which they resort to cope with them. Typically they are educationally and professionally upwardly mobile—or at least with the abilities and aspirations of the upwardly mobile, though society threatens to frustrate their aspirations—and are confronting bewildering, anonymous, cosmopolitan city life for the first time, a city life in which vivid inequalities, consumerism and materialism, foreign mores, and unscrupulous business practices linked to the foreign presence, whether Western or Arab, are glaringly apparent. The women are generally the first generation of women in their family to emerge socially into a sexually integrated world—where men and women are intermingled on the university campuses, in the crowded transport system, and in the professions. In the face of such stresses and novelties, preserving the conventions of dress that prevail in the family at home while adopting the version of that dress that proclaims educational and professional upward mobility appears above all to be a practical coping strategy, enabling women to negotiate in the new world while affirming the traditional values of their upbringing.

Joining Islamic groups or, as is the case for most women, informally affiliating with the trend, then, evidently carries the comfort of bringing the values of home and childhood to the city and its foreign and morally overwhelming ways. This psychological and social dimension appears to be among the most important elements underlying the trend. Inner ease and resolution, often described as a feeling of peace, of centeredness, brought about by the formal or public aligning of oneself with Islam, are prominent features of women's and men's accounts of why they made that alignment and how they feel about it.[35] Affiliation with Islamism also brought comfort by providing a sense of community. Men's groups, which have a formal organization, place great emphasis on brotherhood, mutual support, and sharing and in effect function as extended families—an aspect that is especially attractive to uprooted individuals in an alien environment.[36] Though less likely to be formally organized into groups, the informal sisterhood is doubtless likely to offer a similar sense of community, mutual support, and commonality of values.

Essentially, the adoption of Islamic dress and the affiliation with Islamism express an affirmation of ethical and social customs—particularly with regard to mixing with the opposite sex—that those adopting the dress and affiliation are comfortable with and accustomed to. For women Islamic dress also appears to bring a variety of distinct practical advantages. On the simplest, most material level, it is economical. Women adopting Islamic dress are saved the expense of acquiring fashionable clothes and having more than two or three outfits. The dress also protects them from male harassment. In responding to a questionnaire women stated that wearing Islamic dress resulted in a marked difference in the way they were treated in public places.[37]

These practical advantages partially explain why university and professional women in particular adopt Islamic dress—women who daily venture onto coeducational campuses and into sexually integrated work places on crowded public transport in cities in which, given the strong rural origin of much of the population, sexually integrated social space is still an alien, uncomfortable social reality for both women and men. Thus the ritual invocation through dress of the notion of segregation places the integrated reality in a framework that defuses it of stress and impropriety. At the same time it declares women's presence in public space to be in no way a challenge to or a violation of the Islamic sociocultural ethic.

The dress has a number of other decidedly practical advantages. For example, the fact that wearing it signals the wearer's adherence to an Islamic moral and sexual code has the paradoxical effect, as some women have attested, of allowing them to strike up friendships with men and be seen with them without the fear that they will be dubbed immoral or their reputations damaged. Women declare that they avoided being seen in conversation with a man before adopting Islamic dress, but now they feel free to study with men in their classes or even walk with them to the station without any cost to their reputation.[38] In an age in which arranged marriages are disappearing and women need find their own marriage partners, clothes that enable women to socialize with men to some degree and at the same time indicate their adherence to a strict moral code (which makes them attractive as wives) are advantageous in very tangible ways.

In adopting Islamic dress, then, women are in effect "carving out legitimate public space for themselves," as one analyst of the phenomenon put it, and public space is by this means being redefined to accommodate women.[39] The adoption of the dress does not declare women's place to be in the home but, on the contrary, legitimizes their presence outside it. Consequently, it appears that the prevalence of the Islamic mode among women coming of age in the 1970s and 1980s—women of the second phase—cannot be seen as a retreat from the affirmations of female autonomy and subjectivity made by the generation of women who immediately preceded them. Although the voice of overt feminism and perhaps even feminist consciousness may be absent, the entry of women into the university, the professions, and public space in unprecedentedly large numbers and the availability of education and professional occupations to women from a far broader segment of the population than before cannot be construed as regressive, however apparently conservative the uniform they wear to accomplish these moves comfortably.

Moreover, it appears that the particular language adopted in pursuit of goals of female autonomy and subjectivity, be this the idiom of "feminism" and "Western" dress or that of "Islam" and the "veil," is to an important degree, in these two recent generations as in past generations, a function

of class and the urban-rural divisions of society. The pursuit of these goals
in terms of the language of Western dress, secularism, and explicit "feminism" was evidently typical predominantly of the urban middle classes—
and consequently "feminism" as a political movement may perhaps justly
be described as "elitist or sectional, and cut off from the grass roots of
society"—whereas women's pursuit of those same goals in the language of
Islamism and the veil appears to represent the quest for autonomy at the
grass-roots level.[40] To that extent, the criticism that the older generation
of urban middle-class feminists is directing at the new generation of women
and their "return to the veil" is yet another version of the old class warfare.
One way of describing the process that has led in recent decades to the
emergence of Islamic dress and affiliations with Islamism as a dominant
discourse of social being is in terms of its marking a broad demographic
change—a change that has democratized mainstream culture and mores
and led to the rise and gradual predominance of a vocabulary of dress and
social being defined from below, by the emergent middle classes, rather
than by the formerly culturally dominant upper and middle classes. This
change to a sociocultural vernacular is facilitating the assimilation of the
newly urban, newly educated middle classes to modernity and to a sexually
integrated social reality. From this perspective Islamic dress can be seen as
the uniform, not of reaction, but of transition; it can be seen, not as a return
to traditional dress, but as the adoption of Western dress—with modifications to make it acceptable to the wearer's notions of propriety. Far from
indicating that the wearers remain fixed in the world of tradition and the
past, then, Islamic dress is the uniform of arrival, signaling entrance into,
and determination to move forward in, modernity.

Viewed as expressing personal and familial mores, habits of dress, and
ethics and as reflecting the layperson's understanding of Islam, veiling and
the Islamist trend offer the preceding generation of feminists and other
critics no better ground for denouncing them than Amin or Shaʿrawi had
to attack the veil. Unfortunately, however, establishment Islam (institutional and legal Islam) articulates a different Islam from the ethical message
that the layperson justifiably hears or reads in the Quran, and unfortunately, that Islam, intolerant of all understandings of the religion except its
own, which is authoritarian, implacably androcentric, and hostile to
women, has been and continues to be the established version of Islam, the
Islam of the politically powerful. These profoundly different meanings of
Islam both exist simultaneously, the personal meaning as a source of ethical
and spiritual comfort for those raised within traditional backgrounds and

the political and historical meaning as the system of law and government imposed by the politically dominant; and these meanings are at the root of the profoundly different views of Islam held by the preceding generation of feminists and the current generation of women adopting Islamic dress. They are seeing and arguing about two different Islams.

That a profound gulf separates lay Islam, the Islam to which women are declaring their allegiance by affiliating with Islamism, from establishment Islam is a subject that has received little investigation. In discussions women's adoption of Islamic dress is commonly assumed to denote an affiliation with "conservative" ethical and social habits, and discussants generally also assume that the affiliation automatically connotes support for male dominance and female subservience. Consequently, investigations into the possible "feminist" positions taken by women adopting Islamic dress— positions supportive of female autonomy and equality articulated in terms totally different from the language of Western and Western-affiliated feminism—have yet to be conducted.

Among the few systematic investigations of "veiled" women's views on the roles of women is the one done by Zeinab Radwan and her associates, cited above. Radwan questioned both veiled and unveiled university students on a range of questions relating to women's education and women's roles in the home and in marriage, in the workplace, and in public and political life. The results of the inquiry indicate, as Radwan stresses, that veiled women are consistently more conservative and less "feminist" than their unveiled sisters. For example, more unveiled than veiled women believed that women's education was important (93 percent and 88 percent respectively), and more unveiled than veiled women believed that women had the right to pursue education to the highest levels (98 percent and 92 percent). Similarly, on the question of whether women might work outside the home, more unveiled than veiled women agreed that such work was acceptable (95 percent and 88 percent), and more unveiled than veiled women said they themselves would work on graduating (88 percent and 77 percent). On the matter of women's work, it is worth noting, the responses from both groups suggest that a gap existed between what the women said they believed in general and what they said was appropriate for themselves. Thus a majority in both groups agreed with the proposition that the purpose of educating women was to enable them to be good wives (54 percent of the unveiled and 76 percent of the veiled), and only a small minority in either group thought that the purpose was to prepare women for jobs (5 percent and 2 percent); at the same time, a large majority in both groups, as I just noted, not only agreed that women were entitled to work if they wished or needed to but also stated that they themselves would seek jobs. Both groups thought the most appropriate work for women was in education (43 percent among the unveiled and 51 among the veiled), followed by medicine (excluding nursing; 31 percent of the unveiled and 48 percent of the veiled).[41]

With regard to political life, again more unveiled women than veiled believed women and men should have the same rights and duties in public life (81 percent and 53 percent), and more unveiled than veiled agreed that women should have the right to occupy the highest positions in the land (90 percent and 63 percent). Asked whether there should be equality between women and men in marriage, 66 percent of unveiled women and 38 percent of veiled women agreed that there should.[42]

Radwan is correct, then, in pointing out in her report that veiled women's responses were consistently more conservative and less feminist. But these figures are, if anything, even more striking for the *similarities* they reveal between the two groups of women, veiled and unveiled, and for their indication that the overwhelming majority of veiled women support women's rights to education and to work, that a majority support equality in public life and equal political rights, and that a substantial proportion even support equality in marriage. In all these matters veiled women's views do not conform to the conventional notion of them as committed to the view that women's place is in the home nor to the view that women are second-class citizens without political rights or rights to paid employment outside the home. Even though the majority agreed with the proposition that the purpose of educating women was to make them better wives, the sum of their responses on matters of women's roles and rights indicates that most were consistently *for* education, *for* the right to employment, *for* avenues of professional achievement being open to women, and *for* equal political rights, with only the matter of equality in the marital relationship failing to be supported by more than half the veiled women investigated.

Not only do these responses not conform to the notion that women's place is in the home, identified with traditional Islam, but they do not conform with the views of women encoded in the sharicʿa, although they do accord with some interpretations of the role of women put forward by the Muslim Brethren and others, like Zeinab al-Ghazali. Muslim canon law as conventionally interpreted and as legally in force in Egypt today permits polygamy and easy divorce for men, among other things. Given the notion of the different rights of men and women within marriage articulated in these legal ideas, what place is there for any belief among veiled women, let alone among 38 percent of them, in marital equality?

This disparity between the views of veiled women and those of the shariʿa and Islam as conventionally interpreted suggests that perhaps these women have only a vague idea regarding the technicalities enshrined in establishment Islam and the shariʿa with respect to women and are relying on their own understanding of and feelings about Islam in forming their ideas, or perhaps they are aware of the technicalities of traditional interpretations but contest them—as Zeinab al-Ghazali did with respect to her own life. Some activities being pursued by some veiled women, such as reclaiming of the right to attend prayer in mosques, appear to support the view that some veiled women are to some extent challenging the practices of establishment Islam with respect to women. But little research is available on some Muslim women's return to the mosques and its significance.

The questionnaire unfortunately did not ask the women about their views on conventional and legal Islamic interpretations of polygamy or the male right to divorce and women's general lack of rights in the commonly practiced forms of marriage. They were asked, however, whether they would approve an across-the-board imposition of shariʿa law as part of a package designed to elevate society to "a higher level of Islamic consciousness" (the package would also include improved religious education for children and adults). Sixty-seven percent of the veiled women agreed to the introduction of a general program of reform that included the imposition of shariʿa law. Astonishingly, as many as 52.7 percent of the unveiled women also agreed to this proposal.

Given the openness of the veiled women to the idea of women's having jobs, holding high political office, having access to all levels of education, and sharing equality in political and civil matters and even, for a substantial number of them, in marriage, this endorsement of shariʿa law seems to connote a faith in the inherent justice of Islam and a faith that this justice must be reflected in the laws of Islam, plus a vagueness as to what the shariʿa might in fact be. The willingness of unveiled women to endorse the imposition of shariʿa law is even more striking given the distinctly "feminist" views and the views on women's autonomy that the majority of the unveiled women expressed. The findings of Radwan and her survey group appear to indicate that the belief that Islam is fundamentally just and that that justice must inhere somewhere in its laws, combined with a vagueness as to the content of Islamic law, is not confined to veiled women but rather prevails among the young female population more generally. Unfortunately, neither group was asked to state their understanding of shariʿa law regarding women. Nor were they asked, more simply, how they would view being married to a man who chose to take additional wives.

That women, veiled and unveiled, are vague as to the technical content of Islamic law and doctrine would not in fact be a surprising finding. Investigators of men's groups report that typically they found a core of vagueness in men's ideas about the technicalities of Islam. They report that not only did the broad membership of Islamic male organizations often seem "poorly informed about many doctrinal matters" despite a passionate dedication to religion but that the most overtly and militantly political men among them were also poorly informed. Even such politically central members of men's Islamic associations as those arrested in connection with the assassination of a cabinet minister in 1977 appeared to be not "particularly knowledgeable about the technicalities of their religion" and, despite having strong feelings on political matters, not to have clear ideas about their political objectives or programs.[43] One analyst who conducted interviews among Islamic militants reports:

> When the militants are persuaded to spell out their ideology, attitudes, and feelings, the listener comes away with an overall clear impression of what they are against but with only a vague, though colorful, impression of what they would do if they were in power. They have deep-seated hostility towards the West, Communism, and Israel. Any ruler who deals with or befriends any of them would be betraying Islam. Excessive wealth, extravagance, severe poverty, exploitation, and usury have no place in a truly Muslim society. They disapprove of nearly all the regimes in the Arab and Muslim worlds. They attribute many of the decadent aspects of behavior in Egypt either to Western influence or to the squandering of oil money, and they firmly believe that should "true Islam" be implemented, Egypt and the Muslim World would be independent, free, prosperous, just, and righteous societies.[44]

Like the young women, the young men affiliating with Islam are hearing its ethical voice, a voice insistently enjoining Muslims to act justly and fairly, and constantly reiterating the equal humanity of all. The voice they hear is the voice virtually ignored by the framers of establishment Islam (see chaps. 4 and 5), which is the technical, legal, doctrinal Islam about which they seem so little informed.

If the political circumstances were right, if the societies of the Middle East were politically stable and committed to democratic pluralism, to respect for the individual, and to freedom of expression and ideas, this emergence of a generation of educated young people, some of whom are attentive to the ethical, humane voice of Islam and some of whom are not particularly committed to the religious idiom or to veiling and are ready to explore other avenues of thought among the varieties available to citizens of the modern world, could mark a moment of important transformation and intellectual revolution. It could signal the beginning of a period in which the dictates and assumptions of establishment Islam are fundamentally questioned, a period in which explorations and reformulations of the Islamic heritage could lead to a reconceptualization of Islam as a religion and as a system of law and even perhaps to its becoming as intellectually open a system as, for many, Christianity is in many countries today.

Unfortunately, the political circumstances are not right. Unfortunately, too, young people's psychosocial but doctrinally uninformed affiliation with Islam is open to cooptation by groups who, in contrast to the young people, have the unambiguous political intention of instituting authoritarian theocratic political systems committed to the enforcement of establishment Islam in the full panoply of its unmitigatedly androcentric doctrinal and legal rulings. There is no ambiguity within establishment Islam and its laws on the treatment of men and women, on the proper precedence in all matters of men over women, or on their different, and women's distinctly inferior, rights before the law. Nor is there any doubt or ambiguity about the willingness of establishment Islam, yesterday or today—once ensconced in political power—to eliminate those who challenge its authority or its particular understanding of Islam, including other Muslims intent on heeding the ethical over the doctrinal voice.

For this reason the alarm with which many Arab women, including feminist women, view the Islamist trend and the return of the veil is justified. It would be unreasonable to fault the young women of today for adopting Islamic dress, as if the dress were intrinsically oppressive—which is how the veil, at least, was viewed by the former colonial powers and by members of the indigenous upper and middle classes who assimilated colonial views. It would be even more unreasonable to fault them for adopting Islamic dress as a means of affirming the ethical and social habits they are accustomed to while they pursue their education and professional careers in an alien, anomic, sexually integrated world. In fact, the emergence of women capable of forging a path of political, educational, professional, and economic autonomy for themselves, as veiled women are doing, pragmatically invoking an idiom intelligible and meaningful to the majority within their societies, in itself represents a moment of perhaps unprecedented potential for Muslim women. Yet without their particularly intending to, their affiliation with a cultural and ethical Islamism lends support and strength to Islamist political forces which, if successful in realizing their objectives, would institute authoritarian theocratic states that would undoubtedly have a devastatingly negative impact on women.

The controls on women, the limitations on their participation in the economy, their exclusion from many fields of activity in their society, including politics, their subjection to a code of law with fundamental inequalities and, worse, systematic cruelty—all were features of many previous Muslim societies, just as they are features of theocratic societies and groups politically committed to Islamization today. Indeed, the modern Muslim state, able to make use of the mechanisms and technologies of the West, from passports to computerized accounts, is in a position to enforce its laws and to police women with unprecedented vigilance. Women's freedom of movement within the areas in which they reside, women's dress, women's rights to travel and to work and to choose where to work, are strictly supervised and controlled in several Middle Eastern countries today, most stringently in Saudi Arabia but elsewhere as well, not only by the regular police force but also by a "moral" police, whose special functions include watching over how women dress and where they go and enforcing such laws as those that prohibit women from driving cars, wearing short sleeves, or appearing in the street bareheaded. Women in such countries, by law subject to the authority of individual men and thus practically the prisoners of guardians, parents, and husbands, are also captives of the state.

In many Arab countries men, too, if they are political dissidents, may be controlled, deprived of freedoms, and ill-treated and abused in various ways by the state. For both men and women the human rights situation, and the absence of freedoms and political rights, renders most Arab societies today bleak places to live, even "culturally and politically desolate and oppressive," to use the words of an Arab émigré.[45] Women, however, can be oppressed and deprived of rights not just for being dissidents but merely for being women. The abuses of and controls over men are generally meted out covertly, but the controls meted out to women, their incarceration at home and in their countries, their deprivation of the right to work and earn a living, to participate politically, or to see their children if divorced, are generally not covert but the explicit laws of the land. That is to say, the citizens in many Muslim states need protection from the state; human rights and political rights are areas that need crucial reform, but reform in these areas alone would not be enough to eliminate the oppression of women or give them the necessary protection from either the state or the individual men to whom the state gives control over much of women's lives.

States in which Islamic groups have recently seized power and reinstituted Islamic laws have thus far invariably enacted laws imposing severe
new restrictions on women and sometimes also laws resulting in savage
injustice and inhumanity toward women. Laws imposing restrictions on
women and giving men increased control over "their" women are typically
among the first "Islamic" measures introduced by such groups upon coming to power. This is not surprising. Widespread discontent and frustration
invariably form pronounced elements in the societies in which Islamic
groups are able to seize power; and imposing restrictions on women, limiting their access to education or jobs—and thus increasing the availability
of both for men as well as increasing the availability of women's domestic
and personal services to men—and giving men increased control over
"their" women are easy and obvious ways to distract and appease men's
discontent and temporarily alleviate economic distress.

For examples of what might occur for women following the seizure of
power by Islamist groups one must turn for the present to countries outside
the Arab Middle East: Iran and Pakistan. Studies of Iranian women in
postrevolutionary Iran confirm the documented reports of Haleh Afshar,
who has devoted several works to investigating the plight of Iranian
women.[46] The laws instituted in Iran after the Islamic revolution, in Afshar's words, have deprived Iranian women of "most of their hard-earned
civil rights and . . . reduced them to the status of privatised sex objects
required by the new religious order to be at the disposal of their husbands
at all times."[47] Immediately upon taking power, Ayatollah Khomeini began
a campaign to "drive women back into the sphere of domesticity." Within
months women had been redefined as "unequal" and "impetuous" and
biologically and naturally inferior. "Their mere presence in public was described as 'seditious'" and "they were required to don the Islamic *hijab*,
covering them from top to toe and to return to the home" (258). Defiance
of the rule to wear the hijab was punishable by seventy-four lashes. Worse
still, the promulgation of such decrees created an atmosphere licensing
male aggression toward women: some fanatical groups attacked with
knives and guns women whom they considered inadequately covered (264–
65).

The new laws of Iran do not admit women's evidence in court unless
corroborated by men. Women who insist on giving evidence are assumed
(according to Afshar's account) to be lying and are liable to punishment
for slander. Women judges were dismissed and women barred from attending law schools, and they are not admitted to scientific and most tech-

nological university faculties. They have been subjected also to a campaign intended to drive them out of office jobs, and they are discouraged from working outside areas regarded as appropriate to women, such as nursing and education. They have not been formally banned from the labor market, but this is not surprising given Iran's enormous losses in war and the shortage of manpower.

Gains made before the revolution in matters of marriage were revoked. The permissible age for girls to marry was dropped from eighteen to thirteen, and fathers and paternal relatives regained the right to have custody of children in case of divorce or the death of the father, boys at two and girls at seven, and husbands regained the right to bar their wives from employment (269). The male right to be polygamous and to divorce at will was fully restored, resulting, among other things, in "an epidemic of often short-lived, polygamous marriages; frequently between older men taking a younger bride for a fling and retaining the old one for work" (273). Although Iran is a Shiite country, whereas Arab Middle Eastern countries are predominantly Sunni, the differences between the two branches of establishment Islam in many matters affecting women, including such rulings as those mentioned above, are minimal.

The same kinds of ideas were beginning to be implemented in Sunni Pakistan under Gen. Zia ul-Huq, who seized power and declared martial law in 1977. Ul-Huq announced his intention to Islamize the penal code and to move toward Islamization generally. In 1980 he issued the first of a series of directives ordering all women government employees to veil. Consequently, not only were they compelled to wear a veil or lose their jobs but all men became, in effect, judges of women's modesty. Male aggression toward women in matters of dress was implicitly legitimized, and the harassment of women at work and in the streets increased.

Researchers have found that in Pakistan "the vilification of women increased . . . in direct proportion to the spouting of self-righteous declarations of a new Islamic order." Television programs, for instance, increasingly depicted women as "the root and cause of corruption" and as "those who forced poor men into accepting bribes, smuggling or pilfering funds," and they depicted working women as the cause of "lax morality and the disintegration of family and social values."[48] The views of a prominent Islamist in the government regarding the place of women in Muslim society were aired on television and in the press. These included his beliefs that women and non-Muslims should be debarred from all decision-making bodies, that "all working women should be retired and pensioned off," and that women should "never leave the confines of their homes except in emergencies," and that no one should be punished for rape until total absence of female visibility had been achieved in society.[49]

The idea of a separate university education for women began to be given priority, the government proposing to upgrade the women's colleges of home economics to university status—the object of this move being, women activists believed, to push women into subjects, such as home economics, considered suitable for them and to deny them places in mainstream universities teaching mainstream subjects. The move thus responded to male protests that women were taking up places at the country's better universities that should be freed up for men.[50]

Islamization of the penal code, introduced in 1979, and in particular the laws governing the conviction and punishment for adultery and rape, also had some appalling consequences for women. Four adult male Muslim eyewitnesses were required to convict anyone of adultery or rape, and the testimony of women for either was excluded. Women who accuse men of rape or who become pregnant are thus open to punishment for adultery, while men go unpunished for lack of evidence. The researchers whose work I report here cite a number of cases of monstrous brutality and injustice meted out by the Islamic courts under the penal code.

All the above laws and decrees, those of both Iran and Pakistan, directly reflect or are entirely compatible with shari'a views as interpreted by establishment Islam. There is every reason to believe that any government declaring itself committed to Islamization, along either Sunni or Shia lines, would introduce similar laws for women.

Sixty-seven percent of the veiled university students responding to the questionnaire in Egypt agreed to the proposal that shari'a law should become the law of the land, and 53 percent of the unveiled women agreed. It is surely extremely doubtful that either group has any idea of the extremes of control, exclusion, injustice, and indeed brutality that can be, in the present order of things, legitimately meted out to women in the name of Islam.

CONCLUSION

IN THE DISCOURSES OF GEOPOLITICS THE REEMER-
gent veil is an emblem of many things, prominent
among which is its meaning as the rejection of the
West. But when one considers why the veil has this
meaning in the late twentieth century, it becomes obvious that, ironically, it was the discourses of the West,
and specifically the discourse of colonial domination,
that in the first place determined the meaning of the
veil in geopolitical discourses and thereby set the terms
for its emergence as a symbol of resistance. In other
words, the reemergent veil attests, by virtue of its very
power as a symbol of resistance, to the uncontested
hegemonic diffusion of the discourses of the West in
our age. And it attests to the fact that, at least as re-
gards the Islamic world, the discourses of resistance
and rejection are inextricably informed by the languages and ideas developed and disseminated by the
West to no less a degree than are the languages of those
openly advocating emulation of the West or those who,
like Frantz Fanon or Nawal El-Saadawi, are critical of
the West but nonetheless ground themselves in intellectual assumptions and political ideas, including a belief in the rights of the individual, formulated by

235

Western bourgeois capitalism and spread over the globe as a result of Western hegemony.

Islamic reformers such as al-Afghani and ʿAbdu and the militant Islamists of today; intellectuals radically critical of the West, including Marxists such as Fanon, Samir Amin, and El-Saadawi; and liberal intellectuals wholeheartedly embracing the colonial thesis of Western superiority and advocating the importance of emulating the West all differ fundamentally in their political stance, but they do not differ in the extent to which, whether they acknowledge it or not, they draw on Western thought and Western political and intellectual languages. The revitalized, reimagined Islam put forward by the Islamic militants or by ʿAbdu and his contemporaries is an Islam redefining itself against the assaults of the West but also an Islam revitalized and reimagined as a result of its fertilization by and its appropriation of the languages and ideas given currency by the discourses of the West. In the discourses of the Arab world comprehensively, then, whether they are discourses of collaboration or resistance, the goals and ideals they articulate and even the rejection of and often-legitimate anger at the West that they give voice to are formulated in terms of the dominant discourse—Western in origin—of our global society.

This is of particular relevance to Islamist positions. Marxists, secularists, and feminists generally concede, tacitly if not overtly, their grounding in Western thought, but Islamists, arguing for what they claim to be a restoration of an "original" Islam and an "authentic" indigenous culture, make their case, and conduct the assault on secularism, Marxism, or feminism on the grounds that these represent alien Western importations whereas Islamism intends the restoration of an indigenous tradition. But today, willy-nilly, as the Indian psychologist and critic Ashis Nandy has remarked, the West is everywhere, "in structures and in minds," and Western political ideas, technologies, and intellectual systems comprehensively permeate all societies.[1] There is no extricating them, no return to a past of unadulterated cultural purity—even if in this ancient and anciently multicultural part of the world such a project had ever been other than chimerical.

The Islamist position regarding women is also problematic in that, essentially reactive in nature, it traps the issue of women with the struggle over culture—just as the initiating colonial discourse had done. Typically, women—and the reaffirmation of indigenous customs relating to women and the restoration of the customs and laws of past Islamic societies with respect to women—are the centerpiece of the agenda of political Islamists. They are the centerpiece of the Islamist agenda at least in part because they were posed as central in the colonial discursive assault on Islam and Arab culture. I described in an earlier chapter how in the late nineteenth century the discourses of colonial domination coopted the language of feminism in attacking Muslim societies. Male imperialists known in their home societies for their intransigent opposition to feminism led the attack abroad against the "degradation" of women in Muslim societies and were the foremost champions of unveiling. The custom of veiling and the position of women in Muslim societies became, in their rhetoric, the proof of the inferiority of Islam and the justification of their efforts to undermine Muslim religion and society. This thesis and the societal goal of unveiling were, in addition, adopted and promoted (as I also described earlier) by the upper classes in Arab societies whose interests lay with the colonial powers; and they were opposed and the terms of the thesis inverted (and the importance of veiling and other indigenous practices insisted on) in the discourse of resistance.

The notion of returning to or holding on to an "original" Islam and an "authentic" indigenous culture is itself, then, a response to the discourses of colonialism and the colonial attempt to undermine Islam and Arab culture and replace them with Western practices and beliefs. But what is needed now is not a response to the colonial and postcolonial assault on non-Western cultures, which merely inverts the terms of the colonial thesis to affirm the opposite, but a move beyond confinement within those terms altogether and a rejection or incorporation of Western, non-Western, and indigenous inventions, ideas, and institutions on the basis of their merit, not their tribe of origin. After all and in sober truth, what thriving civilization or cultural heritage today, Western or non-Western, is not critically indebted to the inventions or traditions of thought of other peoples in other lands? And why should any human being be asked to do without some useful invention, political, technological, or of any kind, because it originated among some other tribe or, conversely, be compelled to practice a custom that has nothing to recommend it or even much against it for no better reason than that it is indigenous?

Rejection of things Western and rage at the Western world—an attitude that noticeably does not include the refusal of military equipment or technology—is understandable. Arabs have suffered and continue to suffer injustices and exploitation at the hands of colonial and postcolonial Western governments. But neither rage as a politics nor the self-deception and doublethink involved in relying on Western technologies—and indeed drawing on the intellectual and technical paraphernalia of the Western world in all aspects of contemporary life while claiming to be intent on returning to a culturally pure heritage—and in selectively choosing which aspects of the past will be preserved (for example, the laws controlling women) are persuasive as policies capable of leading the Arab world from entrapment in powerlessness and economic dependence.

Similarly, with respect to the more distant past and the proclaimed intention of restoring "original," "authentic" Islamic ways for women, the Islamist position is again problematic. It assumes, first, that the meaning of gender inhering in the initiatory Islamic society and in Muhammad's acts and sayings is essentially unambiguous and ascertainable in some precise and absolute sense and that the understanding of gender articulated in the written corpus of establishment Islam represents the only possible and uncontested understanding of the meaning of gender in Islam. The evidence reviewed in the preceding pages lends support to neither assumption, however. The meaning and social articulation of gender informing the first Islamic society in Arabia differed significantly from those informing the immediately succeeding Muslim societies, including most particularly those of the society that contributed centrally to the articulation of the founding institutional, legal, and scriptural discourses of dominant Islam—Abbasid Iraq. The meanings of gender specific to Abbasid society and the distinctive meaning that the notion "woman" acquired in that society (a society in which the traditions of a number of religions and cultures, including the Judaic, Christian, and Iranian, blended inextricably and were absorbed into Islamic thought) were inscribed into the literary, legal, and institutional productions of the age—productions that today constitute the founding and authoritative corpus of establishment Muslim thought. The androcentric and misogynist biases of this society affected in particular the different weight given to the two divergent tendencies within the Islamic message. As I argued earlier, even as Islam instituted, in the initiatory society, a hierarchical structure as the basis of relations between men and women, it also preached, in its ethical voice (and this is the case with Christianity and Judaism as well), the moral and spiritual equality of all human beings. Arguably, therefore, even as it instituted a sexual hierarchy, it laid the ground, in its ethical voice, for the subversion of the hierarchy. In the Abbasid context, the regulations instituting a sexual hierarchy were given central emphasis while the ethical message stressing the equality of all human beings and the importance of justice went largely unheeded and remained, with respect to women, essentially unarticulated in the laws and institutions that were now formulated.

Unheeded by the dominant classes and by the creators of establishment Islam, that ethical voice was, in contrast, emphasized by some often-marginal or lower-class groups who challenged the dominant political order and its interpretation of Islam, including its conception of the meaning of gender and the arrangements regarding women. From the start, the interpretation of the meaning of gender in the dominant society and other key issues, such as the proper political and social organization of Muslim societies, were contested. Establishment Islam's version of the Islamic message survived as the sole legitimate interpretation not because it was the only possible interpretation but because it was the interpretation of the politically dominant—those who had the power to outlaw and eradicate other readings as "heretical."

It is this technical, legalistic establishment version of Islam, a version that largely bypasses the ethical elements in the Islamic message, that continues to be politically powerful today. But for the lay Muslim it is not this legalistic voice but rather the ethical, egalitarian voice of Islam that speaks most clearly and insistently. It is because Muslim women hear this egalitarian voice that they often declare (generally to the astonishment of non-Muslims) that Islam is nonsexist. Only within the politically powerful version of Islam (and in its reflection in Western Orientalist literature)—a version with no greater claim to being regarded as the only possible interpretation of Islam than Papal Christianity has to being regarded as the only possible interpretation of Christianity—is women's position immutably fixed as subordinate. Just as with other monotheistic (and indeed non-monotheistic) religions, what the import of Islam was and what its significance for human societies might be are subjects that yielded varieties of interpretations in past societies and that again today are open to a range of interpretations, including feminist interpretations.[2]

Thus, the Islamist position with respect to the distant past is flawed in assuming that the meaning of gender informing the first Islamic society is reducible to a single, simple, unconflicted meaning that is ascertainable in some precise and absolute sense, as well as in assuming that the legacy was open to only one interpretation on matters of gender and that the correct interpretation was the one captured and preserved in the corpus of Muslim thought and writing and constituting the heritage of establishment Islam, created decades and indeed centuries after Muhammad, in the societies of the Middle East. In making these assumptions Islamists overlook the complexity of a gender system diversely and comprehensively articulated in social mores, verbal prescriptions, and the interplay between these, on the one hand, and the critical role of interpretation, on the other. Underlying the above assumptions—and in particular the belief that the laws developed in Abbasid and other societies of early Islam merely preserved and precisely elaborated the pristine originary meaning of Islam—is the notion that ideas, systems of meaning, and conceptions of gender traveled to and were transmitted by other societies without being blurred or colored by the mores, culture, and gender systems of the societies through which they passed. In a similarly literalist approach, Islamists assume that identifying the rulings regarding gender current in the first Muslim society—rulings presumed to be ascertainable in some categorical fashion—and transposing and applying them to modern Muslim societies would result in the recon- stitution of the meaning of gender inhering and articulated in that first society. Such an assumption fails to recognize that a society's rulings in matters of gender form part of a comprehensive and integral system, part of a society's variously articulated (socially, legally, psychically) discourse on gender, and thus that the transposition of a segment of the Arabian Muslim society's discourse (even if this were absolutely ascertainable) to the fundamentally different Muslim societies of the modern world is likely to result not in the reconstitution of the first Arabian Muslim understand- ing of gender but rather in its travesty.

The meaning of gender as elaborated by establishment Islam remained the controlling discourse in the Muslim Middle East until about the be- ginning of the nineteenth century. Unambiguously and on all levels—cul- tural, legal, social, and institutional—the social system it devised and informed was one that controlled and subordinated women, marginalized them economically, and, arguably, conceptualized them as human beings inferior to men. So negatively were women viewed within this system that even women of the spiritual stature of Rabiʿa al-ʿAdawiyya still could be deemed inferior to the least spiritually developed man in the eyes of an establishment spokesman like the theologian al-Ghazali. Evidently, dissent from this dominant view existed and found formal expression in the thought of such groups as the Sufis and the Qarmatians and in the thought of a rare philosopher, like Ibn al-ʿArabi. Evidently, too, informal resistance to the dominant culture was to be found within families and among in- dividuals. That families economically in a position to contractually impose monogamy on their daughter's spouse or otherwise protect her interests in marriage sometimes did impose such terms is one indication of familial and personal resistance to the view of the dominant culture on the place and rights of women. Similarly, that some families educated their daughters despite the lack of any formal avenue for the education of women not merely to the point of literacy but to the point where they could become distinguished scholars and eminent women of learning is another kind of evidence of resistance among people to the prescriptions and dicta of the dominant view of women.

The unraveling of this system began to occur with European economic encroachment in about the early nineteenth century. From that point forward, the consonance that had thitherto pertained in the Muslim Middle East between the discourse on gender espoused by establishment Islam and the social and institutional articulation of that discourse began to be steadily eroded. That erosion, leading to the gradual foundering of the old order and institutions, continues into our own day.

Muslim women have no cause to regret the passing of the customs and formulas of earlier Muslim societies or the foundering of the old order and its controlling and excluding institutions. In the course of the last century or so women in a significant number of Arab countries have attained civil and political rights and virtually equal access to education, at least insofar as public policies are concerned; cultural prejudices, however (as in other parts of the world, Western and non-Western), and inadequate resources continue to hold back women's education in some areas. Again, in a significant number of Arab countries women have gained or are gaining entry into virtually all the professions, from teaching and nursing to medicine, law, and engineering. Developments in these matters have occurred at slightly different rates in different countries, but broadly speaking, most Middle Eastern nations have moved or are moving toward adopting the Western political language of human and political rights and toward according these rights to women as well as to men.

There are two kinds of exceptions to this tendency. One is an exception with regard to a geographic region. The societies in the Arabian Peninsula, the area in the Middle East least subject to European economic, cultural, or political domination and least open generally to other cultures and ideas, continue to resist the current of change. Moreover, in response to increasing exposure to global influences in recent decades, the societies in the region, particularly Saudi Arabia, have attempted to erect yet-more-impregnable cultural and ideological walls. Although the peninsular countries have opened up education to women, in most other ways the old strictures remain firmly in place, and modern ideas about rights such as the right to vote, constituting part of contemporary political thought, have made no inroads. (Kuwait, however, prior to its invasion by Iraq, was beginning to move toward important changes for women.)

The other exception to the trend toward amelioration and extension of rights to women in Middle Eastern countries other than those of the Arabian Peninsula is with respect to Islamic family law—the laws governing men's and women's rights in marriage, divorce, and child custody. These laws have remained profoundly resistant to change. Even though for a good part of this century liberals and feminists in many Muslim societies have persistently mounted attempts to introduce reforms, the laws developed in highly misogynist societies in the first three or four centuries of Islam continue to govern the relations between men and women. Only a few countries—Iraq, Syria, and Tunisia—have introduced modifications in their laws that improve on the laws of establishment Islam in varying degrees.

Family law is the cornerstone of the system of male privilege set up by establishment Islam. That it is still preserved almost intact signals the existence of enormously powerful forces within Middle Eastern societies determined to uphold male privilege and male control over women. Among political Islamist movements such forces are gaining ground. Where Islamist movements have led to the institution of "Islam" as the formal basis of political power—Iran, Pakistan under Zia ul-Huq—the governments have proceeded to transform the countries, as well as women's homes, into prison houses for women, where the confinement of women, their exclusion from many fields of work, and their unjust and inhumane treatment are the proclaimed laws of the land. In addition, the misogynist rhetoric they let loose into the social system implicitly sanctions male violence toward women and sets up women—rather than the corruptions and bankruptcies of the government—as targets of male frustration at poverty and powerlessness. Besides the costs to women themselves, limiting their access to remunerative work deprives their societies of the creativity and productivity that women throughout the world have proven themselves to be capable of.

Clearly, the Islam such governments set up bears no relation to an Islam reinterpreted to give precedence to the ethical voice of Islam. With respect at any rate to women, it is the technical, legalistic legacy of establishment Islam that political Islamism institutes once it gains power. There is one difference between these modern enforcers of technical Islam and their predecessors who developed the laws being reinstituted today. The encoders of the earlier Islamic period, hostage to societies in which misogyny and androcentrism were the uncontested and invisible norms, strove to the best of their abilities to render Islamic precepts into laws that expressed justice according to the available measures of their times. In contrast, their descendants, today reinstituting the laws devised in other ages and other societies, are choosing to eschew, when it comes to women, contemporary understandings of the meanings of justice and human rights, even as they adopt modern technologies and languages in every other domain of life.

Deferring justice to women until rights and prosperity have been won for all men, perpetuating and reinstituting systems immoral by contemporary standards in order to pander to male frustrations—these are sterile and destructive to no less an extent than the politics of rage and the disingenuous rhetoric of rejecting the West in favor of a return to indigenous culture while allowing the mental and technological appurtenances of the West to permeate society without barrier.

Just as the discourses within Arab societies are enmeshed in the discourses of the West and thoroughly implicated, in particular, in the history of colonialism and the discourses of domination that colonialism unleashed upon the Muslim Middle East, so, too, is the study of Muslim Arab women as it is pursued today in the West so enmeshed and implicated. As I described in an earlier chapter, the discourse of patriarchal colonialism captured the language of feminism and used the issue of women's position in Islamic societies as the spearhead of the colonial attack on those societies. Imperialist men who were the enemies of feminism in their own societies, abroad espoused a rhetoric of feminism attacking the practices of Other men and their "degradation" of women, and they used the argument that the cultures of the colonized peoples degraded women in order to legitimize Western domination and justify colonial policies of actively trying to subvert the cultures and religions of the colonized peoples. That posture was perfectly exemplified by Lord Cromer. Famous in England for his opposition to feminism, in Egypt, where he was British consul general, Cromer was a principal advocate of the need to end Islamic degradation of women and a declared champion of the importance of unveiling. It was the practice of veiling and the Islamic degradation of women that stood in the way, according to the imperialist thesis, of the "progress" and "civilization" of Muslim societies and of their populaces being "persuaded or forced" into imbibing "the true spirit of Western civilization."

That thesis was accepted and promoted not only by chauvinist male servants of empire but generally by members of Western civilization and also by natives of the upper and upper-middle classes inducted into the ideas of Western culture. European feminists critical of the practices and beliefs of the men of their societies with respect to themselves acquiesced in and indeed promoted the European male's representations of Other men and the cultures of Other men and joined, in the name of feminism, in the attack on the veil and the practices generally of Muslim societies. Whether the attack on Muslim customs and societies, and especially on their practices regarding women, was made by imperialist men who were supporters of male dominance, by missionaries, or by feminists and whether it was made in the name of "civilizing" the natives, or Christianizing them, or of rescuing women from the religion and culture in which they had the misfortune to find themselves, invoking the issue of women served to license, and to impart an aura of moral legitimacy to, denouncing and attacking the customs of the dominated society and insisting that it change its ways and adopt the superior ways of the Europeans.

It was in this discourse of colonial "feminism" that the notion that an intrinsic connection existed between the issues of culture and the status of women, and in particular that progress for women could be achieved only through abandoning the native culture, first made its appearance. The idea was the product of a particular historical moment and was constructed by the discourses of patriarchal colonialism in the service of particular political ends. As the history of Western women makes clear, there is no validity to the notion that progress for women can be achieved only by abandoning the ways of a native androcentric culture in favor of those of another culture. It was never argued, for instance, even by the most ardent nineteenth-century feminists, that European women could liberate themselves from the oppressiveness of Victorian dress (designed to compel the female figure to the ideal of frailty and helplessness by means of suffocating, rib-cracking stays, it must surely rank among the more constrictive fashions of relatively recent times) only by adopting the dress of some other culture. Nor has it ever been argued, whether in Mary Wollstonecraft's day, when European women had no rights, or in our own day and even by the most radical feminists, that because male domination and injustice to women have existed throughout the West's recorded history, the only recourse for Western women is to abandon Western culture and find themselves some other culture. The idea seems absurd, and yet this is routinely how the matter of improving the status of women is posed with respect to women in Arab and other non-Western societies. Whether those societies did or did not, will or will not, abandon the ways of one culture in favor of those of another is commonly presented in Western-based literature as the crux of the matter of progress for women. To this day, the struggle against the veil and toward westernization and the abandoning of backward and oppressive Arab Muslim ways (the agenda propounded by Cromer and his like as the agenda to be pursued for Muslim women) is still commonly the framestory within which Western-based studies of Arab women, including feminist studies, are presented.

The presumption underlying these ideas is that Western women may pursue feminist goals by engaging critically with and challenging and redefining their cultural heritage, but Muslim women can pursue such goals only by setting aside the ways of their culture for the nonandrocentric, nonmisogynist ways (such is the implication) of the West. And the presumption is, too, that Islamic cultures and religion are fundamentally inimical to women in a way that Western cultures and religions are not, whereas (as I have argued) Islam and Arabic cultures, no less than the religions and cultures of the West, are open to reinterpretation and change. Moreover, the different histories of feminism in the Western world and in the Middle East suggest that the significant factors in Western societies that permitted the emergence of feminist voices and political action in those societies somewhat before their emergence in the Middle East were not that Western cultures were necessarily less androcentric or less misogynist than other societies but that women in Western societies were able to draw on the political vocabularies and systems generated by ideas of democracy and the rights of the individual, vocabularies and political systems developed by white male middle classes to safeguard their interests and not intended to be applicable to women. That women in Western societies are the beneficiaries of the political languages and institutions of democracy and the rights of the individual is commonly assumed to be proof that Western cultures are less androcentric or misogynist than other cultures, but political vocabularies and political and civil rights are quite distinct from the cultural and psychological messages, and the structures of psychological control, permeating a society. The notion that non-Western women will improve their status by adopting the culture, ways of dress, and so on of the West is based on a confusion between these different spheres. Of course, Arab Muslim women need to reject, just as Western women are trying to reject, the androcentrism of whatever culture or tradition in which they find themselves, but that is quite different from saying they need to adopt Western customs, goals, and life-styles.

The study of Muslim women in the West is heir to this history and to these discourses and to the ideas and assumptions they purveyed: it is heir to colonialism, to colonialism's discourses of domination, and to its cooptation of the ideas of feminism to further Western imperialism. Research on Middle Eastern women thus occurs in a field already marked with the designs and biases written into it by colonialism. Consequently, awareness of this legacy, and of the political ends silently being served by the assumptions, the narratives, and the versions of history and culture with which the Western discourse on Arab women is already inscribed, needs itself to be the starting point of any such investigation. At least, such awareness is essential if we are to avoid complicity in the reinscription of the Western discourse of domination and if the study of women and the ideas of feminism are to be prevented from functioning yet again as a tool serving the political ends of Western domination. Of course we must also be wary of reinscribing the contentions of the Arabic narrative of resistance, which entails the wholesale affirmation of indigenous culture and with it the acceptability of injustice to women because indigenous. But few investigators working in the West are in danger of this latter possibility. The discourse of Islamic resistance, although a discourse of power within the Middle East, commands little authority here: a point that underscores the fact that discourses of power nest one within the other, the dominant discourse in the Middle East nesting within—indeed a dependent discourse of—the globally dominant discourse of the West.

The success of Western feminism, or at any rate its success in gaining legitimacy in the academy (what practical gains it has made particularly for women of the more economically deprived classes and for women of color is a more problematic matter), has meant that scholarship on women that is produced within a Western framework is itself now to some extent a discourse of authority in relation to other societies.[3] It would be a pity if this very success should lead, as Western-based feminists direct their gaze toward other women, to the elaboration of a literature rearticulating the old formulas in new guise and reinscribing the old story of the inferiority of Arabs and Muslims, supported now with the apparatus of scholarship. It would be a pity if instead of striving to disengage itself from such designs, feminism should fall once more to inadvertently serving the political ends of the Western political order and of Western-style male dominance. At the very least, perpetuating this approach would lead to the alienation of a younger generation of Arab women and men from feminism. The designs and manipulations of Western discourses, and the political ends being served by the deployment of feminism against other cultures, are today no longer hidden and invisible: on the contrary, to many non-Western people they are transparently obvious.

There can be few people of Arab or Muslim background (including, and perhaps even particularly, the feminists among them) who have not noticed and been disheartened by the way in which Arab and Muslim "oppression" of women is invoked in Western media and sometimes in scholarship in order to justify and even insidiously promote hostility toward Arabs and Muslims. It is disheartening, too, that some feminist scholarly work continues to uncritically reinscribe the old story. Whole books are unfortunately still being published in which the history of Arab women is told within the framework of the paradigm that Cromer put forward—that the measure of whether Muslim women were liberated or not lay in whether they veiled and whether the particular society had become "progressive" and westernized or insisted on clinging to Arab and Islamic ways. In its contemporary version this essentially still-colonial (or colonial and classist) feminism is only slightly more subtle than the old version. It may be cast, for example, in the form of praising heroic Arab feminist women for resisting the appalling oppressions of Arab culture and Islam. Whereas this is its stated message, the unstated message when the inherited constructs of Western discourse are reproduced unexamined is often, just as in colonial days, that Arab men, Arab culture, and Islam are incurably backward and that Arab and Islamic societies indeed deserve to be dominated, undermined, or worse.

In the context of the contemporary structure of global power, then, we need a feminism that is vigilantly self-critical and aware of its historical and political situatedness if we are to avoid becoming unwitting collaborators in racist ideologies whose costs to humanity have been no less brutal than those of sexism. It may be, moreover, that in the context of Western global domination, the posture of some kinds of feminism—poised to identify, deplore, and denounce oppression—must unavoidably lend support to Western domination when it looks steadfastly past the injustice to which women are subject in Western societies and the exploitation of women perpetrated abroad by Western capitalism only to fix upon the oppressions of women perpetrated by Other men in Other societies.

In its analyses of Western societies, feminism, or rather the many feminisms that there now are, has moved far beyond the somewhat simplistic approach of deploring and denouncing. Feminist analysis of Western societies now comprehends a variety of subtle and complicated analytical perspectives and positions. Among the most illuminating is the critique of the way in which feminism is implicated in the dominant political languages of Western societies and its inadvertent complicity in the ideologies and social systems that it explicitly criticizes; also illuminating is the critical analysis of the erosions and costs for women wrought by advanced capitalism. Elizabeth Fox-Genovese, for instance, writing of U.S. society, observes that the history of the twentieth century "confirms that sexism, instead of receding with the triumph of modernity, has probably become more general and more difficult to locate in any single institution. If the so-called sexual revolution has loosened the grip of the nuclear family on female sexuality, it has not indisputably weakened sexism or acceptance of conventional gender roles." Late capitalist society, she notes, "has contributed a bitter twist to the centuries of female oppression. Consumerism, suburban residence patterns, declining family size, increased male occupational mobility, increased female education, declining parental control over children . . . rising divorce rates, and a host of other changes have been interwoven in a dense network of isolation and anxiety." Fox-Genovese fears that feminism itself, in its uncritical adoption of the ideals of individualism, may come one day to be seen as having "done the dirty work of capitalism—of having eroded the older communities and bourgeois institutions that blocked the way to a sinister new despotism."[4]

Research on Arab women is a much younger field. Analysis of this complexity is rare in work on Arab women, in which it is often assumed that modernity and "progress" and westernization are incontestably good and that the values of individualism are always unambiguously beneficial. The sum of what is currently known about women and gender in Arab societies—the many and different Arab societies and cultures that there are—is minuscule. The areas of women's lives and the informal structures they inhabit that are still unexplored are vast. And perhaps the posture of studying other cultures in order to identify their worst practices is not after all likely to be the best way to further our understanding of human societies. The noted Indian anthropologist T. N. Madan, reflecting on the ambiguous legacy of anthropology and the contribution the discipline might nevertheless make to a common human enterprise, rather than serving Western interests, suggests that a productive starting point could be looking to other cultures in an attitude of respect and in acknowledgment of their affording opportunities for critiquing and enhancing awareness of the investigator's culture. The study of anthropology "should not merely tell us how others live their lives: it should rather tell us how we may live our lives better," and ideally it should be grounded in the affirmation "that every culture needs others as critics so that the best in it may be highlighted and held out as being cross-culturally desirable."[5] Perhaps feminism could formulate some such set of criteria for exploring issues of women in other cultures, including Islamic societies—criteria that would undercut even inadvertent complicity in serving Western interests but that, at the same time, would neither set limits on the freedom to question and explore nor in any way compromise feminism's passionate commitment to the realization of societies that enable women to pursue without impediment the full development of their capacities and to contribute to their societies in all domains.

NOTES

Introduction

1. Wiebke Walther, *Woman in Islam,* trans. C. S. V. Salt (London: George Prior, 1981).
2. Ira Marvin Lapidus, *A History of Islamic Societies* (Cambridge: Cambridge University Press, 1988). For a lucid account of the usefulness of analyzing gender in the study of history see Joan W. Scott, "Gender: A Useful Category of Historical Analysis," *American Historical Review* 91, no. 5 (1986): 1053–75.
3. Lapidus, *History of Islamic Societies,* 3.
4. *The Translation of the Meanings of Sahih al-Bukhari* (in Arabic and English), 9 vols., trans. Muhammad M. Khan (Medina: Dar al-fikr, 1981), 7:80.
5. See, for example, Fouad Ajami, *The Arab Predicament* (Cambridge: Cambridge University Press, 1981), 13–15.
6. On the status of minorities see Bernard Lewis, *The Jews of Islam* (Princeton: Princeton University Press, 1984).
7. Even the law as formulated in early Islam at times differentiated between women on the basis of class, permitting husbands, for instance, to beat wives with varying degrees of severity according to their class. It never became the wife's prerogative to beat the husband, however, whatever her class. Judith Butler, *Gender Trouble: Feminism and the Subversion of Identity* (New York: Routledge, 1990), esp. chap. 1, offers a useful discussion of the problematics for feminist theory inhering in analyses made in terms of the category "women."
8. Nancy F. Cott, *The Grounding of Modern Feminism* (New Haven: Yale University Press, 1987), 5.

Chapter 1: Mesopotamia

1. See James Mellaart, *Çatal Hüyük: A Neolithic Town in Anatolia* (New York: McGraw-Hill, 1967).

2. On these subjects see the following works in particular: Thorkil Jacobsen, *Towards the Image of Tammus and Other Essays on Mesopotamian History and Culture,* ed. William L. Moran (Cambridge: Harvard University Press, 1970); Edwin O. James, *The Cult of the Mother-Goddess: An Archeological and Documentary Study* (London: Thames and Hudson, 1959); S. N. Kramer, *From the Tablets of Sumer* (India Hills, Colo.: Falcon Wing Press, 1956).

3. Among the important works discussing theories of the origin of male dominance are Robert Briffault, *The Mothers: The Matriarchal Theory of Social Origins* (New York: Macmillan, 1931); Frederick Engels, *The Origin of the Family: Private Property and the State,* ed. Eleanor Leacock (New York: International Publishers, 1972); Rayna Rapp Reiter, "The Search for Origins: Unravelling the Threads of Gender Hierarchy," *Critique of Anthropology* 2, nos. 9–10 (1977): 5–24; Gayle Rubin, "The Traffic in Women: Notes on the Political Economy of Sex," in *Toward an Anthropology of Women,* ed. Rayna Rapp Reiter (New York: Monthly Review, 1978); and Gerda Lerner, *The Creation of Patriarchy* (New York: Oxford University Press, 1986).

4. I have here summarized, necessarily somewhat tersely and in broad outline, the speculations of feminist and other scholars as to the institutionalization of patriarchy.

5. "The Code of Hammurabi," trans. Theophile J. Meek, in *Ancient Near Eastern Texts Relating to the Old Testament,* ed. James B. Pritchard (Princeton: Princeton University Press, 1950), 170–71; and "The Middle Assyrian Laws," trans. Meek, also in *Ancient Near Eastern Texts,* ed. Pritchard, 184. Hereafter cited in the text as "Code" and "Laws."

6. The term *seignior* is a translation of *awilum,* sometimes also translated as "noble" or "burgher."

7. S. N. Kramer, *The Sumerians: Their History, Culture and Character* (Chicago: University of Chicago Press, 1963), 322. Kramer translates and comments on the text as follows: "If a woman said to a man . . . (unfortunately the text is unintelligible at this crucial point), her teeth were crushed with burnt bricks, (and) these burnt bricks (upon which her guilt was inscribed) were hung up at the great gate (for all to see)."

8. Ilse Seibert, *Woman in the Ancient Near East,* trans. Marianne Herzfeld; ed. George A. Shepperson (Leipzig: Edition Leipzig, 1974), 18. For an interesting discussion of these ideas see Lerner, *Creation of Patriarchy,* 104–5.

9. Seibert, *Woman in the Ancient Near East,* 51.

10. Lerner, *Creation of Patriarchy,* 139.

11. Seibert, *Woman in the Ancient Near East,* 19.

12. Lerner, *Creation of Patriarchy,* 74 (quotation), 74–75.

13. Seibert, *Woman in the Ancient Near East,* 19–20. On naditum see R. Harris, "The Naditu Woman," in *Studies Presented to A. Leo Oppenheim* (Chicago: University of Chicago Press, 1964).

14. Seibert, *Woman in the Ancient Near East,* 19, 21, 14.

15. See Lerner, *Creation of Patriarchy,* esp. chaps. 8, 9; Seibert, *Woman in the Ancient Near East,* 18; A. L. Oppenheim, *Letters from Mesopotamia* (Chicago: University of Chicago Press, 1967), 45.

16. Seibert, *Woman in the Ancient Near East,* 27–28.

17. A. L. Oppenheim, "The Babylonian Evidence of Achaemenian Rule in Mesopotamia," in *The Cambridge History of Iran,* vol. 2, ed. Ilya Gershevitch (Cambridge: Cambridge University Press, 1985), 572; and Oppenheim, *Letters from Mesopotamia,* 45.

18. Seibert, *Woman in the Ancient Middle East,* 51 (quotation); J. M. Cook, "The Rise of the Achaemenids and Establishment of Their Empire," in *Cambridge History of Iran,* 2:226 (quotation). Cook writes that among the Achaemenids the harems were guarded by eunuchs and that no males were allowed to enter, except for doctors, who were usually foreigners. "Rise of the Achaemenids," 226–27.

19. Michael G. Morony, *Iraq after the Muslim Conquest* (Princeton: Princeton University Press, 1984), 134–35.

20. A. Perikhanian, "Iranian Society and Law," in *Cambridge History of Iran,* vol. 3 (2 parts), ed. Ehsan Yarshater (Cambridge: Cambridge University Press, 1983), pt. 2: 656.

21. Ali-Akbar Mazaheri, *La Famille iranienne aux temps anté-islamiques,* Librairie Orientale et Américaine (Paris: G. P. Maisonneuve, 1938), 110.

22. Ibid., 104.

23. Perikhanian, "Iranian Society and Law," 3, pt. 2: 650.

24. Ibid., 648–49.

25. Ibid.

26. Ehsan Yarshater, "Mazdakism," in *Cambridge History of Iran,* 3, pt. 2: 991.

27. Ibid., 998 (quotations). One author, for example, points out that activities attributed to two Mazdakian women—Khurrama, Mazdak's alleged wife, and another woman—suggest an improvement in the condition of women among the Mazdakians and speculates that Mazdak's teachings probably favored women's marrying outside their own class and called for the abolition of harems, the release of additional wives, and more relaxed laws regarding levirate marriages, which women were compelled to enter into without full rights. Ibid., 1000–1001. To orthodox Zoroastrians such ideas would have appeared dangerously disruptive of both the line of male descent and class distinctions.

28. Perikhanian, "Iranian Society and Law," 3, pt. 2: 637.

29. Ibid., 634.

30. J. P. Asmussen, "Christians in Iran," in *Cambridge History of Iran,* 3, pt. 2: 946.

252 NOTES TO PAGES 22–30

31. Sebastian P. Brock and Susan Ashbrook Harvey, trans., *Holy Women of the Syrian Orient* (Berkeley: University of California Press, 1987), 64–65; hereafter cited in the text.

Chapter 2: The Mediterranean Middle East

1. Elaine Pagels, *Adam, Eve, and the Serpent* (New York: Random House, 1988), 88–89. As Peter Brown has noted, "Renunciation [of sex] and baptism into the church declared the power of sex null and void." *The Body and Society: Men, Women and Sexual Renunciation in Early Christianity* (New York: Columbia University Press, 1988), 80.
2. José Grosdidier de Matons, "La Femme dans l'empire byzantin," in *Histoire mondiale de la femme*, 4 vols., ed. Pierre Grimal (Paris: Nouvelle Librairie de France, 1967), 3:28 (quotation), 28n1, 28–30.
3. Judith Herrin, "In Search of Byzantine Women: Three Avenues of Approach," in *Images of Women in Antiquity*, ed. Averil Cameron and Amelie Kuhrt (London: Croom Helm, 1983), 169 (quotation), 171; Angeliki E. Laiou, "The Role of Women in Byzantine Society," *Jahrbuch der österreichischen Byzantinistik* 31, no. 1 (1981): 243.
4. Herrin, "In Search of Byzantine Women," 169.
5. Laiou, "Role of Women in Byzantine Society," 249.
6. De Matons, "La Femme dans l'empire byzantin," 14.
7. For example, de Matons attributes seclusion to "Oriental influences." Ibid., 13–15.
8. Sarah B. Pomeroy, *Goddesses, Whores, Wives, and Slaves: Women in Classical Antiquity* (New York: Schocken, 1975), 81; Helene P. Foley, "Women in Greece," in *Civilization of the Ancient Mediterranean*, 3 vols., ed. Michael Grant and Rachel Kitzinger (New York: Scribner, 1988), 3:1302.
9. Pomeroy, *Goddesses*, 83, 69; Foley, "Women in Greece," 3:1303.
10. Foley, "Women in Greece," 3:1311.
11. Pomeroy, *Goddesses*, 72.
12. Aristotle, *Politica*, trans. Benjamin Jowett, in *The Works of Aristotle*, 12 vols., ed. W. D. Ross, vol. 10 (Oxford: Clarendon Press, 1921), 1.5.1254b.
13. Aristotle, *Historia animalium*, trans. D'Arcy Wentworth Thompson, in *Works of Aristotle*, ed. Ross, vol. 4, ed. J. A. Smith and W. D. Ross (Oxford: Clarendon Press, 1910), 9.1.608b.
14. Aristotle, *De generatione animalium*, trans. Arthur Platt, in *Works of Aristotle*, ed. Ross, vol. 5, ed. J. A. Smith and W. D. Ross (Oxford: Clarendon Press, 1912), 1.20.728a, 2.4.738b.
15. Pomeroy, *Goddesses*, 125.
16. Sarah B. Pomeroy, *Women in Hellenistic Egypt: From Alexander to Cleopatra* (New York: Schocken, 1984), 171; hereafter cited in the text.
17. Dorothy J. Thompson, *Memphis under the Ptolemies* (Princeton: Princeton

University Press, 1988); Naphtali Lewis, *Greeks in Ptolemaic Egypt* (Oxford: Clarendon Press, 1986).

18. Jean Vercoutter, "La Femme en Egypte ancienne," in *Histoire mondiale de la femme,* ed. Grimal, 1:119.

19. Ibid., 1:143. Other authors describe the position of women in similarly positive terms. Christiane Desroches Noblecourt, for example, writes: "The Egyptian woman was the happy citizen of a country where sexual equality seems to have been, from the start, considered as completely natural and so profoundly rooted an idea that the problem seems never even to have been raised." *La Femme au temps des pharaons,* 2 vols. (Paris: Stock/Laurence Pernoud, 1986), 2:170.

20. Noblecourt, *La Femme au temps des pharaons,* 2:171, 216; Jacques Pirenne, "Le Statut de la femme dans l'Ancienne Egypte," in *La Femme,* 3 vols., Recueils de la Societé Jean Bodin pour l'histoire comparative des institutions, vols. 11– 13 (Brussels: Editions de la Librairie Encyclopédique, 1959–62), 1:74.

21. C. J. Eyre, "Crime and Adultery in Ancient Egypt," *Journal of Egyptian Archaeology* 70 (1984): 101–2.

22. Ibid., 95, 96. For the discussions on adultery see Vercoutter, "La Femme en Egypte ancienne," 1:136–37; and Noblecourt, *La Femme au temps des pharaons,* 2:215–16.

23. Noblecourt, *La Femme au temps des pharaons,* 2:211.

24. Vercoutter, "La Femme en Egypte ancienne," 1:121, 152.

25. On these topics see Susan Ashbrook Harvey, "Women in Early Syrian Christianity," in *Images of Women in Antiquity,* ed. Cameron and Kuhrt; and Elaine Pagels, *The Gnostic Gospels* (New York: Vintage Books, 1981).

26. Jean Bottero, "Mésopotamie et Israel," in *Histoire mondiale de la femme,* ed. Grimal, 1:238, 242, 243, 247.

27. See, for instance, Judith Plaskow, "Blaming the Jews for the Birth of Patriarchy," in *Nice Jewish Girls: A Lesbian Anthology,* ed. Evelyn Torton Beck (Trumansburg, N.Y.: Crossing Press, 1982), 250–54.

28. Sarah B. Pomeroy, "Infanticide in Hellenistic Greece," in *Images of Women in Antiquity,* ed. Cameron and Kuhrt, 207; Bonnie S. Anderson and Judith P. Zinsser, *A History of Their Own: Women in Europe from Prehistory to the Present,* 2 vols. (New York: Harper and Row, 1988), 1:30, 82.

29. Anderson and Zinsser, *History of Their Own,* 1:82.

30. Peter Brown, "Late Antiquity," in *From Pagan Rome to Byzantium* (originally in French), ed. Phillippe Ariès and Georges Duby (Cambridge: Harvard University Press, 1987–), 1:298–99. See also Brown, *Body and Society,* 80–81.

31. James A. Brundage, *Law, Sex, and Christian Society in Medieval Europe* (Chicago: University of Chicago Press, 1987), 85–86.

32. Rosemary Ruether, "Misogynism and Virginal Feminism in the Fathers of the Church," in *Religion and Sexism: Images of Woman in the Jewish and Christian Traditions,* ed. Ruether (New York: Simon and Schuster, 1974), 157.

33. An important work on the creation of constructs of history with respect to the

ancient Mediterranean is Martin Bernal, *Black Athena: The Afroasiatic Roots of Classical Civilization* (New Brunswick, N.J.: Rutgers University Press, 1987).

34. Gerda Lerner, *The Creation of Patriarchy* (New York: Oxford University Press, 1986).

Chapter 3: Women and the Rise of Islam

1. *The Quran: The Revelation Vouchsafed to Muhammad the Seal of the Prophets* (in Arabic and English), trans. Muhammad Zafrulla Khan (London: Curzon Press, 1971; rpt., 1985). All quotations from the Quran in this chapter are from this translation.

2. W. Robertson Smith, *Kinship and Marriage in Early Arabia* (Cambridge: Cambridge University Press, 1885); W. Montgomery Watt, *Muhammad at Medina* (Oxford: Clarendon Press, 1956), 272–73.

3. Watt, *Muhammad at Medina,* 375.

4. *The Translation of the Meanings of Sahih al-Bukhari* (in Arabic and English), 9 vols., trans. Muhammad M. Khan (Medina: Dar al-fikr, 1981), 7:44. Here and below I have translated the Arabic rather than use the precise wording of Khan's rendering. Wherever possible, I have used works that give both Arabic and English texts.

5. Watt, *Muhammad at Medina,* 277–79, 376–77; Gertrude Stern, *Marriage in Early Islam* (London: Royal Asiatic Society, 1939), 61–62, 172–73.

6. Abu'l-Faraj al-Isfahani, *Kitab al-aghani,* 20 vols. (Bulak: Dar al-kutub, 1868), 16:106; Stern, *Marriage in Early Islam,* 39–43. For a further discussion of marriage and divorce in pre-Islamic Arabia see Laila Sabbaqh, *Al-marʾa fi al-tarikh al-ʿarabi fi tarikh al-ʿarab qabl al-islam* (Damascus: Manshurat wizarat al-thaqafa waʾl-irshad al-qawmi, 1975), esp. chap. 2.

7. Watt, *Muhammad at Medina,* 384 (quotation); Muhammad Ibn Saʿd, *Biographien/Kitab al-tabaqat al-kabir,* 9 vols., ed. Eduard Sachau (Leiden: E. J. Brill, 1904–40), 8:4. Ibn Saʿd is hereafter cited in the text.

8. *Sahih al-Bukhari,* 7:45–46.

9. See Nabia Abbott, *Studies of Arabic Literary Papyri,* 3 vols., Oriental Institute Publications, vols. 75–77 (Chicago: University of Chicago Press, 1957–72).

10. *Sahih al-Bukhari,* 1:298; Ahmad ibn Muhammad ibn Hanbal, *Musnad,* 6 vols. (Beirut: Al-maktab al-islami lil-tibaʿa waʾl-nashr, 1969), 6:42.

11. *Sahih al-Bukhari,* 1:1–4.

12. Khadija is described in the same text as a woman "of honor and power and a hirer of men" (Ibn Saʿd, 8:9).

13. Gertrude Stern, "The First Women Converts in Early Islam," *Islamic Culture* 13, no. 3 (1939): 293.

14. W. Montgomery Watt, *Muhammad at Mecca* (Oxford: Clarendon Press, 1953), 102–5.

15. ʿUmar Ridda Kahhalah, *Aʿlam al-nisa: fi aʿlami al-ʿarab waʾl-islam,* 3 vols. (Damascus: Al-matbaʿa al-hashimiyya, 1940), 1:280; Stern, "First Women Converts," 291.

16. ʿAbd al-Malik ibn Hisham, *Al-sira al-nabawiyya,* 2 vols., ed. Mustapha al-Saqqa, Ibrahim al-Ibyari, and Abdel Hafiz Shalabi (Cairo: Al-babi al-halabi, 1955), 1:356. I quote here Alfred Guillaume's *Life of Muhammad: A Translation of Ishaq's* Sirat Rasul Allah (New York: Oxford University Press, 1955), 161.

17. Ibn Hisham, *Al-sira al-nabawiyya,* 2:441.

18. Nabia Abbott, *Aishah, the Beloved of Muhammad* (Chicago: University of Chicago Press, 1942), 3 (quotation); Maxime Rodinson, *Mohamad,* trans. Ann Carter (New York: Penguin Books, 1971), 55.

19. Stern, *Marriage in Early Islam,* 34.

20. Ibn Hisham, *Al-sira al-nabawiyya,* 1:487.

21. Ibid., 1:498–99.

22. William Muir, *The Life of Muhammad from Original Sources* (Edinburgh: J. Grant, 1923), 175–76, 201; Abbott, *Aishah,* 50, 68.

23. Ibn Hanbal, *Musnad,* 6:211.

24. Abbott, *Aishah,* 2, 7–8, 31–35.

25. *Sahih al-Bukhari,* 7:88; Watt, *Muhammad at Medina,* 381.

26. Other women besides Khadija are mentioned in the early texts as trading in their own right, for example, ʿAisha bint Mukhariba, in Ibn Saʿd, 8:220. See also Watt, *Muhammad at Medina,* 290.

27. *Sahih al-Bukhari,* 4:85–86; Nabia Abbott, "Women and the State on the Eve of Islam," *American Journal of Semitic Languages* 58 (1941): 273. See also Ilse Lichtenstadter, *Women in the Aiyam al-Arab* (London: Royal Asiatic Society, 1935).

28. Stern, *Marriage in Early Islam,* 111ff.

29. Ibn Hanbal, *Musnad,* 6:271.

30. Abbott, *Aishah,* 25.

31. *Encyclopaedia of Islam* (Leiden: E. J. Brill, 1913–), s.v. "masdjid"; *Sahih al-Bukhari,* 1:257; Watt, *Muhammad at Medina,* 285.

32. Henri Lammens, *Fatima et les filles de Mahomet* (Rome: Scripta Pontificii Instituti Biblici, 1912), 53–54.

33. *Encyclopaedia of Islam,* new ed. (Leiden: E. J. Brill, 1960–), s.v. "hidjab"; Stern, *Marriage in Early Islam,* 108–10; E. Abrahams, *Ancient Greek Dress* (Chicago: Argonaut Press, 1964), 34; *Jewish Encyclopedia* (New York: Funk and Wagnalls, 1901), s.v. "veil."

34. Stern, *Marriage in Early Islam,* 114–15.

35. See also Abbott, *Aishah,* 45, 49–54; Stern, *Marriage in Early Islam,* 114.

36. Abbott, *Aishah,* 56–58.

37. Abbott, "Women on the Eve of Islam," 275–76.

38. Ibid., 264–66.

39. Abbott, *Aishah,* 68–69.

40. Abbott, "Women on the Eve of Islam," 279–80.

41. Ibid., 281–84.

42. F. Beeston, "The So-called Harlots of Hadramaut," *Oriens* 5 (1952): 16–17.

43. Ibid., 16ff.

44. Wiebke Walther, *Woman in Islam,* trans. C. S. V. Salt (London: George Prior, 1981), 78.

45. Abbott, *Aishah,* 11, 84, 95–97.

46. *Encyclopaedia of Islam* (1913–), s.v. "'Omar ibn al-Khattab"; Abbott, *Aishah,* 88; Stern, "First Women Converts," 299.

47. See also Abbott, *Aishah,* 94.

48. Ibid., 160–69.

49. For an analysis of the strong parallels between Islamic and Judaic formulations of marriage see Judith Romney Wegner, "The Status of Women in Jewish and Islamic Marriage and Divorce Law," *Harvard Law Journal* 5, no. 1 (1982): 1–33.

Chapter 4: The Transitional Age

1. *The Holy Qur'an,* trans. A. Yusuf Ali (Jeddah: Dar al-Qiblah for Islamic Literature, 1982). All translations from the Quran in this chapter are from this translation.

2. Aristotle argued that women were innately and by social role different from and inferior to men, and he rejected the idea that virtue could be the same for both sexes. For his discussion on women, men, and virtue see Aristotle, *Politica,* trans. Benjamin Jowett, in *The Works of Aristotle,* 12 vols., ed. W. D. Ross, vol. 10 (Oxford: Clarendon Press, 1921), 1.13.12596–1260a.

3. *The Translation of the Meanings of Sahih al-Bukhari* (in Arabic and English), 9 vols., trans. Muhammad M. Khan (Medina: Dar al-fikr, 1981), 4:343, 1:197, 7:103. The controversy is discussed in detail in B. F. Mussalam, *Sex and Society in Islam* (Cambridge: Cambridge University Press, 1983); see esp. chap. 3. On Islamic attitudes to conception and abortion see my "Arab Culture and Writing Women's Bodies," *Feminist Issues* 9, no. 1 (1989): 41–56.

4. Abu Hamid Muhammad ibn Muhammad al-Ghazali, *Ihya 'ulum al-din,* 5 vols. (Cairo: Mu'assasat al-halabi wa shurakah lil-nashr wa'l-tawzi', 1967–68), 4:514.

5. *The Foundations of the Community,* trans. W. Montgomery Watt and M. V. McDonald, vol. 7 of *The History of Tabari (Tarikh al-Rusul wa'l-muluk),* Bibliotheca Persica, ed. Ehsan Yarshater, SUNY Series in Near Eastern Studies, ed. Said Arjomand (Albany: State University of New York Press, 1987), 130.

6. Muhammad Ibn Sa'd, *Biographien/Kitab al-tabaqat al-kabir,* 9 vols., ed. Eduard Sachau (Leiden: E. J. Brill, 1904–40), 8:301–4; Nabia Abbott, "Women and the State in Early Islam," *Journal of Near Eastern Studies* (April 1942): 118; William Muir, *The Caliphate: Its Rise, Decline and Fall,* rev. ed., ed. T. H.

Weir (Edinburgh: John Grant, 1924), 122; Muir, *Annals of the Early Caliphate* (London: Smith and Elder, 1883), 109; and Abbott, "Women and the State on the Eve of Islam," *American Journal of Semitic Languages* 58 (1941): 277.

7. E. A. Salem, *The Political Theory and Institutions of the Khawarij,* Johns Hopkins Studies in the Historical and Political Sciences, ser. 74, no. 2 (Baltimore: Johns Hopkins University Press, 1956), 86–87.

8. Ibid., 100.

9. Ibid., 87, 18.

10. Abbott, "Women in Early Islam," 111.

11. In some versions it is anonymous "women" who raise the question, in some it is his wife Umm Salama, and in others it is Muhammad's wives generally. Ibn Saʿd, *Kitab al-tabaqat,* 8:144. See also Abbott, "Women in Early Islam," 110. Less important but also indicating women's outspokenness is ʿAisha's remark to Muhammad: "Your Lord hastens to satisfy your desire!" (see chap. 3).

12. Nabia Abbott, *Aishah, the Beloved of Muhammad* (Chicago: University of Chicago Press, 1942), 97, 204, 201; Ibn Saʿd, *Kitab al-tabaqat,* 8:92; Ahmad ibn Muhammad ibn Hanbal, *Musnad,* 6 vols. (Beirut: Al-maktab al-islami lil-tibaʿa waʾl-nashr, 1969), 6:73, 95, 178; *Encyclopaedia of Islam,* new ed. (Leiden: E. J. Brill, 1960–), s.v. "Aisha bint Abi Bakr." See also Arthur Jeffrey, *Materials for the History of the Text of the Qurʾan* (Leiden, 1937), 231–33, 83–85. Umm Salama also had variants attributed to her; see Jeffrey, *Materials,* 235, 85.

13. Al-Baghdadi lists thirty-one learned women; see al-Hafiz Abi Bakr Ahmad ibn ʿAli al-Khateeb al-Baghdadi, *Tarikh Baghdad,* 14 vols. (Cairo: Matbaʿat al-saʿada, 1931), 14:430–47.

14. Abbott, "Women in Early Islam," 125; Abbott, *Aishah,* 85; *Encyclopaedia of Islam,* s.v. "Hafsa."

15. Abbott, *Aishah,* 121, 122.

16. Ibid., 154.

17. Ibn Sʿad, *Kitab al-tabaqat,* 8:167–68.

18. Ibid., 8:193–95; ʿUmar Ridda Kahhalah, *Aʿlam al-nisa: fi aʿlami al-ʿarab waʾl-islam,* 3 vols. (Damascus: Al-matbaʿa al-hashimiyya, 1940), 2:944–49. Kahhalah is hereafter cited in the text.

19. Jean-Claude Vadet, "Une Personnalité féminine du Higāz au Ier/VIIe siècle: Sukayna, petite-fille de ʿAli," *Arabica* 4 (1957): 276.

20. Nabia Abbott, *Two Queens of Baghdad: Mother and Wife of Harun al-Rashid* (Chicago: University of Chicago Press, 1946; Midway Reprint, 1974), 16.

Chapter 5: Elaboration of the Founding Discourses

1. Nabia Abbott, *Two Queens of Baghdad: Mother and Wife of Harun al-Rashid* (Chicago: University of Chicago Press, 1946; Midway Reprint, 1974), 8–9.

2. Nabia Abbott, *Aishah, the Beloved of Muhammad* (Chicago: University of Chicago Press, 1942), 197; Henri Lammens, *Fatima et les filles de Mahomet*

(Rome: Scripta Pontificii Instituti Biblici, 1912), 53–54; Ahmad Amin, *Fajr al-islam* (Cairo: Maktabat al-nahda al-misriyya, n.d.), 88; *Shorter Encyclopaedia of Islam,* ed. H. A. R. Gibb and J. H. Kramers (Leiden: E. J. Brill, 1974), s.v. "Hasan ibn Ali ibn Abi Talib."

3. Michael G. Morony, *Iraq after the Muslim Conquest* (Princeton: Princeton University Press, 1984), esp. parts 2 and 3; hereafter cited in the text.

4. Elizabeth Fox-Genovese, *Feminism without Illusions: A Critique of Individualism* (Chapel Hill: University of North Carolina Press, 1991), 193.

5. Abbott, *Two Queens of Baghdad,* 67.

6. Phillip K. Hitti, *History of the Arabs,* 2d ed., rev. (London: Macmillan, 1940), 342; Abbott, *Two Queens of Baghdad,* 138.

7. Bernard Lewis, *The Arabs in History* (London: Arrow Books, 1958), 109. For further discussion of these ideas and some examples see Wajida ʿAbdullah al-Atraqji, *Al-marʾa fi adab al-ʿasr al-ʿabbasi* (Baghdad: Dar al-rasheed lil-nashr, 1981), 44, 136–37.

8. Abbott, *Two Queens of Baghdad,* 140, 73, 130–31 (quotations). Presenting one's husband with concubines was in fact the commended practice of the day. Al-Jahiz, a literateur of the age, observed: "If she has a slave whom she knows the king desires and who would make him happy, it is the duty of a royal woman to make a gift of her to him. . . . If she does this it is her due that the king should advance her over his other women and elevate and honor her." *Kitab al-taj fi akhlaq al-muluk,* ed. Fawzi ʿAtawi (Beirut: Al-shirka al-libnania lil-kitab, n.d.), 150.

9. Al-Atraqji, *Al-marʾa fi adab al-ʿasr al-ʿabbasi,* 66.

10. Abbott, *Two Queens of Baghdad,* 10.

11. In the legal code elaborated in this age a slave was considered legally an object in some respects and a human being in others. See *Encyclopaedia of Islam,* new ed. (Leiden: E. J. Brill, 1960–), s.v. "ʿAbd."

12. H. F. Amedroz and D. S. Margoliouth, eds. and trans., *The Eclipse of the Abbasid Caliphate: Original Chronicles of the Fourth Islamic Century,* 7 vols. (Oxford: Basil Blackwell, 1920–21), 3:41 (Arabic text). That this anecdote was told of several different sovereigns probably means, as J. C. Burgel notes, not that it was not true but that it happened more than once. "Love, Lust, and Longing: Eroticism in Early Islam as Reflected in Literary Sources," in *Society and the Sexes in Medieval Islam,* ed. Afaf Lutfi al-Sayyid Marsot (Malibu, Calif.: Undena Publications, 1979), 105.

13. Abu Bakr al-Khuwarizmi, *Rasaʿil* (Bombay, 1885), 19.

14. Al-Atraqji, *Al-marʾa fi adab al-ʿasr al-ʿabbasi,* 89 (quotation), 95.

15. Men, too, were sold for sexual exploitation, but not so commonly or routinely. A study of the social and psychological meaning and consequences of slavery in Muslim societies, such as Orlando Patterson's study of slavery in Western societies, *Slavery and Social Death: A Comparative Study* (Cambridge: Harvard University Press, 1982), has yet to be undertaken. Still to be explored

is the impact of the use of eunuchs on Islamic societies and the ways in which the conceptualization and definition of eunuchs related to and perhaps affected the conceptualization and definition of maleness and femaleness.

16. Margaret Smith, *Studies in Early Mysticism in the Near and Middle East* (London: Sheldon Press, 1931), 162–63.

17. See Morony, *Iraq after the Muslim Conquest*, 447, 453; *Shorter Encyclopaedia of Islam*, s.v. "al-Kur'an." Misogyny in its vast variety finds abundant expression in Muslim literature in this and other periods. Its systematic exploration has so far been confined to an examination of this or that specific instance. For one such examination see Denise A. Spellberg, "Nizam al-Mulk's Manipulation of Tradition: 'Aishah and the Role of Women in the Islamic Government," *Muslim World* 67, no. 2 (1988): 111–17.

18. An interesting work on marginal classes of society is Clifford Edmund Bosworth, *The Mediaeval Islamic Underworld* (Leiden: E. J. Brill, 1976).

19. Noel J. Coulson, *A History of Islamic Law* (Edinburgh: Edinburgh University Press, 1964), 10–11, 17. The summary of the history of Islamic law given in the following pages is based on ibid., chaps. 1–3; and on Joseph Schacht, *An Introduction to Islamic Law* (Oxford: Clarendon Press, 1964), chaps. 4–10.

20. Coulson, *History of Islamic Law,* 18–19.

21. Ibid., 30–31.

22. Ibid., 34.

23. Ibid., 36–37.

24. Ibid., 39–49, 77–78; Schacht, *Introduction to Islamic Law,* 28–30.

25. Coulson, *History of Islamic Law,* 85.

26. Ibid., 97; Noel J. Coulson, *Conflicts and Tensions in Islamic Jurisprudence* (Chicago: University of Chicago Press, 1969), 25–30.

27. Noel J. Coulson and Doreen Hinchcliffe, "Women and Law Reform in Contemporary Islam," in *Women in the Muslim World,* ed. Lois Beck and Nikki Keddie (Cambridge: Harvard University Press, 1978), 37–38.

28. See Basim F. Musallam, *Sex and Society in Medieval Islam* (London: Cambridge University Press, 1983); and my "Arab Culture and Writing Women's Bodies," in *Feminist Issues* 9, no. 1 (1989).

29. See *Encyclopaedia of Islam,* new ed. (Leiden: E. J. Brill, 1960–), s.v. "al-Kur'an."

30. Theodor Noldeke, *Geschichte des Qorans,* 3 vols. in 1, ed. F. Schwally (Leipzig, 1909; Hildesheim: G. Olms, 1961), ii, 57–62.

31. *Encyclopaedia of Islam,* s.vv. "al-Kur'an" and "kira'a"; and David S. Powers, *Studies in Qur'an and Hadith: The Formation of the Islamic Law of Inheritance* (Berkeley: University of California Press, 1986).

32. Margaret Smith, *Rabi'a the Mystic and Her Fellow-Saints in Islam* (Cambridge: Cambridge University Press, 1928), 14 (first brackets in original).

33. Ibid., 36.

34. Ibid., 9, 16.

35. Annemarie Schimmel observes that Sufism was ambivalent toward women, noting, for example, that the title of a poem by the Persian mystic Sana'i, *Banat an-na'sh* (Daughters of the bier), "points by its very name to the fact that daughters are better on a bier than alive." Some male Sufis, she says, "were absolutely antagonistic to or disinterested in women, even to the point that they would not touch food cooked by a woman," and "early Islamic asceticism and the mystical writings based on these ascetic ideals were as inimical to women as is any ascetic movement in the world of religion, be it medieval Christianity or early Buddhism. It was easy for the Muslim ascetics of the eighth and ninth centuries to equate woman and *nafs,* 'the lower self that incites to evil' . . . since the word *nafs* is feminine in Arabic. Furthermore, as they saw in woman, as it were, the nafs principle personified they also represented (like their Christian colleagues) the world as a hideous ghastly old hag." *Mystical Dimensions of Islam* (Chapel Hill: University of North Carolina Press, 1975), 426, 428; "Women in Mystical Islam," in *Women and Islam,* ed. Azizah Al-Hibri (Oxford: Pergamon Press, 1982), 146. Schimmel does grant, however, that Sufism was more favorable to women than other branches of Islam.

36. Smith, *Rabi'a,* 9.

37. Jamal J. Elias, "Female and Feminine in Islamic Mysticism," *Muslim World* 77, nos. 3–4 (1988): 214. A background of extreme poverty or slavery was apparently typical of many women mystics. For a discussion see ibid., 210.

38. A. J. Arberry, *Muslim Saints and Mystics* (London: Routledge and Kegan Paul, 1979), 51.

39. This story made its way to medieval Europe where, in one text, the account was accompanied, Schimmel reports, by an illustration showing what she describes as an Oriental woman with a torch and a ewer. See Schimmel, "Women in Mystical Islam," 147.

40. Bernard Lewis, *The Arabs in History* (London: Arrow Books, 1958), 109. See also Ibn al-Jawzi, "Kitab al-muntazim fi tarikh al-muluk wa'l-umam," in *Akhbar al-Qarammita fi al-Ahsa', al-Sham, al-Iraq, al-Yaman,* 2d ed. (Damascus: Dar hasan, 1982), 255–72.

41. On Qarmatian women see *Encyclopedia of Religion and Ethics* (New York: Scribner and Sons, 1961), s.v. "Carmatians"; and M. J. De Goeje, *Mémoire sur les Carmates du Bahrein et les Fatimides* (Leiden: E. J. Brill, 1886).

42. Ibn al-'Arabi, *Sufis of Andalusia: The Ruh al-Quds and al-Durrat al-Fakhirah of Ibn al-'Arabi,* trans. R. W. J. Austin (London: Allen and Unwin, 1971), 142–43.

43. Henry Corbin, *Creative Imagination in the Sufism of Ibn 'Arabi* (originally in French), trans. Ralph Manheim, Bollingen Series 91 (Princeton: Princeton University Press, 1969), 137–39.

44. Ibn al-'Arabi, *The Bezels of Wisdom,* trans. R. W. J. Austin (New York: Paulist Press, 1980), 35; see also Fazlur Rahman, *Islam,* 2d ed. (Chicago: University of Chicago Press, 1979), 146.

45. Ibn al-ʿArabi, *Bezels of Wisdom*, 274; R. W. J. Austin, "The Feminine Dimensions in Ibn ʿArabi's Thought," *Journal of the Muhyiddin Ibn ʿArabi Society* 2 (1984): 8–9.

Chapter 6: Medieval Islam

1. Goitein writes: "It would be hazardous to use letters and documents left by European Jews of the Late Middle Ages for an overall picture of the society to which they belonged. . . . Not so with regard to the Mediterranean society of the period with which we are concerned here. Despite the high degree of legal and civic autonomy enjoyed by them at that time, and despite their status as semi-foreigners . . . in this period they mingled freely with their neighbours and, therefore, cannot have been very much different from them. For, as the Arab proverb has it, 'People are more akin to their contemporaries than they are to their own forefathers.' It stands to reason that a twelfth-century Jewish doctor, who worked in a government hospital in Cairo or Aleppo, was in most respects representative of the medical profession of his time in general, while a Jewish glassmaker, or silk-weaver, or metal founder would use the same techniques and occupy approximately the same social position as his Christian or Muslim fellow workers. Mutual help, as expressed in small, but not too small, loans is attested in the Geniza as prevailing between members of different faiths but of the same or similar professions." *A Mediterranean Society: The Jewish Communities of the Arab World as Portrayed in the Documents of the Cairo Geniza*, 5 vols. (Berkeley: University of California Press, 1967–), 1:70–71.

2. For example, when noting the death of a nine-year-old girl, Muhammad Shams al-Din al-Sakhawi mentions that she had been married. *Kitab al-nisaʾ*, vol. 12 of *Al-dawʾ al-lamiʿ li ahl qarn al-tasiʿ*, 12 vols. (Beirut: Maktabat al-haya, n.d.), 163; hereafter cited in the text. Al-Sakhawi was born in Cairo. He composed a twelve-volume biographical dictionary of notables of his century, devoting a volume to women. For an informative study of the volume on women see Huda Lutfi, "Al-Sakhawi's *Kitab al-Nisaʾ* as a Source for the Social and Economic History of Muslim Women during the Fifteenth Century A.D.," *Muslim World* 71, no. 2 (1981): 104–24.

3. See William Muir, *The Mamluke or Slave Dynasty of Egypt: 1260–1517 A.D.* (London: Smith, Elder, 1896), 217; and Ahmad Abd ar-Raziq, *La Femme au temps des Mamlouks en Egypte*, 2 vols. (Cairo: Institut Français d'Archéologie Orientale du Caire, 1973), 2:183.

4. See Muir, *Mamluke or Slave Dynasty*, 225; and Abd ar-Raziq, *La Femme au temps des Mamlouks*, 2:125–28. On the Mamluks see also Carl F. Petry, *The Civilian Elite of Cairo in the Later Middle Ages* (Princeton: Princeton University Press, 1981).

5. Abd ar-Raziq, *La Femme au temps des Mamlouks*, 2:166–69.

6. Carl F. Petry, "A Paradox of Patronage during the Later Mamluk Period," *Muslim World* 73, nos. 3–4 (1983): 201.

7. Gabriel Baer, "Women and Waqf: An Analysis of the Istambul Tahrir of 1546," *Asian and African Studies* 17, nos. 1–3 (1983): 10, 27. On the high mortality rate among Mamluk men see Muir, *Mamluke or Slave Dynasty,* 226.

8. On the wealth of Mamluk women see Abd ar-Raziq, *La Femme au temps des Mamlouks,* 1:16–19, 57–58, 65.

9. For numerous examples of endowments by women see Abd ar-Raziq, *La Femme au temps des Mamlouks,* 1:319–27. Khatun Tughay, for example, established a convent that included stipends for her female slaves. Abu'l-Abbas Ahmad ibn ʿAli ibn ʿAbd al-Kadir al-Husaini, Taki al-Din al-Maqrizi, *Kitab al-mawaiʿz waʾl-iʿtibar fi dhikr al-khitat waʾl-athar,* 2 vols. (Baghdad: Maktabat al-muthana, [1970]), 2:425.

10. Goitein, *Mediterranean Society,* 3:260. Al-Sakhawi sometimes names as many as three or four husbands for his subjects (46, 140–41, 72, 104, 113, 7–8); and Edward William Lane says remarriage was common among Cairenes in nineteenth-century urban Egypt, as does Judith E. Tucker for Egyptian peasantry in the same period. Lane, *The Manners and Customs of the Modern Egyptians* (London: Everyman, 1966), 188; Tucker, *Women in Nineteenth-Century Egypt* (Cambridge: Cambridge University Press, 1985), 53.

11. Alexander Russell says that "a woman of birth, conscious of family consequence, is apt to be haughty and petulant, and her relations sometimes make it one of the marriage articles, that the husband shall not take another to his bed." As a result, he observes, "among people of rank, as well as the rich merchants, there are many who marry a slave in preference to a free woman; choosing to forego the pecuniary, and indeed all advantages of alliance, rather than submit to the conditions on which such females are obtained." *The Natural History of Aleppo, Containing a Description of the City, and the Principal Natural Productions in Its Neighborhood. Together with an Account of the Climate, Inhabitants, and Diseases, Particularly of the Plague,* 2 vols. (London: Printed for G. G. and J. Robinson, 1794), 1:271.

12. Goitein, *Mediterranean Society,* 1:73–74; Russell, *Natural History of Aleppo,* 1:271, 277; Lane, *Manners and Customs of Egyptians,* 185, 188; Tucker, *Women in Nineteenth-Century Egypt,* 53; Haim Gerber, "Social and Economic Position of Women in an Ottoman City: Bursa, 1600–1700," *International Journal of Middle East Studies* 12, no. 3 (1980): 232.

13. For example, see Russell, *Natural History of Aleppo,* 1:277; and Lane, *Manners and Customs of Egyptians,* 185.

14. I have here summarized the findings presented in "Slave Dealers, Women, Pregnancy and Abortion: The Story of a Circassian Slave-Girl in Mid-Nineteenth Century Cairo," by Ehud R. Toledano, who worked with the documents in the case. *Slavery and Abolition* 2, no. 1 (1981): 53–69.

15. Goitein, *Mediterranean Society,* 3:324. I have not seen any evidence on this subject with respect to Coptic women—whose experiences we currently have least information on.

16. Al-Maqrizi, *Khitat,* 2:454. Other women who founded charitable institutions include Alf bint Salih, a Bulqani, who instituted a school "for orphans and widows," and Khadija bint Yusef, whose mother was a Bulqani and who established a *zawiya* (similar to a ribat). Khadija took up residence there with "many widows" and was buried there when she died. Al-Sakhawi, *Kitab al-nisa',* 7–8, 113.

17. Al-Maqrizi, *Khitat,* 2:427–28.

18. Gerber, "Social and Economic Position in Bursa," 233; Tucker, *Women in Nineteenth-Century Egypt,* 99; Abraham Marcus, "Men, Women and Property: Dealers in Real Estate in Eighteenth-Century Aleppo," *Journal of the Economic and Social History of the Orient* 26, pt. 2 (1983): 145; Ronald C. Jennings, "Women in the Early Seventeenth-Century Ottoman Judicial Records—The Sharia Court of Anatolian Kayseri," *Journal of the Economic and Social History of the Orient* 18, pt. 1 (1975): 61–65.

19. Marcus, "Men, Women and Property," 144, 146; Jennings, "Women in Ottoman Judicial Records," 99. For similar findings see also Tucker, *Women in Nineteenth-Century Egypt,* 83; and Gerber, "Social and Economic Position in Bursa," 234.

20. Women sold three times more than they bought in Kayseri and two times more in Aleppo. Women also sold more often than they bought in Bursa. Jennings, "Women in Ottoman Judicial Records," 99; Marcus, "Men, Women and Property," 144; Gerber, "Social and Economic Position in Bursa," 240.

21. Goitein, *Mediterranean Society,* 1:266; Marcus, "Men, Women and Property," 151, 146–47.

22. Marcus, "Men, Women and Property," 145; Jennings, "Women in Ottoman Judicial Records," 102; Gerber, "Social and Economic Position in Bursa," 234–35; Tucker, *Women in Nineteenth-Century Egypt,* 82–83.

23. Gerber, "Social and Economic Position in Bursa," 233; Tucker, *Women in Nineteenth-Century Egypt,* 99; Jennings, "Women in Ottoman Judicial Records," 61–65.

24. Goitein, *Mediterranean Society,* 3:342, 1:100–102. However, somewhat confusingly, Goitein also states: "Spinning and weaving, the labors theoretically incumbent on all women, are hardly ever mentioned, except with regard to individuals who were professional weavers." Ibid., 3:341.

25. Tucker, *Women in Nineteenth-Century Egypt,* 85. In the records examined by Gerber, twenty of 123 estates, or 16 percent, listed property, such as a loom, showing that women practiced some kind of artisanship, mostly spinning and weaving. In a 1678 survey of silk-spinning implements that he reports on, 150 of 300 such implements in Bursa were owned and/or operated by women. Another document, which records an attempt to reduce the tax on silk-spinning implements, says that most workers in the occupation were "poor women." "Social and Economic Position in Bursa," 237–38. See also Margaret Meriweather, "Women and Work in Nineteenth-Century Syria" (Paper presented at the Middle East Studies Association Conference, 1986).

264 🐛 NOTES TO PAGES 112–15

26. Tucker, *Women in Nineteenth-Century Egypt*, 86.
27. Lane writes: "The young daughters of persons of the middle classes are some-times instructed with the boys in a public school; but they are usually veiled, and hold no intercourse with the boys. I have often seen a well-dressed girl, reading the Kur-an in a boys' school." *Manners and Customs of Egyptians*, 64n1. Tucker also notes that for girls to attend kuttabs was not considered an "innovation" in the nineteenth century. *Women in Nineteenth-Century Egypt*, 110. Russell notes that girls "when about seven years old . . . are sent to school to learn to sew and embroider." After the age of nine they no longer went out to school, but "if their education did not end there, teachers would be brought to the harem." *Natural History of Aleppo*, 1:264.
28. Al-Sakhawi mentions a number of women who were taught by their father (8, 19, 15, 31, 45, 21). One was taught by her aunt Zubaida (21). Another was taught by her husband (44).
29. Al-Sakhawi did have women teachers (see, e.g., 78–79, 124). On al-Suyuti and women teachers see Elizabeth M. Sartain, *Jalal al-Din al-Suyuti* (Cambridge: Cambridge University Press, 1975), 127. Al-Sakhawi only rarely notes of a woman that she was "heard" from behind a veil or partition (e.g., 22). Pre-sumably the term *hijab*, which can mean either "veil" or "partition," meant "partition" here. The fact that al-Sakhawi notes that Hajar and "old women" did not veil suggests that younger women did.
30. See also Peter Gran, *Islamic Roots of Capitalism: Egypt, 1760–1840* (Austin: University of Texas Press, 1979), 129.
31. See, e.g., George Makdisi, *The Rise of Colleges* (Edinburgh: Edinburgh University Press, 1981); A. S. Tritton, *Materials on Muslim Education in the Middle Ages* (London: Luzac, 1957); and Ahmad Shalaby, *History of Muslim Education* (Beirut: Dar al-kashshaf, 1954).
32. James Augustus St. John, *Egypt and Mohammed Ali; or, Travels in the Valley of the Nile*, 2 vols. (London: Longman, Rees, Orme, Brown, Green and Long-man, 1834), 2:335. See Petry, *Civilian Elite of Cairo*, 247.
33. See Goitein, *Mediterranean Society*, 1:127–30; Abd ar-Raziq, *La Femme au temps des Mamlouks*, 1:43–87; Lutfi, "Al-Sakhawi's *Kitab al-nisa*," 117; Tucker, *Women in Nineteenth-Century Egypt*, 82–83. On women employed in maristans see Petry, *Civilian Elite of Cairo*, 140–41.
34. Russell, *Natural History of Aleppo*, 1:263. See Abd ar-Raziq, *La Femme au temps des Mamlouks*, 1:45. In eighteenth-century Cairo prostitutes were also licensed by a government official to whom they paid a tax. André Raymond, *Artisans et commerçants au Caire au XVIIIe siècle*, 2 vols. (Damascus: Institut Français de Damas, 1973–74), 2:609. See also Gabriel Baer, *Egyptian Guilds in Modern Times* (Jerusalem: Israel Oriental Society, 1964), 84–85. On pros-titution and the state in nineteenth-century Egypt see Tucker, *Women in Nine-teenth-Century Egypt*, 150–55. On low-status jobs see Ira Marvin Lapidus, *Muslim Cities in the Later Middle Ages*, Harvard Middle East Studies (Cam-bridge: Harvard University Press, 1967), 82–83.

35. Saʿid Abdel Fattah ʿAshur, *Al-mujtamaʿ al-misri fi ʿasr al-salateen al-mamaleek* (Cairo: Dar al-nahda al-ʿarabiyya, 1962), 167.

36. Abu ʿAbdullah Muhammad ibn Muhammad al-ʿAbdari ibn al-Hajj, *Al-madkhal*, 4 vols. (Cairo: Al-matbaʿa al-misriyya, 1929), 2:141.

37. Goitein, *Mediterranean Society*, 1:118–20, 3:359; Russell, *Natural History of Aleppo*, 238–39; Lane, *Manners and Customs of Egyptians*, 189.

38. S. D. Goitein, "The Sexual Mores of the Common People," in *Society and the Sexes in Medieval Islam*, ed. Afaf Lutfi al-Sayyid Marsot (Malibu, Calif.: Undena Publications, 1979), 46.

39. Goitein, *Mediterranean Society*, 3:128.

40. Ibid., 4:153–54; Abuʾl-Abbas Ahmad ibn ʿAli ibn ʿAbd al-Kadir al-Husaini, Taki al-Din Ahmad ibn ʿAli al-Maqrizi, *Kitab al-suluk li maʿrifat duwal al-muluk*, 4 vols. in 12, ed. Muhammad Mustapha Ziadeh (Cairo: Matbaʿat lajnat al-taʾ-leef waʾl-tarjama waʾl-nashr, 1936–73), 3:503; Ibn al-Hajj, *Al-madkhal*, 1:242.

41. Goitein, *Mediterranean Society*, 1:114, 115, 161, 3:341, 343; ʿAshur, *Al-mujtamaʿ al-misri*, 116–17; Russell, *Natural History of Aleppo*, 1:242; Tucker, *Women in Nineteenth-Century Egypt*, 82–83.

42. Ibn al-Hajj, *Al-madkhal*, 2:54–55; al-Maqrizi, *Kitab al-suluk*, 4, pt. 2: 1032–33.

43. Goitein, *Mediterranean Society*, 3:343; Abd ar-Raziq, *La Femme au temps des Mamlouks*, 1:35; Russell, *Natural History of Aleppo*, 1:254; Lane, *Manners and Customs of Egyptians*, 343, 506.

44. Ibn al-Hajj, *Al-madkhal*, 3:246.

45. On the damina see Abd ar-Raziq, *La Femme au temps des Mamlouks*, 1:86.

46. Ibn al-Hajj, *Al-madkhal*, 1:267–68.

47. Al-Maqrizi, *Kitab al-suluk*, 4, pt. 2: 619; 2, pt. 1: 51.

48. Ibn al-Hajj, *Al-madkhal*, 1:272–75; al-Maqrizi, *Kitab al-suluk*, 4, pt. 2: 614.

49. Al-Maqrizi, *Kitab al-suluk*, 4, pt. 2: 1032–33.

50. De Lacy O'Leary, *A Short History of the Fatimid Caliphate* (London: K. Paul, Trench, Trubner; New York: E. P. Dutton, 1923), 173.

51. See Abd ar-Raziq, *La Femme au temps des Mamlouks*, 2:217.

52. Ibn al-Hajj, *Al-madkhal*, 2:172–73.

53. *The Complete Letters of Lady Mary Wortley Montagu*, 2 vols., ed. Robert Halsband (Oxford: Clarendon Press, 1965), 1:347–48; hereafter cited in the text.

54. Russell, *Natural History of Aleppo*, 1:267. Toledano notes this type of investment with respect to upper-class women in nineteenth-century Istanbul. "Slave Dealers, Women, Pregnancy and Abortion," 59–60.

55. Russell, *Natural History of Aleppo*, 1:270; Baer, "Women and Waqf," 23–24.

56. Russell, *Natural History of Aleppo*, 1:247–48.

57. *Aspects de la vie quotidienne en Egypte: A l'Epoque de Mehemet-Ali, première moitié du XIXe siècle, d'après les souvenirs d'une fille du peuple, en Egypte, 1834–36, de Suzanne Voilquin*, ed. Rouchdi Fakkar (Paris: Maisonneuve et Larose, 1975), 72–73.

Chapter 7: Social and Intellectual Change

1. Fatima Mernissi, *Beyond the Veil* (Cambridge: Schenkman, 1975), 12.
2. European merchants aggressively competed for local markets. French merchants, for example, reportedly set out to learn the types and colors of fabrics that Egyptians preferred and sent samples back to France to have them copied. In Iraq imported cloth from British India made the greatest inroads in domestic production. See Roger Owen, *The Middle East in the World Economy, 1800–1914* (London: Methuen, 1981), esp. chap. 1; and Charles Issawi, "Egypt since 1800: A Study in Lopsided Development," in *An Economic History of the Middle East, 1800–1914,* ed. Issawi (Chicago: University of Chicago Press, 1966), 359–74.
3. Afaf Lutfi al-Sayyid Marsot, *Egypt in the Reign of Muhammad Ali* (Cambridge: Cambridge University Press, 1984), 17.
4. Judith E. Tucker, *Women in Nineteenth-Century Egypt* (Cambridge: Cambridge University Press, 1985), 86–88, 101.
5. For example, when the British, embroiled in the Napoleonic wars, needed grain for their army, Muhammad 'Ali agreed to sell it to them. To pay for the grain, British merchants stepped up their exports to Egypt, flooding the country with cheap British textiles, an influx that caused a number of local workshops to close down and brought about the loss of livelihood or essential supplemental income for both women and men. Marsot, *Egypt in the Reign of Muhammad Ali,* 166.
6. There is some debate about the reason for the failure of Muhammad 'Ali's attempts to industrialize, particularly with regard to the textile industry. Afaf al-Sayyid Marsot and others have argued that the European powers played a major role in ensuring these failures: they had an interest in keeping Egypt a supplier of raw materials and a consumer of their own goods and not letting it become a competitor in the production of finished products. See Marsot, *Egypt in the Reign of Muhammad Ali,* esp. 175, 259.
7. Mona Hammam, "Women and Industrial Work in Egypt: The Chubra el-Kheima Case," *Arab Studies Quarterly* 2, no. 1 (1980): 51–54. See also Moustapha Fahmy, *La Révolution de l'industrie en Egypte et ses conséquences sociales au XIXe siècle (1800–1850)* (Leiden: E. J. Brill, 1954), 64–65, 69.
8. Marsot, *Egypt in the Reign of Muhammad Ali,* 122; Tucker, *Women in Nineteenth-Century Egypt,* 27, 41; Judith E. Tucker, "Decline of the Family Economy in Mid-Nineteenth Century Egypt," *Arab Studies Quarterly* 1, no. 3 (1979): 260.
9. Judith E. Tucker, "Egyptian Women in the Work Force: An Historical Survey," *Middle East Research and Information Project,* no. 50 (1976): 7, 8.
10. For a discussion of the fate of freed slaves see Tucker, *Women in Nineteenth-Century Egypt,* 188–91.
11. J. Heyworthe-Dunne, *An Introduction to the History of Education in Modern Egypt* (London: Frank Cass, 1968), 105.

NOTES TO PAGES 134–38 ❦ 267

12. Muhammad Kamal Yehya, *Al-judur al-tarikhiyya li tahrir al-mar'a al-misriyya: fi al-'asr al-hadith* (Cairo: Al-hayy'a al-misriyya al-'ama lil-kutub, 1983), 69; Jamal Mohammed Ahmed, *The Intellectual Origins of Egyptian Nationalism* (London: Oxford University Press, 1960), 13; Yacoub Artin, *L'Instruction publique en Egypte* (Paris: Ernest Leroux, 1890), 120 (quotation).
13. She served as principal from 1834 to 1836. Heyworthe-Dunne, *Introduction to the History of Education,* 32.
14. For an account of their training see Laverne Kuhnke, "The 'Doctoress' on a Donkey: Women Health Officers in Nineteenth-Century Egypt," *Clio Medica* 9, no. 3 (1974): 194–96.
15. Ibid., 200; Artin, *L'Instruction publique,* 131; Yehya, *Al-judur,* 85.
16. Artin, *L'Instruction publique,* 134.
17. Mai Ziadeh, *'Aisha Taymour* (Beirut: Mu'assassat nufal, 1975), 60–61.
18. Artin, *L'Instruction publique,* 160–61.
19. Mary Louisa Whately, *Child-Life in Egypt* (Philadelphia: American Sunday-School Union, [1866]), 40–45; Heyworthe-Dunne, *Introduction to the History of Education,* 334.
20. Anouar Abdel Malek, *Egypt: Military Society; The Army Regime, the Left, and Social Change under Nasser,* trans. Charles Lam Markmann (New York: Random House, 1968), 154, 313; Yehya, *Al-judur,* 77; Heyworthe-Dunne, *Introduction to the History of Education,* 335–36.
21. Fritz Steppat, "National Education Projects in Egypt before the British Occupation," in *Beginnings of Modernisation in the Middle East,* ed. William R. Polk and Richard L. Chambers (Chicago: University of Chicago Press, 1968), 287 (quotation), 288; Yehya, *Al-judur,* 71–72.
22. *Al-a'mal al-kamila li Rifa'ah Rafi' al-Tahtawi,* ed. Muhammad 'Amara (Beirut: Al-mu'assasa al-'arabiyya lil-dirasat wa'l-nashr, 1973), 2:356, 360, 393. On al-Tahtawi's feminism see also ibid., 2:562; Charles Vial, "Rifâ'a al-Tahtâwî (1801–1873), précurseur du féminisme en Egypte," *Maghreb Machrek* 87 (January–March 1980).
23. Yehya, *Al-judur,* 70. John Stuart Mill, author of the first feminist book by a European male (*The Subjection of Women,* 1869), wrote a similar document for his wife, repudiating the rights the law unjustly gave him over her property and person.
24. Steppat, "National Education Projects in Egypt," 293.
25. Robert L. Tignor, *Modernisation and British Colonial Rule in Egypt, 1882–1914* (Princeton: Princeton University Press, 1966), 324.
26. Elizabeth Cooper, *The Women of Egypt* (Westport, Conn.: Hyperion Press, [1914]; rpt. 1981), 165.
27. J. M. Ahmed, *Intellectual Origins of Egyptian Nationalism,* 30; Ijlal Khalifa, *Al-haraka al-nisa'iyya al-haditha: qissat al-mar'a al-'arabiyya 'ala ard misr* (Cairo: Al-matba'a al-'arabiyya al-haditha, 1973), 107; Tignor, *Modernisation and British Rule in Egypt,* 345–46; Cooper, *Women of Egypt,* 169.

28. Turkey sent student missions to Europe and opened military and medical schools about the same time as Egypt. A school for midwives had been founded there in 1842, and by the 1860s the Turkish government had begun to establish schools for girls, generating a rhetoric explaining the need for girls' education to justify its doing so. When opening a teacher-training college in the 1860s, for instance, the minister of education declared that children were "in their mother's care until they reached school age and that for this reason women should learn how to read and write." He observed that "there was nothing in the Koran to stop Moslem women from learning or acquiring a trade for themselves or even from becoming technicians." By 1895 the college had 350 students. A. Afetinan, *The Emancipation of the Turkish Woman* ([Paris]: UNESCO, [1962]), 38; Fanny Davis, *The Ottoman Lady: A Social History from 1718 to 1918* (New York: Greenwood Press, 1986), 51.

29. Davis, *Ottoman Lady,* 50, 93.

30. Charles C. Adams, *Islam and Modernism in Egypt* (New York: Russell and Russell, 1933), 13. On the intellectual history of the era see also Albert Hourani, *Arabic Thought in the Liberal Age, 1798–1939* (Cambridge: Cambridge University Press, 1983); and Peter Gran, *Islamic Roots of Capitalism: Egypt, 1760–1840* (Austin: University of Texas Press, 1979).

31. I cite here Adams's concise synopsis of ʿAbdu's views: *Islam and Modernism in Egypt,* 152. For ʿAbdu's further views on polygamy, divorce, and the veil see *Al-aʿmal al-kamila lil-Imam Muhammad ʿAbdu,* 6 vols., ed. Muhammad ʿAmara (Beirut: Al-muʾassasa al-ʿarabiyya lil-dirasat waʾl-nashr, 1972), 2:68–90, 105–30, 227–31.

32. *Al-aʿmal al-kamila lil-Imam Muhammad ʿAbdu,* ed. ʿAmara, 2:365.

33. From Muhammad ʿAbdu, "The Error of Intellectuals," quoted in Adams, *Islam and Modernism in Egypt,* 49.

34. Khalifa, *Al-haraka al-nisaʾiyya,* 24, 40, 50, 111–12.

35. Ibid., 23.

36. Byron D. Cannon, "Nineteenth-Century Arabic Writing on Women and Society: The Interim Role of the Masonic Press in Cairo—*Al-Lataʾif,* 1885–1895," *International Journal of Middle East Studies* 17, no. 4 (1985): 475, 477 (quotation), 476, 483.

37. Leila Ahmed, *Edward William Lane and British Ideas of the Middle East in the Nineteenth Century* (London: Longman, 1978), 45.

38. Yehya, *Al-judur,* 73.

39. Qassim Amin, *Tahrir al-marʾa,* in *Al-aʿmal al-kamila li Qassim Amin,* 2 vols., ed. Muhammad ʿAmara (Beirut: Al-muʾassasa al-ʿarabiyya lil-dirasat waʾl-nashr, 1976), 2:18.

40. Mukhtar Tuhami, *Thalath maʿariq fikriyya: al-sahafa waʾl-fikr waʾl-thawra* (Cairo, 1976), 36.

41. A. B. De Guerville, *New Egypt* (London: William Heinemann, 1906), 146;

Beth Baron, "Unveiling in Egypt: Fashion, Seclusion, and Change" (Unpublished paper).

42. Khalifa, *Al-haraka al-nisa'iyya,* 112.

Chapter 8: The Discourse of the Veil

1. See J. N. Anderson, "Law Reform in Egypt: 1850–1950," in *Political and Social Change in Modern Egypt,* ed. P. M. Holt (London: Oxford University Press, 1968), 209–30; and Noel J. Coulson and Doreen Hinchcliffe, "Women and Law Reform in Contemporary Islam," in *Women in the Muslim World,* ed. Lois Beck and Nikki Keddie (Cambridge: Harvard University Press, 1978), 37–51.

2. Robert L. Tignor, *Modernisation and British Colonial Rule in Egypt, 1882–1914* (Princeton: Princeton University Press, 1966), 324.

3. Ibid., 324–6.

4. In Dante's *Divine Comedy,* for instance, in which Muhammad is relegated to one of the lowest circles of hell, Muhammad is associated with a figure whose transgressions similarly were in the area of what he preached with respect to women. See *The Comedy of Dante Alighieri,* trans. Dorothy Sayers (Penguin Books, 1949), Canto 28, 346–47, 251. For some accounts of early Western representations of Islam see Norman Daniel, *Islam and the West* (Edinburgh: Edinburgh University Press, 1966); and R. W. Southern, *Western Views of Islam in the Middle Ages* (Cambridge: Harvard University Press, 1962).

5. *The Complete Letters of Lady Mary Wortley Montagu,* 2 vols., ed. Robert Halsband (Oxford: Clarendon Press, 1965), 1:318. She corrects "our Vulgar Notion that they do not own women to have any Souls" but perpetuates a modified version of that error in writing, " 'Tis true, they say they [women's souls] are not of so elevated a kind, and therefore must not hope to be admitted into the paradise appointed for the Men." Ibid., 1:363. For her statements on polygamy and the parallel "inconstancy" of European men see ibid., 1:329. Montagu also points out in this context that Muslim women of the upper classes owned property in their own right and thus were less at the mercy of men than their Christian sisters. For her remarks on the veil see ibid., 1:328.

6. Timothy Mitchell's *Colonising Egypt* (Cambridge: Cambridge University Press, 1988) offers an interesting and valuable exploration of the issues of colonialism and its discursive designs.

7. Edward Said, *Orientalism* (London: Routledge and Kegan Paul, 1978).

8. For discussions of the uses of anthropology to colonial theory and its uses in reinforcing sexist views of women see Mona Etienne and Eleanor Leacock, "Introduction," in *Women and Colonisation: Anthropological Perspectives,* ed. Etienne and Leacock (New York: Praeger Publishers, 1980), 1–24; Susan Carol Rogers, "Women's Place: A Critical Review of Anthropological Theory," *Comparative Studies in Society and History* 20, no. 1 (1978): 123–62; Elizabeth

Fee, "The Sexual Politics of Victorian Social Anthropology," in *Clio's Consciousness Raised,* ed. M. Hartman and L. Banner (New York: Harper Torchbooks, 1974), 86–102.

9. Earl of Cromer, *Modern Egypt,* 2 vols. (New York: Macmillan, 1908), 2:146; hereafter cited in the text.

10. A. B. De Guerville, *New Egypt* (London: William Heinemann, 1906), 154.

11. Cromer Papers, cited in Judith E. Tucker, *Women in Nineteenth-Century Egypt* (Cambridge: Cambridge University Press, 1985), 122.

12. Cromer was so prominent in the antisuffrage movement that it was sometimes called the Curzon-Cromer combine after Cromer and Lord Curzon, first marquis of Keddleston. See Constance Rover, *Women's Suffrage and Party Politics in Britain, 1866–1914* (London: Routledge and Kegan Paul; Toronto: University of Toronto Press, 1967), 171–73; see also Brian Harrison, *Separate Spheres: The Opposition to Women's Suffrage in Britain* (New York: Holmes and Meier Publishers, 1978).

13. Rev. Robert Bruce, in *Report of the Centenary Conference on Protestant Missions of the World Held in Exeter Hall, London (June 9–19th),* 2 vols., ed. James Johnston (New York: F. H. Revell, [1889]), 1:18–19; Annie van Sommer and Samuel M. Zwemer, eds., *Our Moslem Sisters: A Cry of Need from Lands of Darkness Interpreted by Those Who Heard It* (New York: F. H. Revell, 1907), 27–28; van Sommer and Zwemer, eds., *Daylight in the Harem* (Edinburgh: Oliphant, Anderson and Ferrier, 1911), 149–50.

14. Qassim Amin, *Tahrir al-mar'a,* in *Al-a'mal al-kamila li Qassim Amin,* 2 vols., ed. Muhammad 'Amara (Beirut: Al-mu'assasa al-'arabiyya lil-dirasat wa'l-nashr, 1976), 2:71–72; hereafter cited in the text. All quotations from *Tahrir al-mar'a* are from vol. 2.

15. For a discussion of Amin's family life see Mary Flounders Arnett, *Qassim Amin and the Beginnings of the Feminist Movement in Egypt* (Ph.D. diss., Dropsie College, 1965).

16. 'Amara, "Hadith 'an al-a'mal al-kamila" (Discussion of the works of Amin), in *Al-a'mal al-kamila li Qassim Amin,* ed. 'Amara, 1:133. 'Amara mentions that the work was the outcome of a gathering in Geneva in 1897 attended by Muhammad 'Abdu, Sa'd Zaghloul, Lutfi al-Sayyid, and Qassim Amin. Indeed, 'Amara points to particular sections that he believes were written by Muhammad 'Abdu. Ibid., 1:139.

17. Perhaps passages such as the above were contributed by 'Abdu or by others— Sa'd Zaghloul or Lutfi al-Sayyid—who have also been mentioned as collaborating with Amin. See Afaf Lutfi al-Sayyid Marsot, *Egypt and Cromer* (London: John Murray, 1968), 187.

18. Mukhtar Tuhami, *Al-sahafa wa'l-fikr wa'l-thawra, thalath ma'ariq fikriyya* (Baghdad: Dar ma'mun lil-tiba'a, 1976), 28.

19. Among the more interesting pieces on the subject are Judith Gran, "Impact of the World Market on Egyptian Women," *Middle East Research and Infor-*

mation Report, no. 58 (1977): 3–7; and Juan Ricardo Cole, "Feminism, Class, and Islam in Turn-of-the-Century Egypt," *International Journal of Middle East Studies* 13, no. 4 (1981): 394–407.

20. Tuhami, *Thalath maʿariq fikriyya,* 42–45.

21. Talʿat Harb, *Tarbiyet al-marʾa waʾl-hijab,* 2d ed. (Cairo: Matbaʿat al-manar, 1905), e.g., 18, 19, 25, 29.

22. Frantz Fanon, *A Dying Colonialism,* trans. Haakon Chevalier (New York: Grove Press, 1967), 65. A useful discussion of the interconnections between thesis and antithesis and the ways in which antithesis may become locked in meanings posed by the thesis may be found in Joan W. Scott, "Deconstructing Equality-versus-Difference: Or, the Uses of Poststructuralist Theory for Feminism," *Feminist Studies* 14, no. 1 (1988): 33–49.

23. Ataturk, speech at Kastamonu, 1925, quoted in Bernard Lewis, *The Emergence of Modern Turkey* (London: Oxford University Press, 1961), 165. For further discussions of Turkish articulations of the issue see S. Mardin, *The Genesis of Young Ottoman Thought* (Princeton: Princeton University Press, 1962); and O. Ozankaya, "Reflections of Semsiddin Sami on Women in the Period before the Advent of Secularism," in *Family in Turkish Society,* ed. T. Erder (Ankara: Turkish Social Science Association, 1985).

24. Guity Nashat, "Women in Pre-Revolutionary Iran: A Historical Overview," in *Women and Revolution in Iran,* ed. Nashat (Boulder, Colo.: Westview Press, 1982), 27.

25. One problem with rebuttals of the Islamicist argument voiced by women of Muslim background (and others) generally, but not exclusively, based in the West is the extent to which they reproduce the Western narrative and its iteration in native upper-class voice without taking account of the colonialist and classist assumptions in which it is mired. This silent and surely inadvertent reinscription of racist and classist assumptions is in rebuttals offered from a "Marxist" perspective as much as in rebuttals aligned with the Western liberal position. See, for example, Mai Ghoussoub, "Feminism—or the Eternal Masculine—in the Arab World," *New Left Review* 161 (January–February 1987): 3–18; and Azar Tabari, "The Women's Movement in Iran: A Hopeful Prognosis," *Feminist Studies* 12, no. 2 (1986): 343–60. The topic of Orientalism and the study of Arab women is addressed with particular acumen in Rosemary Sayigh, "Roles and Functions of Arab Women: A Reappraisal of Orientalism and Arab Women," *Arab Studies Quarterly* 3, no. 3 (1981): 258–74.

26. See Deniz Kandiyoti, "Women and the Turkish State: Political Actors or Symbolic Pawns?" in *Women—Nation—State,* ed. Nira Yuval-Davis (London: Macmillan, 1989), 126.

Chapter 9: The First Feminists

1. Robert L. Tignor, *Modernisation and British Colonial Rule in Egypt, 1882–1914* (Princeton: Princeton University Press, 1966), 375–81; P. J. Vatiokis,

The History of Egypt: From Muhammad Ali to Sadat (London: Weidenfeld and Nicolson, 1969), 231; Salama Musa, *The Education of Salama Musa,* trans. L. O. Schuman (Leiden: E. J. Brill, 1961), 29. Musa is hereafter cited in the text.

2. Jamal Mohammed Ahmed, *The Intellectual Origins of Egyptian Nationalism* (London: Oxford University Press, 1960), 66.

3. Tignor, *Modernisation and British Rule in Egypt,* 377.

4. For one account of this incident see ibid., 280–82.

5. J. M. Ahmed, *Intellectual Origins,* 63.

6. The British, it will be recalled, did not open secondary schools for girls until 1917.

7. See Beth Baron, "Unveiling in Egypt: Fashion, Seclusion and Change" (Unpublished paper).

8. Elizabeth Cooper, *The Women of Egypt* (Westport, Conn.: Hyperion Press, [1914]; rpt. 1981), 169.

9. Beth Baron, "Mothers, Morality and Nationalism in pre-1919 Egypt" (Unpublished paper). See also Ijlal Khalifa, *Al-haraka al-nisaʾiyya al-haditha: qissat al-marʾa al-ʿarabiyya ʿala ard misr* (Cairo: Al-matbaʿa al-ʿarabiyya al-haditha, 1973), chap. 3. Among the founders of the Society for the Advancement of Woman was Fatima Rashid, wife of Muhammad Farid Wajdi, owner of the nationalist paper *Al-dustur.* Baron, "Mothers, Morality and Nationalism."

10. Margot Badran, *Harem Years: The Memoirs of an Egyptian Feminist,* trans. Badran (New York: Feminist Press, 1987), 99, 93–95. The quotation is on p. 93.

11. Afaf Lutfi al-Sayyid Marsot, "The Revolutionary Gentlewomen in Egypt," in *Women in the Muslim World,* ed. Lois Beck and Nikki Keddie (Cambridge: Harvard University Press, 1978), 272–74.

12. Valentine Chirol, *The Egyptian Problem* (London: Macmillan, 1920), 168, 169 (quotation); Khalifa, *Al-haraka al-nisaʾiyya,* 156–57.

13. Fina Gued Vidal, *Safia Zaghloul* (Cairo: R. Schindler, n.d.), 32.

14. Khalifa, *Al-haraka al-nisaʾiyya,* 155.

15. Chirol, *Egyptian Problem,* 168.

16. Ibid.

17. Noel J. Coulson and Doreen Hinchcliffe, "Women and Law Reform in Contemporary Islam," in *Women in the Muslim World,* ed. Beck and Keddie, 40–44; J. N. D. Anderson, "Law Reform in Egypt, 1850–1950," in *Political and Social Change in Modern Egypt,* ed. P. M. Holt (London: Oxford University Press, 1968), 225.

18. Badran, *Harem Years,* 7, 80 (quotation).

19. Bahiga ʿArafa, *The Social Activities of the Egyptian Feminist Union* (Cairo: Elias Modern Press, 1964), 4–5, 51, 8; Badran, *Harem Years,* 134.

20. Afaf Lutfi al-Sayyid Marsot, *Egypt's Liberal Experiment, 1922–1936* (Berkeley: University of California Press, 1977), 199.

21. See Khalifa, *Al-haraka al-nisaʾiyya,* for an account of these women.
22. Baheeja Sidky Resheed, Taheya Mohamad Asfahani, and Samia Sidky Mourad, *The Egyptian Feminist Union* (Cairo: Anglo-Egyptian Bookshop, 1973), 12, 24.
23. Bahithat al-Badiyya, *Al-nisaʾiyyat, majmuʿat maqalat fi al-jarida fi mauduʿ al-marʾa al-misriyya,* 2 vols. (Cairo: Al-maktaba al-tijariyya al-kubra, 1925), 1:24–27; hereafter cited in the text.
24. Charles C. Adams, *Islam and Modernism in Egypt* (New York: Russell and Russell, 1933), 235–36.
25. For these elegies see al-Badiyya, *Al-nisaʾiyyat,* 2:39–45.
26. Malak Hifni Nassef, *Athar Bahithat al-Badiyya, 1886–1918,* ed. Majd al-Din Hifni Nassef (Cairo: Wizarat al-thaqafa waʾl-irshad al-qawmi, al-muʾassasa al-misriyya al-ʿama lil-taʾleef waʾl-tarjama waʾl-tibaʿa waʾl-nashr, [1962]), 54, 52–53.
27. For a preliminary discussion of some of these issues see my "Between Two Worlds: The Autobiography of a Turn-of-the-Century Egyptian Feminist," in *Life/Lines,* ed. Celeste Schenck and Bella Brodski (Ithaca: Cornell University Press, 1988).
28. See Mahmoud Bakheet el-Rabie, "Women Writers and Critics in Modern Egypt, 1888–1963" (Ph.D. diss., University of London, 1965).
29. Clara Boyle, *Boyle of Cairo* (Kendal: Titus Wilson, 1965), 42.
30. Ibid., 37–38.
31. Emine Foat Tugay, *Three Centuries: Family Chronicles of Turkey and Egypt* (London: Oxford University Press, 1963), 117. For further dark hints about Nazli's excesses see Nubar Pasha, *Mémoires* (Beirut: Librairie du Liban, 1983), 21, 122–23.
32. Huda Shaʿrawi, *Muthakirat Huda Shaʿrawi,* ed. Abdel Hamid Fahmy Mursy (Cairo: Al-hilal, 1981), 83.
33. Cited in Mary Flounders Arnett, "Marie Ziyada," *Middle Eastern Affairs* (August–September 1957): 291.
34. " 'Our country,' . . . throughout the greater part of its history has treated me as a slave; it has denied me education or any share in its possessions. . . . If you insist upon fighting to protect me, or 'our' country, let it be understood, soberly and rationally between us, that you are fighting to gratify a sex-instinct I cannot share, to procure benefits I have not shared. . . . In fact, as a woman, I have no country." Virginia Woolf, *Three Guineas* (London: Penguin Books, 1978), 125.
35. Arnett, "Marie Ziyada," 293.

Chapter 10: Divergent Voices

1. Amir Boktor, *School and Society in the Valley of the Nile* (Cairo: Elias Modern Press, 1936), 122, 153; see also Joel Beinin and Zackary Lockman, *Workers*

on the Nile: Nationalism, Communism, Islam and the Egyptian Working Class, 1882–1954 (Princeton: Princeton University Press, 1987), 167.

2. *Annuaire Statistique: 1932–33* (Cairo, 1934), table 5; Ruth F. Woodsmall, *The Study of the Role of Women: Their Activities and Organisations in Lebanon, Egypt, Iraq, Jordan and Syria, October 1954–August 1955,* directed by Woodsmall with the assistance of Charlotte Johnson (New York: International Federation of Business and Professional Women, 1956), 25 (quotation); Ijlal Khalifa, *Al-haraka al-nisaʾiyya al-haditha: qissat al-marʾa al-ʿarabiyya ʿala ard misr* (Cairo: Al-matbaʿa al-ʿarabiyya al-haditha, 1973), 25.

3. Charles Issawi, *Egypt at Mid-Century* (London: Oxford University Press, 1954), 55.

4. Ibid., 261n2. For a discussion of this debate see Giora Eliraz, "Egyptian Intellectuals and Women's Emancipation, 1919–1939," *Asian and African Studies* 16 (1982): 95–120.

5. Soha Abdel Kader, *Egyptian Women in a Changing Society, 1899–1987* (Boulder, Colo.: Lynne Rienner, 1987), 102.

6. Issawi, *Egypt at Mid-Century,* 262, 71.

7. Mona Hammam, "Women and Industrial Work in Egypt: The Chubra el-Kheima Case," *Arab Studies Quarterly* 2, no. 1 (1980): 55; P. J. Vatiokis, *The History of Egypt from Muhammad Ali to Sadat* (London: Weidenfeld and Nicolson, 1969), 324; Issawi, *Egypt at Mid-Century,* 62.

8. Robert Mabro and Samir Radwan, *The Industrialisation of Egypt, 1939–1973: Policy and Performance* (Oxford: Clarendon Press, 1976), 28; Issawi, *Egypt at Mid-Century,* 60, 262.

9. Vatiokis, *History of Egypt,* 329.

10. Richard P. Mitchell, *The Society of the Muslim Brothers* (London: Oxford University Press, 1969), 73; hereafter cited in the text.

11. Afaf Lutfi al-Sayyid Marsot, *Egypt's Liberal Experiment, 1922–1936* (Berkeley: University of California Press, 1977), 236.

12. See Mitchell, *Society of Muslim Brothers,* chap. 7.

13. Selma Botman, "Women's Participation in Radical Politics in Egypt, 1939–52," in *Khamsin: Women in the Middle East* (London: Zed Books, 1987), 22. See also Botman, *The Rise of Egyptian Communism, 1939–1970* (Syracuse, N.Y.: Syracuse University Press, 1988).

14. Ahmed Abdulla, *The Student Movement and National Politics in Egypt, 1923–73* (London: Al-Saqi Books, 1985), 241–42n40.

15. Botman, "Women's Participation in Radical Politics," 23 (quotations), 20.

16. Valerie J. Hoffman, "An Islamic Activist: Zeinab al-Ghazali," in *Women and the Family in the Middle East,* ed. Elizabeth Warnock Fernea (Austin: University of Texas Press, 1985), 234; hereafter cited in the text.

17. Zeinab al-Ghazali, *Ayam min hayati* (Cairo: Dar al-shuruq, n.d.), 26. Chap. 2 of the work, meticulously translated by Hoffman (whose translation often coincides with mine), is presented after Hoffman's account of her interview with al-Ghazali in "Islamic Activist."

18. Al-Ghazali, *Ayam min hayati*, 37.
19. Ibid., 35–40.
20. Ibid., 39.
21. Cynthia Nelson, "The Voices of Doria Shafik: Feminist Consciousness in Egypt, 1940–1960," *Feminist Issues* 6, no. 2 (1986): 16; hereafter cited in the text.
22. Derek Hopwood, *Egypt: Politics and Society, 1945–1981* (London: Allen and Unwin, 1985), 84–90.

Chapter 11: The Struggle for the Future

1. Ghulam Nabi Saqib, *Modernisation and Muslim Education in Egypt, Pakistan and Turkey: A Comparative Study* (Lahore: Islamic Book Service, 1977), 233, 237; *The Charter* (Cairo: U.A.R. Information Department, 1962), 57, 84.
2. Primary education had been declared compulsory by previous governments, in the 1920s and again in the 1940s, but little had been done to implement general education. Amir Boktor, *The Development and Expansion of Education in the United Arab Republic* (Cairo: American University of Cairo Press, 1963), 27.
3. In the 1970s more than 60 percent of the primary schools operated more than one shift, and there were about forty students per teacher. Khalid Ikram, *Egypt: Economic Management in a Period of Transition* (Baltimore: Johns Hopkins University Press, 1980), 118.
4. Mahmud A. Fakhsh, "The Consequences of the Introduction and Spread of Modern Education: Education and National Integration in Egypt," *Middle Eastern Studies* 16, no. 2 (1980): 45; Ikram, *Egypt*, 117, 130.
5. Fadwa El Guindi, "Veiled Activism: Egyptian Women in the Contemporary Islamic Movement," *Femmes de la Méditerranée Peuples Meditérranéens* 22–23 (January–June 1983): 84; Fahim I. Qubain, *Education and Science in the Arab World* (Baltimore: Johns Hopkins University Press, 1980), 71; Saqib, *Modernisation and Muslim Education*, 254; Ikram, *Egypt*, 130.
6. Ikram, *Egypt*, 119; Earl L. Sullivan, *Women in Egyptian Public Life* (Syracuse, N.Y.: Syracuse University Press, 1986), 34, 35, 195n48; Sullivan, "Women and Work in Egypt," in *Women and Work in the Arab World*, ed. Sullivan and Karima Koraysem, Cairo Working Papers in Social Science, vol. 4, monograph 4 (Cairo: American University of Cairo Press, 1981), 14, 29–33, 37; and Peter C. Dodd, "Youth and Women's Emancipation in the U.A.R.," *Middle East Journal* 22, no. 2 (1968): 161. Over the same period agricultural employment, once the major occupation for women, reportedly declined, probably because of urban migration. Figures are inexact, however, for women not employed full time tend not to be counted, and most women worked on their own farms. Indeed, the figures with respect to working women, including those in agriculture and domestic service, are generally unreliable, because there is a pronounced tendency to underreport female workers. The women employed in industry increased from 3 percent (1961) to 11 percent (1971) of the work

force, although clerical work mostly accounted for the increase. Sullivan, "Women and Work in Egypt," 17–18.

7. Mahmoud Abdel-Fadil, "Educational Expansion and Income Distribution in Egypt, 1952–57," in *The Political Economy of Income Distribution in Egypt*, ed. Robert L. Tignor and Gouda Abdel-Khalek (New York: Holmes and Meier Publishers, 1982), 355.

8. Ikram, *Egypt*, 110, 130.

9. John Waterbury, *Egypt: Burdens of the Past, Options for the Future* (Bloomington: Indiana University Press, 1978), 78; Ikram, *Egypt*, 105.

10. See Waterbury, *Egypt*, 61.

11. Ikram, *Egypt*, 110–11.

12. Waterbury, *Egypt*, 58, 56; Ahmad Taha Ahmad, *Al-mar'a kifahha wa 'amalha* (Cairo: Dar al-jamahir, 1964), 156–58.

13. See, in particular, Saad Eddin Ibrahim, "Social Mobility and Income Distribution in Egypt, 1952–1977," in *Political Economy of Income Distribution*, ed. Tignor and Abdel-Khalek, 381.

14. Ikram, *Egypt*, 142, 113, 145.

15. Waterbury, *Egypt*, 127–28; see also Ikram, *Egypt*, 148–49.

16. See Fakhsh, "Consequences of Modern Education," 49–51.

17. In the fifty years from the late 1920s to the late 1970s literacy for males rose from about 19 percent to 57 percent, and for women it rose from a near-negligible 4 percent to about 30 percent; by the end of the period over half of all males and nearly a third of all females were literate. Amir Boktor, *School and Society in the Valley of the Nile* (Cairo: Elias Modern Press, 1936), 104; Sullivan, "Women and Work in Egypt," 24, 26; and also Sullivan, *Women in Egyptian Public Life*, 34.

18. Aziza Husein, a veteran worker for family planning and on other issues concerning women, describes how the Family Planning Association began in the 1970s a systematic effort to reform the Personal Status Laws and drafted a document making some changes helpful to women, whose passage was facilitated by Sadat. After his death the amendment was struck from the law and later reinstituted in modified form. Husein, "Recent Amendments to Egypt's Personal Status Law," in *Women and the Family in the Middle East*, ed. Elizabeth Warnock Fernea (Austin: University of Texas Press, 1985), 230.

19. Mervat Hatem, of Howard University, is currently working on a book covering this period.

20. Andrée Chedid, *From Sleep Unbound*, trans. Sharon Spencer (London: Serpent's Tail, 1987), 80. The critique of male dominance in the twentieth century has come from Arab men as well as women. See, e.g., Hisham Sharabi, *Neopatriarchy: A Theory of Distorted Change in Arab Society* (New York: Oxford University Press, 1988), 41n51.

21. Joel Beinin and Zackary Lockman, *Workers on the Nile: Nationalism, Communism, Islam and the Egyptian Working Class, 1882–1954* (Princeton: Princeton University Press, 1987), 271.

22. Nazih N. M. Ayubi, "The Political Revival of Islam: The Case of Egypt," *International Journal of Middle East Studies* 12, no. 4 (1980): 490.

23. Saad Eddin Ibrahim, "Anatomy of Egypt's Militant Islamic Groups: Methodological Notes and Preliminary Findings," *International Journal of Middle East Studies* 12, no. 4 (1980): 426.

24. John Alden Williams, "A Return to the Veil in Egypt," *Middle East Review* 11, no. 3 (1979): 53.

25. Waterbury, *Egypt,* 151.

26. Saad Eddin Ibrahim, *The New Arab Social Order* (Boulder, Colo.: Westview Press; London: Croom Helm, 1982), 18.

27. Ibid., 92–93; and Sullivan, "Women and Work in Egypt," 34.

28. See Ibrahim, *New Arab Social Order,* chap. 4, for some discussion of this.

29. Ibid., 89; Fouad Ajami, "The Open Door Economy: Its Roots and Welfare Consequences," in *Political Economy of Income Distribution,* ed. Tignor and Abdel-Khalek, 505.

30. For further descriptions see Ayubi, "Political Revival of Islam," 494; and Fadwa El Guindi, "Veiling Infitah with Muslim Ethic: Egypt's Contemporary Islamic Movement," *Social Problems* 28, no. 4 (1981): 474.

31. Williams, "Return to the Veil in Egypt," 49–50.

32. Ibrahim, "Anatomy of Islamic Groups," 438.

33. Zeinab ʿAbdel Mejid Radwan, *Thahirat al-hijab bayn al-jamʿiyyat* ([Cairo]: Al-markaz al-qawmi lil-buhuth al-ijtimaʿiyya waʾl-jinaʾiyya, 1982), 40, 42, 37, 40, 81–82.

34. Ibrahim, "Anatomy of Islamic Groups," 21.

35. Fifty percent of the women gave inner peace as the principal effect of adopting Islamic dress. Other responses were that wearing Islamic dress put an end to their being harassed in public places by men (19.5 percent) and that people treated them with new respect (20 percent). Radwan, *Thahirat al-hijab,* 92.

36. Ibrahim, "Anatomy of Islamic Groups," 448.

37. Safia K. Mohsen, "New Images, Old Reflections: Working Middle-Class Women in Egypt," in *Women and the Family in the Middle East,* ed. Fernea, 69; Radwan, *Thahirat al-hijab,* 92.

38. Mohsen, "New Images, Old Reflections," 69.

39. El Guindi, "Veiled Activism," 87–88.

40. Sharabi, *Neopatriarchy,* 137, thus defines, with considerable persuasiveness, all dominant political movements in Arab societies in this century prior to the emergence of Islamism. See also ibid., chap. 9.

41. Radwan, *Thahirat al-hijab,* 94, 99, 104, 95, 101.

42. Ibid., 112, 107, 113.

43. Ayubi, "Political Revival of Islam," 493–94; Ibrahim, *New Arab Social Order,* 21.

44. Ibrahim, *New Arab Social Order,* 22. See also his "Anatomy of Islamic Groups." For a succinct and evocative account of the vague and pregnant uto-

pianism and promise of Islamic fundamentalism see Sharabi, *Neopatriarchy,* chap. 9, esp. pp. 139–47.

45. Sharabi, *Neopatriarchy,* 155.

46. Afshar's further studies pertinent to this subject (in addition to the work cited in the following pages) include "The Iranian Theocracy," in *Iran: A Revolution in Turmoil,* ed. Afshar (London: Macmillan, 1985), 220–44; and "Khomeini's Teachings and Their Implications for Iranian Women," in *The Shadow of Islam,* ed. A. Tabari and N. Yeganeh (London: Zed Press, 1982), 75–90, a collection that has other useful articles on the subject. Further useful studies of women in contemporary Islamic republics include Farah Azari, ed., *Women of Iran: The Conflict with Fundamentalist Islam* (London: Ithaca Press, 1983); Eliz Sanasarian, *The Women's Rights Movement in Iran: Mutiny, Appeasement, and Repression from 1900 to Khomeini* (New York: Praeger Publishers, 1892); Guity Nashat, ed., *Women and Revolution in Iran* (Boulder, Colo.: Westview Press, 1983); Val Moghedem, "Women, Work and Ideology in the Islamic Republic," *International Journal of Middle East Studies* 20, no. 2 (1988); Patricia J. Higgins, "Women in the Islamic Republic of Iran: Legal, Social, and Ideological Changes," *Signs* 10, no. 31 (1985): 477–95; and Minou Reeves, *Female Warriors of Allah* (New York: E. P. Dutton, 1988). There are numerous works on Islamism, or the Islamic Revival; among the most useful are Ali E. Hillal Dessouki, *Islamic Resurgence in the Arab World* (New York: Praeger Publishers, 1982); R. Hrair Dekmejian, *Islam in Revolution* (Syracuse, N.Y.: Syracuse University Press, 1985); Fred Halliday and Hamza Alavi, eds., *State and Ideology in the Middle East and Pakistan* (New York: Monthly Review Press, 1988); Sheeren Hunter, ed., *The Politics of Islamic Revivalism* (Bloomington: Indiana University Press, 1988); Bruce B. Lawrence, *Defenders of God* (San Francisco: Harper and Row, 1989); James P. Piscatori, *Islam in the Political Process,* ed. Piscatori (Cambridge: Cambridge University Press, 1983); Emmanuel Sivan, *Radical Islam: Medieval Theology and Modern Politics* (New Haven: Yale University Press, 1985).

47. Haleh Afshar, "Women, State and Ideology in Iran," *Third World Quarterly* 7, no. 2 (1985): 256; hereafter cited in the text.

48. Khawar Mumtaz and Farida Shaheed, *Women of Pakistan: Two Steps Forward, One Step Back?* (London: Zed Books, 1987), 82.

49. Ibid., 83–84.

50. Ibid., 89.

Conclusion

1. Ashis Nandy, *Intimate Enemy: Loss and Recovery of Self under Colonialism* (Delhi: Oxford University Press, 1983), xi.

2. I just referred to Orientalism's reproducing—and thereby also endorsing, even if inadvertently, in its own account of Islam—dominant Islam's view of itself as the sole possible and only legitimate version of Islam. Orientalism is most

familiar as the West's mode of representing, and misrepresenting, the Islamic world as a domain of otherness and inferiority; it is also familiar as a field of domination. But it should be noted that the discourses of Orientalism and those of establishment Islam are androcentric discourses of domination and that consequently in some ways they complement or endorse each other, even as in other ways they are at war.

3. For critiques of the politics of Western or white feminism and women of the non-Western world and women of color see Gayatri Chakrovorty Spivak, *In Other Worlds: Essays in Cultural Politics* (New York: Methuen, 1987); and bell hooks, *Feminist Theory: From Margin to Center* (Boston: South End Press, 1984).

4. Elizabeth Fox-Genovese, *Feminism without Illusions: A Critique of Individualism* (Chapel Hill: University of North Carolina Press, 1991), 137–38, 14, 31.

5. T. N. Madan, "Anthropology as Cultural Reaffirmation" (The first of three papers delivered as the William Allan Neilson Lectures at Smith College, Northampton, Mass., October 1990), 5–6.

INDEX

Surnames beginning with *al-* are alphabetized under the element that follows the *al-*.

Literature: Abbasid, 83, 85; by women, lack of, 104; by women, 140, 178, 187, 190, 214–16. *See also* Discourses; Journalism by women; Poetry by women
Loans made by women, 110, 111
Love and affection: of fathers for daughters, 16, 85–86, 105–6, 107, 200; in Mesopotamia, 16–17; between Muhammad and his wives, 51–52; of God, 98, 100; of mistresses for slaves, 121–22; in marriage, 136–37, 157–58, 185; between women, 185–86
Lower classes: and alternatives to orthodoxy, 97–98, 115–16, 260 n. 37; employment, 115, 131; marriage patterns, 117; pilgrims, 120; effects of modernization on, 131, 132–33; and veiling, 165, 216, 221–22, 225; and politics, 173, 178, 193, 213–14, 225. *See also* Class; Middle classes; Upper classes

Madan, T. N., 248
Magazines for women, 140–41. *See also* Journalism by women
Maimuna, 58
Makarius, Miriam, 141
Male dominance: as "natural," 11, 29; in pre-Islamic societies, 12, 13, 17, 28–29, 32, 33, 45; women need male guardians, 20, 30, 42, 49, 63, 89, 109; does not inevitably lead to misogyny, 32–33; legitimized in Islam, 45–46, 62, 64, 116, 163, 183, 199, 242; in European society, 123, 161, 162, 165–66; effect of European encroachment on, 127–28, 142; and emotional relationships, 158–59, 183; and Islamicist movements, 199, 200, 231–32. *See also* Androcentrism; Independent women; Marriage; Men; Patriarchy
Mamluks, 104, 105–6
al-Ma'mun, 84
al-Mansur, 78
al-Maqrizi, 110
Marcus, Abraham, 111
Marj al-Saffar, battle of, 70

Marriage: in Mesopotamia, 13, 14, 15, 19–20, 251 n. 27; reproduction as its purpose, 19–20, 30; within social classes, 20; alternatives to, 22–24, 98, 187; arranged for children, 26, 52; companionship as its purpose, 30, 33; in pre-Islamic Egypt, 31–32, 33; in pre-Islamic Arabia, 41, 42, 43–45, 62; and establishment Islam, 44–46, 52, 61–64, 66, 75, 76, 99, 233; Muhammad's, 49–52, 53, 56, 76; women's ability to control, 76–78, 83, 84, 89, 91, 107, 199–200; less popular than concubinage, 83; Qarmatian, 99; universal, 104, 187; of educated women, 134; modern patterns, 224, 233, 242. *See also* Age at marriage; Children; Contracts, marriage; Divorce; Monogamy; Polygyny
Matrilineality, 41, 43, 44
Mazdakism, 21, 251 n. 27
Mecca: commerce in, 43, 53; opposition to Muhammad in, 47–49; Muslim conquest of, 57, 58; pilgrimage to, 61, 96–97, 109, 113, 114, 119–20
Medical workers, female, 27, 121, 123, 134–35, 143, 153, 173, 184, 191, 211, 227. *See also* Health care; Midwives
Medina, 49, 50, 52–53
Men: affection for women, 16, 85–86, 105–6, 107, 136–37, 157–58, 185, 200; promote women's education, 138; their views of women, 157–58; as feminists, 157–58, 180–82. *See also* Androcentrism; Fathers; Gender in Islam; Male dominance; Women
Mernissi, Fatima, 128
Mesopotamia and pre-Islamic Iraq: and core discourses of Islam, 3; early history, 12; status of women, 12, 13, 34; laws, 13; influence on Judaism, 34
Middle classes: marriage patterns, 107, 117; women's economic activities, 110–11, 195, 208; education, 113, 195; pilgrims, 120; and colonialism, 145–46; expansion of, 209, 213–14; and Islamic dress, 221–22, 225. *See also* Class; Upper classes

Reza Shah, 164
Ribats (convents), 110, 114–15, 262 n. 9, 263 n. 16
Ridda, Rashid, 142
Rifaat, Alifa, 183, 214
Rights of women: in Mesopotamia, 13–14, 15; concepts of, do not spread, 18–19, 33, 34, 35; women as things, 21; in Classical Greece, 28–29; in pre-Islamic Egypt, 29–33; struggle for, 166–68, 196, 203–5, 214, 241, 245; and Islamicist movements, 195, 196–97, 198–99, 203, 227, 236. *See also* Divorce; Egalitarianism; Feminism and feminists; Law; Marriage; Oppression of women; Property rights of women
Royalty: marriage practices of, 77–78, 83, 186; Egyptian, in politics, 131, 135, 156, 191, 204. *See also* Harems
Rural life: agricultural labor, 132, 191, 211, 275 n. 6; agricultural reform, 132–33, 204, 209; and education, 211; migration from, 213, 221–23, 224, 225, 275 n. 6; and veiling, 216, 221–22. *See also* Lower classes; Urban life
Russell, Alexander, 115, 121–23, 262 n. 11, 264 n. 27

al-Sadat, Anwar, 212, 217, 219–20, 276 n. 18
Safia, 73, 75
Said, Edward, 150
al-Saʿid, Amina, 185, 190, 197
Sajah bint ʿAws, 59
al-Sakhawi, Muhammad Shams al-Din, 104, 107–8, 109, 112, 113–14, 118–19, 261 n. 2, 264 n. 29
Salma bint Malik, 58–59
Sami, Semseddin, 138
Sasanian empire: and the rise of Islam, 4, 19, 77; use of the veil in, 5; harems in, 14, 19, 80; and decline in women's status, 17–19; Persian migration to Iraq, 80–81
Saudia Arabia, 217, 218, 231, 241
Sawda, 49, 50, 54, 60

al-Sayyid, Ahmad Lutfi, 149, 177
Schimmel, Annemarie, 260 n. 35
Scholars, women as, 110, 113–15, 240–41. *See also* Education of women; Literature; Teachers, women as
Schools for girls: sewing, 112, 136, 264 n. 27; *kuttabs*, 113, 135, 136, 264 n. 27; state-sponsored, 134–35, 137–38, 144, 160; missionary, 135–36, 138, 143, 160; secondary, 137–38, 171, 177, 189, 272 n. 6; Muslim benevolent society, 138, 144, 160; feminist, 177. *See also* Education of women
Segregation of women: in pre-Islamic societies, 5, 17, 18, 26–29, 32, 35, 55; as the ideal, 27; architecture of, 28, 116–17; Western attitudes toward, 36, 153, 154, 160, 161; Muhammad's wives, 43, 53–55, 61; Muslim institution of, 60, 61, 62, 127; at the mosque, 60–61; during Abbasid era, 79–80, 99; and education, 113, 160; women's presence on the streets, 118–20, 142, 143, 169, 204, 221, 223–24, 231, 233–34; effect on women's lives, 161; modern breakdown of, 218–19, 222–23, 230. *See also* Travel by women; Veil and its discourse
Sewing, 112, 136. *See also* Textile production
Sexuality, women's, 185–86; as male property, 12, 14, 15, 20, 45, 52, 62; wife-whore contrast, 12, 14–15; and legal status of rape, 14, 234; determines her place in class system, 15; as her defining characteristic, 18, 22, 24, 26, 35–36, 66, 93; as sinful or shameful, 18, 23, 35–36, 116, 120; state's interest in regulating, 32; male legal right to, 92–93. *See also* Bodies; Male dominance; Marriage; Misogyny
Shabth ibn Ribʿi, 75
Shafik, Doria, 179, 183, 185, 188, 196, 197, 207
Shams, 99
Shariʿa: status of non-Muslims, 7; and pre-Islamic law, 16, 28; jurisdiction of, 146; reform of, 168, 198; and women's